COLLEGE OF MARIN LIBRARY
KENTFIELD, CALIFORNIA

ETHICS
AFTER
BABEL

ETHICS AFTER BABEL

THE LANGUAGES OF MORALS AND THEIR DISCONTENTS

JEFFREY STOUT

BEACON PRESS · BOSTON

Beacon Press
25 Beacon Street
Boston, Massachusetts 02108

Beacon Press books
are published under the auspices of
the Unitarian Universalist Association of Congregations.

© 1988 by Jeffrey Stout
All rights reserved
Printed in the United States of America
95 94 93 92 91 90 89 88   1 2 3 4 5 6 7 8

Text design by Dennis Anderson

Library of Congress Cataloging-in-Publication Data
Stout, Jeffrey.
Ethics after Babel.
Bibliography: p.
Includes index.
1. Ethics.   I. Title.
BJ1012.S848   1988   170   87-42847
ISBN 0-8070-1402-8

To Livy, My Parents, and Nan

Therefore is the name of it called Babel; because the Lord did there confound the language of all the earth: and from thence did the Lord scatter them abroad upon the face of all the earth.

—Genesis 11:9

The view dies hard that Babel was the occasion of a curse being laid upon mankind from which it is the business of the philosopher to deliver us, and a disposition remains to impose a single character upon significant human speech.

—Michael Oakeshott

CONTENTS

PREFACE

A few years ago the local martial arts club posted a list of the five "Codes of Human Conduct" on a bulletin board in the gymnasium where I play basketball. The list gave both "contemporary" and "ancient" interpretations for each of the five items, as follows:

1 The Spirit of Contribution   Loyalty to Country
2 The Spirit of Respect   Obedience to Parents
3 The Spirit of Harmony and   Honor Friendship
  Unity
4 The Spirit of Determination   No Retreat in Battle
5 The Spirit of Humanity   In Killing, Choose with Sense
                                      and Honor

You will have no trouble guessing which column is which. Evidently, somebody felt the need to translate the ancient codes into a language suited to twentieth-century Americans. Need I say that something seems to have been lost in the translation? The conceptual distance between the two columns is great—enough so in the fifth case to be amusing. Should it also be troubling?

The two columns betoken nothing so simple as a disagreement over the truth of particular moral propositions. Liberals might dissent from traditional opinions about patriotism or filial piety. Pacifists might object to ancient injunctions to kill with honor. But the differences go beyond that level. They point, it would seem, to distinct moral languages, organized around different central concepts and at home in different social settings.

The idea that there are distinct moral languages, disparate conceptualities within which to understand and appraise conduct, character, and community, has become a commonplace in recent humanistic scholarship. Consider a few examples:

• The Sinologist Jacques Gernet depicts the impact of Christianity on China as a function of disparities between distinct languages with different "logics, " "modes of thought," and "visions of the world and man."

• French feminists like Luce Irigaray speak of a unique morality, expressive of female sexuality, which produces a language unlike that of men.

• Historians of political theory like J. G. A. Pocock and Quentin Skinner report the emergence of new moral and political languages in early modern Europe.

• The historian of religious ethics James Turner Johnson asks whether "the language of natural law" or some other language should be employed by the just-war theorist.

• A theologian like Stanley Hauerwas declares "rights language . . . insufficient on grounds of social theory," and defends instead the language of character and community.

• The sociologist Peter Berger describes the interlocking concepts of honor, insult, and chastity as "obsolescent," claiming that they have been displaced in the modern world by a language of dignity which makes sense only on the assumption that human identity is "essentially independent of institutional roles."

• The philosopher Alasdair MacIntyre condemns "contemporary moral utterance" because of its protracted disagreements and "conceptual incommensurability."

• The sociologist Robert Bellah finds, to his disappointment, that individualism has become the "first language" of American moral self-understanding and that the languages of biblical and civic republican traditions are endangered.

• The philosopher Richard Rorty avers that "what counts as cruelty and injustice is a matter of the language that is spoken" and speculates that "what is most important for human life is not what propositions we believe but what vocabulary we use."

Such talk may be in fashion, but it also inspires discontents: discontents about objectivity and relativity in ethics, about the possibility of understanding or criticizing cultures unlike ours, about how secular morality relates to the religious traditions concerning which philosophers nowadays say so little, and about the health of a culture like our own, in which we seem at times to have too many moral languages for coherent public discourse. These are the discontents addressed in this book. My approach is philosophical, since I am an ethicist and philosopher of religion by training. But a wide range of issues and authors, some of them from fields I study but do not practice, like anthropology and theology, come up for discussion.

I have tried to express myself on these matters without talking down to people outside the guild or producing a technical treatise for experts only. While being as clear as I can for the benefit of newcomers, I do not avoid technical distinctions when they seem essential to an argument. A couple of chapters, earmarked in the introduction, are harder going than the rest. The introduction also lays out the overall strategy of the book and explains the division into three parts—one on the spectres of skepticism, nihilism, and relativism in ethics, a second on the relation between secular moral philosophy and the religious traditions, and a third on the fate of moral discourse in our society in particular. The last will hold the most interest for many readers, some of whom may consider sparing themselves a deliberate journey through intervening (at times daunting) philosophical terrain. Nevertheless, I have found such a journey indispensable in my search for fresh perspective on our predicament.

I considered keeping mention of other authors to a minimum. It seemed better, in the end, to say more—for four reasons. The first was to provide needed commentary on authors who deserve it. The second was to make this book useful in colleges and universities by treating authors already being read in courses with titles like "Moral Relativism," "Religion and Morality," and "Communitarians and Liberals." My third and fourth reasons, however, were more compelling. As I went along, I increasingly felt the need to test, clarify, and refine my views in extended dialogue with others who see the issues differently. And I discovered that much of what I wanted to say, expecially about rhetorical and literary dimensions of ethical writing, could only be said in close readings of particular works.

These four reasons explain not only my decision to discuss other authors at some length but also my choice of authors and the amount of space allotted to each. They explain, for example, my decision to say quite a bit about the writings of professional philosophers, particularly Anglo-American ones, although I don't want to imply that they are the only people who deserve a hearing on the topics under discussion. Many readers find philosophical literature forbidding and confusing. This has not prevented it, however, from exerting influence outside the discipline—even, perhaps especially, when it is poorly understood. My hope is to make the literature somewhat more accessible while appraising some of its most interesting arguments and assumptions and its (sometimes hidden) figures of speech and stories about the past. Whatever my own reservations about standard approaches to those topics, which will become apparent as we proceed, I want to call attention to what can be learned from serious engagement with contemporary philosophy and to show that it can be read as a kind of literature with its own dramatic tensions and political implications.

I make no attempt at exhaustive coverage. Authors who fail to challenge my main argument or who supply no distinctions essential to advancing it are often simply ignored. Concerning authors like John Rawls and Jürgen Habermas—whose work, though relevant, has already generated an extensive secondary literature—I have said relatively little. At various points, I have had to choose representative authors or works to illustrate a general approach or set of assumptions. So some books that might seem like obvious candidates for lengthy commentary—like Neil Cooper's *The Diversity of Moral Thinking* (Oxford: Clarendon Press, 1981)—are forced to give their proxy to others. A natural line of counterargument will be to say that I've selected unfair samples, that I should have chosen Gewirth in place of Donagan to speak for the Kantians, or Hauerwas in place of MacIntyre to play the role of Jeremiah to pluralistic society. I can only hope that critics will show how their preferred representatives would make a difference in the outcome when they join the argument. Doing so will benefit us all.

It may seem odd that Part 2, which explores the prospects for a new dialogue between secular moral philosophy and the religious traditions, contains only a single chapter on academic theology. It happens, however, that the theologians most interested in dialogue with secular moral philosophy since Kant have largely accepted the very philosophical assumptions which, on my account, have made genuine dialogue difficult or impossible. They therefore supply surprisingly little assistance for my project. Chapter 8 speculates on why this might be so. It also directs attention toward religious thinkers of other kinds—thinkers more apt to be philosophically interesting precisely because they are not trying to sound like philosophers (of a certain sort) themselves.

I came to Princeton University in 1972, and over the years since then I have learned a great deal from my teachers, colleagues, and students here. Some of it is reflected in this book. I wish the notes could tell the full story of indebtedness, but even where space allows, memory sometimes fails. Early drafts of chapters from Parts 2 and 3 were written when I was on leave for a year as the university's John Witherspoon Bicentennial Preceptor. The book was brought close to completion during another leave, also funded by Princeton, in 1986. I am grateful for both sabbaticals and especially to friends who helped my family cope with illnesses that interrupted the second.

Many Princeton colleagues have commented helpfully on drafts of one or more chapters: David Bromwich, Malcolm Diamond, Mary Douglas, Victor Preller, Paul Ramsey, Chava Weissler, and Bernie Yack. A former colleague, Richard Rorty, and two former editors, Stanley Hauerwas and Alasdair MacIntyre, have been especially generous with comments and encouragement from the beginning. My criticisms of their work, implicit and explicit, should not hide how much I owe them or the high esteem in which I hold them.

I presented papers based on material from Parts 2 and 3 at Yale University, Harvard University, Indiana University, the University of Houston, and the University of North Carolina at Greensboro. My thanks to all those who responded to my views on those occasions or who took the time to converse with me at some length by other means, especially Timothy Jackson, Gene Outka, and Jock Reeder. I have also benefited from the careful attention given to my manuscript by John Bowlin, L. Gregory Jones, and two anonymous readers toward the end. Warm thanks to my editors at Beacon Press and Lorraine Fuhrmann of Princeton's administrative staff for other kinds of help, no less essential.

This book includes reworked material from the following essays: "The Philosophical Interest of the Hebrew-Christian Moral Tradition," *The Thomist* 47/2 (1983): 165–96; "Moral Abominations," *Soundings* 66/1 (1983): 5–23; "The Voice of Theology in Contemporary Culture," in *Religion and America: Spirituality in a Secular Age*, ed. Mary Douglas and Steven M. Tipton (Boston: Beacon Press, 1983), pp. 249–

61; "Virtue Among the Ruins," *Neue Zeitschrift für Systematische Theologie und Religionsphilosophie* 26/3 (1984): 256–73; "Liberal Society and the Languages of Morals," *Soundings* 69/1–2 (1986): 32–59; and "A Lexicon of Postmodern Philosophy," *Religious Studies Review* 18/1 (1987): 18–22. I thank the editors and publishers of these publications for kindly granting permission to reprint sections of those essays here.

I also owe gratitude, of an entirely different order, to my family: parents and grandparents, brother and sister, in-laws, wife, and children. They have all given me love and support and fellowship for which I am deeply thankful. My wife and children have done their part not least of all by tolerating the demands my peculiar vocation makes upon them. They have also taught me much about cabbits, the virtues, medical care, baseball, and other matters of importance treated in these pages.

INTRODUCTION

Kafka returns to it repeatedly, inviting us to view its labyrinthine galleries from within. Borges finds a library there that includes everything, including your obituary. The tower of Babel, for all its antiquity, continues to exert its power over the imagination.[1] Whenever we desire to penetrate the strangeness of alien speech or dispel the confusion of tongues, the image of the ruined tower recurs. It is, among other things, a symbol of our moral condition. This book is about the desires and disappointments of Babel, thus construed.

When authors like Stanley Hauerwas, Alasdair MacIntyre, and Basil Mitchell begin their books by proclaiming that modern moral discourse has suffered a great catastrophe, leaving us in conceptual disarray, they cannot help echoing Babel.[2] They are saying that pluralism is just another name for confusion. When skeptics, nihilists, and relativists argue that the disarray is not new, that it has accompanied moral discourse as long as anyone can remember, they merely place Babel before the dawn of history. They do not cease to invoke Babel's name, confusion, in their descriptions of moral speech. And when philosophers seek to overcome the confusion of tongues by constructing great systems or aspiring to a God's-eye view, satirists mock them for mirroring Babel's pretensions. To Jacques Derrida, the collapsing tower, its internal structure partly exposed by God's act of deconstruction, "does

1

not merely figure the irreducible multiplicity of tongues; it exhibits an incompletion, the impossibility of finishing, of totalizing."³

Michael Oakeshott calls the story of Babel our "most profound" myth about the perils of "finding a shortcut to heaven." The penalty for having tried to see the world from God's perspective, he says, is a "chaos of conflicting ideals, the disruption of a common life."⁴ And that is how our moral discourse often appears to us, whether or not we take the story literally. What can we make of this apparent chaos? Are we presumptuous to hope to rise above it?

I mention the story here at the outset for several reasons. First of all, it calls the facts of moral diversity vividly to mind, and I want to reflect on the extent to which they deserve to be called chaos or confusion. Second, and equally important, the story warns against the philosopher's urge to look down upon the fray from God's point of view in the heavens or to devise a universal language in which all moral differences can be stated and resolved. I shall meditate on that warning at length. Finally, however, I want to ask whether we should think of ourselves as having lost a prior moral and linguistic unity at all.

Genesis says that once upon a time "the whole earth had one language and few words." Is this perhaps an ancient author's wish for unity, projected wistfully upon a forgotten past? Granted that there are many moral languages in use around us, each with its own assumptions about reality and complicit in a distinct way of life, and granted that our condition is often one of discord and misunderstanding, do we have good reason to regret coming on the scene belatedly—*after* an age of coherent discourse and community?

Actually, Genesis itself seems of two minds about whether the heyday of Babel was such a time. By the end of Genesis 10, Noah's descendants are already speaking their own languages, living in their own lands. The redactor has not bothered to explain how the whole earth could be speaking one language by the beginning of Genesis 11, just before God wreaks havoc on Babel. What happened to all those languages in the sudden transition from one chapter to the next? Perhaps the plurality of nations has simply been lost from view, obscured by a narrator's poor memory or ethnocentricity. But if the many nations did become "one people," how was this unification accomplished? Did Nimrod—"the first on earth to be a mighty man" and whose kingdom began at Babel—use his might to impose a single character upon all human speech? If so, then the condition of ethics during the heyday of Babel may not have been so good.

My concern, in any event, is not with ancient history, nor with the story of Babel itself, but with contemporary worries about the languages of morals, for which Babel serves as a trope. Put prosaically, if generally, my topic is this: the significance of disagreement and conceptual diversity in ethics. Why should this topic call forth mythic images, great literature, and profound philosophy? More to the point, why might it deserve serious and extended attention from us?

At one level, the answer to these questions is obvious. We disagree with each other on matters of moral importance—matters like abortion, nuclear weapons, the treatment of dying patients, and the distribution of wealth—and these disagreements can be painful. At times, failure to resolve them rationally leads to bloodshed. We therefore have good reason to be concerned with obstacles to rational persuasion. Yet, all too often, we fail even to understand what others are saying to us. Our differences go deeper than mere disagreement over propositions. Their concepts strike us as foreign. We do not speak the same moral language. Our capacity to live peaceably with each other depends upon our ability to converse intelligibly and reason coherently. But this ability is weakened by the very differences that make it necessary. The more we need it, the weaker it becomes, and we need it very badly indeed.

This thought alone would make my topic important. Further reflection, however, reveals additional reasons for taking the topic seriously. For one thing, the trouble we have conversing intelligibly and reasoning coherently with each other can easily erode our confidence in the idea that truths or justified beliefs *can* by attained in ethics. Three spectres haunt the philosophy of moral diversity—skepticism, nihilism, and relativism. Each, in its own way, involves loss of confidence in our ordinary talk of moral truth and justification, and each can have worrisome effects on how we live our lives.

Part 1 of this book is about the spectres of moral diversity. Complete loss of confidence is one kind of temptation to be avoided. The aspiration to a God's-eye view is another. But it proves extremely difficult to find the mean between these extremes. They often seem like our only options. I argue at some length that they are not.

In the first two chapters, I consider the relatively limited kind of moral diversity represented in disagreement over propositions. I ask whether moral disagreement is as complete as it sometimes seems and whether it differs in any crucial respect from disagreement in areas like science, where our confidence in truth and justification rarely flags. Chapter 1 sets out my position on the implications of moral disagreement in simple terms. Chapter 2 responds to objections and introduces qualifications. Some of the objections are motivated by philosophical concerns discussed in the technical literature, so that chapter contains the more difficult, though ultimately more interesting, arguments and distinctions.

Chapter 3 turns from one kind of moral diversity to another—from disagreement over propositions to the sort of differences motivating talk about distinct moral languages. This is where I explicate the idea that there are distinct moral languages and consider implications for our conception of comparative ethics, moral philosophy, constructive moral thought, and moral change. I also give an account of the difficulties of expressing alien concepts in familiar terms—difficulties which have made some people doubt the possibility of understanding or interpreting the moralities of other cultures or periods.

The first three chapters touch upon various things we may mean by "moral relativity." The fourth goes further to study different sorts of critical moral judgments we make about people, acts, practices, and institutions in other cultures. It suggests that the general question, "Is moral relativism true?" needs to be traded in for a list of more manageable questions, including questions about particular concepts like blame, justice, what ought to be the case, what one ought to do, and so on. These concepts fall at various points on a spectrum, depending on what we need to know to employ them in a particular kind of case. While delineating the spectrum of relativity, I have my say on the kinds of moral relativism defended by philosophers Gilbert Harman, David Wong, and Bernard Williams.

Skepticism, nihilism, and relativism, as I use the expressions here, have to do with worries about morality *as such*, worries often exacerbated by reflection on the facts of moral diversity. Can moral philosophy say anything insightful and interesting about specific moral languages and the difference they make? Part 2 takes up the fate of one kind of morality or moral language—the religious kind. I propose to treat religious ethics as the crucial test for the ability of any secular philosophy to account for moral diversity. If moral philosophy speaks of itself as, by definition, secular in orientation, what can it say about the difference that constitutes its own identity? In point of fact, it has of late said almost nothing. Religious ethics has gone into eclipse in recent moral philosophy. We need to ask why.

This question brings us to another reason for examining the topic of moral diversity. For in coming to terms with particular kinds of moral difference, we jeopardize not only our assumptions about the uniformity of ethics but also our conception of what makes us distinctive. Failure even to confront specific differences can promote a false sense of unity, condemning us to ignorance of whatever diversity there may be. Failure to work through the differences we acknowledge can foster harmful stereotypes of the "other" and dangerous illusions about ourselves.

When moral philosophy aspires to universality, it often takes as its subject matter what various critics have derisively called "Esperanto." The ground rules of this supposedly universal language, once displayed clearly in abstraction from the vagaries of particular traditions, are then said to be definitive of practical reason itself. Esperanto becomes *the* language of morals, its rules the deep structure of morality as such. Nonconformity to the rules becomes a sign of viciousness or irrationality. Then the diversity of moral languages ceases to matter. In fact, it becomes virtually invisible. A religious tract, speaking of idolatries or abominations unheard of in Esperanto, will either be deemed irrelevant to the moral philosopher's properly delimited subject matter or, insofar as it does pertain, flatly condemned as a product of fallacy and superstition.

"Fallacy" and "superstition" are modern moral philosophy's derogatory names for the religious "other" against which it defines itself as rational and secular. They are the signs posted by the Enlightenment at the boundaries of the discipline. Even philosophers who want to take down the signs, out of lingering sympathy with religious tradition, still often leave the boundaries undisturbed. Part 2 attempts to exert pressure upon those boundaries from two directions. Chapters 5 and 6 press from within by deconstructing the arguments and rhetorical devices of two Esperantists who try to do justice to religious ethics. Chapters 7 and 8 push from without by bringing long-neglected concepts and traditional religious concerns to bear on secular philosophical interests.

Part 1, I have said, pertains to worries about morality as such, worries about what follows from the facts of moral disagreement and conceptual diversity. Part 3 pertains to similar worries about morality in one society in particular—our own, one so hospitable to diversity it is called "pluralistic" or "liberal." Influential books, defending an outlook sometimes dubbed "communitarian," find our pluralistic ways seriously deficient. Alasdair MacIntyre goes as far as to say that the "new dark ages" have come to pass, that the only way to restore the common good and the virtues to their proper place is to withdraw into small communities not divided by fundamental moral disagreements and competing moral concepts.

The standard brand of liberal opposition to this conclusion is Esperantist. Some readers may expect my criticisms of Esperanto to lead naturally to endorsement of MacIntyre's conclusion. I intend nothing so simple as that. Rather, I aim to complicate matters by considering nonstandard versions of liberalism. The most important of these, for my purposes, are inspired by Augustine's theology and Dewey's pragmatism. Chapter 9 introduces the communitarians and begins the job of criticizing them. Chapter 10 introduces nonstandard alternatives and begins the job of integrating insights from Augustinian theologians, pragmatic liberals, and communitarians alike.

Some readers will worry that if I preserve too much from pragmatic liberalism, I'll be unable to make good on commitments made in Part 1. Pragmatism, they will charge, brings such noxious consequences as moral aphasia and nihilism in train. Chapter 11 responds to the charges by discussing various senses of pragmatism and disowning the troublesome senses I'd rather do without. It makes contact with some of the harder parts of Chapter 2 and thus poses similar challenges to readers relatively unfamiliar with the literature.

Chapter 12 completes my efforts at eclectic but selective retrieval by saving something from MacIntyre. I argue that while we had better dispense with his sense of belatedness and his account of moral diversity, we can benefit greatly from his concept of social practices, his understanding of their relation to institutions, and his distinction between internal and external goods. Such tools allow us to redescribe pluralistic society and reappraise its characteristic problems, breaking free from both the "terminal wistfulness" of the communitarians and the complacency of liberal apologetics.

The upshot of Part 3 is rejection of what both liberals and communitarians often accept, our society pictured as a way of managing conflict of interest among individuals utterly unconnected by agreement about the good. Liberals like what they see in this picture. Communitarians despise what the liberals like. But if the picture is mistaken or misleading, then the debate between them is largely misplaced. Part 3 looks beyond the current debate and sketches the general outlines of a picture in which the opposition, "liberal versus communitarian," is beside the point.

According to the picture I propose, our problems do not result from the confusion of tongues in a society that has fallen from the coherence and community of an earlier age. The plurality of moral languages in our society is closely related to the plurality of social practices and institutions we have reason to affirm. Our moral languages exhibit a division of conceptual labor, each doing its own kind of work. But they also sometimes get in each other's way. Some languages, in particular those of the marketplace and the bureaucracies, creep into areas of life where they can only do harm. They tend to engulf or corrupt habits of thought and patterns of interaction that we desperately need. Protecting them is a grave problem, worthy of the best social criticism and political experimentation we can muster.

At the end of the book, you will find a lexicon of selected philosophical and theological terms. It is intended not only to help beginners over hurdles but also to summarize some of the conceptual clarification essential to my arguments. Hobbes once said that when you get your definitions right, everything else goes right too; he concluded that the prudent philosopher would be well advised to put the definitions first, as he did in *Leviathan*. I've put mine last, on the theory that most of my definitions won't be intelligible to someone who hasn't first worked through my arguments, or most of them, anyway.

Irving Howe describes one of the great challenges of the political novel in these words:

to make ideas or ideologies come to life, to endow them with the capacity for stirring characters into passionate gestures and sacrifices, and even more, to create the illusion that they have a kind of independent motion, so that they themselves—those abstract weights of idea or ideology—seem to become active characters. . . .[5]

It is, essentially, the same challenge encountered by moral philosophy (or philosophically inclined social criticism) when it doesn't take refuge in dryness, mere technique, or sheer formality.[6] Like the novelist, the philosopher needs to drive ideas "into a complex relation with the kinds of experience that resist reduction to formula—and this once done, supreme difficulty though it is, transforms [those] ideas astonishingly."[7]

But the philosopher's task is in some respects more difficult, because the novelist typically possesses more compelling means for rendering the concrete details of experience.

As Howe sees it,

The political novel . . . is peculiarly a work of internal tensions. To be a novel at all, it must contain the usual representation of human behavior and feeling; yet it must also absorb into its stream of movement the hard and perhaps insoluble pellets of modern ideology. The novel deals with moral sentiments, with passions and emotions; it tries, above all, to capture the quality of concrete experience. Ideology, however, is abstract, as it must be, and therefore likely to be recalcitrant whenever an attempt is made to incorporate it into the novel's stream of sensuous impression. The conflict is inescapable: the novel tries to confront experience in its immediacy and closeness, while ideology is by its nature general and inclusive. Yet it is precisely from this conflict that the political novel gains its interest and takes on the aura of high drama.

Moral philosophy is animated by the same conflict. But because it begins with ideas and arguments, not with the stream of sensuous impression, its challenge is to find its own way to confront the stubborn intuitions embedded in the moral lives of ordinary people, the unwelcome objections that might defeat its generalizations, the strangeness of alien words and ways. Both kinds of writer are sometimes forced to journey, by book's end, "through places of the head and heart undreamed of" in the original plan, pressing their "predispositions and yearnings and fantasies" against the reality of moral experience, the diversity of human life.[8]

At its best, ethical reflection achieves a mixed diction. It cannot do without isms and generalizations, its repertoire of technical distinctions and bizarre examples. Otherwise, it simply falls silent before diversity, unable to articulate a movement of argument, to express a sense of relation between part and whole, or to make its points with sufficient precision. But the abstractions all count for nothing if they are not brought down from the tower, back to earth. When a strong philosopher or social critic connects them with the manifold of human affection, opinion, and action, the result can have as much high drama and draw us as thoroughly into dialectical action as any other kind of literature. It can also, of course, reveal as much as any novel about the peculiar complicities, blind spots, and insensitivities of its author as a human being.

So here is further reason to reflect at length on the significance of moral diversity, on the languages of morals and their discontents, on the desires and disappointments of Babel. Few topics subject moral philosophers, social critics, and their readers to so severe a test. None makes the temptations of moral reflection in our age more strongly felt: the comforts of false unity and transcendence; the cynicism and demoralization often lurking behind brave refusals of consolation; the urge to lose oneself in playful aestheticism or the rigor of professional technique; the tendency to either denigrate or romanticize one's fellow citizens, one's ancestors, or members of distant cultures; the evasions implicit in self-congratulation or revolutionary exaltation; the wishful thinking of utopian proposals and wistful thoughts of days gone by.

It is therefore a topic ideally suited to display what philosophers and social critics do. Could it be that they do something for us that novelists don't?

1

THE SPECTRES OF MORAL DIVERSITY

1

MORAL DISAGREEMENT

Disagreement and diversity in ethics beget worries. If ethics does not have an agreed basis in universal rational principles or even in the concepts we should use in framing our principles, aren't we compelled to become moral nihilists, denying that there are any moral truths at all? Or moral skeptics, denying that we can have justified beliefs about whatever moral truths there may be? Or moral relativists, confining the notions of ethical justification and truth within groups otherwise united on fundamentals? Is there not too much disagreement in ethics, especially in contrast to science, for us to go on confidently employing the notions of justification and truth, especially when considering societies far removed from ours? In short, mustn't we abandon the traditional conception of moral judgment and reasoning as either objective or rational?

The malaise implied in these questions does not depend on explicit arguments for nihilism, skepticism, relativism, and associated doctrines. One needn't include Westermarck, Protagoras, or J. L. Mackie on the syllabus to get students troubled over disagreement and diversity in ethics. One need only assign a series of authors—theological, utilitarian, Kantian, Aristotelian—who disagree among themselves on the standard list of moral problems. Before long, some freshman will start saying that there's no such thing as a truth of the matter or a justified belief in ethics, that the most one can demand of a morality is internal consistency, that any moral system not guilty of self-contradiction is as good as any other. Students who began by agreeing in turn with each author they read often end up thinking that the only way to avoid intellectual promiscuity is to stop giving themselves to *any* author, however persuasive.

For that matter, many of our fellow citizens enter public debate on behalf of settled convictions only to find themselves repressing a sense of bad faith when they can't defend themselves beyond a certain point against people whose convictions and backgrounds differ from theirs. They find themselves saying, somewhat defensively, that there's a leap of faith or ultimately subjective element at the bottom of *everybody's* moral convictions, explaining their inability to argue further by saying that they're no worse off than anybody else. The instructor then points out that using this defensive tactic makes it easier for Khomeni and Qaddafi and Botha to use it too. The move that initially seemed attractive because it extended the comfort of equal standing with one's critics seems to extend the same comfort to scoundrels and fanatics. Keeping company with them is no comfort at all.

Have we nothing to say to the scoundrels and fanatics? Have we no authentic grounds for judging them and their practices evil? Can we even understand those whose moral concepts differ from our own? Such questions arise within the realm of ordinary moral discourse. Many people utterly innocent of philosophy have shared the discontents they express. In the next several chapters, I want to look closely at these and related worries—worries of a sort that draw people to moral philosophy in the first place. It would be foolish to engage in this project without attending carefully to what philosophers have been saying about such worries, but I want to stress that one needn't be a philosopher or a student of philosophy to find the worries worrisome and thus worthy of serious thought.

I won't disprove moral nihilism or moral skepticism. No knockdown argument, intended to demolish opposing positions, will be given. My aim is much more modest, as are my means. I will try to show simply that the facts of moral diversity don't *compel* us to become nihilists or skeptics, to abandon the notions of moral truth and justified moral belief. I shall not try to silence nihilists or skeptics or to demonstrate the incoherence of what they say. Neither shall I consider all the possible reasons nihilism or skepticism might seem forced upon us. I shall rather proceed on two assumptions: first, that most of us wouldn't embrace nihilism or skepticism unless we felt we had to; and second, that the facts of moral diversity are at least a leading cause, if not the leading cause, of nihilistic or skeptical compulsions in ethics.

The second assumption helps explain the philosophical import of my project without claiming too much for it. The first attempts to locate the burden of proof. Instead of asking,"Why *not* be a moral nihilist or skeptic, given the facts of moral diversity?" I intend to ask, "Why feel one *must* be?" My answer will be that we needn't feel compelled to accept nihilistic or skeptical conclusions because of moral diversity. Not that moral diversity isn't more extensive, and in some respects more troubling, than many enemies of nihilism and skepticism pretend. In Part 2 we will find reason to suspect that secular moral philosophy has often repressed diversity, rendering it invisible and unchallenging, rather than taking its full measure and working through a relation to significantly different moral traditions. But if I am right, there are ways to deflate the spectres of nihilism and skepticism without taking false comfort in an artificial unity.

As for moral relativism, the third spectre of moral diversity, my strategy will be to divide and conquer. I'll try to show that many things might be meant by the claim that morals are relative, that these various things need to be meticulously disentangled from one another, and that once they are separated and examined with care we are not left with any compelling threat to the possibility of moral judgment *per se* in cross-cultural settings. The argument will be cumulative. It will take many twists and turns. Some objections to it will not be met until Parts 2 and 3. So I must beg for patience.

I'll begin by concentrating on moral disagreement, leaving what I'll call "conceptual diversity" until later. To pose the issue in a reasonably concrete way, I want to consider the views of Stanley Hauerwas and C. S. Lewis. Neither is a professional philosopher, but each nonetheless has quite a bit to say about the extent and significance of moral disagreement. And they seem, initially at least, as far apart as they could be on the matter.[1] Lewis believes in the natural law as a universal, transcultural standard of morality. Hauerwas criticizes appeals to any such standard, claiming that all moral reasoning is a radically contextual affair, situated within specific traditions and dependent upon their contingent assumptions and forms of life. Lewis plays down the extent to which people disagree on specifically moral grounds. Hauerwas plays it up. The differences between the two authors seem as stark as they are important. Lewis is typically viewed as a champion of moral objectivity and rationality. Hauerwas is often denounced as giving comfort to nihilism, skepticism, and relativism. Each has reached a wide audience outside the academy. Their apparently disparate views not only illustrate the broad cultural interest of our topic but also help establish the need for philosophical reflection. What, on reflection, do their differences come to?

I

Let me begin by calling attention to similarities between Lewis and Hauerwas, similarities one is apt to miss. For one thing, both Lewis and Hauerwas believe that there are moral truths and that people can know them. Hauerwas doesn't think his position forces him to deny that. For another thing, both of them believe that our knowledge of moral truths, like our knowledge of mathematics, wouldn't be possible unless we were taught a certain sort of vocabulary, trained in its use by more experienced members of our culture, and capable of acquiring certain habits of thought and action through imitation, reprimand, encouragement, criticism, and so forth. Furthermore, both of them agree that disagreement on moral issues occurs from one person or culture or period to the next, that some of this disagreement is very hard to resolve by rational means, and that failure to resolve such disagreement sometimes leads to tragic consequences—like resort to warfare.

Both authors would affirm the rationality of morals, if this means that we are entitled to go on using the notions of moral truth and justification with confidence, the facts of moral disagreement notwithstanding. Lewis, however, would suspect that Hauerwas's way of stressing diversity and the dependence of moral reasoning upon particular cultural traditions makes it too hard to defend this affirmation. And Hauerwas would suspect that Lewis's talk of a transcultural natural law unwittingly invites nihilism or skepticism by making it seem as if the objectivity or rationality of morals depended on something universal and certain that turns out, on examination, to be a fiction. Both then would worry that the other does something that invites nihilistic or skeptical doubts—the one by providing so little universal grounding for moral reasoning that it threatens to collapse, the other by requiring more universal grounding than could ever be supplied.

Debates over the significance of moral disagreement often reach an impasse like this, with neither side explicitly defending nihilistic or skeptical conclusions but each suspecting the other of nihilistic or skeptical tendencies. We need to see what can be done to break the impasse.

Lewis begins his discussion of these matters by noting that when people disagree about moral issues, they in fact behave as if they were differing over the truth of something. They tend to offer each other reasons, and these reasons typically appeal to standards or considerations they agree upon. If people were merely expressing feelings, rather than quarreling about the truth of something, it would be odd to say that they disagreed, and it's hard to see how they could quarrel or disagree over something without being united by substantial agreement on other matters.

Lewis says that unless you and the person you're arguing with have some sort of agreement about right and wrong, it doesn't make sense to try to convince each other that your own view was right. I think Lewis is right about that, although somebody might dismiss his point by saying, "Okay, then, I guess we shouldn't have been trying to convince each other after all. It's a case where disagreement goes all the way down, leaving us with nothing in common to appeal to. In such cases, where disagreement goes all the way down, there may be argument, but it will be pointless and fruitless. There is no ground for agreement."

Lewis responds to this sort of point by saying that while there have been differences among moralities, "these have never amounted to anything like a total difference" (p. 19). There is truth in this claim, as I'll show in a moment, but Lewis's argument is less than persuasive. He says, for example, that anyone who takes the trouble to look will be struck mainly by the similarities among moralities. Not so. Hauerwas is struck mainly by the differences. So am I.

Lewis asks us to imagine "a country where people were admired for running away in battle, or where a man felt proud of doublecrossing all the people who had been kindest to him." He adds that you "might just as well try to imagine a country where two and two made five" (p. 19). Now there is something to this. We can, of course, imagine a country of pacifists, where people are admired for running away from battle. But Lewis really wants us to imagine a country in which courage counts as a vice instead of a virtue, and that is a hard thing to imagine. The injunction to be courageous does indeed keep cropping up in one morality after another, if not always with the same emphasis and rarely with the same specification of courageous acts. The reason the injunction is so widespread seems to be that courage is a virtue needed to pursue any aim that involves dangers or some kind of unwelcome experience. [2]

So Lewis does seem to put his finger on an example that shows the differences among moralities not to be total. On the other hand, people don't usually appeal to the belief that courage is a virtue to settle moral disagreements, so this kind of similarity may not do much to remove the deeper worry. Agreeing that courage is a virtue doesn't help us resolve our disagreement about which things to count as courageous. Many things that I consider courageous will strike you as rash (and thus vicious). It will have to be agreement on other sorts of things that will help there.

What about the man who felt proud of doublecrossing all the people who had been kindest to him? Can we imagine that? Lewis thinks not, although the problem may be lack of imagination. There have been many movies and novels about such people—spy novels, for instance, and movies about the good thug who felt proud, if not without a touch of mixed feelings, for turning state's evidence against his comrades. But again, Lewis would grant the point; he wants us to imagine a society in which doublecrossing the people who have been kindest to you is thought of, without qualification and in all circumstances, as right or good or virtuous. And that is hard to imagine.

The only society I have read about that seems, after careful inspection, to condone pointlessly cruel behavior is a tribe appropriately named the Ik. But the Ik are best understood, if their ethnographer is right, [3] as a society that has disintegrated under severely unfavorable conditions, which makes them an unfair example to use against Lewis. By analogy, it wouldn't make us doubt the status of science as a rational and objective endeavor if we discovered that a scientist, who had been tortured for ten years, had developed a strong preference for theories that *conflict* with data from the laboratory.

One would probably have trouble finding many people in any culture or epoch who would candidly endorse as morally good plucking out the eyeballs of innocent members of the community merely for the fun of it. We can, of course, imagine a culture in which people endorse eyeball-plucking for some reason other than mere sport. Perhaps it possesses religious significance in certain exotic rites, a significance that makes it seem justifiable against the background of equally exotic assumptions about the origin of the universe. But eyeball-plucking for mere sport is simply too obvious in its pointless cruelty to sit well with any conception of the good that social groups are willing to live with over time.

If we did find a group that seemed to endorse such a practice as a *moral* good, we would be well advised to consider the following possibilities. First, the chances are that we have simply misunderstood them. There are probably many cases where societies initially seem to condone pointlessly cruel behavior but where deeper understanding would lead us to see the point and to withdraw the assumption that it is cruelty as such which they are endorsing. Second, if charitable consideration only increases our sense that they hold false views about pointless cruelty, we will want to ask how they came to hold views so different from ours. We may find that through no fault of their own they take false presuppositions for granted in their moral reasoning. Otherwise, we shall either have to classify them with the Ik as irrational or vicious (or both) and inquire into the causes of their failings, or we shall have to change *our* minds about the morality of pointless cruelty. Whichever of these responses we elect, we are still assuming that morality is, at least in principle, an endeavor in which truth and justification are at issue.

But why assume that we probably misunderstand a society if we seem to disagree with them totally about moral matters? Lewis doesn't help much with this question. Donald Davidson does.[4] The following argument is essentially his.

If you and I disagree about some proposition, moral or nonmoral, we will at least have enough in common to make sense of that proposition. We couldn't disagree about it if we couldn't make sense of it. If you push the disagreement down too far, it tends to disappear by becoming merely verbal. Suppose you and I disagree about clocks. I say that clocks are vehicles one drives to work, that nearly all new clocks nowadays cost many thousands of dollars, and that one needs a license to operate them legally. You hold the more orthodox opinions about clocks. Here is a case where apparent disagreement goes so deep that it becomes merely verbal. We begin by assuming that we're disagreeing about clocks, but it soon becomes clear that we don't share enough beliefs about what we're each calling clocks to identify a common subject matter to disagree over. No doubt, you will begin to wonder whether it makes more sense to say that my word *clock* should be translated into your language as *car*, thus making most of what I say about both clocks and cars true and reasonable by your lights.

We can find a related phenomenon in comparative ethics. If you start by interpreting some other society as differing from yours *all the way down* on what is right or good and what is not, you'll have trouble saying why the disagreement is about rightness or goodness after all. If somebody applies terms like *right, good,* and *desirable* in ways *completely* unlike the way you do, you have no good reason to translate the terms as *right, good,* and *desirable.* So there's no such thing as evidence of total disagreement about rightness and goodness, any more than there is about clocks and cars.

What follows from this argument? It does follow that any two people who disagree about a given moral proposition will inevitably have a lot of common ground, just as Lewis claims.[5] It does not follow that we can isolate a small set of general principles on which all societies necessarily agree, on pain of irrationality, principles of the kind Lewis seems to have in mind when he speaks of the natural law. Nor do I know of any good argument that can establish substantive principles as universally acceptable. For what principles count as rationally acceptable depends on what is presupposed in a context. We can always imagine some change in presuppositions that would make acceptance of a given substantive principle seem unreasonable, and comparative ethics gives us many examples of cultures whose presuppositions differ from ours in ways that make substantive principles surprisingly unlike ours reasonable in their context. We shall discuss the case of Hinduism in Part 2.

On the other hand, there is a limit to how much disagreement on moral matters we can reasonably posit between any two people (or cultures). It is a vague limit, but a limit nonetheless. Positing too much disagreement on moral matters simply changes the subject. As R. W. Beardsmore has argued:

although it is not possible to exclude *a priori* any feature of an object as a possible criterion of its goodness, we *can* say that if anything is to count as a criterion, then it must in principle be possible to see some relationship between it and the other things which count as criteria of goodness.[6]

If somebody's criteria of goodness were said to differ completely from ours, we would then lack any good reason for concluding that we were in fact disagreeing about goodness. By the same token, if somebody's opinions on moral matters across the board were said to have no overlap with ours whatsoever, it is not clear why we should hold our opinions to be about moral matters at all.

This argument allows us to preserve something from both Lewis and Hauerwas while breaking the apparent impasse between them. Recognizing the extent of real disagreement and our inability to establish foundational principles that every rational agent is bound to accept should make us share Hauerwas' suspicions about the idea that, in justifying our moral beliefs, we can appeal to a transcultural natural law. Lewis does seem to be seeking comfort against the spectres of skepticism and nihilism by imposing a false unity upon moral belief, a unity reinforced by belief in God as Author of the Law. But if every disagreement in fact makes sense only against a background of agreement to which the disputants can appeal, Lewis is right in saying that there is a limit to moral disagreement—a limit beyond which talk of disagreement, in ethics as elsewhere, becomes unintelligible. And this is a limit we can recognize without either imposing a false unity upon moral belief or seeking comfort in theology.

It may be that Hauerwas, in failing to recognize such a limit, feels a need to seek a kind of metaphysical comfort of his own, also theological in character. Moral diversity, as he portrays it, is a chaos of competing options against which he braces himself with bracing thoughts. The extent of moral diversity, for him, is quite literally a sign of the human condition after Babel. The comfort, the strong medicine which sustains a Christian's confidence against the spectres of diversity, comes essentially from beyond the chaos—namely, from God himself. "For we believe that at Pentecost God has undone what was done at Babel."[7] That is, no doubt, a comforting thought—for Christians. But if we cannot accept such comfort, yet share Hauerwas's suspicions about a position like Lewis's, must we simply give in to skepticism, nihilism, or radical relativism? Not if there is a middle way between false unity and sheer chaos.

II

I, no less than Lewis or Hauerwas, believe that there are moral truths. For example, I hold that slavery—understood as the coercive practice of buying, selling, and exercising complete power over other human beings against their will—is evil. I accept the proposition that slavery is evil as true.[8] This proposition hasn't always been believed to be true, of course, just as it hasn't always been held to be true that the earth is roundish, but the *truth* of the matter is that the earth is roundish. The point I'm making now isn't a point about slavery or about the earth but a point about morality and moral propositions. We can share Hauerwas's doubts about appealing to the Moral Law, his emphasis on moral diversity, and his insistence that all justification depends on context without denying that moral propositions are capable of being true or false. Moreover, we needn't think that believing a proposition makes it true.[9] The proposition about slavery mentioned a moment ago didn't become true only when people started believing it to be true. If slavery, as defined a moment ago, is evil, it makes perfect sense to say that it has always been evil—wherever and whenever it can be found in the historical record.

Obviously, people have disagreed, over time, about the evil of slavery. One need not hold, however, that the differences among moralities have been slight in order to employ the notion of moral truth with confidence. We have not yet come across anything to suggest that the facts of moral disagreement, even as Hauerwas sees them, should force us to abandon talk of moral truth. Even much wider disagreement over the truth of moral propositions than Lewis acknowledges would still presuppose that moral propositions have truth-value. If "the natural law" or "the moral law" is just a fancy name for all the moral truths, known and unknown, then neither Hauerwas nor I need object to belief in it.

I do object to the idea that we can explain what it is for moral propositions to be true by saying that they correspond to the Law, since the relation of correspondence invoked by such an explanation doesn't seem clear enough to explain anything. This, however, is another, quite different, issue. To say that a moral proposition corresponds to the Moral Law doesn't obviously add anything more than a well-worn figure of speech—anything of explanatory value—to saying that the proposition is true. For it to do so, we would have to be able to say what such correspondence consists in. Yet this is precisely what philosophers have had trouble saying. There would be no problem here if we knew what it would be like to look directly, without help from variable tradition-bound presuppositions, at the Moral Law and then back again at our beliefs, surveying the relations for instances or failures of correspondence. But we don't know what it would be like to do that, so talk of correspondence as an *explanation* of truth cannot help us.

Nor does it obviously help to say that *testing* our moral beliefs for truth or for rational acceptability is a matter of comparing them with some transcendent thing-in-itself, the Natural Law. In any event, all we have to go on in testing our moral beliefs is our own culture's best view of what moral truth or justified moral belief consists in (for example, as expressed in its sacred scripture or most profound moral philosophy and enriched by flights of imagination or fresh experiences in the world). A transcendent thing-in-itself, even if we suppose it exists, wouldn't help until we described it in our own terms—at which point we would no longer be appealing to a thing-in-itself but rather to a belief about the truth of the matter in question. When we test our beliefs for truth or rational acceptability, we appeal not to the thing-in-itself—to which, by definition, we could never have access—but rather to further beliefs not currently in question.

Even if you augment your own culture's collective wisdom about morality by comparative study of distant cultures, so that you have been persuaded to abandon some propositions long held true in your culture and to embrace wisdom from abroad, it will now be a new and (we may hope) improved version of your own culture's collective wisdom you'll need to take into account as you reason about which moral propositions to hold true or justified. You can't somehow leap out of culture and history altogether and gaze directly into the Moral Law, using it as a standard for judging the justification or truth of moral propositions, any more than you can gaze directly into the mind of God. You can, if you possess the requisite virtues, search your available resources for all relevant considerations and deliberate wisely. You can even expand your own culture's horizons in a way that brings new or long-neglected considerations into view. What you can't do, if you are human, is have your judgment determined solely by the matter under consideration without relying on beliefs, habits of description, and patterns of reasoning that belong to a cultural inheritance.

The important point to understand here is that doubts about explanations or criteria of moral truth are not necessarily doubts about moral truth—about whether moral statements that have proposition-like form are really propositions and thus have truth-value. Rejecting a theory of truth or the idea that moral philosophy needs one is not (and should not be) to reject the concept of truth. Doubting whether a Moral Law or Realm of Values is needed to give moral propositions something to be true *of* in order to keep the bottom from falling out of moral objectivity isn't the same as doubting that moral propositions have truthvalue. Recently, much misleading talk about nihilism and moral realism has been fostered by failure to appreciate this.

I find it enlightening when a deft philosopher of language like J. L. Austin or Donald Davidson explains how the term *true* functions in our language by showing the contribution it makes to speech-acts or by reflecting on sentences such as "'Slavery is evil' is true if and only if slavery is evil." When I express the suspicion that philosophy cannot explain the nature of truth or what it is for a moral proposition to be true, I am saying that I fail to see what remains to be explained about the concept of truth after we know all there is to know about how the term *true* is used. I have no trouble with the notion that we need criteria of truth, in the sense of norms that help us determine which sentences to accept as true. What I doubt is that correspondence to a culture-transcendent thing-in-itself, like the Moral Law or a Realm of Values, will be of much help, either as a criterion or an explanation, to us human beings who are not culture-transcendent, whose every knowing is culturally embedded. But neither my suspicion about explanations of truth nor my doubt about the helpfulness of certain criteria commits me to abandoning the term *true*. The term functions perfectly well in our discourse, as far as I can tell. Like most of us, I use it wholeheartedly, no less in moral contexts than elsewhere.

In fact, my talk of moral disagreement makes sense only if I grant that there is some truth of the matter in ethics to disagree over and only if I am prepared to say of people who disagree with me over the truth of moral propositions that it is they who are wrong. But if there are flatearthers, people who are wrong about important scientific truths, why shouldn't there be societies that are wrong about important moral truths? To say that there are such societies is not necessarily to say that their members are unjustified in believing and behaving as they do. One can be blameless, epistemically and morally, and still hold and act on false beliefs, whether in science or in ethics. We need impute no dishonor to those who disagree with us. Nor need we lack humility when we conclude that our beliefs are true, and, by implication, that those who disagree with us hold false beliefs. To hold our beliefs is precisely to accept them as true. It would be inconsistent, not a sign of humility, to say that people who disagree with beliefs we hold true are not themselves holding false beliefs.

Presumably, some of the moral propositions that we embrace, however justified we may be in accepting them under current epistemic circumstances, will someday be discovered to be false. That is, they are false now, even though we don't know it yet, even though we're now justified in accepting them as true. Humility does require recognition that some of our beliefs are surely wrong. But that is no reason, in itself, for withdrawing any particular truth-claim or for shunning the notion that people who disagree with a truth-claim we have made accept a falsehood. Granting that those who disagree with us could possibly be right after all does not involve admitting, here and now, that they are right. Nor does it require us to use the terms *true* and *false* in anything but a straightforward manner. Some of the sentences, including moral ones, that we are now warranted in asserting and justified in believing are not true. We know this from observing human history and learning the facts of finitude. If we knew which ones were false, we would immediately cease believing them. But knowing that some are false isn't the same as knowing which are false. So we go on accepting each one as true until we have reason for doubting something in particular. And all the while, we also believe that something, we know not what, will need correction.

This general doubt, inspired by humility, doesn't make anything in particular doubtful. The appropriate moral to draw from such possibilities is rather this, that justification and truth require different treatment. More precisely: the phrases "is justified" and "is true" function differently in our language. Notice that sentences like these seem perfectly in order:

1. He, given his context, is justified in believing that p but the proposition that p is false.
2. I used to be justified in believing that p but the proposition that p is false and always was.
3. I am now justified in believing that p but the proposition that p could turn out to be false.

We could construct analogous instances by substituting "warranted in asserting" for "justified in believing," and they would make equally good sense. It is therefore severely misleading at best to express doubt about certain traditional theories of truth by saying that truth is merely warranted assertibility. What, then, could the pragmatists who said that truth is warranted assertibility have been driving at? No doubt, they were not blind to the absurdity of denying, for example, that I can be warranted in asserting a proposition at a given time and later discover the proposition to have been false. Their point, I take it, was that seeking to hold or to assert true propositions involves neither more nor less than seeking to hold or to assert rationally justified or warranted propositions. We can accept this point, however, without allowing that truth *is* warranted assertibility.

To see why, consider how odd it would be to say:

4. I am now warranted in asserting (justified in believing) that *p* but the proposition that *p* is false.

When I am speaking of a proposition that I, here and now, take myself to be warranted in asserting or justified in believing, it will normally be a proposition that I, here and now, will accept and assert as a truth. If not, my rationality or candor will be suspect. First-person, present-tense statements about justified belief or warranted assertibility do tend to match up well with the relevant assertions about what is true. Granted, the match doesn't obtain when the statements about justified belief or warranted assertibility are in the second or third person or the past tense (as in 1 and 2 above), nor when first-person, present-tense statements about justified belief or warranted assertibility are paired with assertions about what *could* be the case (as in 3).

But where the match does obtain, it has significance. For when I, here and now, face the problem of what propositions to deem true and seek criteria for determining this, the propositions I accept as true, if I am being reasonable, will be the ones I am justified in believing. The propositions I assert to be true, if I am being reasonable and candid, will be the ones I am warranted in asserting. And the criteria I use for judging truth will be the ones I use for determining which propositions I am justified in holding true.[10] Because it is always the first-person, present-tense perspective from which we judge truth, the pragmatists' point, though not their dictum, is well taken. We might capture the truth in the dictum by saying: Truth, for us, here and now, is always warranted assertibility. But it would be better to avoid the dictum altogether while appreciating the point.[11]

One reason to avoid the dictum altogether is that even the qualified version may be taken to imply that when I say (here and now) that such-and-such a proposition is true, this should be taken to *mean* that the proposition is warranted or justified. Any such characterization of the meaning of truth-claims, however, is plainly false. I believe that slavery is evil. I have just told you what I believe about the moral standing of slavery. The proposition "Slavery is evil" is true. Now I have just told you that the truth-condition of a proposition obtains. That's not the same as telling you that the proposition is justified in my context or that I am justified in believing it or warranted in asserting it. If I went on to tell you that I am justified in believing that slavery is evil or warranted in asserting that the proposition "Slavery is evil" is true, these additional claims could be false even if my statement about the truth of the proposition is true (and vice versa). So truth does not *mean* justified belief or warranted assertibility, even in a restricted class of grammatical contexts.

Nor, the dependence of justification on epistemic context notwithstanding, does the claim that I am justified in believing that slavery is evil simply mean that "Slavery is evil" is actually a sentence my peers would allow me to assert without challenge. Sabina Lovibond has written that "when we ask a question about some aspect of reality, we are not asking for a report on the state of public opinion with regard to that question, we are asking to be told the *truth* about it." [12] Something similar can be said regarding justification. If you ask me whether the proposition that slavery is evil is justified, you're not asking me for a report on the state of public opinion. When I answer that the proposition is justified, I presuppose standards native to my own context, standards constituted in part by consensus on certain matters as well as by shared intentions and desires. But I am not telling you what the consensus on slavery is. And while our justificatory practice would be impossible in the absence of widespread agreement on a great many things, I can always buck the consensus on something in particular. Furthermore, I can be right in doing so—both in the sense of believing a truth and in the sense of being justified in believing it.

Suppose I am a very early abolitionist, the first to recognize an incoherence in the stock defenses of slavery heretofore accepted by all parties. I rise to the pulpit one Sunday and declare that slavery is evil. No one else has said or thought this before. Yet because the stock defenses of slavery are incoherent in the way I have just recognized, I am in fact justified in believing slavery to be evil. In such a situation, as Lovibond puts it, "I'm right and everyone else is wrong." [13] I'm still using standards that belong to my context, standards which have their authority in part because others who share my context agree on certain things—things like a principle requiring a morally relevant reason for intentionally treating some people in ways we would not wish to be treated ourselves. If we weren't initiated into a community of agreement on various matters, we wouldn't be able to carry on at all. Take all agreement away and we would simply be dumb and brutish. A certain level of public agreement is, therefore, a condition of the possibility of being justified in believing something. But when I claim that my belief is justified, I'm not telling you what the state of public opinion is—either at the level of standards or at the level of their application to cases.

Moreover, by presupposing standards not currently in doubt among members of my community, I'm using or relying on those standards in a way that commits me to their authority. This is what places me within the logical space of normative discourse—the only space in which expressions like "is justified" and "is true" can be used, not merely mentioned. We are wise, then, to avoid making sensible, "pragmatic" points about truth and contextually sensitive, "historicist" points about justification by uttering dicta that seem like attempts to reduce normative terms (like "is justified" or "is true") to nonnormative expressions (like "is what your peers will let you get away with" or "forms part of some widely accepted social institution").[14]

But what, then, do the terms "is justified" and "is true" mean? If I find the standard theories unacceptable because their definitions lack explanatory power, are unduly reductive, or are otherwise troublesome, why not just propose my own theory about how justification and truth should be defined and thus end the suspense? My answer is that such a definition wouldn't tell us anything about these notions we hadn't already grasped by learning how the relevant terms function in our language and by learning how to use them ourselves. Once we know the subtle details of actual usage, a theoretical definition of such a concept is likely to cause more problems than it solves and unlikely to be both informative and nonreductive. It would be better to have none at all.

III

Is moral relativism true? That depends on what we mean by relativism. Confusing the various senses of relativism is part of what fuels concerns over the significance of moral diversity. We've just discussed senses in which the justification of moral propositions is relative. I claimed that which moral propositions you're justified in believing depends upon or is relative to where you find yourself in culture and history. All justification is relative in this way—scientific as well as moral. It doesn't follow, however, that the truth of a given proposition is relative. Furthermore, while justification is relative, it isn't relative to arbitrary, subjective choice on the part of an individual.

I maintain that the world isn't flat and that slavery is evil. We are now justified in believing both of these propositions, in holding them true. That is to say, we have good reason, given what else we're taking for granted at the current stage of inquiry and given the experience and wisdom we've accumulated so far, to believe that the world isn't flat and that slavery is evil. Anybody who wanted to deny these propositions in our context would have to bear the burden of proof.

It's clear, however, that people who lived thousands of years ago don't deserve epistemic blame for believing that the world is flat. There's a clear sense in which they were justified in so believing. Given the reasons and evidence available to them, it was rational to believe that the world is flat. Given the reasons and evidence that have since become available, and on which we draw in justifying our current beliefs about the shape of the earth, we would be unreasonable to doubt that the earth is in fact roundish.

We're now justified in believing slavery to be evil. Part of what justifies this belief is a failure, over the long haul of moral reasoning, to make clear what could conceivably justify treating people assigned to the role of slave in ways that we do not tolerate for other people. Some of the beliefs that used to underlie the practice of slavery—such as the belief that no society could survive without slavery and the belief that God had designated certain classes of people as slaves after the Flood— have not survived critical scrutiny. Let us suppose that most of these considerations were sufficiently evident to people even in the American South a hundred years ago that the proponents of slavery in that context weren't justified. Their reasons and arguments just weren't good enough, in the presence of reasons and counterarguments on the other side, for them to be justified in believing that slavery is morally legitimate. But we may imagine a time, or discover one through historical inquiry, when belief in slavery was justified, relative to available reasons and evidence.

Justification in morality, as in science, is relative—but relative to one's epistemic circumstance, including reasons and evidence available at the current stage of inquiry, not to the arbitrary choice of individuals. Just as an arbitrary change in scientific criteria wouldn't make it more reasonable for me to believe that the earth is flat, neither can an arbitrary change in moral principles make it more reasonable for me to believe that slavery is good. Being justified in believing something is a normative relation that exists among a given proposition, the person who accepts it, and a cognitive context. If I am justified in accepting a proposition, then the proposition, my context, and I are related in the required way. The relation is as objective as can be, not subject to worrisomely arbitrary subjective manipulation. What may make it seem subjective is that some of the facts about it are facts about the human subject involved. Facts about what my peers take for granted, about judgmental dispositions acquired by members of my society during successful training in the relevant practices, about the history of casuistical precedents in my tradition, about evidence available to me, and so on, all will be relevant features of the context, features open to objective inquiry.

This relativity does not carry over, at least in a case like the proposition that slavery is evil, to truth. What we're justified in believing about the evil of slavery varies according to the evidence and reasoning available to us in our place in culture and history. But the truth of the proposition that slavery is evil doesn't vary in the same way. It wasn't true several millennia ago that the earth was flat. When we say that it was true for people of the time that the earth was flat, we mean only that they believed it was true, not that the earth really was flat and only later became round. Similarly, slavery didn't become evil only when people discovered what was wrong with it. Perhaps it became blameworthy then, but the discovery involved coming to know a truth about slavery—namely, that it was evil all along.

I hope this makes clear why some authors can sound relativistic for long stretches and then suddenly sound nonrelativistic about moral truth, especially when speaking as moralists. They need not be guilty of contradiction, for we can take them, charitably, to be able to see the difference between justification and truth. The facts of moral disagreement may well give us reason to insist upon the relativity of justification, since that insistence will help us explain forms of disagreement which might otherwise remain puzzling. But this insistence needn't render justification merely arbitrary or subjective, and it can swing free of concerns over moral truth.

Notice that a willingness to distinguish justification from truth allows us to be forthright in affirming the truth of our convictions without necessarily blaming previous generations or distant cultures for believing differently. We can say that some of their practices were morally evil and that some of their related moral beliefs were false—for instance, beliefs about the treatment of slaves and women and witches—without implying that they were irrational, unreasonable, or blameworthy for behaving and believing as they did. Saying that slavery is evil is not the same thing as imputing blame for practicing it or supporting it or believing it morally unproblematical. We may disagree with our ancestors' moral judgments and thus hold their judgments to be false, explaining the difference by citing intervening historical developments that have significantly changed the epistemic situation. Reflection on such developments may make us want to excuse our ancestors for accepting false beliefs and hence for acting on them. If so, we shall say that they were justified but wrong.

We shall not always want to be so charitable, of course, even on reflection. At times, we will be forced to explain a point of disagreement with our ancestors' moral beliefs not by saying that they were justified in holding beliefs we now deem false but rather by saying that negligent reasoning, ideological rationalization, or wishful thinking led them to hold false beliefs. If, after extending the benefit of the doubt to third-century Athenians, we can find nothing in their epistemic circumstances to excuse their beliefs about slavery, we will conclude that they weren't justified in holding those beliefs.

We may even conclude that some of their true beliefs were held for bad or insufficient reasons. Just as people can hold false beliefs for good reasons, they can hold true beliefs for bad reasons. Someone who held a true theory of the shape of the earth in the twelfth century B.C.E. would probably have to be judged unreasonable.[15] Someone who was largely right about the treatment of slaves in third-century Athens might well have been so by accident or for merely self-interested reasons. Two things follow from such possibilities. First, similarity in belief on certain topics between two groups sometimes is harder to explain than dissimilarity. Second, even if a given group holds beliefs we deem true, we may still need to consider whether such factors as negligent reasoning, ideological rationalization, and wishful thinking are at work.[16]

We have been discussing cases of apparent moral disagreement with our ancestors or with other cultures. So far we have considered cases in which we explain away the apparent disagreement by charitable reinterpretation of ancient or alien opinion, cases in which we count such opinion justified but false, and cases in which we feel forced to ascribe irrationality or other forms of viciousness to the people with whom we disagree. It is very important, however, to keep in view another possibility, only implicit until now. We might, after all our dialogue with the dead or the foreign, decide to change *our* minds on the moral issue in question. Another group's ideological distortions, once we perceive them, may help us uncover ours. Or we may learn from the people we are studying by discovering reasons for their moral judgments we have forgotten or never known, reasons that persuade us that their judgments, and not ours, are true.[17] Or perhaps we will come to admire them as people and wish to be like them, adopting some analogue of their way of life. Indeed, much of the point of comparative ethics lies in possibilities like these. To neglect them is to make comparative inquiry into an exercise in self-congratulation—an imperialistic discipline in which one announces, with perfect *hubris* and without ever questioning one's own views, where the great unwashed have gone wrong.

2

OBJECTIONS AND REPLIES

Objection: The previous chapter, although it purports to affirm justification and truth in ethics, is in fact committed to the very tendencies
that undermine realism in both ethics and science, for it dispenses with
things-in-themselves, with reality that transcends us as knowing beings.
In ethics, this approach does away with the Moral Law, a Realm of
Values, or the idea of culture-transcendent Moral Facts. In science, it
is the World that is lost. Such consequences prove the absurdity of the
tendencies that lead to them.

Reply: To say that testing or justifying beliefs always involves appeal to
further beliefs and not appeal to things as they are in themselves, independent of all human description, is an epistemological, not an ontological remark. In other words, it tells you something about the grammar of testing and justifying, not about what there is. If I say that testing
beliefs about the physical world inevitably takes objects under descriptions, that at any given time there is no justificatory appeal beyond the
world-as-we-are-currently-describing-it, I am not expressing doubt, say,
that rocks and trees would have existed even if language-users had
never come along to describe them. Idealism, the ontological thesis
that the existence of the world depends upon the descriptive capacity of
minds, *is* absurd. But I reject idealism. I also reject nihilism, by which
I mean the thesis that there are no moral truths.

33

Objection: Claiming that there is no culture-transcendent Moral Law sounds suspiciously like an ontological thesis.

Reply: I have deliberately avoided putting it in that way, hoping to sidestep misunderstanding. I have no problem with the idea of a culture-transcendent Moral Law if it commits us merely to such notions as these: that there are moral truths; that any given moral proposition may in fact be true even though none of us knows that it is; that no one could possibly know all the moral truths without knowing the (perhaps infinite) set of moral vocabularies in which all moral propositions could be formulated (including some not yet invented); and that what an omniscient being would know in knowing the truth-value of all possible moral propositions in all possible moral vocabularies might plausibly be called the Moral Law. The problems come when we appeal to the Moral Law, in our explanations or criteria of moral truth, in a way that requires denying that we are necessarily employing culturally embedded categories as we do. For then the implied sense of the phrase "culture-transcendent Moral Law" is: "a set of moral truths one could know or understand without making use of a moral vocabulary." And there is no such thing. This may sound like a negative ontological claim, a claim about what there isn't, but the point is really epistemological—namely, that a certain sort of appeal involves an epistemological impossibility. In this sense, a "culture-transcendent Moral Law" is, like the unknowable thing-in-itself, a creature of epistemology—and well lost. The only sort of object whose existence is being denied is an object one would posit only for (bad) epistemological reasons, an object defined in epistemological terms. This denial leaves everything outside epistemology, including common sense, just as it is.

Objection: This just isn't so. Common sense is committed to a culture-transcendent Moral Law.

Reply: Surely, not in the sense just stipulated, the sense at issue. Nobody believes in "a set of moral truths one could know or understand without making use of a moral vocabulary" until after exposure, direct or indirect, to philosophy. One has to be initiated into epistemology to acquire such notions. What belongs to common sense is the idea that there are moral truths, not a conception of moral truths tailored to essentially post-Kantian epistemological purposes.

Objection: The position being defended obviously claims to reject nihilism. It is hard to find anyone who wants to bear that label. The question is whether the position implies nihilism, whatever the intent of its defenders.

Reply: Granted. But it remains to be shown that the position in fact implies nihilism. To think that what I have said about *explanations* and *criteria* of moral truth commits me to nihilism in any interesting sense is to confuse separate issues. I claim that positing a transcendent Moral Law (or the like) does not help explain what it is for a moral proposition to be true. Nor, I claim, does such a posit help as a criterion for judging the truth of moral propositions. Neither of these claims, separately or in conjunction, implies that there are no moral truths. One can, of course, merely stipulate that these two claims render any associated view nihilistic, but that would beg the question. The label doesn't stick unless the person applying it can demonstrate that our talk of moral truth, to which I subscribe without reservation, fails to make sense unless we adopt the disputed explanation of what it is for moral propositions to be true. This has not been done.

Objection: It is fine to have the truth or justification of a proposition asserted. No attempt has been made in these chapters, however, to justify the proposition that slavery is evil or that eyeball-plucking for sport is unjust. In the absence of any such attempt, we have nothing but assertion, where what we need is argument.[1]

Reply: We don't always have to justify a proposition (show it to be true), or even be able to justify it, to be justified in believing it or for it to be justified. Some propositions acquire a kind of epistemic authority that needs no support from recitation of justifying reasons or demonstrations of truth, provided specific grounds for doubt do not arise. The propositions about the shape of the earth, the evil of slavery, and the injustice of whimsical eyeball-plucking may now have such authority. I hope so. I would worry about someone who claimed to find such propositions doubtful. In fact, as Wittgenstein pointed out, there are many propositions that we are justified in believing but wouldn't know how to justify. Anything we could say on behalf of such a proposition seems less certain than the proposition itself. By now, it is hard to debate with flat-earthers. What real doubt do they have that can be addressed with justifying reasons? The same may hold for debate with moral fanatics, a matter to which we shall return in Part 3. None of this is to say, of course, that I couldn't supply justifying reasons for some of the moral propositions in my examples. I hinted at some in my discussion of slavery. But we ought to be suspicious of people who want reasons even when they can't supply reasonable doubts.

Objection: The previous chapter's willingness to compare moral and scientific propositions—the one about slavery and the one about the shape of the earth—raises a question the moral skeptic will want to exploit. For when we do compare morality and science, we find that morality utterly lacks the kind of agreement and rational means for securing it that we find in science, and this lack is precisely what all the fuss is about.

Reply: That may be what much of the fuss is about, but it is by no means obvious that the question does the damage skeptics think it does. It would be foolish not to concede that there are important differences between science and morality. What the skeptic needs to show, however, is that the differences, such as they are, should undermine our confidence in speaking of justification and truth in ethics, and this isn't as easily shown as one might think. While it is clear that moral judgments are not tested exactly as scientific hypotheses are, it is much less clear that the notion of testing fails to apply to moral judgments. It begs the question to assume that only testing of a kind found uniquely in science, in which a certain sort of observation employing physicalistic descriptions of the world plays a crucial role in securing agreement, can provide a basis for talk of justification and truth.

We must be careful not to exaggerate the contrast between morality and science by taking for granted either an excessively narrow view of scientific reasoning or an inflated estimation of scientific agreement. People who exaggerate the differences between morality and science often picture scientific rationality and concord in a way that has been under severe attack in the philosophy of science for nearly forty years, conveniently neglecting such phenomena as the theory-ladenness of observation and the protracted disputes that have marked scientific revolutions.

Many people who have doubts about morality move too quickly from recognizing that moral reasoning fails to conform to a certain model of rationality or objectivity to concluding that it's not a rational or objective endeavor at all. These people are too sure thay know what rationality or objective truth is. They take that for granted, find (quite rightly) that morality doesn't live up to their standard, and then despair for morality. They need to ask whether morality exhibits a kind of rationality or objectivity they weren't looking for at the start. Moral skeptics, shall we say, are like a critic who has imagined the ideal novel but who is constantly disappointed by the actual novels coming across her desk for review. They don't measure up to her model of what the perfect novel should be like. But is that a fault in the books or a fault in her model? If you want to make morality look bad by comparison with science, you must first defend a picture of scientific disagreement, not just take one for granted, and then make the terms of the comparison fair.

Objection: Not everybody who contrasts science and ethics stacks the deck in this fashion. Consider, for example, Gilbert Harman, who goes out of his way to call attention to such phenomena as the theory-ladenness of scientific observation. For Harman, what scientists perceive in the laboratory depends to some extent on the theories they hold. The scientist does not test theories against "pure observations." Observations necessarily employ available vocabularies and partake in the commitments implicit in background theories. Only with such vocabularies and theories in place is scientific observation possible. "Similarly," Harman says, "if you hold a moral view, whether it is held consciously or unconsciously, you will be able to perceive rightness or wrongness, goodness or badness, justice or injustice. There is no difference in this respect between moral propositions and other theoretical propositions." Still he maintains that "observation plays a role in science that it does not seem to play in ethics." In science, "you need to make assumptions about certain physical facts to explain the occurrence of the observations that support a scientific theory," but the same does not hold in ethics, where "you do not seem to need to make assumptions about any moral facts to explain the occurrence of . . . moral observations." Ethics, he concludes, is "cut off from observation" and therefore problematic. [2]

Reply: It will be helpful to discuss one of Harman's examples, a case in which children pour gasoline on a cat and ignite it. Most of us would be inclined to respond immediately—without moving through a series of inferential steps—by saying that the children acted viciously. Harman grants that there are moral observations in this sense. He also grants that "moral principles might help to explain why it was *wrong* of the children to set the cat on fire." If we "observe" that the children are wrong to set the cat on fire, and the best explanation of the wrongness of their act involves the notion that acts deriving solely from malicious cruelty are wrong, the observation lends credence to the explanation. It is important to see that Harman is not denying this. So even if he is right in holding that there are important disanalogies between science and ethics, he is not saying that observation is irrelevant to ethics.[3]

Objection: Fair enough. But "moral principles," Harman thinks, "seem to be of no help in explaining *your thinking* that" the children were wrong (p. 8). To explain your thinking that the children were wrong, according to Harman, we need only make certain assumptions about your "sensibility," your "psychological set." We needn't make any assumptions about the moral truth of the matter. In contrast, says Harman, when a physicist observes a vapor trail, which he takes to be a proton, in a cloud chamber, his observation supports the theory he is testing "only because, in order to explain his making the observation, it is reasonable to assume something about the world over and above the assumptions made about the observer's psychology" (p. 7). Assuming that a proton actually passed through the chamber helps explain the physicist's thinking that it did. If it didn't, we couldn't use his thinking that it did as evidence for the theory he is testing.

Reply: It isn't clear that Harman's contrast survives critical scrutiny. In particular, it isn't clear that we never need to make assumptions about moral truth in accounting for moral observations. Suppose we have two people, Charles Manson and Archbishop Tutu, each of whom has witnessed the children reducing a cat to ashes, and two observers of the cloud chamber, a Hindu metaphysician ignorant of modern science and a leading physicist. The sensibilities of each pair differ. Difference in sensibility helps explain why Manson is amused at the cat-burning while Tutu observes cruelty. Difference in sensibility also helps explain why the physicist's report includes talk about a proton while the Hindu's includes nothing of the sort. Up to a point, differences in sensibility provide all the explanation needed in both cases. But in each case, we shall want to go further if we sense that the observations in question have some bearing on what beliefs *we* should hold in physics or ethics. At that point, we will no longer be able to abstract from moral and scientific appraisal of the various observations, treating their truth or falsity as unimportant for our purposes. We shall then need to make judgments of our own about truth and falsity, invoking or assuming the relevant standards of competence in judgment.

In both morals and science, the role of competent observer is defined largely by the acquisition of a certain sensibility or "psychological set"—beliefs, goals, desires, dispositions. Whether someone's observation counts as evidence for evaluating a theory depends on whether that person qualifies as a competent observer. To the extent that Tutu is a competent moral judge and the physicist a competent practitioner of physics, their observations become relevant to the assessment of theories and principles in their respective domains. Once we grant, however, that both men are competent observers, it becomes unclear why the moral truth of the matter in Tutu's case shouldn't contribute to our explanation of why he immediately judged the children wrong upon seeing their act. Assuming that the children really did exhibit malicious cruelty in pouring gasoline on the cat—that malicious cruelty was the moral fact of the matter—does help explain Tutu's thinking that the children were wrong, provided that malicious cruelty is wrong, Tutu is a competent moral judge, and he was in a good position to know all the morally relevant details.

We know that we'd side with Tutu against Manson, and our explanation of the difference in their immediate responses would be morally incomplete if it failed to mention differences in competence. We are inclined to say that Manson is morally deviant and to cite deficiencies in his sensibility because we need an account of why his immediate responses to vicious acts take no cognizance of their viciousness. In saying this, we are operating within the logical space of a moral language, relying on standards of appraisal and patterns of authority. It is within this logical space that the truth of the proposition, "The children exhibited malicious cruelty," helps explain why a morally competent observer took the children to be wrong. Only if we stand outside that logical space, abstracting from the question whether it is true that the children were wrong and from the assessment of moral principles that might have some bearing on this question, does it seem sufficient to appeal simply to differences in sensibility, without introducing the normative notion of competence, in accounting for why Tutu's response to cat-burnings differs from Manson's. To admit that Tutu is competent in the relevant sense implies that in cases of this sort, where all competent observers agree, he can generally be depended on to observe *rightly*. The truth of his observation therefore helps explain why he, given his competence, made that observation.

When Harman says that the physicist's "making the observation *supports* the theory only because, in order to explain his making the observation, it is reasonable to assume something about the world over and above the assumptions made about the observer's psychology," he is standing within the logical space of scientific language and presupposing the physicist's competence. Only on the assumption that the physicist is competent does his observation support the theory. The Hindu metaphysician's observation would neither support the theory nor undermine it. And only if we assume that the physicist is competent and place ourselves within the logical space in which it makes sense to speak of something as "support" for a theory does it make sense to introduce the terms of the theory ("A proton was going through the cloud chamber") in order to explain the physicist's observation. If we make a similar assumption about competence in the moral case and place ourselves within the logical space of a moral language, it does seem to make sense to introduce the truth of a moral proposition as part of our explanation of Tutu's thinking that the children were wrong. When we have made that assumption and entered that logical space, we shall want to say not simply that Tutu and Manson have different sensibilities but also that Tutu is sensitive and wise whereas Manson is viciously deranged. But it will be difficult to explain what makes them different on that (normative) score without making assumptions about the *truth* of moral propositions like, "It really is a sign of viciousness to set cats (or people) on fire for the fun of it."[4]

If a moral theory implied that raping women was generally a good thing, morally speaking, all competent moral judges in our community would reject that theory as false. Of course, it is hard to imagine such a moral theory being seriously proposed in the first place, just as it is hard to imagine a situation in which one's observations of children setting a cat on fire would play a crucial role in assessment of an ethical outlook. But if you are a competent moral judge and have worked extensively with rape victims, your moral observations of what rape has done to their lives might well be relevant to the appraisal of propositions concerning what, morally speaking, ought to be done for them. The fact that rape has severely adverse effects upon the women subjected to it will help explain why a judge of your competence finds it so evil.

Objection: This argument simply begs the question. What needs to be shown is why we ought to enter with such confidence into the logical space of moral judgment—the space where it seems obvious that the truth of a moral proposition about cruelty helps explain the observations of supposedly competent judges.

Reply: The only way to get people to enter this logical space is through successful moral training. No simple argument will do it. But the same is true for the logical space of scientific judgment. My argument is intended simply to point out the parallels. A comparison between morality and science begs the question whether "ethics is problematic" if it begins by adopting a kind of alienation from the logical space of moral judgment that it does not adopt with respect to science.

Objection: Reference to "immediate moral judgments" and "moral observation" smacks of intuitionism. But intuitionism has long been out of favor—and for good reason.

Reply: One must be careful to specify the sort of immediacy involved. I maintain that there are immediate moral judgments or observations in the sense of reports we are disposed to make without moving through a series of inferential steps. Noninferential reports need not possess the other sorts of immediacy typically associated with intuitionism. They need not be incorrigible, indubitable, infallible, immediately demonstrable, self-justifying, prelinguistic, or possible in the absence of extensive training. The idea that there can be noninferential reports (such as the idea, mentioned several paragraphs back, that some propositions can *be* justified in a certain context even though we don't know how to justify them) recovers a grain of truth from intuitionism without reverting to disreputable forms of immediacy.[5]

Objection: On close examination, morality simply lacks the level of agreement found in science, a level of agreement that could justify confident references to standards of competent judgment.

Reply: The comparison must be fair. It won't do to cite a few beliefs held by all of us who have had introductory physics courses and then to contrast that depth of agreement with the depth of disagreement over abortion.[6] It would be fairer to compare the propositions from Physics 101 with our now widely shared moral beliefs about slavery. Neither would have commanded wide assent in the Middle Ages. Both have involved hard-won victories in which reasoning played a heavy role in bringing about change in belief. Disagreement over an issue like abortion might then be compared with disagreement among cosmologists over the origin of the universe. It's not yet clear what, if anything, is going to settle these disagreements, although neither one seems impossible in principle to resolve by rational means.

Objection: Lovibond suggests in the first half of *Realism and Imagination in Ethics* that we should junk the sharp, metaphysical distinction between science and ethics, according to which ethics can make no legitimate claim to objectivity or truth, but that we should nonetheless develop a more subtle, phenomenological description of differences between the "pull of objectivity" or level of agreement in the two realms. When we look closely at the two realms, however, the differences seem great, as even Lovibond seems forced to admit.

Reply: There are differences, but even Lovibond tends to exaggerate them. She says, for example, that while "there is agreement among competent users of natural-scientific language in their (potential) verbal responses to new experiences . . . this kind of agreement is absent in morals" (p. 81). This comment pays insufficient heed to turbulent and prolonged debates in the history of natural science. Equally important, it neglects the areas in which competent users of moral language would be likely to agree in their (potential) responses to new experiences. New types of pointless cruelty would, of course, be greeted with abhorrence by everybody who (a) qualifies as a competent moral judge and (b) does not suffer from false empirical and metaphysical assumptions.

Objection: Adding conditions (a) and (b) begs the question by guaranteeing a level of agreement that tends to be absent.

Reply: Conditions (a) and (b) are needed to make the comparison with science fair, since we could easily increase the level of disagreement in science by counting quacks or imaginary Hindu metaphysicians as scientists.

Objection: If there were really so much agreement in ethics, it would not be so hard to recognize. A sharp distinction between morality and science on this score is a matter of prereflective common sense.

Reply: We have little trouble noticing scientific agreement, perhaps because most of us stop taking science courses before we get into areas of heated debate. We never get to use scientific discourse, as scientists do, to express dissent or to work away for years at resolving a disagreement. If we have more trouble noticing moral agreement, the reason may be that we are initiated into a moral consensus as very young children. By the time we begin reflecting on differences between morality and science, we are already sufficiently expert as moral critics to spend much of our time using moral language to engage our fellows in debate. Ethics courses do not bother to rehearse countless platitudes assented to by nearly everybody in our culture. The first week's reading is already in disputed territory. Inside the classroom or out, skilled users of moral language typically leave platitudes unstated or even forgotten, calling them to mind or putting them into service only when they prove useful in resolving disputes, celebrating holidays, or correcting the unskilled.[7] We forget that it is a background of agreement on platitudes that makes moral disagreement intelligible.

Objection: The account of moral observation offered a moment ago leans heavily on the notion of a competent moral judge. But agreement on what constitutes a competent moral judge is hard to come by. The example of Tutu is a case in point. Many of Tutu's moral judgments are highly controversial. Many people, including not only white South Africans who support apartheid but also black South Africans who oppose divestment, would want to challenge Tutu's practical wisdom. Scientists have no similar problem getting agreement on what constitutes a competent observer in the laboratory.

Reply: Scientists do have similar problems during periods of scientific revolution, when epistemic circumstances do not clearly indicate which of two research programs ought to be pursued and proponents of each program question their opponents' wisdom and competence. But I have no stake in denying that what makes a competent moral judge is often highly contested and, in some settings, more contestable than analogous questions in science. What accounts for the difference? One factor is that the question of what makes somebody a competent moral judge is closely connected to the very subject matter a moral judge is called upon to make judgments about, such as the question of what makes a virtuous person. In natural science, there is no such close connection and therefore less reason to worry over circularity.

Another factor is this: Science has been professionalized. Modern scientific practice tends to be confined to institutions that impose strict limits on who qualifies as a legitimate practitioner. Morality, in contrast, tends to be less tightly bound to such institutions—ecclesiastical ones in particular—than it used to be. Morality, we might almost say, has been de-professionalized, Cardinal Ratzinger's efforts to the contrary notwithstanding. Part of the point of moral discourse in pluralistic societies is to include blacks, women, religious minorities, and atheists in public debate over such matters as who would make a competent moral judge or what judgments such a person would reach concerning policies like apartheid and divestment. But relaxing institutional limits on who counts as sufficiently competent to enter public moral debate has an inevitable consequence—namely, that the standard of ideal moral competence becomes more contestable. We still, in practice, affirm a standard of minimal competence when we disregard fanatics or discipline children. And we recognize throughout the debate that while many views are presented, not everyone's judgment carries the same weight. Disagreement takes place within limits, and patterns of authority, however informal, remain.

The level of visible disagreement in science and ethics, then, is determined less by subject matter than by institutional arrangements for encouraging or stifling debate. Science has profited from its willingness to exclude quacks from the ranks of qualified practitioners, although some people, like Paul Feyerabend, may be right in thinking that its institutional arrangements have been much too rigid. Liberal society has profited from its willingness to expand the boundaries of public moral debate beyond a narrow elite. The danger here may be that our notion of moral competence will become so contested that we lose our ability to declare with confidence that Charles Manson (or a two-year-old child) simply fails to judge rightly in cases where all competent moral observers agree. But this is a worry about morality under specific historical conditions, not a worry about morality as such.

Objection: It doesn't matter whether ethics is problematic *per se* or because the level of agreement required to sustain rational moral discourse has eroded over time. What matters is that ethics is problematic—that, whatever the reason, ethics does in fact now lack the level of agreement that would allow us to speak with confidence of moral beliefs as justified or true.

Reply: In Part 3, I shall return to the claim, articulated most forcibly by Alasdair MacIntyre, that ethical discourse has fallen, over time, into nearly complete disarray. MacIntyre thinks that the objectivity of ethical discourse could be salvaged if we had quite different institutional arrangements and insisted upon high standards of moral competence for all participants in public debate. Quite likely, somewhat different institutional arrangements and higher standards of competence would indeed help restore our confidence in ethics. And this marks an important difference between MacIntyre's claim and that of the radical moral skeptic, for it suggests that greater historical and sociological sensitivity will help explain the phenomena to which the skeptic calls attention. But, as we shall see, MacIntyre shares the skeptic's tendency to move too quickly from specific instances of disagreement to the conclusion that all is lost.

Disagreements over Tutu's judgments on divestment go far deeper than disagreements over his judgments on apartheid or disagreements over whether Manson is vicious. We shouldn't place all such disagreements on a par. We shouldn't suppose that relatively deep discord in one area infects all regions of moral belief with doubt. Nor should we suppose that failure to achieve perfect uniformity of opinion on a given moral issue—failure to bring the likes of Botha and Manson into the consensus on apartheid or wanton cruelty—ought to undermine our confidence that we hold justified true beliefs on that issue.

Objection: Lovibond says that we should exchange the fact-value distinction for a fact-value continuum "based on the more or less extensive role played by intellectual authority-relations within different regions of discourse" (p. 68). This suggests that scientific judgments cluster at one end of the continuum (the factual side), moral judgments at the other (the value side). The admission undercuts her wholehearted affirmation of justification and truth in ethics.

Reply: It would be better to say that there is a continuum of epistemic authority, with moral and scientific judgments alike to be found at every point along the way. Just how heavy is the concentration of moral or scientific judgments at a given point on the continuum? The right way to answer this question, as Lovibond grants, is to describe the respective language-games (p. 68). We should not assume in advance what the answer should be.

Objection: Reflection on knotty moral dilemmas, as every reader of Sartre knows, demonstrates that moral judgments, unlike scientific ones, express arbitrary choices.

Reply: When people point to disagreement over a knotty moral dilemma in order to make this sort of point, they tend to overlook the fact that the dilemma poses a problem for moral reflection only because we can perceive the significance and weight of genuine moral considerations on both sides. Renford Bambrough makes the following argument against Sartre's use of such a dilemma:

> When Sartre presents the case of the young man who has to choose between supporting his mother and supporting the struggle for freedom against tyranny he represents himself a supporting the conclusion that moral judgments express unreasoned choices. . . . Yet Sartre is able to paint the dilemma in considerable detail, and each detail is itself a sample of the moral knowledge that Sartre is trying to deny us. In showing or saying that one consideration balances another he reveals his own recognition of the nature and force of the various considerations, and appeals to our own recognition of their nature and force.[8]

Dilemmas of this kind show us, sometimes quite vividly and poignantly, where our moral uncertainties, and thus our probable areas of moral disagreement, are. But they don't show that there's no such thing as moral truth or justified moral belief. In fact, as Bambrough points out, they trade on the assumption that certain moral beliefs are justified and true in making their point. Such dilemmas are rather like cases where scientists get inconclusive data back from the laboratory. One school, given its theoretical commitments and perhaps even its practical interests, interprets the data in one way. Another school interprets it differently. Neither can be ruled out as unjustified, at least for the time being. This does not mean that there is no truth of the matter. Epistemic circumstances will change, new data will come to light, and it will become clear to everybody who counts as a competent judge which interpretations of the data are to be favored.

Analogously, the hardest cases in ethics are those in which two or more moral conclusions are tied for first place, given the current epistemic situation, and skilled casuists, try as they may, cannot reach agreement on how to break the tie. It is not surprising, here as in the scientific arena, that differences in training, interest, and prior commitments lead some casuists to favor one conclusion while others do not. Just as we're suspicious of scientists who write off troublesome data when they ought to be looking for new ways to explain them, we're also suspicious of moralists who are too quick to write off the considerations that give one side of a dilemma its force. Epistemic circumstances may well change, making it obvious that one conclusion should win out over its competitors. If not, and division continues to separate competent judges, we may entertain the possibility that, objectively speaking, there is no single best response to the dilemma, that someone who says there is a best response is speaking a moral falsehood, out of touch with the truth of the matter. We should not confuse doubting that there is a single best thing to do in a given case with doubting that there is a moral truth of the matter with respect to that case.

In ethics, the information that would break a tie between two competing outlooks often remains out of reach because the kind of experimentation needed to produce that information couldn't be performed without changing our entire lives. The ideal test of a novel ethical outlook would involve persuading people to live by it for an extended period and then observing the difference it makes, in practice, to real human beings. If an outlook has already been put into practice over time, historians and anthropologists can often help us with relevant forms of observation. (Ethics is not to be sharply distinguished from social science.) If an outlook has not been put into practice, hard moral data on it can be obtained only by reforming society. That's a costly form of experimentation—and time-consuming, to say the least. So, where the historians and anthropologists cannot help, we typically rely on imagination of the sort displayed in novels at their best. (Ethics is not to be sharply distinguished from imaginative art, either.) Physicists, meanwhile, rely on hard data from the laboratory and feel free to direct their research toward areas in which available technology can assist observation.

Objection: In moral reasoning, we presuppose certain more or less widely shared desires and goals as well as beliefs, and our arguments tend to be persuasive only to people who share substantially similar desires and goals. This shows that morality is essentially subjective in a sense that science is not.

Reply: Only if scientific persuasion is not similarly dependent on shared desires and goals. Yet scientists do presuppose certain desires and goals having to do with prediction and control, and they fashion systems of beliefs that help to satisfy them. It is agreement on the good, Hilary Putnam has argued, that in no small part makes it possible to get agreement on criteria for assessing systems of beliefs as more or less successful scientific theories.[9] People from distant tribes or distant generations who lack the relevant concerns with prediction and control tend, unsurprisingly, not to hold systems of beliefs we would count as scientific. The fact that some people do not share precisely our desires and goals—the fact that most people throughout human history have not—doesn't normally raise doubts about the status of scientific reasoning. Why should morality be any different?

With such desires and goals in place, we continuously adjust our systems of beliefs about various sorts of things, looking for explanatory scope and power, elegance, consistency, and so on. We give up a specific belief—say, about the flatness of the earth—when doing so rounds out our total view of things in the right way (for example, by eliminating an unacceptable tension with new information coming through the telescope). We then find ourselves forced to give up certain other beliefs that had presupposed that one, and we replace them with others. All of this strikes us, for the most part, as unproblematically objective.

In moral reasoning, we also make changes as we go along, responding reasonably or unreasonably to new information and considerations. As in science, we strive for reasons that will be persuasive beyond the circle of people who hold the same configuration of beliefs, desires, and intentions we do. We strive to eliminate certain sorts of inconsistency, revising principles to account for strongly held views about cases, using principles that have so far withstood scrutiny to shed light on new and uncertain cases. The process resembles the scientific one in structure.

Typically, the beliefs and intentions we assess in moral reasoning presuppose—and thus need to be responsive to changes in—beliefs of other kinds. We change our view of the good, for example, if changes in our factual beliefs convince us that our previous aims were unrealistic. That's a perfectly rational, objective affair. If we learn that a given aim cannot in fact be achieved, we then have compelling reason to abandon that aim, to conclude that a vision of the good which incorporates that aim is false. For example, if we determine that God does not exist and that we therefore have no sufficient reason for believing the traditional theistic claims about the nature of humanity and the universe, we can safely reject the pursuit of perfect fellowship with God as the good toward which humanity should strive. If, on the other hand, we had decisive confirmation of traditional theistic claims, we would be perfectly justified, given what else we believe, in concluding that certain related claims about the good life are true. It follows that the notions of justification and truth are relevant to at least one of the characteristic sorts of question to which moral reasoning is addressed.

Suppose we did manage to secure universal agreement on questions such as what people are like, what conditions would lead to the greatest satisfaction of the desire for fellowship, whether we were created by a loving God, whether there really are witches (to use an example from C. S. Lewis), and so on. Is it obvious that we would still have trouble attaining rational agreement on most moral questions?[10] If not, then we must ask whether the facts of moral disagreement place the status of moral reasoning as such in question. For then the trouble would be not so much with morality or moral reasoning itself, but rather with these other topics, ranging from mundane empirical facts to metaphysical speculation. If we could somehow get agreement on those, we would surely be justified in eliminating from consideration nearly all currently popular proposals concerning the good life. We would be justified in deeming such proposals false, for they would proffer aims that presuppose false beliefs about the way things are.

Objection: There would still be some room for disagreement over the good life, even after agreement had been secured on matters of empirical fact and metaphysical speculation.

Reply: Perhaps, but there is another dimension of realistic appraisal of claims about the good. Many of our desires can be fulfilled only if other people share intentions with us over time. This fact places constraints not only on the kind of reasons we will use in trying to persuade others but also on what can reasonably be intended in the first place. Some intentions, to be reasonable, need to be intentions that others can be brought to share. It is unreasonable for me to intend something if (a) that intention cannot be achieved unless others intend likewise and (b) I know that others cannot be brought to intend likewise. This gives me a reason to employ arguments that will be persuasive to others. But it also makes it reasonable for me to begin with intentions that others can in fact be brought to share.

I may desire to be worshiped as the greatest basketball player ever, but because I know that I can't convince people that I am the greatest basketball player ever and therefore can't persuade other people to form the intention to worship me as such, I cannot reasonably embrace, as part of my vision of the good to be pursued, the aim of being worshiped in that way. This keeps some of my intentions, although not necessarily my desires, within limits. Because I see that others cannot be brought to share the intentions of Stout-worship, I cannot reasonably incorporate the demand for Stout-worship into my vision of the good to be pursued. Hence, the claim that such an intention is part of the good I ought to pursue is false.

In contrast, my desire to live in just fellowship with others does not run into the same problems. As in the previous case, the intention to live in just fellowship with others cannot be achieved unless others can be brought to share it. If other people cannot be brought to share such an intention, the intention itself, and thus any vision of the good that incorporates it, must be rejected. But because most of us desire to enjoy the benefits of just fellowship with others, we have reason for trying to become the kind of people for whom the good of fellowship in justice is achievable—people who in fact share the intentions and dispositions needed to achieve it. In some areas, then, there is a kind of rational pressure both toward agreement of intentions among persons and toward those kinds of discourse and education that will promote such agreement. Nothing could qualify as the truth about the good if it designated a way of life that involved intentions people would refuse to share over time. A vision of the good could be true only if it included a realistic conception of goods essentially held in common by virtue of shared, and thus sharable, ends.

Objection: Imagine that we have ruled out all ways of life that are unrealistic. We have discounted as false all visions of the good that presuppose false empirical or metaphysical judgments. And we have rejected those involving essentially shared intentions that people undeceived by empirical and metaphysical falsehood would have no good reason to share. Wouldn't another, even more important, source of disagreement about the good remain? It is conceivable that someone with perverse desires and dispositions will still have reason to differ with those whose desires and dispositions are not perverse.

Reply: This only brings us back to the parallel between the moral judgments of the Ik and the perverse propensities of the scientist who spent too long at the hands of the torturer. Scientific judges, no less than moral judges, qualify as competent only if they possess the virtues that make competent judgment of the relevant kind possible. So the possibility of perverse desires and dispositions adds nothing new.

Objection: Suppose you were able to persuade everybody to adopt the intentions involved in Stout-worship. Surely, that would not make the way of life good, morally speaking.

Reply: Granted. The example was intended only to show that conceptions of the good can be disqualified as unrealistic if they cannot be adopted by a group over time under realistic conditions. Conceptions of the good can also be disqualified on other grounds. The cult of Stout-worship is disqualified on many grounds. I am not the greatest basketball player ever. Worshiping me as such would involve accepting a false supposition. It is also false that being the greatest basketball player of all time would make someone worthy of worship. A competent moral judge is someone who knows how to use notions like desert in the right way. He or she would know, for example, that finite beings, even if they are great basketball players, do not deserve to be worshiped. So there are good reasons for my difficulty in getting other people to convert to Stout-worship. It involves getting them to accept false suppositions about my abilities and about desert. A rightly informed competent judge—someone who not only knew all the information but also had successfully acquired the virtues necessary to genuinely moral observation, inference, and action, someone capable of making sound moral judgments—would never convert to the cult. Therefore, to get people to convert, I would either have to deceive them or corrupt them. Any conception of the good that could become widely shared only by such means is disqualified.

Objection: What explains the truth of the notion that finite beings do not deserve to be worshiped? Surely, a specific conception of the good. But now the proposed view seems circular. It relies heavily on the notion of a competent moral judge, another name for a virtuous person, in order to define the good as a way of life such a judge would accept if ideally well informed. And yet it defines the virtuous person, in part, as someone who would make certain judgments whose truth can be explained only by assuming a conception of the good.

Reply: The circle is virtuous. The concepts of a competent moral judge, a virtuous person, the good life, and desert are all moral notions. One cannot acquire them singly. Fully understanding any involves fully understanding them all. This is the same thing as acquiring the ability to apply the relevant terms as a competent moral judge would. If you have doubts about any one of these concepts, I can help you only by tracing connections between it and the others. None is prior to all the others. For some purposes and in some contexts, I shall take one concept as primitive. For other purposes and in other contexts, I shall take another as primitive. It depends on the kind of doubt being addressed. There is no viciousness in such circularity. When I trace those connections with you, I assume that you have already acquired many of the skills, desires, habits, dispositions, beliefs, and so on, of a competent moral judge. If you have not, you need education, not persuasion. That is, you need to be formed into the kind of person who can see a certain sort of activity as unjust, the kind of person for whom moral reasons have motivating force. Becoming that sort of person is not distinct from acquiring a conception of the good. I can persuade you only if you already have reasons of the kind I could appeal to in trying to resolve your doubts, reasons accessible only within what I have called the logical space of moral judgment. To stand outside that space is to be the sort of person who can profit from persuasion only after a long period of training in the relevant skills of observation, inference, and action.

Objection: Rationality alone, then, gives people no reason to enter the logical space of moral judgment, acting and believing accordingly.

Reply: I do not hold that everyone has reasons for acting morally or for believing the moral truth. Infants do not. The insane do not. Some extremely vicious people do not. Extremely vicious people can be rational in some ways, and thus be sane in some sense, without adopting a moral point of view and acquiring moral motivation. They might be quite good at reasoning in the way physicists reason about physics or in terms of self-interest. Rationality of any kind involves the acquisition of particular skills and virtues. One can acquire the skills and intellectual virtues of a physicist, one can reason as a physicist reasons and thus be rational in a certain sense, without being able to reason well in certain other areas, such as morality. To be rational in moral matters involves acquiring moral reasons and the virtues of a skilled moral reasoner. Someone who is perfectly rational, in one sense of this phrase, would be someone who has already acquired the relevant moral virtues, the virtues of a wise person. This only shows, of course, that the expression "rationality alone" is a useless abstraction. It treats rationality as if it were a single capacity external to morality, instead of as a family of capacities to reason in various ways, some of which are moral ways.

Objection: If a competent moral judge is a virtuous person, someone whose desires and other attitudes have been formed in a particular way, that makes moral requirements merely hypothetical. That is, it makes them conditional on having certain desires. They seem, however, to impose categorical demands, just as Kant said.

Reply: I follow John McDowell in distinguishing between two senses in which a moral demand might be categorical. Moral demands are not categorical in the sense that everyone, including the vicious and the ill-formed, can recognize them as binding. But moral demands may still be categorical in another sense—namely, that they require us to act for one sort of reason as opposed to another. A virtuous person does the just thing because it is just, not in order to be rewarded for behaving justly, nor even in order to be a just person. Still, being a virtuous person involves having desires of one sort and not another. For example, a virtuous person does not have desires of a sort that regularly interfere with deliberation so as to make wise judgment impossible. And a virtuous person does desire to achieve the good, where the good includes his or her own good properly conceived. This would indeed need to be mentioned in any full specification of the virtuous person's "psychological set." Insofar as such a specification is part of the explanation of why the virtuous person acts, it does of course form part of the reasons for action in the broadest sense. But in acting justly, the virtuous person intends the act under the species "just act," not as a means to the satisfaction of some desire over and above the desire to act justly. Furthermore, I agree with McDowell that actions required by justice are, for the genuinely virtuous person, demanded in a way that silences other considerations, as it were, *categorically*, although this is not the place to argue the point.[11]

Objection: The proposed view, despite appearances, turns out to be nihilistic after all. Moral propositions are true or false all right, but only by virtue of the virtuous person's projections onto the real world. It is only the world as it appears to a person of a certain sort, a person who possesses what Hume would call artificial virtues, that contains moral truths thus understood.

Reply: As I shall argue in more detail in the next chapter, truth is a property of interpreted sentences, and interpreted sentences belong to languages, which are human creations. The world-as-it-is-in-itself is, by definition, the world apart from the application of interpreted sentences by human beings—the world described for epistemological purposes as undescribed. It therefore includes no truths. To accept or discover the truth about something is to have acquired a language in which interpreted sentences can be applied in a certain way. It is therefore to make use of human artifice, to possess certain habits, beliefs, and so on. That is the only road to truth about anything. When the objection refers to mere projection, what is missing is something intelligible that projection might be contrasted to—something that is both a possible road to truth and yet not reliant on human artifice and the judgment of people who have acquired skills and virtues, people to whom things will appear in a certain light. In the absence of a suitable contrasting term, reference to "projection" ought to be dropped as misleading. The scientist is equally dependent upon artifice and projection in this innocuous sense.

Objection: But there is a middle way between the paradoxical notion of the world described for epistemological purposes as undescribed and the world conceived as that which appears to us in a certain way, thanks to our projections onto it. For science forms what Bernard Williams has called an "absolute conception" of reality.[12] The absolute conception is not that of the world as it is in itself. It is rather a conception that abstracts from properties, description of which essentially involves reference to a subject's perspectives, perceptions, or aspects thereof. The absolute conception is itself admittedly a human artifact, and human beings can acquire this conception of the world only through training, by acquiring certain virtues and vocabularies, by becoming a certain sort of person. But it conceives of the world strictly in terms of what used to be called primary qualities. Real science is about the world thus conceived. While there is a weak sense in which the world thus conceived is a projection, there is also an interesting sense in which it is not. For the absolute conception, rightly developed, gives us beliefs about the world as it really is, untainted by secondary qualities donated by our subjectivity. Morality gives us no such thing. It therefore makes sense to call moral knowledge merely projective, a realm in which we can be true to our convictions but not speak truly of reality. Its truths are truths about how the world appears to a kind of person, not about the world conceived absolutely.

Reply: As the objection admits, the world of the absolute conception is the world described in a particular fashion—a highly austere fashion. Moral truths are not about the world thus conceived. I grant this happily. Moral discourse employs its own vocabularies of description, vocabularies that must refer to matters other than primary qualities in order to perform their function in moral thought and speech. The question is what of interest follows from this fact. That moral vocabularies fail to refer to reality? Only if objects and their primary qualities uniquely possess reality, but we have been given no reason for supposing that. A physicist who makes a claim about the behavior of subatomic particles is not typically making an elliptical statement about how those particles would appear to a well-informed and properly disposed observer. Similarly, if I assert that Manson's murder of Sharon Tate was unjust, I am not saying that Manson's murder of Sharon Tate would seem unjust to any fully informed, virtuous person. I'm making a direct assertion about the moral truth of the matter. In doing so, I stand within the logical space of moral judgment, which establishes its own sort of objectivity, a sort relevant to its own concerns, through its own kind of abstraction from irrelevant descriptions and "merely subjective" considerations.[13] The sort of objectivity involved in the physicist's absolute conception of the world is neither higher nor lower than this but simply oriented toward different concerns.

Objection: Given the position as developed so far, how could "Manson's murder of Sharon Tate was unjust" not mean the same thing as "Manson's murder of Sharon Tate would seem unjust to any fully informed, virtuous person"?

Reply: Because pointing out connections in our discourse between, say, the notion of justice and the notion of a virtuous person or a competent moral judge is not equivalent to saying that the two propositions mentioned in the objection have the same meaning. I have not been offering conceptual analyses of moral expressions, definitions that could be substituted for moral terms without altering the sense of sentences including them. In particular, I have not shown how to reduce them to expressions about how things would seem to ideal observers. No claim about synonymy enters in. In fact, I hold that moral expressions would have to be used to specify what an ideal observer would be like. So this is not an "ideal observer" theory of ethics in the standard sense.

Objection: It is still conceivable that, even under the imaginary ideal circumstances, moral judges whose desires, dispositions, and beliefs were ideally shaped by education, and who were therefore ideally competent, would not easily agree on a single best way of life.

Reply: This only brings us back to the possibility that more than one moral option may, objectively speaking, be tied for first place, in which case they would be equally worthy of adoption and that would be the truth of the matter. We seem to have found no contrast between morality and science that would support skeptical worries.

Objection: If deprived of a damaging contrast between morality and science, skeptics are free to extend their suspicion about justification and truth in ethics to encompass science as well.

Reply: Extended all the way, as consistency seems to demand, skepticism seems to self-destruct, leaving the skeptic skeptical about skepticism. That's a reason for using the notions of justification and truth with renewed confidence in both science and morals, for viewing scientific and moral reasoning, despite their differences, as two aspects of a single rational and objective process in which we criticize and revise our propositional attitudes.

Objection: What we have, then, ironically enough, is a picture of human nature. According to this picture, people believe, desire, intend, and so on, criticizing and revising these attitudes as they go along. Taken together, an individual's propositional attitudes have a structure. It is not the structure of a building resting on permanent foundations. It is more like Otto Neurath's famous boat, which can never be brought into dry dock for complete overhaul but can be repaired, plank by plank, while remaining at sea. The process of criticism and revision— of plank repair, if you will—is carried out on board, at sea. It depends on leaving nearly everything intact at any given moment to stay afloat. But the picture is altogether too optimistic. We could have real confidence in the notions of truth and justification, whether in ethics or any domain of scientific inquiry whose conclusions might have normative import, only if we could bring the boat into dry dock, stand on firm ground not fabricated by us, and peer with suspicion at the rot of human desire and self-deception. No ship's captain can bring the full extent of such rot into view while still at sea. Too much of it is below the surface of consciousness. And any process of reconstruction dependent on such a structure is, in effect, imprisoned by it, constrained by that structure to preserve its fundamentals. Neurath's boat is actually a floating prison, the prison house of language, a ship of fools. The process you call "criticism and revision," insofar as it remains merely immanent, has no access to fresh lumber. Its only hope is to rearrange the already rotting planks that keep it, for the moment, from sinking. Because it can never really provide a new hull, it has to settle, in the end, for repainting the hull's interior surface. Your picture is the story used by the unhappy consciousness to comfort itself once the hope for dry dock is lost.

Reply: I have no quarrel with the notion that I am offering a picture of human nature if we can agree to mean by this a way of describing human beings, a collection of truth-claims not dependent on the distinctions between necessary and contingent truths or on the metaphysics of "natures" and "essences." Is my picture optimistic? Not in the sense implied. I have been defending the idea that we should go on using the notions of moral truth and justified moral belief with confidence. It doesn't follow that we ought to hold any particular belief with confidence, nor that we ought to relax suspicion in our appraisal of human beings and their attitudes. To the contrary, I have urged humble acknowledgment of fallibility, irrationality, and corruption. Even justified beliefs, I have said, often turn out to have been false all along. Even true beliefs, I have said, can be held for bad reasons. Even the farthest reaches of scientific theory, I have said, are shaped by the force of corruptible (and often unconscious) human desire.

But notice that in order to say these things, I have had to rely at every point on the notions of truth and justification. I have had to show confidence in something, at least implicitly, in order to limn the limits of justified confidence. Notice, too, that the objection implicitly relies on thses notions as well. The objection would lack force if it did not present its claims about human beings and my picture of them as true and justified claims. If the objection is meant to justify the truth-claim that we ought not have any confidence in the notions of justification and truth, it self-destructs before doing damage to the picture I propose.

Aside from a few remarks asbout slavery and malicious cruelty, I have thus far said little about which moral propositions I take to be true and justified or about which human attitudes I find dubious. Rest assured, I am not making apology for conservatism. My point is rather that conservatives and radicals are, so to speak, in the same boat. Be as radical as you please, extend suspicion about human attitudes as far as they can intelligibly go without self-destructing—as far as your favorite radical social critic has actually managed to take it—and you will still need to suppose that you are justified in believing some moral propositions true. You will therefore still be justified in showing confidence in the notions of moral truth and justification themselves.

The objection implies that if conservatives and radicals are in the same boat, and that boat is Neurath's, then they are equally imprisoned by the terms of the consensus within which their debate is carried on. But the image of Neurath's boat, as developed in the objection, is misleading in that it suggests too little scope for criticism and revision. Neurath's boat can travel the open seas, trade with foreign places, and

send parties ashore in search of virgin timber. Its crew can take un-
imagined treasures on board, plunder shipwrecks for usable gear, and
invent an engine to pull weight once pulled by oar. It can become a
prison, but it needn't.

What it can't do is be hauled into dry dock. This may seem troubling, as if all the incremental work done on board were useless apart
from the hope for a complete overhaul performed on really solid
ground and with a full view of the vitiated structure. But why should
it? Suppose the crew once pinned its hopes on reconstruction in dry
dock but those hopes now seem utopian. Does it make sense to abandon all hope, all confidence in incremental acts of criticism and revision? Wouldn't that be a case of thinking that only everything could be
enough?

In believing, desiring, and intending, we can do well or poorly. All
too often, we fall short of our best. We neglect available evidence. We
believe, against available evidence, what we merely wish were true. We
deceive ourselves with rationalizations. We fail to desire genuine goods
or to desire them in proportion to their actual goodness. We intentionally do what we believe we shouldn't and wish we wouldn't. We remain
blind to our own motivations more often than we care to admit.

The doings of a perfectly vicious being, however, wouldn't even be
recognizable as actions. They would display no discernible pattern of
motivation. Our failings, to be counted as such, need a niche in a
network not entirely out of whack, just as our disagreements or doubts,
to be intelligible, require a background of truths taken for granted. The
standards that matter, as we judge each of these failings, must themselves be within human reach. They cannot be impossibly utopian or
unconnected with ordinary belief without becoming irrelevant. The
best we can do, as we engage in the process of criticism and revision,
is the most we can reasonably hope for or desire. That means applying
the standards we've got as rigorously as we can, all the while trying to
improve them as we go. It also means accepting our lot as finite beings.
It would be foolishness and masochism to despair over being in Neurath's boat. Such despair is itself a kind of vice, a lingering trace of the
desire to be like God.

3

THE LANGUAGES OF MORALS

The most influential book of moral philosophy written in the 1950s was probably *The Language of Morals* by R. M. Hare.[1] "Ethics," Hare wrote in his preface, "is the logical study of the language of morals." *Logical* study, not historical or comparative. The *language* of morals, not the content of moral belief. *The* language of morals, not somebody's particular moral language, not the language of this or that moral tradition.

It would be hard to win wide assent today for Hare's definition of ethics. Ethical theorists still sometimes think of themselves as engaged in logical study, but there is noticeably less conviction that the logical analysis of moral language can be clearly distinguished from historical and comparative study or from the interpretation and appraisal of moral belief. If meaning is use, and use changes along with belief, then the analysis of meaning requires the skills of the historian. And if comparative study reveals significant conceptual diversity in ethics across classes, cultures, and historical periods, as many ethicists now hold, it makes less sense to speak as if there were a singular and uniform subject matter in view. Accordingly, we hear less and less talk about *the* language of morals, more and more about a plurality of moral languages, each with its own characteristic concepts and patterns of reasoning. Moral diversity is the order of the day.

In the first two chapters, we have been looking closely at different sorts of moral disagreement. Moral disagreement is only one kind of moral diversity. We need now to consider another. If two cultures employ quite different moral languages, each with its own characteristic concepts and styles of reasoning, might they not have too little in common even to disagree? Could they understand one another at all? If so, how? What bearing, in general, should the prospect of diverse moral languages have on our conception of moral philosophy, constructive moral thought, and moral change?

I

Let me begin with another question, one we've touched on already. Can the proposition that slavery is evil be true (and not merely believed to be true) in our cultural setting and false in another? I have suggested that even deep disagreement between two cultures over the truth of this and similar propositions provides less impetus toward a relativistic conception of moral truth than might initially be supposed. If you and I disagree about the truth of a moral proposition, we must at least have in common whatever background of concepts and beliefs is required to give it sense. That turns out to be quite a lot, although not necessarily enough to resolve the disagreement. Pressed beyond a certain point, the point at which a relativistic conception of truth becomes tempting, apparent disagreement merely changes the subject, so that it no longer makes sense to say that precisely the same proposition is true in one setting but false in another. As Chris Swoyer has put it, "the relativist seems unable to tell a convincing story about *what it is* that can be true in a relative sense." For "a difficulty arises in trying to maintain simultaneously that two frameworks are sufficiently different for one thing to be true in one while false in the other *and* that they are sufficiently alike to share something which could thus vary in truth value."[2] Two groups that differed radically enough in belief to tempt us to speak of relative truth would necessarily lack the resources for expressing or entertaining "one and the same" proposition whose truth-value was relative. Be that as it may, however, there remain other possibilities to consider. Swoyer makes clear, for example, that his argument leaves open the possibility that "truth might be relative in a weak sense"— namely, that "there could be things that were true in one framework which were not expressible and a fortiori not true in another" (p. 105).

Imagine that we have just returned from several years of anthropological fieldwork in two social groups, each of which has now spent many generations essentially isolated from the outside world. One group, the Old World Corleones, keeps alive the ethos of ancient Sicily, as depicted in the novels of Mario Puzo. Unlike their American cousins, they know nothing of cosmopolitan ways. The other group, the Modernists, descends from a band of Kantian explorers who got lost in the jungles of Brazil in 1831. The Corleones go on at length about purity, honor, and role-specific virtues and obligations. The Modernists do not exactly dissent from propositions employing such concepts. They do not even entertain such propositions. Instead, their moral talk is all about human rights, respect for persons, freedom, and what individuals (not strictly identified with their social roles) morally ought to do. If their ancestors once spoke about the topics that matter so much to the Corleones, the Modernists have long since forgotten. Most moral propositions entertained in the one culture have no analogues in the other. They don't share enough conceptual ground, it seems, to disagree with, or to translate, each other's sentences.

Would the discovery of societies that conformed to these stereotypes establish that moral truth is relative in Swoyer's weak sense? I think Swoyer is right to suppose that two groups could each be uttering some true propositions not expressible in each other's languages, but the point needs to be made carefully. The Corleones currently lack conceptual resources needed to express various true propositions believed by the Modernists and vice versa. What does it add to say that such propositions are true in their respective frameworks? Where wouldn't they be true? Presumably, if we did find another language with the conceptual resources for straightforward translation of Corleone moral propositions—say, English as spoken by Mario Puzo—those propositions would be true there, too, if they were true at all.

Of course, we can interpret a sentence only by establishing its relation to other interpreted sentences. In determining what someone means by uttering a sentence, we make assumptions about that person's beliefs, desires, and other attitudes and about a framework of platitudes and presuppositions widely shared by members of that person's linguistic cohort. But once we have an interpreted sentence, a proposition, to deal with, it is simply true or false, not true or false in that framework. Its actual truth-value will be preserved by accurate translation into other languages.

What Swoyer is driving at, though, seems to be that one and the same proposition, whatever its truth-value, might be expressible in one language or framework but not in another. The notion of truth-in-a-framework is dispensable. Truth needn't be relative for expressibility to be relative. Here too, however, we need to be careful—for two reasons. First, asking whether propositions are expressible in a language might seem to imply that propositions are timeless, nonlinguistic entities, whose content might explain what we accept in accepting a sentence as true. We might then be tempted to think of "expression" as a relation between something nonlinguistic and something linguistic, or of understanding a sentence as a complicated process of decoding something linguistic into something nonlinguistic. If, however, we take a proposition to be simply an interpreted sentence—a sentence that can be given a home in a language game—we can safely avoid such commitments and temptations. Then Swoyer's problem of expressibility can be seen as merely the question of which languages possess the conceptual resources for translating particular fragments of which other languages. Translation relates two languages to each other, not two languages to some third thing, a language-independent meaning or proposition.

What is it for a language to possess the conceptual resources for translating a fragment of another language? Just as I see no explanatory value in postulating language-independent propositions as part of an account of translation,[3] I see no point in thinking of the concepts held by someone as an *explanation* of how that person uses words. To have a concept, on my Wittgensteinian view, *is* to have the ability to use a word in accordance with established patterns of usage in a group. So it wouldn't add anything of explanatory value to say that my son uses words as he does because of the conceptual resources of his language. My talk of "propositions" is shorthand for interpreted sentences. "The conceptual resources of a language" is shorthand for the many ways in which words are used by members of a certain community.

If you start using a word in new ways, and so establish a new pattern of observation-reports, inference, and intention-formation in your group, you have a new concept—and new conceptual resources for translating the speech of other groups. A language possesses the conceptual resources for translating a fragment of another if the established patterns of usage among members of the two groups are similar enough to allow us to say that "so-and-so" in the one language means "such-and-such" in the other. How much similarity is that? That needs to be settled case by case, according to the purposes for which the translations are designed. Setting the standard high, as some purposes would require, will make us demand virtually perfect correspondence. Then we shall say that another group has our concept, R, if and only if they use some expression in precisely the ways we use our expression, "R." Wherever we would employ "R" in an observation, they employ "V." "R" has precisely the same effects on inference and on intention-formation in our discourse as "V" has in theirs, given the overall scheme of translation we have reason to adopt. For most purposes, however, we tolerate minor dissimilarities, especially those that have negligible effects on truth-conditions. "Meaning," as Hilary Putnam has said, "is a coarse grid laid over use."[4] I would emphasize *coarse*.

The second reason for being careful in speaking of propositions as expressible in some languages but not others is that the meaning of "languages" in this context is ambiguous. Are we thinking of a language synchronically, as a static system frozen in time, or diachronically, as something that changes over time? In our example, the Modernists cannot, by stipulation, express most of the propositions of Corleone moral discourse in Modernese. That means they cannot do so now. But the Modernists may end their cultural isolation and send out their own ethnographers to study the Corleones. In time, ethnographers from Modernity can learn the moral language of the Corleones as Corleone children do—from the ground up. That option is always open when initial efforts at direct translation fail. If the Modernists then wish to translate Corleone moral discourse into their own native tongue, they are free to enrich Modernese by weaving sentences and using words in unfamiliar ways, creating new linguistic contexts within Modernese for expressing Corleone thoughts.

Swoyer's notions of inexpressibility, then, can be traded in for untranslatability. And untranslatability may be overcome by hermeneutical innovation. If, at a given time, a proposition expressible in one language, L_1, is not expressible in another, L_2, this need not be so at some later time. L_2, after all, can be developed hermeneutically.[5] Inexpressibility cannot seal us off permanently from those whose concepts differ from ours unless we treat languages as static systems not subject to hermeneutical enrichment. Natural languages actually in use are not static systems. That is why cultures are not, simply by virtue of conceptual diversity, hermeneutically sealed. Nothing in the nature of conceptual diversity itself prevents one culture from developing the means for expressing an alien culture's moral propositions or grasping their truth.

Notice that we should probably have an easier time translating Corleone and Modernist moral discourse into our language than they would have translating each other's utterances. Our language is already rich enough to express most Corleone and Modernist moral propositions. We have concepts like purity and honor although they are less central in our speech than in the Corleones'. We may need to work at imagining what it would be like to operate only with such concepts, to see how a reasonable Corleone could find a certain insult an affront to his honor, an act demanding vengeance. No doubt, we shall need extended commentaries and cautionary remarks as well as translations of sentences to render Corleone moral discourse fully intelligible in our books about it. And if we encounter a concept for which we have no natural equivalent, we may need to begin by transliterating a term or two while writing longer commentaries and footnotes, thicker thick descriptions.

If Corleones and Modernists come to write about each other, they will have to rely heavily on transliteration from the start, adding very long commentaries and footnotes indeed, helping readers through something like a process of learning a first language. Their native tongues will offer relatively little in the way of handy parallels to alien ways. But these are artificial examples, with difficulties added for illustrative purposes. We, in contrast, like most societies that engage self-consciously in comparative ethics, can find traces of many sorts of moral concepts surviving in our own speech—a ready reservoir of analogues for any translation or thick description. We can also call on our long history of dealing with other cultures and translating what they say, which has amply enriched our conceptual resources for dialogue with strangers. Although some of those dealings now give us little cause for pride, we do not labor under the serious disadvantage of prolonged cultural isolation, with all the conceptual impoverishment that can entail. (This comforting thought gives new meaning to Whitman's praise of English as "the medium that shall well nigh express the inexpressible.")

There are, to be sure, dangers aplenty awaiting any comparative ethicist. There are dangers, for example, in making foreign sentences seem too familiar too quickly, the dangers of ethnocentric interpretation. There are dangers as well in assigning foreign populations a prefabricated role as if the Other, as if their linguistic practices existed merely to provide a reverse-image of ours in an already-scripted intercultural drama.[6] We shall be taking a closer look at such dangers in Part 2. For the moment, however, I want to stress that we cannot help looking for similarities in an alien culture that might provide a foothold for interpreting the rest. If we didn't begin by assuming some similarities, interpretation could hardly get started.

Some of our initial assumptions may turn out to be wrong, of course, making us look excessively ethnocentric or Romantic in retrospect, but we wouldn't do better by making no assumptions about similarity at all. Nor should we abandon the hope that comparative inquiry may be more than an imperialistic culture's projection on the Other, that it may correct our possibly quite vicious stereotypes, teach us about what makes us truly distinctive, or enhance our sense of human possibility through the discovery of differences. Without such aims, comparative ethics would have little point. The trick is to leave our initial posits of similarity and the terms in which we contrast ourselves with others open to question, while developing as much sensitivity to detail as we can muster and refusing to rest content with our interpretations until we have dealt rigorously with the dangers endemic to cross-cultural interpretation. The kind of detail disclosed in thick description has a way of overturning mistaken early expectations about the patterns of similarity and difference.

If, however, coming to understand another society's moral language can involve acquiring the ability to observe, infer, and act in new ways, must we go on to become like the people we are studying to understand them? Suppose the Corleones know nothing of physics beyond what we would call common sense. Modernists, though expert physicists, draw no subtle moral distinctions whatsoever. They just apply the only formulation of Kant's categorical imperative they still remember, and do that simplemindedly. Corleone ethnographers will run into deep trouble in Modernity's physics laboratories. They will have to become physicists—acquiring new skills of observation, inference, and experimental intervention—to learn the language of physics in any depth. This suggests how difficult genuine cross-cultural understanding can be. Understanding moral expressions could be equally demanding. If talk of the virtues is highly developed among the Corleones, it might be every bit as opaque to Modernist ethnographers as Modernity's language of physics is to the Corleones. Modernist ethnographers might have to become like a Corleone sage, passing through many rites of passage and much casuistic catechism, to appreciate the subtleties of moral distinctions in his language.

It doesn't follow, however, that understanding another culture's moral language necessitates adopting the moral beliefs held by its members.[7] Knowing how to use words as they do need not commit me to using words as they do. If I can imitate Corleone moralizing, describe it in thick detail, predict what Corleones will say about new cases, make sense of their past behavior by ascribing beliefs and desires that fit in nicely with my translations of their moral sentences, and so on, then I understand their moral language. I might still refuse to join in when they moralize. I might vigorously dissent from their beliefs about women and strangers. Their claims about the necessity of vengeance might never influence my own moral reasoning.[8]

II

Ian Hacking has encountered something like Swoyer's problem of expressibility. He says:

Translation is hard when one gets to whole new ranges of possibility that make no sense for the favored styles of reasoning of another culture. It is there that ethnographers begin to have problems. Every people has generated its own peculiar styles. We are no different from others, except that we can see, more clearly from our own written record, the historical emergence of new styles of reasoning.[9]

New ways of using words, including new styles of reasoning, make new propositions expressible—or, as Hacking puts it (in a turn of phrase that deftly avoids making propositions sound like timeless, nonlinguistic entities), bring new "candidates for truth and falsehood" into being. "Understanding the sufficiently strange is a matter of recognizing new possibilities for truth-or-falsehood, and of learning how to conduct other styles of reasoning that bear on those possibilities" (p. 60).

Hacking helps me say what authors who refer to distinct moral *languages* might have in mind and why the plurality of moral languages might be philosophically interesting over and above the kind of moral diversity displayed in disagreement over a proposition. There would be no point in asserting the plurality of moral languages without offering some notion of how moral languages, in the relevant sense, are to be individuated.

If contemporary French and contemporary German can each express all moral propositions expressible in the other—if neither saddles translators with problems that make translation hard in the way Hacking describes—we should not count them, for present purposes, as distinct moral languages or vocabularies. When Quentin Skinner details the emergence of the language of human rights, when James Johnson asks whether the language of natural law is well-suited for discussing the ethics of war, and when Peter Berger claims that the concept of honor is increasingly obsolescent, they are not pointing to differences like the ones that separate the speech of shopkeepers in Paris from the speech of shopkeepers in Bonn today. Differences between French as spoken in 1500 and French as spoken in 1950, or between German as spoken by the bourgeoisie and German as spoken by the proletariat, may be more germane.

Let us say that moral languages, in the relevant sense, can be individuated by reference to the sets of candidates for truth and falsehood they make available. Not that moral languages are merely sets of candidates for truth and falsehood: we do many things with our moral vocabularies, and entertaining candidates for truth and falsehood is only one of them. My point is not to *identify* a moral language with the set of candidates it makes available, as if there were nothing to a moral language but that. My point is rather to *individuate* moral languages by reference to sets of candidates, thereby making sense of what people like Skinner, Johnson, and Berger say about them. According to such authors, the language of human rights and the language of honor differ. How can we tell that they do? Because words are used in significantly different ways by the respective groups and this makes translation hard. What counts as a significant difference in the ways words are used? Any difference that substantially alters what propositions are up for grabs as true-or-false.

The notion of a moral language, thus delineated, remains vague. We know not to count a very slight difference in up-for-grabs propositions as a new moral language. And we know that the propositions entertained within the language of human rights and the language of honor are different enough to support references to distinct moral languages. Between these extremes, no doubt, there will be some twilight. No harm in that. We need a principle of individuation that shares the vagueness of the notion being explicated. A sharp line of demarcation would be pointless. Nobody is asking for a precise count of moral languages. And we need no general criterion for saying when a new moral language has come into being. Historians can decide that case by case, guided by the dramatic contours and explanatory demands of their narratives. What matters, philosophically, is that there are clear cases, cases in which it clearly makes sense to speak of distinct moral languages. If you accept my delineation of the notion, these will be cases in which two groups differ morally not primarily because one group denies propositions the other asserts but rather because their respective forms of discourse put forth different possibilities to disagree over.

Note that any rich fragment of a moral language qualifies, according to the proposed principle of individuation, as a moral language. We can multiply moral languages just by dividing existing ones into suitably rich fragments. Sometimes we don't count the fragments, as when we speak simply of *the* moral language of a certain group.[10] But the language of human rights and some attenuated form of the language of honor are both fragments of our moral language. Speaking in this way makes the fragments count. How many moral languages do we speak then? Never mind. There's no point in asking. Whether we should count fragments and how rich a fragment should be to be counted separately, like the question of how big a change must be to count as significant or how much more hair I must lose to qualify as bald, are questions worth answering only in contexts where an answer would serve a specific purpose. Once we know the purpose, the answers come easily.

Our moral language encompasses various fragments. Some are analogues to fragments of Corleone moral discourse. Others are analogues to fragments of Modernese. In each case, parallels to our own activities of moral reasoning and judgment are needed to make sense of the idea that we are considering a *moral* language. Could there be a society whose moral language had no parallels to ours? The problem lies in imagining what could count as evidence that a society had a moral language at all unless there were some substantial overlap in patterns of moral reasoning and judgment. Here Davidsonian considerations become relevant again.[11] We can imagine a group that has no moral language, although no actual case within our species comes to mind and it's hard to know whether we would view members of such a group as persons. But the important point is this: to say that another society has a moral language is to say that it has views on at least some of the topics we denominate as moral. A society that never assessed conduct, character, or community as good or bad, right or wrong, honorable or dishonorable, just or unjust, as contributing to or detracting from human well-being, and so on across the board, would simply not possess a moral language. It follows that within morality, given how the reference of the term *morality* is fixed in our discourse, there are limits to conceptual contrast.

They are, however, adjustable limits. If Modernist ethnographers set out to study Corleones before they came to study us, they might conclude early on that the Corleones have no moral language. The extension of the phrase *moral language* in Modernese would be narrower than it is in our discourse, because of the relative austerity of Modernist morality and their history of cultural isolation.[12] But when the Modernist ethnographers get around to us, the parallels between our discourse and theirs will make them want to say that we do have a moral language. Coming to understand the complexity of our moral language, however, may well make them revise their earlier assumption that the Corleones have none. For when they can recognize the relevant parts of Corleone discourse as analogous to a fragment of our moral language, the extension of the phrase *moral language* in Modernese can be broadened to include heretofore unanticipated possibilities. By enriching their conception of morality through comparative inquiry, the Modernists will have come to see the Corleones as having had a moral language after all. The limits of conceptual contrast within the moral sphere, as marked off within Modernese, will have been expanded.

We, too, may have our conception of morality broadened in the course of comparative inquiry. In Part 2, I shall argue for a broader conception than Kantians tend to embrace. It would be a mistake, however, to think that we should be seeking the broadest possible conception. We could, of course, let any discourse on any topic count as moral discourse, but that would make the notion useless, not richer. A broader conception is richer only if it allows us to tell better stories of how we got to be where we are, to engage in more fruitful dialogue with other cultures, and to make sense of all extant moral languages as members of a single family connected by intelligible relations of family resemblance. And this means that the limits of conceptual contrast within the moral sphere, although adjustable, are real constraints. We can expand those limits somewhat, with good reason and much profit, but not any old way and not too much—not if we want to have good reason and much profit.

The Modernist discovery that the Corleones have a moral language consists of the discovery of new relations of family resemblance. Until ethnographers from Modernity studied us, they couldn't see how Corleone talk about honor could belong to the same family as Modernist talk about human rights. Now that their horizons have been broadened, Modernity's ethnographers can employ what Charles Taylor calls a "language of perspicuous contrast." Possessing such a language allows us to view our moral discourse and that of another culture

as alternative possibilities in relation to some human constants at work in both. It would be a language in which the possible human variations would be so formulated that both our form of life and theirs could be perspicuously described as alternative such variations. Such a language of contrast might show their language of understanding to be distorted or inadequate in some respects, or it might show ours to be so (in which case, we might find that understanding them leads to an alteration of our self-understanding, and hence our form of life—a far from unknown process in history); or it might show both to be so.[13]

Thus, Modernity's ethnographers might come to see Corleone and Modernist moral discourse as members of the same family, instances of the same kind of thing. Each is an alternative possible variety of moral language. How far one or the other or both may be distorted or inadequate is a matter to be determined by moral inquiry. And this inquiry is possible only within some moral language or another. The more perspicuous the contrasts and comparisons it makes possible, the better.

III

So it matters what moral language we use—and not only because the moral language we use influences what forms of discourse in other cultures we can rightly regard as languages of morals. It matters also because the moral language we use in daily life has much to do with what that life is like, with what we are like. To belong to a society in which the language of honor is dominant and the language of human rights has no place is to be a certain sort of person. It is to live a moral life that revolves around knowing one's position in the hierarchical social order of an extended family, executing the role-specific duties appropriate to that position, showing the kind of respect Don Corleone (and not Kant) demands from others, repaying insult with vengeance. The texture and contours of such a life will be determined, say, by whether one is the first son of Don Corleone or the second, his son or his daughter, a member of his family or a stranger, someone who has shown him respect or someone who once insulted him.

To live one's life on these terms, as one not alienated from the form of life, is to presuppose that justice *is* vengeance, that the distinction between first and second sons or between sons and daughters does bear on moral choice, that one loses the right to respect from others if one does not repay insults with vengeance, that an insult to a member of your family is an insult to you. It is to be complicit in a way of life. It is to make certain assumptions about moral truths. It is to speak a language in which sentences such as these are candidates for truth and falsehood: "Amerigo Bonasera is in debt to the don for the vengeance visited upon those who dishonored his daughter." "Luca Brasi is a man of unquestioned loyalty to the Corleones." It is to be someone unlike Kant or Hauerwas or St. Francis or Charles Manson, not only in the acts one is willing to do or the assumptions one makes or the beliefs one holds but in the candidates for truth and falsehood one entertains, the terms in which one lives one's life.

If moral philosophy is reflection on the languages of morals, it can claim no uniform and unchanging subject matter. The next culture heard from or the latest wrinkle in our own form of life can yield new candidates for truth and falsehood, ways of living in the world we hadn't anticipated, and quite possibly new kinds of people for us to be. That is why each generation needs to write its own moral philosophy. Until some version of moral Esperanto triumphs and the anthropologists, historians, and novelists die out, there is no way of telling what fresh tasks will be placed before us. Moral philosophy is not practiced from the vantage point of omniscience, above history. It begins, for any of us, at some particular site, where some moral languages are in use. Perhaps other languages are being invented or imagined, or are retained in memory without being put to use, or are accessible to study if we put our minds to it. Still others, however, are beyond the scope of our reflection—long forgotten or yet to be imagined. It matters, then, where moral philosophy begins.

Let us say that moral philosophy, thus conceived, is a kind of reflexive ethnography. It begins at home, with languages in use, and then reaches out to other possibilities, accessible from its particular historical position. Its first method is participant-observation, its initial aim the understanding of all-too-familiar uses of words and related goings-on.

It benefits from thick description, from dredging up old documents, from long visits to strange places, from flights of artistic imagination— from all the ways in which new possibilities of moral observation, inference, and action can be brought into view. We must begin in a particular place, but that need not and should not condemn us to stay at our starting point. Breadth of vision remains a good to be pursued, even if our perspective can never be eternity.

The ethical heritage of Western culture is not a closed system, a single seamless language, needing only to be received, applied to our situation, and passed on to the next generation. As Mary Midgley has put it,

> From Socrates and Christ through Rousseau and Marx onward, half the business of Western culture has been self-criticism. In fact it is (as those names make obvious) not a single culture at all, but a debating-ground, not a monolith but a fertile confused jungle of sources—Greek and Roman and Jew, Celt and Viking, Arab and Slav, Indian and American. Within that jungle we have to choose, and hard work it is, which is why we sometimes feel like writing the whole thing off. [14]

Nor, as Midgley goes on to say, are other cultures essentially uniform. To find oneself in a cultural tradition is the beginning, not the end, of critical thought. There is no simple opposition between tradition and critical reason or between conservatism and reform. Our task is not simply to bring as many possibilities into view as we can but also to judge what is worth preserving, what requires reformulation, and what must be left behind. And we have nothing to go on but the critical resources of the tradition itself, extending its horizons with the help of history, anthropology, and creative art.

It would be comforting, of course, to think that we could rise above Midgley's "confused jungle of sources," climbing to the vantage point of universal reason. If you are favorably disposed toward tradition, you might then picture yourself as employing pure reason to extract a tradition's essential philosophical core. If you make tradition the seat of superstition and prejudice, you could view yourself as employing reason to set tradition aside. But either way, you would be trying to make the complexities and contingencies of tradition inessential to ethical thought, something one could in principle do without. Tradition would be at best what it was for Kant, a historical vehicle of pure reason, necessary only because we still have farther to go on the road of moral progress, but eventually to be transcended altogether. At worst, it would be something to be despised or ignored—as inessential now as it will be in the long run.

The philosopher's wish to rise above tradition, above the particularity of any historical location, serves us no better than the naive traditionalist's wish to be relieved of the responsibilities of critical thought. It tends, in fact, to focus attention too narrowly on one strand of moral language wrongly thought to have been purified of historical contingency—local custom masquerading as universal speech. But Esperanto is not God's language. (Let's hope not, anyway.) And the philosopher's constructive proposals, although couched in Esperanto, themselves draw secretly upon the same jungle of sources the philosopher wishes to escape. That is why even the most austere and abstract moral language can make some connection with ethical cares and concerns. Any version of moral Esperanto is itself a product of a process in which one begins with bits and pieces of traditional linguistic material, arranges some of them into a structured whole, leaves others to the side, and ends with a moral language ready to use, possibly a quite novel one.

Let us call this process of moral figuration *bricolage* and the person who carries it out a moral *bricoleur*, alluding to Claude Lévi-Strauss's use of the terms.[15] The *bricoleur*, Lévi-Strauss says in introducing the term, is "someone who works with his hands and uses devious means" (p. 16). He does odd jobs, drawing on a collection of assorted odds and ends available for use and kept on hand on the chance they might someday prove useful. That, for Lévi-Strauss, is how the primitive mind operates. It uses a limited, heterogeneous repertoire of inherited bits and pieces (p. 17). It makes do with "whatever is at hand," "with a set of tools and materials which is always finite and is also heterogeneous because what it contains bears no relation to the current project, or indeed to any particular project, but is the contingent result of all the occasions there have been to renew or enrich the stock or to maintain it with the remains of previous constructions or destructions." I like this image, but I use it ironically because part of my purpose is to deny Lévi-Strauss's distinction between savage minds and the rest of us, at least in moral thinking. As I see it, we are all *bricoleurs*, insofar as we are capable of creative thought at all. In alluding to Lévi-Strauss's usage, I wish to disentangle it from a binary opposition, an overly sharp contrast with the engineer.[16]

All great works of creative ethical thought (and some not so great), whether or not their idiom is Esperanto, involve moral *bricolage*. They start off by taking stock of problems that need solving and available conceptual resources for solving them. Then they proceed by taking apart, putting together, reordering, weighting, weeding out, and filling in.[17] Recent moral philosophy tends to favor a particular kind of *bricolage*—the kind that draws sharp lines around a secularized moral language, dismissing all else as inessential, and then reducing what is left to a single principle employing a single essential concept. In Part 2, we shall be studying an example of this type in detail. But we shall also see that there are other means of moral figuration, other ways of arranging and rearranging fragments of moral language in relation to each other and to the whole. We may speak of these ways as *tropes*, borrowing a language of perspicuous contrast indebted to Vico but which has recently been used mainly by literary theorists to study kinds of writing apparently far removed from the prose of moralists and ethical theorists.

Fear not. There is no jargon-laden theory in the offing.[18] If I wanted to pursue the parallels to literary theory, I could say that the master trope of much recent moral philosophy is *metonymy*, because of its predilection for reducing the full range of moral concepts and considerations to the essentials embedded in foundational principles. I could then go on to speak of some traditions of casuistry as *metaphorical*, in the sense that they attempt no reduction to foundational concepts and principles but dwell instead on the play of similarity and difference from one case of conscience to another. I might then look for other examples to illustrate the tropes of *synecdoche* (Hegel?), in which fragments are integrated nonreductively into a whole greater than the sum of its parts, and *irony* (J. L. Mackie?), in which "language folds back upon itself and brings its own potentialities for distorting perception under question."[19] In that fashion I could round out a neat typology students could learn by heart and apply with their eyes only half open. I'd rather not. We need no exhaustive typology of tropes, and the technical terms can safely be ignored for present purposes. My claim is simply that how the various fragments of moral language are related to each other and to the whole can be every bit as important as which parts are selected for retention or available for use in the first place.

This claim entails a warning. We fail to do justice to an instance of creative moral thinking or writing when we force it into the mold of some other moral trope, as when we press too hard with Socratic questioning to uncover foundational concepts and principles that we are convinced must be there, and then perform the reduction ourselves, even if that goes against the grain.[20] That is what happens when we make metonymical moral philosophy our sole language of contrast. Sometimes we simply distort what is going on, seeing foundational principles where there are none. Sometimes we highlight metonymical elements actually present but in a way that makes us miss the significance of the whole.

Take Aquinas, whom we too often remember, misleadingly, as the author of a great system of natural law. This makes him look too much like a precursor of the Esperantists. His real accomplishment was to bring together into a single whole a wide assortment of fragments—Platonic, Stoic, Pauline, Jewish, Islamic, Augustinian, and Aristotelian. He ordered them in such a way that an Aristotelian language of the virtues transmitted largely by Islamic sources becomes the locus of most moral reflection, Platonic-Augustinian themes set a framework for thinking of creation as a whole, and the language of natural law is confined to quite limited tasks. I may be wrong about the priority accorded, respectively, to the various linguistic fragments within Aquinas's ethics, and it is not part of my purpose here to defend my view of the matter. For the moment, my point is that viewing Aquinas as a sort of *bricoleur*, a strong moralist engaging in a kind of selective retrieval and reconfiguration of available moral languages for his own use, helps make sense of what he was doing. It makes a difference not only which elements he had at his disposal, which he selected for retention, and which he weeded out, but also how he reconfigured the fragments into a whole. It need not have been the way that we find most familiar. We need to be looking for different kinds of *bricolage*, different tropes of moral discourse. We shall have no trouble finding them once we begin looking, as I hope to show in discussing other moral thinkers in later chapters. Some will turn out to be every bit as eclectic as Aquinas, and some will prove quite self-conscious about the enterprise in which they are engaged.

Calling attention to the processes of inclusion, exclusion, and reconfiguration at work in creative moral thought should help us avoid thinking of ethical reasoning merely as a procedure for determining the truth-value of moral propositions. There are too many moral truths for any of us to consider.[21] To entertain all of them, one would have to know all the possible moral languages. None of us can do that. We are lucky to master the one we learn early on at home and a few others being spoken in the vicinity. Even a single moral language places countless moral truths before us, far too many to factor into our deliberations, most of them too trivial to concern ourselves with. The moral *bricoleur* needs to declare some propositions true, some false. But there is more to the process than that. *Bricolage* can put new candidates for truth and falsehood to work, recover old candidates from retirement, and alter the current division of conceptual labor. It can give some truths pride of place while making others seem trivial or irrelevant, though nonetheless true.

Philosophers debate whether there are moral truths. I have said there are. Those who agree with me often go on to debate whether such truths are discovered or made. Call the one school realism, the other constructivism. I say we should be both realists and constructivists. How can we be both? We can be realists, of a sort, by affirming that moral propositions, being propositions, have truth-value, that some of them, indeed many of them, can be known to be true, and that coming to know the truth of a moral proposition consists in a kind of discovery. We can be constructivists, of a sort, by asserting with Richard Rorty "that where there are no sentences there is no truth, that sentences are elements of languages, and that languages are human creations."[22] To say that candidates for truth and falsehood in ethics can be brought into being by the creative human effort of moral *bricolage* is not to deny that the candidates thus brought into being really possess truth-value or can be discovered to be true or false by rational means. A Romantic emphasis on the poetic dimension of moral thinking, which I have tried to reclaim in my references to the moral tropes, need not conflict with the emphasis that I placed on the truth of moral propositions in earlier chapters. One couldn't get very far in moral reasoning without knowing the truth of many moral propositions, but truth is only one of the goods we seek in a proposition, and one could know a great many moral truths without knowing which ones were relevant to the problems at hand, worth mentioning in an argument, or capable of conferring order, by virtue of their explanatory scope and power, on the rest of what we believe.

IV

Languages are human creations, yes, but widely used moral languages tend not to be the creations of particular individuals. Glacial shifts in the use of moral language cannot be accounted for simply as systematic attempts at moral *bricolage* by individuals. Locke, Hobbes, Aquinas, Calvin, Marx, Freud, Jefferson, Jane Austin, and Martin Luther King have all left their mark on the language we use, just as architects have left their marks on our cities. But just as the history of our cities must go far beyond the biographies of architects, so too must the history of moral change go far beyond the classic texts of moral *bricolage*. The intentional acts of individual language-builders make a difference, but so do the large-scale social processes to which individual actors respond and contribute, often unwittingly.

Rorty writes:

The mind of Europe did not *decide* to accept the idiom of Romantic poetry, or of socialist politics, or of Galilean mechanics. That sort of shift was no more an act of will than a result of argument. Rather, Europe gradually lost the habit of using certain words and gradually acquired the habit of using others.[23]

Similarly, it is not as if the spirit of the age decided to make the category of honor less central to moral discourse. Seventeenth-century moral philosophers were self-consciously trying to displace the category, but they were responding to a shift already in progress—one that was not primarily the result of their own efforts and arguments. (This is not to say that argument plays no role.)

One source of conceptual change in modern ethics is the blurring of certain inherited distinctions. As new social practices and institutions take hold within a group, distinctions that used to be sharp can become fuzzy. It may become more difficult, for example, to draw a sharp distinction between "us" and "them" or between masculine and feminine roles. And this, in turn, can make certain sorts of moral judgments inapplicable or irrelevant to the new circumstances. So it was with certain judgments concerning honor and, as we shall see in Chapter 7, certain judgments concerning the abominable.[24]

But there are other sources of conceptual change in modern ethics besides the blurring of inherited distinctions. In Chapters 8–12, we shall be paying special attention to the growth of new vocabularies in and around newly configured social practices and institutions in modern societies—the vocabulary of utility associated with the capitalist market; the vocabulary of rights associated with liberal bureaucracies; and the vocabularies of specific virtues, goods, and obligations developed within particular social practices like religious worship, politics, medical care, and baseball. The relation among these vocabularies can, of course, be highly contentious, and the resulting strife can itself create circumstances in which new concepts take root. For now, consider just one way in which this can happen. It has to do with what David Lewis calls the kinematics of presupposition.

Intentional speech-acts have unintended consequences. What I say affects what you can presuppose in discourse with me even if I'm not trying to bring about changes in presupposition. A change in what we can jointly presuppose and subsequent efforts to accommodate that change may have a much greater influence on the future of moral discourse than anything I intended to accomplish. Suppose you and I live in early modern France but we accept conflicting conceptions of God and these conceptions lead our views of the good to diverge. Suppose also that I am in the minority in my geographical region. I cannot win the day for my conception of the good by force, although my party is too numerous to be wiped out altogether. If, under these circumstances, I wish to persuade you to adopt my political proposals, or if I am a weary peacemaker or international lawyer (like Grotius) concerned for other reasons to limit the bad effects of religious strife, I shall not be able to presuppose, at least in dialogue with you, the truth of my religious beliefs at those points where they conflict with yours.

As a result, belief in the existence of a specific sort of God and in certain aspects of a vision of the good ceases to function as a presupposition of our moral discourse with each other. I will have a strong interest in drawing attention to aspects of your religious outlook that might incline you to treat me with tolerance—your conception of conscience perhaps. And I will have an equally strong interest in making arguments that do not take my religious outlook for granted. This may get me arguing in new ways, putting new twists on familiar usages and possibly even bringing new candidates for truth and falsehood into being without trying to do so. A generation or two later, our descendants may be talking about human rights and the natural law, not religious obligations and God's will, when they moralize in public. They may still think God's will is important, but they mention it only at home or in church or on those increasingly rare public occasions when the reference seems likely to increase the chances of persuading those who disagree with them.

This example provides a useful model for construing some of the forces that contributed to one highly significant change in our use of moral language, the secularization of public discourse. Again, while particular authors like Hume and Bentham tried to help this shift along, it was not brought about by individual or collective decision. Nor did it essentially consist in a lowering of religious commitment by individuals. Religious commitment has waxed and waned in varying degrees throughout the period. It now seems to be waxing, in America, at any rate, and in many parts of the Third World. Yet the secularization to which I refer—the secularization of public discourse—didn't occur in people's heads and hearts but rather in the linguistic transactions that took place, under the aegis of certain public institutions, between one person and another. What they had in their heads and hearts mattered. Luther's religious convictions about the nature of the secular order and Locke's religious convictions about conscience, as well as the convictions of eighteenth-century deists and nineteenth-century atheists, all contributed to the secularization of moral discourse. But we need also to keep in mind how heavily the need to persuade one's religious opponents without resort to war has contributed to the process of conceptual change.

Secularized public moral discourse may have made it more likely that disbelief would gain a foothold it didn't previously have, given how much one could now do in the culture without presupposing the existence of a specific sort of God; but it also left ample room for religious phenomena such as millenial sects, the cult of self-improvement, and the multiplication of denominations. Moreover, secularization of this kind may very well be undone by the next epochal shift, despite the wishes of individuals and groups who struggle against new developments or perhaps even aided by the unintended consequences of their resistance. Those who did the most to bring the distinctive features of our moral discourse into being were not atheists, and they were not trying to create conditions in which atheism might have room to flourish. The gap between intended consequences and actual results may be just as wide in future as it was in the past.

Our secularized language of human rights seems in fact to have begun as what the linguists call a *pidgin*—a sparse dialect used entirely for communicating with members of other groups, nobody's native tongue or first language of deliberation but a handy mode of discourse with strangers. But what used to be a pidgin can undergo further development, catch on as a language to be learned in infancy, and function as a subtle medium for deliberation and discourse with friends and family. Linguists call such a language a *creole*. A creole can become, over time, as rich a moral language as one could want—drawing vocabularies from diverse sources and weaving them together, if all goes well, into a tapestry well-suited to the needs of a time and place. Need we reduce our moral discourse to Esperanto or confine ourselves to the scant conceptual resources of a pidgin to make the language of human rights our own? Not if we can give it a place within a language sufficiently rich and coherent to meet our needs. Or so I shall argue in Part 3.

The change I refer to as the secularization of moral discourse, then, was one in which new moral vocabularies took hold in an environment to which they were well adapted, in accordance with the kinematics of presupposition.[25] We shall be trying to assess its significance in later chapters. For now, I cite it only to illustrate that what Rorty has said of our language in general applies to our moral language in particular: it is "as much a contingency, as much a result of a thousand small mutations finding niches (and a million others finding no niche), as are the orchids and the anthropoids."[26]

4

THE SPECTRUM OF RELATIVITY

So far, I have mentioned many different things that might be meant by "the relativity of morals." I have said the justification of a moral belief is relative to epistemic context, but only because all epistemic justification is relative to context. I have said that the interpretation of a moral sentence is relative to a language, but only because to be interpreted all sentences need to be related to other sentences in a language we understand. I have said that the expressibility of moral propositions is relative to a language, but only in the sense that one can't always translate a foreign sentence of a given kind into one's native tongue without spending time in foreign places and enriching the conceptual resources of one's native tongue hermeneutically. I have also said that the truth of some moral propositions, like the proposition that slavery is evil, is not relative in Swoyer's strong sense. A sentence could not simultaneously express precisely this true proposition and also be false, no matter what context, language, or framework it was embedded in.

There was one hint of additional complexity, however, when I suggested that ancient slaveholders might not have been blameworthy for holding slaves even if the institution of slavery has always been evil, that judgments of blame must take into account particular features of an agent's context. This raises the possibility that the truth-value of some moral propositions is indeed relative in an interesting sense. In this chapter, I want to pursue this possibility by considering different sorts of moral judgments we make about people, acts, practices, and institutions in other cultures. What about a culture whose moral concepts and background assumptions are quite different from ours or whose way of life is so distant that it offers no real option for people in our historical circumstances? Does it even make sense for us to say that such a way of life is morally good or bad, just or unjust? that people so distant from our own assumptions or concerns are evil or blameworthy for their treatment of women and slaves? that they ought to have done certain things differently? What conclusions can we draw, generally, about the nature of morality from careful examination of the judgments we make in our moral language about people in other cultures and their actions? Should we conclude, in particular, that moral truth is not one, that there is no single true morality?

I

When I affirmed that the proposition about the evil of slavery is true, always has been true, and would be true in any framework or context, I chose my example carefully. Given my purposes, it would only have clouded the issue to cite an ambiguous sentence, whose truth-value would depend on which of two or more plausible interpretations were assigned to it, such as: "It would be evil for us all to hang together." My interest here is in whether the truth-value of certain *interpreted* sentences is relative. The kind of relativity present in all instances of ambiguity is beside the point. By the same token, it would have been inappropriate to cite a sentence with what philosophers call indexical expressions, such as: "*I* am morally evil," "*This* is morally evil," or "The *current* investment policies of *our* university are morally evil." We are not concerned with sentences whose truth-value depends, for reasons that teach us nothing interesting about morality, on who spoke them, what demonstrative gestures accompanied them, when they were spoken, or the like. No one denies that the truth-value of sentences including indexical expressions is relative to features of context.[1]

Nor does anyone deny that moral sentences often include an implicit indexical element. If I say, "Uttering falsehoods with the intent to deceive is evil," I may be leaving unstated a restriction of the form, "other things being equal" or "under circumstances of the sort being discussed," trusting that this will be clear from the context of the remark. A complete statement of my view would make any such specification of conditions explicit.[2] Thus, the truth-value of a statement with an implicit reference to conditions of this sort will be relative to context; but this is not at issue in the debate over moral relativism. I am stipulating that propositions are fully interpreted, meaning by this that they have already been paired with paraphrases that resolve ambiguity, substitute nonindexical expressions for pronouns, demonstratives, and similar expressions, while making all implicit qualifications explicit.

The proposition in question, then, is that slavery, as defined in the previous chapter, is evil, period. No qualification of the form "under such-and-such conditions" or "other things being equal" is intended. My example needed to be a proposition nearly everyone likely to read this book would interpret fully and straightforwardly, accept without argument as true, and view as moral in content. The point I wanted to make wasn't about the relativity of uninterpreted sentences, the ethics of slavery, or the line between moral and nonmoral propositions. The example also needed to be a proposition whose truth does not seem, intuitively, to be relative in certain other ways. An unqualified proposition about the evil of slavery served my purposes well, for most of us are apt to condemn slavery as evil wherever and whenever we find it practiced, even in cases where those practicing it employ concepts quite different from ours, would fail to recognize our reasons for judging the practice evil, and don't know any better. If, however, you are reluctant to judge slavery *as such* evil, feel free to add the clause, "other things being equal." The addition will make the proposition weaker and thus perhaps easier to believe without further qualification, but the statement still serves my purposes by providing an example of a fully interpreted moral sentence whose truth is not relative.

Some propositions about the evil of some kinds of institution require more qualifications than does the one about slavery. Slavery, I want to say, is intrinsically evil in the sense that no variations in circumstances could make it good or morally indifferent. Polygamy seems to require different treatment. Many of us believe that while every society requires means for regulating sexual activity, and monogamy may be the best means for us, no single means is necessarily best for all societies.[3] Polygamy may be evil under some conditions—for instance where a widely accepted institution of monogamy is in place and there are roughly equal numbers of heterosexual men and women—but not under others. We are not inclined to judge polygamy evil in a situation where most men have been killed at war and there is ample cultural precedent for taking more than one spouse, a condition that might obtain in a certain Bedouin tribe.

David Wong refers in this connection to *environmental relativity*, which he distinguishes from both the kind of relativity that denies that there is "a single true morality" and the kind of relativity involved in judgments with implicit qualifying clauses.[4] He is right, I believe, in saying that environmental relativity does not threaten the notion that there is a truth of the matter about which practices are good or evil, morally speaking. It implies only that some practices which are in fact evil under particular social-historical conditions may not be so under others. There is a sense in which "Polygamy is evil" is true for us but not for the Bedouins just mentioned, a sense not captured by saying that we believe polygamy is evil and the Bedouins don't. But putting it in that way is apt to confuse the issue. It would be less misleading to say simply that in truth polygamy is not intrisically evil, that whether a given instance of polygamy is evil depends on the social-historical conditions in which it is found.

This way of putting it makes clear, however, that environmental relativity differs only in scope from the kind brought out when implicit qualifications are made explicit in ordinary moral judgments. On my view, uttering falsehoods with the intent to deceive is evil, but only under certain conditions (namely, when one owes the truth as a debt of justice). The same holds for practicing polygamy—it, too, is evil only under certain conditions. The case of polygamy seems different only because the relevant conditions are always satisfied, as a matter of fact, in some societies but not in others. To discover that the truth-value of a given proposition is environmentally relative in Wong's sense is simply to discover that, in order to be true, the proposition needs a qualifying clause of the form "under conditions C," where C indicates a general type of social-historical setting instead of a type of moral circumstance one might find in any social-historical setting.

Given my beliefs about polygamy, I need to explain how others came to believe differently. Those within my own society who hold that polygamy is intrinsically evil pose one sort of problem. Bedouins who hold that polygamy is always acceptable, whatever conditions obtain, pose another. In each case, I may point to metaphysical beliefs I take to be mistaken, beliefs about what way of life God or Allah ordained for all humanity, beliefs whose presence helps account for what I take to be moral error concerning polygamy. Or I may point to ignorance of or insensitivity to social-historical conditions unlike one's own. In any event, however, I have differences to explain. Acknowledging environmental relativity is not a way of eliminating moral disagreement altogether. Environmental relativity remains a far cry from the idea that each society has its own moral truth, although it does help explain some of the differences that cause some people to embrace that idea.

Moreover, granting that there is a range of practices and institutions, among which one might be the best, objectively speaking, for a given society to adopt, depending on its social and historical circumstances, does not rule out holding that some practices are simply beyond the pale. Slavery, on my view, is such an institution. It is evil wherever and whenever it is found. Why do I not say, with equal conviction, that all slaveholders deserve blame? Because the truth-value of a judgment about blame is relative to the agent's circumstances in a way that the former judgment's truth-value is not.

In this respect, moral blame is like epistemic justification. People are epistemically justified in believing a proposition if, epistemically speaking, they are doing the best that could be done under the circumstances. They need not necessarily be believing truths, provided they are making proper use of available evidence and concepts, avoiding wishful thinking, and so forth. People are morally justified and hence morally blameless if, morally speaking, they are doing the best that could be done under the circumstances. They may be engaged in practices that we rightly judge to be evil and still be blameless, provided they could not have known the moral truth of the matter, have not been negligent, intend no injustice, and so forth. Before judging a given class of slaveholders blameworthy, we need to know, among other things, what they could have known about the intrinsic evil of slavery. Ignorance on that score, if the ignorance itself is morally blameless, will tend to excuse them for owning slaves.

This helps explain our reluctance to blame people in distant generations and cultures for engaging in practices and institutions we find evil. We cannot assume that their knowledge coincides with ours. Our knowledge about the evil of slavery may depend upon our use of concepts or styles of reasoning they lack; their judgment may have depended on no longer tenable empirical and metaphysical beliefs they had no compelling reason to question. This does not mean, of course, that we may never make judgments of blame across cultural boundaries. It means only that such judgments often require more subtlety, more sensitivity to context, than judgments about whether practices and institutions are evil. Certainly there are some people in every social group—and some actions of every member of every social group—that deserve our moral blame. Ceasing to apply the concept of blame across cultural boundaries is no way to avoid ethnocentrism. But figuring out who deserves blame and in what degree can be a complex matter, much complicated by differences in cultural setting.

In summary, I propose a metaphor. Propositions imputing moral blame and propositions describing people, practices, or institutions as evil fall at opposite ends of a spectrum of relativity. The truth-value of the former, like the truth-value of propositions about epistemic justification, is relative to certain features of the circumstances of the people referred to. The truth-value of the latter is not similarly relative. The closer you get to the former end of the spectrum, the more sensitivity to context a wise interpreter's moral judgments will need to show in judging members of other cultures. Even at that end of the spectrum, however, sound cross-cultural moral judgment remains possible—and often necessary—provided one is sensitive in the required ways and knows what one needs to know to judge well.

II

Gilbert Harman invites us to consider a society in which cannibalism is tolerated. He comments, "We feel uncomfortable about saying that it is morally wrong *of them* to eat human flesh. On the other hand, we also believe that their practice is objectionable."[5] Evidently, Harman has his finger on a distinction not unlike the one we have been discussing. But would a society's toleration of cannibalism be enough, by itself, to make us uncomfortable about saying that it is morally wrong of them to eat human flesh? I think not.

The issue turns on whether we found compelling reason to blame them for engaging in the activity we find objectionable. Suppose the society in question is our local college eating club, which engages in cannibalistic practices as part of its initiation rites and yet has every reason to find the practice objectionable. The fact that the group permits cannibalism would not relieve its members of blame. We ought to blame them for behaving in this way. They perform objectionable acts. They know better. Nothing in their circumstances excuses them. It is therefore wrong *of them* to behave as they do. No doubt, Harman had a different sort of case in mind, a case in which something in the circumstances would excuse members of the group for engaging in the activity. But it is important to recognize that a group's willingness to permit an activity is not enough to excuse its members for engaging in it. They could still be wrong to behave as they do.

On Harman's theory of morality, implicit agreements give rise to moralities, which in turn supply agents with reasons for acting in accordance with the agreements. Imagine that our local college eating club has consciously opted out of its implicit agreement with the rest of us. Its own implicit agreement provides reasons, for those who intend to keep it, to engage in cannibalism—or, to make the case stronger, to torture the innocent as part of its weekly entertainment. Does it not make sense to say that it is wrong *of them* to engage in such practices? I see no reason for thinking so. We can and do blame people for complicity in agreements, even the implicit agreements that might be said to constitute the groups to which they belong.[6] If Harman's theory were right, this would be hard to explain. His theory implies, if I understand it correctly, that we cannot intelligibly impute blame to others or say that it is wrong of them to behave as they do simply because they violate the strictures entailed by implicit agreements to which they do not subscribe. Yet my counterexample suggests that we can. Perhaps Harman's theory places too much weight on agreements as constitutive of morality.

We can, however, detach Harman's genetic "hypothesis," concerning what brings a morality's distinctive reasons into being, from what he calls "a soberly logical thesis about logical form."[7] The logical thesis is that some moral judgments are "inner judgments"—judgments we make about someone only if we believe they are "capable of being moved by the relevant moral considerations." On the highly plausible assumption that not everyone is moved by the considerations that count for us as morally relevant, the truth-value of the inner judgments we make about people is relative. Relative to what? To the reasons they could reasonably find morally relevant, given their epistemic context, the moral language they speak, and so forth. Clearly, this sort of relativity could obtain even if those reasons are not constituted by intentions to abide by implicit agreements.

At least some judgments about blame seem to be inner judgments in Harman's sense, because one thing that can relieve someone of moral blame for an objectionable act is nonculpable ignorance of reasons for finding the act objectionable. According to Harman, judgments about what someone morally ought to do are also inner judgments. In one of Harman's examples, a mobster is directed to kill Bernard J. Ortcutt, a bank manager. The mobster, given his upbringing and social setting, sees no morally relevant reason not to kill Ortcutt. Harman concludes that "it would be a misuse of language to say of him that he ought not to kill Ortcutt or that it would be wrong of him to do so, since that would imply that our own moral considerations carry some weight with him, which they do not. "[8]

Saying this does not commit Harman to denying that the act of killing Ortcutt ought not to be done or that the state of affairs in which Ortcutt is killed ought not to obtain. Of these various "ought" judgments, according to Harman, only the one about what an agent ought to do is an inner judgment. Furthermore, it would not be a misuse of language, in Harman's view (or in mine), to say that the mobster is evil or that the practices and institutions in which the mobster is involved are unjust.[9] We can still sensibly call Hitler evil or vicious, his genocidal policies unjust, and the Third Reich morally despicable even if we find, *per impossibile*, that Hitler and all his fellow Nazis were nonculpably ignorant of the morally relevant reasons.[10]

Not everyone shares Harman's intuitions about which moral "ought to do" judgments involve misuses of language. My own intuitions waver. But Harman strengthens his case by offering a persuasive account of how the term *ought* and related modal auxiliary verbs function in various moral and nonmoral contexts. The account gives strong reasons for taking what one morally ought to do as a four-term relation among an agent, a type of act, a set of qualifying considerations or conditions, and morally relevant reasons for action that can be rightly ascribed to the agent. If the account is correct—and I am inclined to think it is—then what one morally ought to do is a fact, but a relational fact, and the truth-value of judgments about what one morally ought to do is therefore relative to epistemic context, although no less determinate than the corresponding relational facts.[11]

Assuming that Harman is right about this, what follows? On the one hand, it follows that at least some moral propositions are *about* something—namely, relational facts of a certain kind—by virtue of which they are either true or false. And these propositions seem no more problematic, on reflection, than other relational, context-dependent or context-sensitive propositions, including propositions about epistemic justification and explanatory success in science.[12] On the other hand, once we detach the "soberly logical thesis about logical form" from the genetic hypothesis, leaving the latter aside, and underline the differences turned up by Harman's analysis between "ought to do" judgments and moral judgments of other kinds, we are not in a position to proclaim anything so grand or potentially disconcerting as the "truth of moral relativism."

It would be better, more modest and more reassuring, to say that our moral language provides rich resources for making various kinds of moral judgments. These judgments fall at many different places on a wide spectrum, depending on what aspects of personal, social, historical, and epistemic circumstances they require us to take into consideration. Judgments about evil tend to cluster at one end of the spectrum. Judgments about what a person ought morally to do tend to cluster, if Harman is right, closer to the other end, near the judgments about blame. Harman's analysis of moral "ought to do" judgments helps to fill in part of the whole picture, but it does not introduce a kind of relativity entirely unlike the kind that traditional moralists, including those usually labeled absolutists, have long recognized at work in judgments of blame. Nor should the similarity be surprising, for both sorts of judgments have to do with a kind of justification, and justification is relative to context.

All of these judgments, in principle, can properly be applied across cultural boundaries. Some judgments, because of where they fall on the spectrum of relativity, require us to exercise more caution in cross-cultural contexts than others. There may well be contexts in which it would be rash, given how little we know, to make "inner judgments" at all. And our judgments about what an agent in a distant culture ought morally to do, given his or her alien patterns of reasoning, can sometimes diverge sharply from our judgments about what ought to be done (in the sense that appraises the act, not the agent). But the relativity of inner judgments hardly places cross-cultural moral assessment as such at risk. It opens up no abyss that silences moral judgment or swallows up our confidence in moral truth. It only helps us see in more detail the respects in which our moral language is a motley, one well-suited to myriad uses at home and abroad. Which is not to say, of course, that our moral language cannot be improved or that we have nothing to learn, morally speaking, from strangers.

III

In David Wong's terminology, a moral relativist denies what an absolutist affirms, that "there is a single true morality" (pp. 1, 4). One can still be a relativist in Wong's sense while affirming that moral statements have truth-values, that moral arguments can be good or bad, that non-moral facts are relevant to the assessment of moral statements, and that there are moral facts.[13] One can remain an absolutist, according to Wong, while embracing two types of relativity already mentioned: relativity to implicit qualifying conditions and "environmental relativity." The crucial test of the absolutist, Wong thinks, comes in trying to make sense of moral diversity, especially the kind displayed in prolonged and apparently intractable disagreement. How can absolutism be right in positing a single true morality when there are so many moral issues on which rational agreement seems beyond reach?

As Wong sees it, absolutism cannot clear this hurdle. His own strategy, therefore, is to accept relativism, as he defines it, and show how far a relativist can go in accounting for such phenomena as our references, in ordinary language, to "true moral statements" and "good moral arguments." There are true moral statements, good moral arguments, and even moral facts, he concludes, but only *within* moralities. This is because moral statements, properly analyzed, contain a reference to a system of rules adequate with respect to a particular group's ideal of morality. If you morally ought to do such-and-such, and I say so, my statement is true relative to an "adequate moral system" that functions within a group to resolve internal and interpersonal conflicts. All moral facts are relational. All moral statements involve implicit relativity to what, in the context of utterance, counts as an adequate moral system. Their truth-conditions, in other words, include an indexical element, since the extension of the phrase "adequate moral system" varies from context to context. There is no single true morality for this reason: There are many different sets of moral truths, each relative to a different adequate moral system.

Everything hangs, it seems, on whether Wong is right in holding that there is no truth of the matter concerning which moral system is most adequate. If there were a truth of the matter about that, we would have no reason to treat "adequate moral system" as an indexical expression. We would simply say, with the absolutist, that many groups have made false assumptions about what the most adequate moral system is and that these false assumptions help to explain the facts of moral diversity. Why should we steer clear of absolutism on this point? Because, says Wong, it cannot successfully explain the facts of moral diversity. Wong's point seems to be that if there were a truth of the matter concerning which moral system is most adequate, we wouldn't have such prolonged and apparently intractable disagreement about it as we in fact have.

But there is something very odd about Wong's solution to the problem, for if "adequate moral system" is an indexical expression, these prolonged and apparently intractable disagreements among the proponents of various moral systems aren't disagreements at all. There is no point to the debates. It is as if I had said "This is brown," and you had replied "It is not!" but each of us was referring to a different object, making our subsequent remonstrations and arguments over the matter pointless. Furthermore, since most people behave like absolutists when debating which set of rules is the most "adequate moral system," Wong would have us believe that such people are not aware of the expression's actual indexicality. It is as if our merely apparent disagreement over the color of *this* object were further complicated by my failure to recognize *this* as an indexical term.

How could the absolutist be mistaken about the indexicality of "adequate moral system"? The expression is not *learned* as varying in extension, as pronouns and demonstratives are, Wong says: "A competent language user could have 'adequate moral system' or 'the right moral rules' in his or her idiolect, and be completely unaware that it could vary in extension. It is an analysts of moral language, not necessarily as users, that we attach the subscript to 'adequate'" (pp. 44–45).

At this point, we must ask precisely whose moral language Wong is analyzing. Imagine an isolated community of absolutists who have never met a relativist but have a long history of debate over which moral system is most adequate. Will the expression "adequate moral system" function indexically in their language, unbeknownst to them? Wouldn't it be more plausible to say that this expression and its cognates function indexically in only in languages that already, as it were, incorporate commitment to moral relativism? If so, the useful question isn't how the expression functions *simpliciter* or even how it functions in our language but rather whether we should speak a language that incorporates commitment to relativism. To answer that question, we must determine whether there is a truth of the matter concerning which moral system is most adequate. Asking whether "adequate moral system" is really an indexical expression obscures the issue more than it clarifies it.[14]

Why should evidence of protracted disagreement on a given topic tend to show that there is no truth of the matter on that topic and thus nothing to have a real disagreement over? Wong says surprisingly little about this. There has been disagreement over moral relativism for centuries, and it is likely to continue for some time. Does this tend to show that there is no truth of the matter concerning relativism? Hardly. Wong would surely point out that relativism is an exceedingly knotty topic, made up of many intertwined perplexing issues. We have trouble agreeing on relativism in part because of the difficulty in disentangling any one issue from others with which it might easily be confused. Wong is right to work hard at undoing the knots in hope of getting at the truth about moral relativism. Why shouldn't we take much the same attitude toward the problem of what way of life or moral system would really be best?

Wong knows that absolutists need not be rendered speechless by the existence of apparently irresolvable disagreement. He acknowledges several "major methods of explanation" that are available to them (pp. 117–120). One of these places great weight on ignorance and on errors in perception and reasoning. Another stresses that "some moral questions are simply beyond human powers to resolve one way or another, at least as these powers exist in their present state." Yet another emphasizes environmental relativity. Wong holds that such methods are bound to produce results that leave "gaping holes in our theory of the speakers of moral language" (p. 153). Let us see if he is right.

In two revealing passages, Wong says, "There is no *neutral* standpoint from which to eliminate all but one ideal as the most rewarding life for human beings" and "no *neutral*, rational way of weighing" conceptions of human happiness in reference to which one might select a moral system as ideally adequate (pp. 159, 136, italics added). But absolutists need not deny such claims. An absolutist remains free to say that while there is a single true moral system, there is not an Archimedean point, beyond all systems of moral belief, from which human beings could conceivably apply leverage to determine moral truth in perfect neutrality. Absolutism, as Wong has defined it, need not deny that the justification of moral belief is relative to epistemic circumstances, that no road is open to a neutral epistemic standpoint, entirely above the fray. Perhaps Wong underestimates absolutism's ability to explain moral diversity because he conflates relativity of justification with relativity of truth.

An absolutist who avoids conflating these two sorts of relativity can go a long way toward explaining protracted moral disagreement by saying that whereas moral truth is one, people who are raised in different ways, exposed to different models of excellence, trained in the use of different vocabularies, immersed in different traditions, and familiar with different evidence relevant to the determination of moral truth are likely to be *justified* in accepting somewhat different moral beliefs. So long as you and I, given our epistemic circumstances, are justified in reaching different judgments about the most adequate moral system, our disagreement will remain unresolved. In dealing with moral diversity across cultures, historical periods, and social classes, this sort of explanation would seem very plausible indeed in a wide range of cases. Nothing in Wong's argument makes clear how the explanation would be strengthened by saying that there is no truth of the matter concerning the ideally adequate moral system, especially since that would complicate the task by requiring us to explain why so many people have supposed otherwise.

Thus Wong does seem to have underestimated one sort of move the absolutist might make. Now consider another. In discussing a specific instance of disagreement between John Rawls and Robert Nozick on justice, Wong considers the possibility that it may simply be "beyond human powers to resolve" for the time being:

> But in order to make this more than a cover for there being no fact-of-the-matter for the disagreement to be about, absolutists must tell us more about why the truth is beyond our reach in this particular case and not others. What is it about this disagreement that makes it impossible to resolve at this time? (p. 152)

Wong recognizes that in science, disagreements often cannot be resolved at a given time. He does not treat such disagreements as evidence that there is no truth of the matter. But, he says, "we are able to understand why these disagreements occur when they do" (p. 152). "Can we do the same for Rawls and Nozick?" (p. 153) I don't see why not.

If I agree with Rawls on most points, part of my burden will be to show how, if Rawls is mainly right, Nozick could have gotten those points wrong. This may involve admitting that Nozick is justified relative to his epistemic context. More likely, given the fact that Nozick, Rawls, and I share much the same epistemic context, I will need to entertain other possibilities. No doubt, I will attack some of Nozick's arguments, trying to indicate how and where they go wrong. If they go wrong in subtle and intricate ways, and I can show this, there will be no trouble explaining how Nozick could have missed the problems. Moral philosophy isn't easy. If I have too easy a time of it, and Nozick's arguments turn out to be easy targets, I shall have to question his moral or technical competence (in his case, probably the former). This will raise further questions about how he came to be deficient as a moral judge, questions I might endeavor to answer by dabbling in moral psychology, critical biography, and the history of professionalization. If I have too much difficulty on that score, I may have to double back and reassess other judgments, perhaps even going as far as calling my agreement with Rawls into question, either siding with Nozick after all or seeking a third theory of justice that affords a better overall explanation of the strengths and weaknesses of previous theories and theorists. And if I come to see strengths and weaknesses in both Rawls's theory and Nozick's, but see no way at present to choose between them or go beyond them, I shall have good reason to say that the question is, at least for the time being, beyond our powers to resolve.

However it goes, the explanatory task facing me will not be essentially unlike the task facing scientists who wish to explain the unwillingness of their opponents to switch sides. This example shows that absolutists will need to move case by case, relying on their own substantive moral views and assessments of arguments, in deciding how to explain moral disagreement. But the same is true when scientists explain disagreements among themselves. Wong thinks absolutists would have trouble filling in an account of why one case of disagreement, as opposed to another, proves difficult to resolve. Why, however, should they need to do more than show that, relative to the current epistemic situation, each of two theories counts as equally justified, given the strengths and weaknesses of each? What scientist could do more?

At times, Wong seems to want the absolutist to supply a general theory that would define "standards of rationality," give complete statement to a view of the good for humanity, or characterize "the nature of the relations between irreducible moral reality and those who perceive it" (p. 153). But we all get along rather well most of the time without such a theory. It seems gratuitous to demand one of absolutists. It would also be unfortunate to assume, as Wong does, that "when absolutists assert that there is only one valid ideal of the good for man, they believe that validity is grounded in determinate features of human nature, such as reason or distinctive human potentials for satisfying activities" (p. 158). Many absolutists have of course been committed to belief in determinate features of human nature, but no such commitment is built into absolutism as Wong initially defined it.

First, the definition entails no commitment to essentialism, an ontology of "essences" and "natures" founded on the notion of "necessary truths." So the absolutist is free to deny that there are "determinate features of human nature" in any sense that would involve commitment to essentialism. Second, absolutism, as Wong has defined it, need not deny that human nature is (in Wong's word) "plastic"—at least if we take this to mean that what people desire, what they believe, and how they behave, as well as what would make them happy and contribute to their flourishing, tends to vary considerably from one cultural setting to another. How might an absolutist who affirms such plasticity account for it without going over to Wong's view?

This question brings us to the other absolutist's method identified by Wong—namely, appeal to environmental relativity. Recall that, on Wong's definition of absolutism, an absolutist is free to affirm environmental relativity. Wong puts no limitation on how far an absolutist can take environmental relativity without ceasing to be an absolutist. Doesn't this method, if fully exploited, actually make it easy for absolutists to accommodate wide variations in what people are like across cultures, what they find rewarding, and what makes them truly happy? Nothing prevents an absolutist from saying that the most adequate moral system must include provisions for every way in which such variations could prove morally relevant. The moral truth of the matter may be that polygamy is the best way in one social and cultural environment, monogamy the best way in another. Liberal political arrangements could be objectively right under some historical circumstances and not others—a possibility we shall be considering in Part 3. And so on. Fully exploited, environmental relativity seems to allow absolutists to enjoy all the explanatory benefits of Wong's more radical relativism without incurring the costs. So again Wong seems to be underestimating the absolutist's explanatory resources. He seems to be attacking especially vulnerable forms of the position he has set out to refute.

An absolutist, then, can take both the relativity of justification and environmental relativity very far indeed. It may seem odd to speak of such a person as an "absolutist" or as someone committed to the existence of "a single true morality" or "most adequate moral system." But we are simply abiding by Wong's definitions. Perhaps it would be better to leave all isms behind. All three expressions are apt to be misleading, and Wong himself tends to stray from the meanings he stipulates. There is not a single true morality or most adequate moral system in the sense of a "complex of activities arranged in an ideal balance, which any rational and informed person would find the most rewarding" (p. 158), nor in the sense that morality requires exactly the same thing in most areas of life of a professional athlete in today's West that it requires of a tribal princess in thirteenth-century Africa. In what sense is there a single true morality? The single true morality could only be the set of all true fully interpreted moral sentences in all possible moral languages. The whole moral truth is singular in the sense that an omniscient being who accepted each and every sentence in that infinite set would not embrace a contradiction.[15]

The whole moral truth, of course, could never be coterminous with the moral system of a finite human being. One would have to be God to know that much. Moral systems tailored to human needs must accommodate our finitude. They will have to make some candidates for truth and falsehood central, leaving many others peripheral or consigning them to oblivion. Part of my proposed explanation of moral diversity, a part Wong does not consider in his critique of absolutism, involves saying that different groups often speak different moral languages. They not only disagree about moral propositions, they entertain different candidates for truth and falsehood. Taking this tack puts a certain sort of absolutist in a powerful position. Absolutism, taken as the view that there is a single true morality (consisting of all the true propositions in all the possible moral languages), does not conflict with the idea that the actual moral languages are in fact quite various. The notion of distinct moral languages allows this kind of absolutist (my kind) to preserve a nonrelativistic conception of moral truth while granting that different groups concern themselves with different sets of truths.

Part of what an omniscient being would know, I suppose, would be not only which moral sentences in all possible moral languages were true but also which were relevant to what sorts of questions and how much weight they should carry in deliberation. The ideally adequate moral system, we might say, would have to include all true propositions of that order as well (although not necessarily an algorithm for arriving at them). But is it not quite conceivable, Wong wishes to ask, that two or more "ways of life" could be tied for first place as judged by ideally competent, fully informed moral judges? Wouldn't this make them equally true or adequate? And doesn't this possibility, by thrusting indeterminacy into the very heart of moral truth, give us compelling reason to treat "adequate moral system" indexically?

First-place ties are possible, but Wong never says why their possibility lends credence to treating "adequate moral system" as an indexical expression. (Nor does he say why similar considerations wouldn't make "adequate scientific system" an indexical expression. Can't there be first-place ties in science, too?) An absolutist can say that if two systems are tied for first place from the vantage point of omniscience, then the choice between them is morally indifferent, that (in a suitably broad sense of the phrase) "the most adequate moral system" designates each of two ideally good ways of life as possible instantiations of the human good. It might be impossible, pragmatically, to be committed to two such ways of life simultaneously. They would not, however, involve commitment to contradictory propositions. They might compete for converts but not for the title "uniquely true." That title would be reserved for the system that could recognize the full truth in each.

In fact, for all Wong says, an absolutist could also be a Romantic who holds that the truly adequate moral system encompasses many ways of life tied for first place. Such ways would all be just and good, even by each other's lights. They would each enable human beings to achieve what, speaking roughly, we call the good. But they might involve substantially different social practices and moral vocabularies, thereby acquiring direction from distinct combinations of goods not all realizable together. Tolerate genuinely good ways of life, the Romantic absolutist might say, but don't tolerate just any system of rules that manages to catch on within some group as a mechanism for managing internal and interpersonal conflict while satisfying its own, perhaps evil, moral ideal. Let a thousand flowers bloom, but keep killing weeds.

The main motive for resisting radical relativism is not a worry over how to resolve first-place ties. It is rather a concern to preserve the possibility of distinguishing, so to speak, among first-, second-, third- . . . and last-place finishers when the evidence is comparatively clear.

On Wong's theory, any system that (a) functioned within a group as a means for managing internal and interpersonal conflict and (b) satisfied the standards of its own ideal for morality, including its ideal of moral change, would necessarily be adequate, by virtue of a hidden indexicality. Wong rightly points out that not just any system of rules would, as a matter of empirical fact, be likely to meet these two criteria. His criteria do exclude some systems. But they also leave far too many systems in the running, and on equal footing. All contenders allowed to compete finish tied for first. It is too easy to imagine systems that would satisfy Wong's criteria and yet be truly atrocious.

Imagine, for example, a system that encourages abuse of outcastes. Its ideal for morality discourages critical questioning of its metaphysics, which derives the distinctions between a priestly caste and untouchables from false teachings about their cosmic origins. In such a case, satisfaction of its own moral ideal is not enough to make a moral system adequate; this system would be better, not merely better relative to our moral ideal, if it retained its more attractive features but changed its rules for treatment of outcastes. Its ideal for morality would be better, not just better by our lights, if its acceptance did not depend on metaphysical falsehoods and insulation from critical questioning. In saying so, we presuppose our own moral ideal, our own general outlook on moral and metaphysical matters, but we are not making an inherently indexical statement about how things seem by our lights or about what holds relative to our moral ideal. We are making a statement about the truth and adequacy of their moral system.

It may be hard to say with certainty, from our present vantage point, which of the moral systems that satisfy Wong's criteria are the best, but can we not make any qualitative distinctions among them whatsoever? Can we not discern some gradations in overall quality with considerable certainty even now, despite being far less than ideally well-informed or perfectly wise? These are the questions that make Wong's relativism seem too sweeping and simplistic to account for what he calls "our moral experience."

His position has more to commend it than do moral skepticism and nihilism, for Wong is able to accommodate much of our ordinary moral talk, with its references to good moral arguments and true moral statements. But like its skeptical and nihilistic kin, it begins by generalizing too quickly from examples of protracted disagreement and ends with a picture too lacking in color, texture, and shades of gray to be plausible. To be sure, the best-known forms of absolutism are no more successful, relying as they do on implausible theories of human nature and practical reason that are hard to square with the facts of moral diversity. We need a more finely detailed picture with subtle shading to take full measure of both relativity and objectivity in ethics.

IV

If Wong were right, the truth-value of all moral judgments would be relative in a strong sense, and there would be no need to speak, as I have, of a spectrum of relativity. But if he is wrong, as I have just claimed, we need not go all the way to the other extreme, acknowledging no differences with respect to relativity of truth-value among the many moral judgments we make. Speaking of a spectrum of relativity—while also fully exploiting environmental relativity and the relativity of justification—allows us to occupy the middle ground between relativists like Wong and absolutists like Kant, accounting for the strengths and weaknesses of each. We need now to ask whether there are some conditions, not mentioned by Wong, under which it simply doesn't make sense for reflective people to render moral judgments of any kind across cultural boundaries. In an article called "The Truth in Relativism," Bernard Williams has raised the possibility that there are.[16]

What conditions might these be? Roughly, according to Williams, conditions under which the way of life or moral system of another society offers no real option for us. A system is a real option for us if it is either already our system or it would be possible for us to adopt it and live according to it while (a) retaining our "hold on reality" and (b) being able to explain our adoption of that system in light of "rational comparison" between it and the one we now hold (p. 181). When we are confronted with a real option, the confrontation between systems is real. Otherwise, the confrontation is merely notional. Williams's suggestion is that employing the "vocabulary of appraisal" makes sense or has point only in relation to real confrontations, not in relation to merely notional ones. This, he implies, is the truth in relativism, which he elsewhere describes as a "relativism of distance."

Unfortunately, Williams does not explicate conditions a and b in any detail, so it is hard to know how he would apply his distinctions. Condition a seems especially problematic. Would we lose our hold on reality if we went over to Nazism? We certainly would, at least in the sense that, in becoming Nazis, we would have to believe many falsehoods. But I have little trouble making sense of my negative appraisals of Nazism as a moral system, so perhaps this isn't the sort of case Williams had in mind. Maybe he meant something else by losing one's "hold on reality." Assuming he did, I wonder whether he could specify it without reintroducing the concept of "real option" and thus falling into unhelpful circularity.

We may get a clue about what Williams had in mind by working backward from his examples. He says, "The life of a Greek Bronze Age chief, or a mediaeval Samurai, and the outlooks that go with those, are not real options for us: there is no way of living them" (p. 182). Such moral systems are distant from us in a way Nazism is not. There are ways of being a Nazi here and now, even though they involve fanaticism and falsehood in high degree. Some of our neighbors are Nazis. We could join them. Nazism is realistically recognizable as a way of life possible in the twentieth century. The life of a Greek Bronze Age chief, or a medieval samurai, seem not to be. The issue is not simply that one cannot simultaneously live in the twentieth century and at some other time. It is rather that the most one could manage, if one tried nowadays to live the life of a medieval samurai, would be a gross parody. Being a medieval samurai requires a social context we can, as an empirical fact, neither gain access to nor reconstruct.

As Williams puts it,

Even Utopian projects among a small band of enthusiasts could not reproduce *that* life: still more, the project of re-enacting it on a societal scale in the context of actual modern industrial life would involve one of those social or political mistakes, in fact a vast illusion. The prospect of removing the conditions of modern industrial life altogether is something else again—another, though different, impossibility. (p. 182, italics in original)

A small band of enthusiasts could not reproduce the life of a medieval samurai because they could not reproduce the sort of social circumstances in which alone that life could be lived. A much larger band of enthusiasts might try to transform modern social circumstances into a context within which such a life could be lived, but because the clock cannot be turned back in that fashion, Williams thinks, any way of life they actually succeeded in making available as a real option would still not be the life of a medieval samurai.

Let us grant, without pressing too hard for clarification of conditions a and b, that the life of a medieval samurai is not a real option for us and is therefore distant in the relevant sense. What does a "relativism of distance" require us to conclude about such a case? Williams is not claiming that our vocabulary of appraisal cannot be applied to such a case without linguistic impropriety. His claim is rather that in such a case "there is so little to this use, so little of what gives content to the appraisals in the context of real confrontation, that we can say that for a reflective person the appraisal questions do not . . . genuinely arise." If you are confronted with a real option, and you ask whether it is a bad moral system or a good one on the whole, your question will have some point. We know how to judge answers to the question because we know how to relate the question to a real concern—namely, whether this option is worthy of adoption. If, however, the option is not real, it is bound "to lack the relation to our concerns which alone gives any point or substance to appraisal: the only real questions of appraisal are about real options" (p. 183). We will, in such a case, have trouble knowing what would count for or against an answer to the question of appraisal, because we won't know what purpose an answer could serve.

Suppose you are a professor of Japanese history, teaching an introductory course on the life of medieval samurai warriors. One of your students is a cynical sophomore who, unless you awaken his imagination, will remain completely untouched by the material and thus learn nothing about himself or about human possibility. You ask him whether he finds the life of a medieval samurai good or bad. He responds by quoting Williams, whose work he has been reading in a philosophy course. He tells you that the life of a medieval samurai is not a real option for us and that there can be no real question of appraisal concerning it. This is something reflective people know.

If you were such a professor, how would you respond? I would say that really reflective people know how to make notional confrontations seem real. Then I'd ask my sophomore to imagine that while traveling in the vicinity of Japan he is shipwrecked on an isolated island where, much to everyone's surprise, medieval Japanese culture survives intact. When the rescue party finally arrives two years later, he must decide whether to stay. Moral: Notional confrontations can become real in the imagination—real enough, at any rate, to mobilize a reflective person's powers of moral appraisal, thereby giving point to moral questions about distant cultures. One would have to be sophomorically unreflective to resist such thought-experiments. It is no accident that thought-experiments of this kind, often every bit as trite as this one in their use of shipwrecks (or time machines), do heavy duty in humanities courses designed to promote reflective thought. And there is a clear sense in which, within such thought-experiments, real questions of appraisal arise about notional options.

We can arrive at much the same result by another route, eschewing imaginary shipwrecks and time travel. Suppose, after reading the collected works of Alasdair MacIntyre, we all become convinced that the modern age is morally depraved. Yet, we also see that there is no turning back the clock. As MacIntyre once put it, it is too late to be medieval. Might we not, under such circumstances, reasonably regret living under modern conditions and wish we could become medieval again, knowing all the while that we cannot but be modern? Medieval ways would not then be a real option for us, on any reasonable interpretation of Williams's usage, but wouldn't there still be a point in using the vocabulary of moral appraisal in asking whether we should become medieval again if only we could? We need to ask such questions about notional options in order to morally evaluate our actual regrets and wishes. Here we have a kind of case in which counterfactual speculation is essential to moral reasoning about real questions. Williams's relativism of distance seems to fare poorly when subjected to scrutiny.

Furthermore, if Williams's relativism of distance were right with respect to moral appraisal, why shouldn't something analogous hold with respect to our judgments about distant ontological views? It seems clear that most ontological systems that developed during antiquity—the cosmology of Mithraism, for example—are not real options for us. Yet we have no trouble mobilizing our vocabularies of scientific appraisal against them if we wish. Why, if Williams were right, should this be so unless the relativism of distance applied to science? He does not say. Williams gives no indication of believing that it applies to science, but he also gives no reason for supposing that his arguments about real options and notional confrontations wouldn't apply to science as well as to ethics. It would be simpler, clearly, to resist the relativism of distance in science and ethics alike.

Williams has recently put some distance between himself and "The Truth in Relativism." He now grants, in particular, that *just* and *unjust* are

central terms that can be applied to societies as a whole, and in principle, at least, they can be applied to societies concretely and realistically conceived. Moreover, an assessment in terms of justice can, more obviously than others, be conducted without involving the unhelpful question of whether anyone was to blame. The combination of these features makes social justice a special case in relation to relativism.[17]

This admission is intended to leave the relativism of distance in place while treating assessment in terms of justice as an exception to the rule. Williams does not say, however, why expressions like *good, evil, true, false, cruel, vicious,* and related terms in our vocabulary of moral appraisal should not be treated as exceptional on the same grounds. If I am right, all of these terms are more like *just* than like *blameworthy* when used to make moral judgments about distant cultures.

Nor does Williams say why the question of whether anyone was to blame is always unhelpful in cases of purely notional confrontations. Telling the full story of the medieval samurai with any sensitivity may require me to blame someone for knowingly and willingly instituting certain especially cruel and unjust practices. The truth in Williams's remark is simply that judgments of blame and moral judgments of other sorts can often be disconnected. One needn't be in a position to afix blame in order to appraise a way of life as good or bad, just or unjust, on the whole.

It seems safe to conclude therefore that, Williams's arguments notwithstanding, we do need to recognize a broad spectrum of relativity, even concerning judgments about distant ways of life that offer no real option for us. We have every reason to doubt that judgments about justice and injustice are all alone, clustered at one end of the spectrum as the only kind "that transcend the relativism of distance."[18] If so, we should see Williams' admission that one kind of judgment is an exception to the rule as a step toward full recognition of the complexity and richness of the moral language we use in cross-cultural settings. It is only a single step, but a step in the right direction and one that leads naturally to others.

I have now said enough, I hope, to show why the general question, "Is moral relativism true?" ought to be replaced by a long series of more specific, and ultimately less daunting, questions of various sorts—questions that evoke the Wittgensteinian thought that our moral language is a motley. As previous chapters have shown, we need to say quite different things about the justification, interpretation, expressibility, and truth-value of moral sentences. It should now be clear that we need to say quite different things even about the truth-value of different kinds of moral sentences, depending upon the quite various concepts they employ.

It would be fruitless—and no doubt tedious—to develop my account of moral disagreement and conceptual diversity further in abstraction from particular instances of disagreement and diversity that make us care about these issues in the first place. So I shall turn, in Part 2, to the fate of religious ethics—the interpretation and appraisal of religious tradition by secular moral philosophers, the largely untold significance of certain religious assumptions and categories as part of our moral history, and the trials that religious ethics has faced in the modern world.

I have spoken of moral Esperanto as the preferred language of modern moral philosophy. It comes in two main dialects. One is the idiom of Bentham and Mill, in which all genuine moral speech is about calculations of beneficial consequences. The other is an idiom drawn from Kant's *Groundwork*, in which all genuine moral speech is about respect for others as ends-in-themselves.[19] We shall, in Chapters 5 and 6, be looking at recent consequentialist and Kantian moral philosophers, respectively, seeing how they take account of those whose moral speech resists reduction to the "fundamental principles" of the leading varieties of moral Esperanto. In the first case, an enemy of superstition grapples with the language of divine will. In the second, a champion of universal practical reason tries to make sense of Hindus. Both, as it turns out, have trouble—but interesting trouble, from which we can learn.

Chapter 7 in Part 2 examines one kind of moral language—prominent in biblical traditions, many alien cultures, and even in certain strands of our own culture—that has received little comment from ethical theorists during the heyday of Esperanto. My question will be why, and my answer will take us back to reflexive ethnography and the kinematics of presupposition. Chapter 8 is a case study in moral *bricolage* as practiced by one of the most distinguished Christian ethicists in America at the height of his career. His example will show us not only what moral *bricolage* can look like for those who consciously turn their backs on Esperanto but also what difficulties theologians now face in winning a hearing from both fellow intellectuals and fellow believers.

2

THE ECLIPSE OF RELIGIOUS ETHICS

5

RELIGION AND MORALITY

If there are many languages of morals, some of them surely show the influence of religious beliefs and practices. In some languages, for example, talk of moral obligation will coincide with talk of God's commands. Our own moral language not only retains vestiges of Jewish and Christian vocabularies but also bears the marks of attempts to secularize the terms in which we debate matters of public concern—reason enough for us to study the shifting relationships between religion and morality. An account of moral language, undertaken in our culture at this point in its history and sensitive to its context, must sooner or later come to grips with the fate of religious ethics or else risk radical distortion.

It must be said, however, that most moral philosophers in recent decades have felt free to dismiss religious ethics as plainly fallacious and therefore not worthy of serious philosophical study. It was possible for many years to defend this dismissal merely by citing famous arguments from Plato, Hume, Kant, and G. E. Moore. These arguments demonstrated, most philosophers thought, that religion must depend logically on morality, rather than the other way around, and that attempts to derive moral judgments from theological judgments or to define moral concepts in theological terms could not possibly succeed. Doubt about the logic of religious ethics and confidence in the uniformity and autonomy of morality have, for some time now, gone hand in hand.

Not everyone accepted all the arguments. Occasional questions were raised especially about the arguments drawn from Hume and Moore, which seemed to threaten not only religious ethics but much else besides. Yet almost all analytic philosophers saw ethics as the logical study of *the* language of morals. The historical or comparative study of evolving, distinct moral languages or communities of belief did not fall within their purview. To the contrary, they held that while it was certainly possible for people to mix moral and religious concepts, logical study could always separate the two sorts of concepts analytically without threatening the priority and independence of moral language as such. As *moral* philosophers, they therefore felt free to neglect religious ethics in a way one could hardly call benign. Meanwhile, logical positivism and related doctrines gave independent reasons for deeming religious propositions meaningless.

On many counts, then, religious ethics for some time attracted little philosophical attention. Virtually all those who attended to it did so polemically, in the spirit of the Enlightenment's struggle with superstition. Religious ethics remained the "other" against which secular moral philosophy defined itself. Religious ethics was always present, so to speak, in its absence, an absence needed to mark off the boundaries of discussion. Most theologians either ignored the antireligious polemics or were too busy retreating to put up a fight. There was never anything like real dialogue, which might have allowed secular moral philosophy to work through its merely antithetical relation to the religious traditions.

Recently, however, much has changed in philosophy. Developments in the philosophy of language and the theory of knowledge have undermined distinctions that were central to positivistic critiques of religion, and it now seems a good time to ask whether received philosophical opinion on the logical relation between religion and morality needs to be rethought. Rethinking this relation involves asking whether it is *a* relation—something essentially singular, subject to timeless analysis. But if things turn out to be messier than the logician's idiom would suggest, the uniformity and autonomy of morality can no longer be taken for granted. And if a real dialogue with the religious traditions can then be begun, the categories we have used to congratulate ourselves for being more rational than our ancestors and neighbors—categories like the old concept, "superstition" and its twentieth-century counterpart, "fallacious reasoning"—may be placed at risk.

I

Analytic philosophers tended to dismiss religious ethics in passing, and not to argue the matter at length. Kai Nielsen is a notable exception. His *Ethics without God*, a book in which he pulled together arguments he had been making in the journals for some years, can serve as a useful illustration of attempts to establish the essential independence of morality from religion by analyzing the language of morals.[1]

As a secular humanist dedicated to the language of consequentialist ethics, in which appeals to moral absolutes or divine commands have no place, Nielsen has a stake in denying that morality requires a religious foundation; and, Nielsen says, many theologians have claimed that such a foundation is necessary for morality. What exactly is the issue Nielsen is raising? It quickly becomes clear that he is not concerned with a historical question about the origins of morality, nor primarily with an empirical question about what is likely to happen to morality if people abandon religion or stop fearing divine retribution, nor with the question of whether God is in some sense causally responsible for bringing the realm of human morality into being. Rather, he is addressing an epistemological question, a question about the "fundamental criteria" of moral judgment.

Nielsen does not show that this is the sort of question theologians have been answering when they have made the claims he ascribes to them. But his interest in "foundations" and "fundamental criteria" tells us something important about Nielsen's concerns. He further delimits his topic by assuming that the foundation in question will be a criterion defining moral requirement in terms of *God's will*. So his major thesis takes this form: "I shall argue that the fact that God wills something— if indeed that is a fact—cannot be a fundamental criterion for its being morally good or obligatory and thus it cannot be the only criterion or the only adequate criterion for moral goodness or obligation" (p. 2). Nielsen's argument intends to pose an unpleasant dilemma for his theological opponents, forcing them to abandon their position. The idea is basically this. Suppose you are one of Nielsen's opponents. Either you propose a purely theological foundation for morality or you don't. If you do, then you can't get that foundation in place without running into insurmountable difficulties. A purely theological foundation, by definition, includes no moral concepts. They are meant to be defined later, in terms of the foundation. But how can you justifiably give content to your praise of God as morally perfect or be able to justify worship of God—tasks that seem essential to theism—without using moral concepts? How could you even justify awarding the title *God* to a being who deserves it?

If, on the other hand, you don't propose a purely theological foundation, you have granted that we are capable of exercising independent moral judgment after all, in which case morality seems not to depend upon a theological foundation for its justification. If you admit the need to employ moral concepts even in determining which being, if any, deserves the title *God*, then you've already let nontheological ethics in at the ground floor. So things seem to turn out poorly for you either way. Theological convictions are thus rendered entirely ancillary to moral judgment.

It would seem that you cannot slip between the horns of the dilemma as I've just presented it. Either you propose a purely theological foundation for morality or you do not. The dilemma poses an exhaustive and exclusive choice. What about breaking one of the horns? Nielsen devotes nearly all of his argument to showing that unwanted implications do follow for theists who propose a purely theological foundation for morality, that the first horn can't be broken in any way acceptable to theists. This is where he draws upon the stock arguments so often cited by analytic philosophers while dismissing the interest of religious ethics—arguments, for example, that recall Plato's *Euthyphro*.

As Glenn Graber has pointed out, even if these stock arguments work, the most they can do is raise the cost of proposing a purely theological foundation for morality.[2] The theist could simply accept the consequences of a theology that offered no justification for worshipping God, no way of distinguishing God from an omniscient and omnipotent Satan. That would be an unpleasant option, we might say, but still could be the least unpleasant option, since the only alternatives involve placing oneself in the position of judging God.

Let us grant, however, that most people, including most theologians, would find being impaled on Nielsen's first horn sufficiently unpleasant to abandon the proposal of a purely theological foundation for morality. Consider, instead, the possibility of breaking the second horn. Why can't you just say that you have no stake in defending a purely theological foundation for morality? The theologian who grasps the second horn can admit that if morality has a foundation, it isn't purely theological. But that leaves open the possibility that the most adequate morality includes theological elements. Such a morality would be partly but not entirely theological. The nontheological part would suffice to help us recognize the real God. It would also give content to our praise of God's moral perfection. We wouldn't have to say, for example, that "God is good" means simply that God conforms to the will of God. But the theological part, it might be argued, needs to be included to make our morality fully or more nearly adequate. In this case, morality would not require a purely theological foundation but, if it is to be adequate, theological judgments would be essential to it. Doesn't that sound more like what the theologians were probably driving at?

As Nielsen's opponent you might then argue

1. God wills what he does because it is right.

2. "X is right" does not just mean "x is willed by God."

and

3. We do in fact have to use some nontheological judgments in determining which if any being is the true God.

but

4. God's revealed will is nonetheless the best criterion of rightness available to us, given our finitude and his perfection.

and therefore

5. The best available or most adequate morality for us must incorporate theological elements.

This would mean

6. The most adequate morality would in some significant sense depend on theological beliefs.

even though

7. Theology would not be said to supply, all by itself, the foundation for morality.

We need now to ask how this series of claims relates to Nielsen's major thesis. Nielsen denies that God's will can constitute a fundamental criterion of moral goodness or obligation. Does 4 conflict with this denial? Apparently not, since claims 1–7 say nothing about fundamental criteria. Nielsen's opponent can, at this point, either add that conformity to God's will constitutes one fundamental moral criterion and thus one part of the foundation of morality or simply avoid mention of fundamental criteria and foundations altogether, insisting only that this criterion is essential.

Either way, the theologian would be unscathed by Nielsen's dilemma: the second horn would be broken. And it is interesting, if somewhat surprising, to find Nielsen admitting as much by the time he reaches his second chapter. He grants that his argument to that point does nothing to dismantle something like the following picture. The God who commands us is the God who created us. And he created us with certain ends in view—especially that of loving fellowship with God. He made us the way we are as human beings. Given the way we are and the way creation has been structured, we do well to strive for the good for which we were designed and toward which we tend. But because we are finite and fallen, the commands of the perfect God are our best guide to the fulfillment of our own nature—the best criterion of moral goodness and obligation we've got.

Nielsen's only means for ruling out a religious ethics of this kind seems to be his claim that theological beliefs aren't justified anyway—because they're either meaningless or false. He grants that "we should make our moral judgments in light of what the facts are" (p. 31) and that, if a theological account of the way things are is justified, we ought to adjust our moral judgments accordingly. But he adds:

We have no evidence at all for believing in the existence or love of God. None of the proofs works; we (or some of us, at any rate) have religious experiences, but these religious experiences do not establish, even with any probability, that there is an unlimited being, a transcendent cause of the universe. . . . Worse still, the very meaning of the term God is opaque. (p. 31)

Ethics without God has very little to say in defense of such charges. It must be said, on Nielsen's behalf, that the theological beliefs presupposed by Jewish or Christian ethics do need defense if they are going to make any headway with a secular audience. Moreover, it is by no means clear where such a defense is to be found—a matter to which we shall return in a later chapter. But the point I wish to make now is that the unpleasant dilemma which seems initially to be the crux of Nielsen's argument—and in fact forms the center of most analytic discussions of the relation between religion and morality—seems in the end to have remarkably little bearing on the appraisal of religious ethics. It may raise the costs of proposing a purely theological foundation for morality or a reductive definition of moral requirement in terms of God's will. Yet it leaves open the possibility that theology (or some other religious outlook) ought to play a significant role in shaping our moral judgments.

II

What stake need theologians have in claiming that God's will constitutes a *fundamental moral criterion?* Perhaps we should ask, before going any further, what Nielsen means by this expression. He says he means this:"(a) a test or measure used to judge the legitimacy of moral rules and/or acts or attitudes, and (b) a measure that one would give up last if one were reasoning morally" (p. 2). But if this is really what Nielsen means by a fundamental moral criterion, then it must be concluded that his arguments do nothing whatsoever to show that God's will doesn't or shouldn't function as one. For none of his arguments has anything to do with what tests or measures we should give up last in the process of reasoned revision of our moral views. All his arguments have to do with what we would need to know before we could be justified in believing something else.

For example, Nielsen argues that we couldn't know that God is good or that a given being deserved the title of *God* without first knowing, on independent grounds, some criteria of goodness other than being in accord with God's will. This contributes to the larger argument of the first chapter of *Ethics without God*, which shows (at most) that God's will cannot function as a moral criterion all by itself. But even if you would need to know how to use certain other criteria first, in order to know that God is good or that a given being deserved the title *God*, this would do nothing, once you had justified using God's will as a measure, to prevent your treating it as the last criterion you would abandon.

This suggests that Nielsen doesn't really mean what he says he means by a fundamental criterion. For his arguments to have any chance of working, even to modest effect, he has to mean something else. We can begin to specify what he must mean by defining what it is for a proposition to be "more fundamental" than another: A proposition, p, is more fundamental than another proposition, q, if and only if you'd have to be justified in accepting p before you could justify accepting q. If we then take "fundamental moral criteria" to mean the *most* fundamental criteria we employ in moral judgment, they would be such that you could and must be justified in accepting them first— that is, before you proceed to justify other moral beliefs and criteria on that foundation. *The* fundamental moral criterion, if there is one, would then be the most fundamental of all, the criterion on which all the others depend.

The theologian who seeks to break the second horn of Nielsen's dilemma grants that God's will is not the fundamental moral criterion. The fundamental criterion would have to be one we were justified in accepting without being justified in accepting any other moral criteria whatsoever, and the costs of claiming that God's will is the fundamental moral criterion in this sense seem high. But it does not follow from this admission that a criterion connecting moral goodness or obligation to God's will is less fundamental than many (or even most) of our moral judgments. So there may still be a strong sense in which God's will belongs to the foundation of morality—the level of criteria and beliefs on which the bulk of moral judgments depend for their justification.

Furthermore, it is unclear that anything could qualify as *the* fundamental moral criterion, in the sense just defined, since it isn't clear how we could be justified in accepting any criterion without relying upon the acceptability of other moral criteria and judgments. Some philosophers have supposed that what we rely on in justifying the fundamental moral criterion may be judgments about nonmoral value. But I shall bypass that possibility in favor of another, one raised by a parenthetical remark appended by Nielsen to his definition of "a fundamental moral criterion": "In reality, there probably is no single fundamental criterion, although there are fundamental criteria" (p. 2). This remark suggests, interestingly, that many of our moral judgments depend for their justification upon a level of criteria more fundamental than they are, but that within the most fundamental level there are relations of mutual dependence among criteria. Each of the fundamental criteria, in that event, would depend upon others at the same level for its justification.

This would mean, however, that Nielsen's theological opponent is free to make an even stronger claim, namely, that a criterion connecting God's will with moral goodness and obligation belongs to the most fundamental level of moral criteria. For if criteria at the most fundamental level are mutually dependent, then admitting that a given criterion depends upon other beliefs or criteria does nothing to disqualify it as a fundamental criterion. So the possibility of relations of mutual epistemic dependence casts further doubt on the significance of Nielsen's argument. There is a clear and strong sense in which he has failed to justify the major thesis of his book's first chapter.

Once the idea arises that there might be relations of mutual episte-mic dependence, of course, we may begin to entertain doubts about references to "foundations" and "fundamental criteria" as such. We may ask, for example, whether we have any good reason to believe that relations of mutual epistemic dependence are confined to a single, most basic level of moral criteria. To pursue this thought would be, as it were, to uproot the second horn of Nielsen's dilemma completely by calling into question the foundationalist imagery it employs.

The notion that there are such things as fundamental moral criteria in the sense that Nielsen's argument seems to presuppose derives its plausibility from a standard type of moral reasoning. Say I want to justify a highly specific belief about what one ought to do in a given case. What I need, it seems, is another belief from which the specific belief can be derived. The natural candidate will be some more general belief about what one ought to do in cases that are, in all morally relevant respects, like the case at hand. But the more general belief will serve to justify the more specific one only if it too is justified. So it seems that I shall have to cite a still more general rule. And this process will go on, if I'm being rigorous, until I reach the level of my most general moral criterion or criteria. On these principles, it would seem, rest all my more specific moral judgments about what one ought to do.

How, then, might these criteria be justified? Not, evidently, by ap-peal to some further moral criteria, for we have already reached the most basic level of moral criteria. At times, Nielsen has his theological opponent claim not that God's will is the fundamental moral criterion but rather that the fundamental criteria of morality can be deduced from God's revealed will. But anyone who claims this, Nielsen says, must be mistaken, for deducing a proposition from some set of other propositions is just a matter of making explicit what was already there, implicitly, all along. It follows that a moral conclusion can be deduced only from a set of propositions that includes a moral judgment. If the facts about God's revealed will do not already involve moral judgment, the deduction will be fallacious. The proposed deduction seems to work only when a moral judgment is smuggled into the "facts" about God's will. As Nielsen puts it:

One of the basic reasons I have for rejecting either a natural-law ethics or an ethics of divine commands is that both systematically confuse factual and moral issues. We cannot deduce that people ought to do something from dis-covering that they do it or seek it; nor can we conclude from the proposition that a being exists whom people call God that we ought to do whatever that being commands. In both cases we unjustifiably pass from a factual premise to a moral conclusion. (pp. 55-56)

This argument is meant to have general application. One cannot deduce a moral conclusion from nonmoral premises, whether or not the premises are theological. So the theologian might well ask Nielsen why the argument should be thought to pose special problems for theological ethics. Nielsen does not claim to deduce his own moral criteria from nonmoral premises. Why should the theologian? Moreover, Nielsen goes on to say, "Sometimes a moral agent may reach a point at which he can give no further justification for his claims but must simply, by his own deliberate decision, resolve to take a certain position. . . . In the end, we must simply decide" (p. 57). Why, then, are theologians any worse off than Nielsen if, like all moral agents, they move from specific moral beliefs to increasingly general criteria and finally reach a point at which they can give no further justification for their claims and must simply take a stand? Their stand is theological; his is not. But in neither case, Nielsen seems now to be admitting, can further justification be supplied or, indeed, justly be demanded.

This response to Nielsen may offer some comfort to the theologian, but not much and not for long. For while it makes the theological ethicist no worse off than Nielsen is, it seems to leave all of us rather worse off than we would like to be. If all our moral beliefs ultimately depend upon fundamental criteria we simply decide upon, those beliefs seem not to have been justified at all but rather rendered utterly arbitrary. Justification dependent on arbitrary decisions seems to defeat the purpose of justification. If moral agents must finally just pick some set of fundamental principles or other, and must do so without further justification, they could end by picking anything at all—Nielsen's principles, Martin Buber's, or Hitler's.

I don't think, though, that Nielsen really believes that justification is relative to arbitrary decisions of principle. He says that we must simply decide, which sounds worrisome, but says also that our decision may be "deliberate," which does not sound arbitrary. How do we deliberate about which moral criteria to accept if not by deducing them from nonmoral beliefs? Nielsen says that "we do justify moral claims by appeal to factual claims" (p. 56). Justification, then, must not consist essentially in deduction. "We cannot deduce moral statements from factual ones but we all repeatedly use factual statements to back up our moral statements" (p. 31).

Responsible moral agents, Nielsen now seems to be saying, must shape their moral principles in light of the best available understanding of what nature, history, and humanity are like. As our beliefs about the way things are undergo change, especially as they bear on human desires and needs, we struggle to bring our moral beliefs into line. Our moral beliefs are not deducible from nonmoral beliefs, but they are responsive, in a rational way, to changes in our beliefs about the way things are.

But if we accept something like this picture of moral reasoning, why speak of fundamental moral criteria or of the foundation of morality at all? If justification is not essentially deductive, then highly general moral criteria may well be responsive to strong convictions about specific cases as well as to beliefs about the way things are. And when Nielsen goes on to discuss specific cases in his later chapters, he does not simply decide, even in light of his nonmoral beliefs, to accept a set of fundamental moral criteria and then proceed merely to deduce particular conclusions about how to act. He also places another sort of constraint on the fundamental moral criteria he is willing to accept by requiring them to stay in line with strongly held convictions about specific cases. Like the rest of us, he uses intuitions about cases to test criteria.

In practice, then, Nielsen doesn't treat his most general moral criteria as fundamental in any strong sense. If their justification depends upon their coherence with relatively certain convictions about what one ought to do in specific cases, it is misleading to say that general criteria are the foundation on which the more specific convictions depend, as if the relation of epistemic dependence didn't go, much of the time, in the other direction. Sometimes, of course, we do abandon intuitions about specific cases because they conflict with an especially useful and powerful principle. But not always. J. B. Schneewind has put the point well:

Moral philosophers, whatever their theoretical programmes, have in practice always recognized that allegedly basic moral principles depend no less on fairly specific moral propositions than on the other sorts of grounds that have been offered for them; a principle that led to the conclusion that truth-telling was usually wrong, and torturing children normally permissible would be rejected, no matter what kind of proof it might have. But if general principles may sometimes depend on particular moral judgements, and particular judgements sometimes on general principles, then there is no impersonal, necessary order of dependence within the realm of moral knowledge. . . .[3]

If Schneewind is right about this, as I believe he is, then the theologian would be well advised to respond to Nielsen by saying: No, God's will is not the fundamental criterion of morality, but the problem you pose has more to do with foundationalist theories of knowledge than with theological ethics. It is misleading to say that morality has (or requires) any foundation. Religious ethics need have no stake in foundationalism at all. It need not propose a fundamental moral criterion, nor a reductive definition of moral terms, nor a deduction of moral conclusions from nonmoral premises.

III

None of us starts from scratch in moral reasoning. Nor can we ever start over again, accepting only beliefs that have been deduced from certitudes or demonstrable facts. We begin already immersed in the assumptions and precedents of a tradition, whether religious or secular, and we revise these assumptions and set new precedents as we learn more about ourselves and our world. Our starting point is not so much arbitrary as inescapable: we are who we are, the heirs of this tradition as opposed to that one, born into one epoch rather than another, our intuitions shaped by the grammar of our native tongue. We demonstrate our rationality, if at all, by how we move out from that starting point—subjecting this or that assumption or precedent to criticism as real doubts arise, employing old vocabularies or inventing new ones, the better to think and live well.

Accepting this view of moral reasoning makes it seem odd to ask about *the* logical relation between morality and religion. If there is no impersonal, necessary order of dependence within the realm of moral knowledge, there will be no reason to ask whether moral or religious judgments necessarily come first and no reason to think of the philosopher's assessment of religious ethics as part of an atemporal analysis of the language of moral obligation and goodness. There will be good reason, however, to subject specific religious traditions to philosophical scrutiny, to inspect the interaction of particular religious and moral vocabularies under particular historical circumstances. For on this view of moral reasoning, we shall have trouble understanding our own moral language or the justification of our own moral beliefs unless we give them a context in history. And it would be hard, on reflection, to deny religious traditions a significant role in our history.

Have philosophers in fact moved beyond the idea that there is something worth calling *the* logical relation between religion and morality? It must be said that ethical theory is still a long way from the kind of turn toward historical specificity that began to reshape the philosophy of science decades ago. The most rigorous recent philosophical work on religious ethics has come from authors like Philip Quinn and Robert Merrihew Adams, both of whom use their considerable philosophical skills to devise versions of religious ethics that are immune to the stock arguments drawn on by critics like Nielsen. Quinn has gone through many of those arguments one by one, pointing out premises and suppressed assumptions that now seem highly questionable. He has also used the rigor of contemporary analytical techniques, for reasons I cannot fathom, to show how various sorts of divine command theories of ethics look when expressed in the form of modal logic.[4] To my knowledge, he has not gone further than that.

Adams, whose familiarity with Christian tradition is extensive, has come as close as anyone to transforming the philosophy of religious ethics. In the initial version of what he called his modified divine command theory of ethical wrongness,[5] Adams insisted that he was not trying to present an analysis of "what *everybody* means by 'wrong' in ethical contexts" (p. 319). He was not offering a theory of how a term functions in *the* language of morals but was rather analyzing the meaning of a term in "Judeo-Christian religious ethical discourse." This allowed him to avoid the problem of earlier theorists in accounting for the linguistic habits of nonbelievers. And it raised the interesting possibility that we might need to study specific traditions of religious ethical discourse in order to shed light on the philosophy of religious ethics. This was a significant departure from the assumptions that linked Nielsen with an earlier generation's way of framing discussion of religion and morality, but it has not been pursued very far, even by Adams himself.

Adams also modified divine command theory in another way, by explicating the believer's use of "ethically wrong" as what would be contrary to the commands of a *loving* God—a move designed to alleviate the concern that divine command theorists, if so commanded by God, would be willing to make cruelty their ultimate goal. A loving

God, Adams maintained, would command no such thing, so a suitably modified divine command theory raises no such concern. But while he was trying to remove obstacles that might block rational acceptance of a form of religious ethics, Adams was not, in his original defense of the modified theory, trying to produce a positive argument for believing in the loving God presupposed by his form of religious ethics. Even if Adams's claims about the meaning of "ethically wrong" in Judeo-Christian discourse were true, it would not follow that we should adopt the moral language that Jews and Christians speak.[6]

Adams has since shifted ground somewhat, having decided that it would be better to modify his theory again, this time by dropping claims about the *meaning* of moral terms altogether. Drawing on the work of Saul Kripke and others, he has recast his claims as a theory of the *nature* of ethical wrongness.[7] This is not the place to pursue problems in the new version of Adams's theory,[8] but I do want to call attention to two consequences of the remodified version. First, this version is less likely than its predecessor to encourage movement toward historical specificity, since it no longer claims to give an account of what anybody in particular means by moral expressions. Second, by recasting his claims as he has, Adams is now able to use his theory to argue more positively for religious ethics, for the new theory is about the nature of ethical wrongness as such, not merely the nature of ethical wrongness as conceived by Jews and Christians or the use of moral language in Jewish and Christian traditions. If the theory is the best account of ethical wrongness available, we would have a strong reason to believe what that theory presupposes about God's existence and nature.[9]

The problem, of course, is that the best account of ethical wrongness cannot be determined in isolation from other matters—including what independent grounds we may have for believing or disbelieving in a loving God. The best account of ethical wrongness will be part of the best account of everything, on the whole. The best account of everything, on the whole, does not necessarily postulate a loving God. Adding that postulate may be too high a price to pay simply to improve our account of ethical wrongness, even on the assumption (which I find dubious) that we can't gain a highly plausible account of ethical wrongness in other ways. No one is likely to accept Adams's theory of ethical wrongness and adopt the sort of moral language reflected by

Adams's theory unless they already find good reason, outside ethical theory, for believing in a loving, command-issuing, knowable God.[10]

It is becoming increasingly clear, then, that the real philosophical action is going to occur elsewhere—not in debates over the logical status of religious ethics or the Kripkean metaphysics of ethical wrongness, but rather in whatever forces, rational or nonrational, incline people toward religious faith or against it in the first place. A broadly humanistic account of those forces, an account capable of tracing their relation to changing historical circumstances and variations in moral language, remains badly needed and barely begun.

6

REASON AND TRADITION

A survey of ethical theory would show that the question of why one might find the fate of religious ethics important, and thus worthy of detailed philosophical study, has rarely been posed in this century, let alone answered in ways convincing to a secular audience. Theologians, when addressing the faithful, usually either assume the answer to be obvious or give an answer that could serve as motivation only to the faithful. The same theologians, when addressing a general audience on a specific moral problem, typically search for common assumptions in a way that blurs any distinctive contributions of their religious tradition. Secular students of religious ethics tend either to attempt value-free description or to argue on philosophical grounds that the relationship between religion and morality is basically invariant and can be discovered *a priori*. They thus either studiously avoid giving readers reasons for being interested in their subject or make historical investigation of actual religious traditions seem relatively insignificant.[1]

Theologians and those secular academicians who specialize in what is called religious ethics have of course studied the ethical aspects of religious traditions; they have, however, said rather little to show that such study might be justified on grounds that are neither theological nor antiquarian—grounds that would make the various traditions of religious ethics seem philosophically interesting. Philosophers, as we have seen in the preceding chapter, have generally touched on this topic only to set it aside. As long as an essentially autonomous subject matter, the language of morals, was ascendent, religious ethics tended to remain in eclipse.

When, in the late 1970s, Alan Donagan devoted a section of his book, *The Theory of Morality*, to the philosophical interest of the Hebrew-Christian moral tradition, he seemed to be going against the stream.[2] "That the Hebrew-Christian tradition, as a matter of historical fact, has determined the substance of the received morality of the Western world," Donagan wrote, "is sufficient reason for studying it philosophically" (p. 28). This rationale does not presuppose the acceptability of a version of religious ethics, either in its metaphysical commitments or its specifically moral content. Religious ethics could remain philosophically significant even if all its major variants turned out to be unjustifiable in our context, provided only that the context itself could not be fully described and explained without reference to religious tradition.

In Donagan's view, however, a stronger case can be made. He believes that both the central moral claims of the Hebrew-Christian tradition and the metaphysical commitments they presuppose are true. *The Theory of Morality* is, then, a far cry from *Ethics without God*. Yet it is, as we shall see, in one respect remarkably like Nielsen's book. Both books, despite their authors' apparent intentions, raise potentially unsettling questions about the status of supposedly fundamental principles, moral diversity, and relativism in ethics—questions that keep arising, time and time again, in these chapters. Both books point, unwittingly, beyond themselves to issues that now occupy center stage in ethical theory.

I

Definite articles and singular nouns predominate in Donagan's prose. The title of his book promises *the* theory of morality. Our ethical heritage is said to issue from *the* Hebrew-Christian tradition. This heritage consists in *the* common morality, whose content can be derived from *the* fundamental principle, which in turn involves *the* concept of respect. To speak in this way does not rule out the possibility of diversity. Donagan remains free to refer to competing versions of the theory, the various strands within the tradition, to differing interpretations of the common morality. But he only rarely allows such hints of plurality into his speech, and when he does, he always takes pains to convey a sense of underlying uniformity. There may be competing versions of the theory, various strands of the tradition, and differing interpretations of the whole and its parts, but these are presented as entirely commensurable differences, largely matters of detail.

A great deal has been thought, said, and done within what Donagan portrays, apparently without strain, as a single coherent tradition. We must ask how, in his hands, such a thorough integration of seemingly diverse phenomena has been achieved, and, further, whether this integration has been achieved at too great a cost. Donagan's book can be read as an extended figure of speech—literary critics would call it a metonymical reduction—in which some phenomena are systematically excluded from consideration as inessential and the rest are reduced to a single idea that guarantees the essential unity of the whole. We need to understand how this procedure of exclusion and reduction is carried out and to ask whether, in the end, it can be justified. The point, of course, is not simply to understand Donagan but to trace the literary and conceptual means by which a prominent philosophical tradition construes itself and the subject matter of ethics. We are looking at Donagan's book as an example of moral *bricolage*.

A theory of morality, according to Donagan, proposes a rational standard for judging systems of mores, and mores are "generally accepted norms of individual conduct" (p. 1). This definition may seem harmless, but notice that Donagan has already made an important choice, one that elevates individual conduct and its regulation by precepts to a privileged position. *The* theory of morality is the truly rational standard for judging mores. It establishes the limits within which "everybody ought to live, no matter what the mores of his neighbors might be." As such it has the form of law.

Despite Donagan's contention that the "conception of morality as virtue is not an alternative to a conception of it as law" (p. 3), his own theory clearly occupies only a small part of the territory encompassed by traditional theories of the virtues. It is not, as they are, a theory of the traits of character required for living well. Neither does it seek completion, as Aristotle's ethics does, in political theory, in consideration of the kinds of community in which human beings might flourish. The theory limits what pursuit of the good life can be and what forms of community can be tolerated. It therefore has implications for theories of virtue and of politics, but its scope is considerably narrower. It is, moreover, prior to and separable from such theories: they do not place constraints on it as it does on them. The theory of morality constitutes an independent domain, not a chapter that gathers up significance from all that we believe about human excellence and communal life.

This much said, it comes as no surprise to hear: "The Stoics, rather than Aristotle or Plato, are to be credited with forming the first reasonably clear conception of morality: not because they had a theory of divine law, but because they conceived the divine law as valid for all men in virtue of their common rationality" (p. 4). Ethics, on Donagan's view, is a footnote to Stoicism. Morality certainly becomes more distinct, and in that sense clearer, in the Stoic conception than in the Aristotelian. An Aristotelian would want to know, however, why this distinctness should be thought an advantage if it has been gained largely by severing connections with a broader context of concern for the truly good life and by shifting attention away from the *polis* of an actual society to an abstraction like *our common rationality*. Those who side against the Stoics and with Aristotle—including some writers we shall discuss in later chapters—need not be seen as guilty of unclear thinking, of failing to bring the true concept of morality in focus. They may simply have reasoned objections to the Stoic conception as impoverished, antipolitical, and abstract. Yet in Donagan's reconstruction of the tradition, the debate between Aristotelians and Stoics is barely visible. It does not really take place within the tradition at all. Aristotle and his followers do not fit clearly within the tradition because they do not clearly identify the topic of their theories as moral in Donagan's sense.

While the clear conception of morality is "less obvious" in Judaism and Christianity than in Stoicism, there are many signs of its presence—enough, at any rate, for Donagan to dub the tradition Hebrew-Christian. Both Judaism and Christianity have since antiquity distinguished the moral law from "special divine commandments addressed to particular individuals and groups" (p. 4) and from the requirements of pursuing nonmoral religious ideals (p. 246). Part of Mosaic Halachah was, from biblical times forward, held to apply "to gentiles and Jews alike." Similarly, in Romans 2:14–15 St. Paul mentioned a kind of natural law written in the hearts of all men (p. 5). Theologians as different as Aquinas and Calvin echo the same theme. What is more, the voluminous casuistry of the religious moralists provides ample evidence, as Donagan sees it, of something like the Stoic conception.

What makes the clear conception less obvious in Jewish and Christian materials, he says, is that it usually matters little to someone endeavoring to live a religious life whether something is required for strictly religious reasons or is required of rational creatures merely in virtue of their rationality. Thinking "of a religious way of life as a seamless whole, in which common morality is comprehended and sanctified," tends to blur the line between religion and morality (p. 7).

Once again, however, we must try to take note of what has been passed over or pushed toward the periphery. Not everything in Judaism and Christianity that might be thought to have moral implications belongs at the center of the tradition Donagan has in mind. Many figures in the Christian tradition, from the fathers of the early Eastern church to an author like Stanley Hauerwas, will have to be judged peripheral on the same grounds as Aristotle: their devotion to a language of the virtues leaves the conception of morality insufficiently defined. So too will anyone, like Maimonides and the Ockhamists, who finds that natural human reason does not suffice to establish the "common" morality. Thinkers preoccupied with divine commands, rather than with the requirements of universal human reason, will not be counted as significant precursors in the *moral* tradition. The notion that a religious way of life and the common morality form a seamless whole from which morality cannot be abstracted without suffering distortion is not a central part of the heritage Donagan intends to plumb.

"Fortunately," Donagan writes, "the part of Hebrew-Christian morality that depends on beliefs about the nature of God (for example, the prohibition of idolatry) is separable from the part that has to do with the duties of human beings to themselves and to one another" (p. 28). The moral tradition may have been passed on mainly by people who were in fact religious, but it possesses a "philosophical core" (p. 27) "which covers all the topics with which secular moral theory has to do" (p. 28).

Yet from Donagan's perspective, "it is only a slight exaggeration to say that the ages of faith brought forth the idea of a pure moral philosophy but not the thing" (p. 8). Theologians, after all, are prone to "treat the moral law theologically," and this sometimes leads to fuzzy thinking about what unaided natural reason requires:

How else can the Jewish conviction be accounted for that the seventh Noachite commandment is part of common morality? It does not appear to be contrary to our nature as rational creatures to eat a part cut from a living animal, for example, to eat a live oyster, unless it involves cruelty. And how else can the Christian conviction be accounted for that Jesus' severer pronouncements on divorce are morally definitive? (p. 7)

According to Donagan, the thinking that leads to such conclusions can be ignored as inconsistent with the moral tradition at its best. Like the Aristotelian insistence upon treating moral precepts as ancillary to the virtues, it results from a kind of blurred mental vision.

Donagan's reference to Immanuel Kant as "the first major philosopher to work out a complete philosophical theory of morality" (p. 8) and his conscious use of Kant's practical philosophy as exemplary for the execution of his own project (p. 9) should by now be no more surprising than his decision to place the Stoics but not Aristotle and Plato at the heart of the tradition. A tradition construed along Donagan's lines could not help culminating in Kant. Indeed, it is hard to avoid the impression that such a tradition could be pieced together only retrospectively—only, that is, after Kant had been chosen as the great precursor. This is intellectual history in the classic neo-Kantian style, where apparent congruity with Kant's conclusions determines which books will be included in the tradition.[3] The Hebrew-Christian moral tradition turns out to be less inclusive than we might have expected. Whatever fails to anticipate Kant's conception of pure practical reason or the system of precepts that for him defined the moral law, falls outside the tradition.

The tradition, in other words, is the Kantian tradition. Its uniformity is guaranteed by a criterion of selection that excludes in advance the possibility of significant discord. A broader moral history, inclusive of many traditions and much conflict and attentive to a host of interests just beyond the bounds of a "clear" conception of morality, has been curtailed—without any evident sense of loss.

II

I have suggested how Donagan excludes what he finds inessential to morality and to the moral tradition. Let us now examine how he reduces what remains to its underlying essence, the fundamental principle of respect from which the entire content of the common morality, as Donagan interprets it, can be derived. What is the fundamental principle? It is, roughly speaking, the principle that you should love your neighbor as yourself (p. 59). But since philosophers should not speak roughly and are enjoined by their secular calling to steer clear of the theological virtue of *agape* or *caritas* (pp. 61-62), Donagan prefers to avoid the term *love*. Kant, he tells us, had it right: Act always so that you respect every human being, yourself or another, as being a rational creature.

This principle, says Donagan, "is fundamental to an independent field of inquiry" (p. 210). From it, together with the various additional premises required to specify what "falls under the concept of respecting a human being as rational" (p. 66), the precepts of the common morality can be derived. What, then, is the status of the fundamental principle itself? Many of those identified by Donagan as predecessors in the tradition held that the foundation of the common morality is self-evidently true. But Donagan, rather than appealing to self-evident truth, sets out to show that "it is intellectually impossible to get on without" the fundamental principle (p. 210). He elaborates a theory of practical reason that aims to give adequate reason for affirming our own rational nature as an end in itself worthy of respect. The theory is less certain than the principle, but it does, Donagan thinks, legitimate it.

When Donagan says that the fundamental principle "cannot be established by deducing it from others yet more ultimate" and that there is "no substantive principle in its field that does not rest upon it," I take him to mean that the principle cannot depend for its justification upon the very domain that depends upon it. Like Nielsen, he seems to be assuming—in theory, if not in practice—that there is a context-free order of epistemic dependence. The system of moral precepts derives both its content and its justification from the foundation, which must, to avoid vicious circularity, be established on grounds that do not presuppose the acceptability of some or all of the system derived from it.

Yet there seems to be a sense in which the fundamental principle, by Donagan's own admission, derives from a kind of circular reasoning:

In common law, as Edward H. Levi has observed, a "circular motion" is perceptible in the reasoning by which concepts are first elicited from cases and then applied: in the first stage, a legal concept is created by comparing and reflecting on cases; in the second, that concept, more or less fixed, is applied to new cases; and in the third, reasoning by example with new cases goes so far that the concept breaks down, and a new one must be created. Those who accept traditional morality, without necessarily believing that it originated in a divine command, can hardly escape concluding that its concepts were created by just such a "circular" process: and they will read both Hebrew and Greek literature as containing evidences of it. (p. 68)

There is nothing vicious about the circular motion Levi describes. It is merely the dialectical interplay between beliefs about specific cases and beliefs of a more general form, in a continuing process of refinement and revision. Nor is the process a matter of discovery as opposed to justification, relevant only to the historical genesis of our moral views and not to their acceptability. For in order to count as justified or acceptable, any relatively general moral principle must pass the test of confrontation with highly certain and widely shared beliefs of a more specific sort. As we have seen Schneewind arguing in the previous chapter, a principle that runs counter to strong convictions about specific cases must be reformulated or rejected. The most powerful argument on behalf of any principle, whether moral or legal, is that it has repeatedly survived exposure to intuitions about specific cases.

Levi's arguments, like Schneewind's, suggest that there is no context-free order of epistemic dependence in legal reasoning or, by extension, in the kind of moral reasoning it so closely resembles. Such reasoning is not, Levi claims, "simply deductive."[4] Why, then, if Donagan accepts Levi's account of such reasoning as virtuously circular, does he choose to present the tradition as a deductive system "derived from" and "dependent upon" a "fundamental principle"? His answer is that the process described by Levi has reached a point at which a straightforwardly deductive rendering of the tradition is possible.

To accept traditional morality is to accept its fundamental principle as true, and hence to be confident that the concepts in terms of which it is formulated are not liable to break down when applied to new and unforeseen cases. With regard to that principle, although not to the more specific of the specificatory premises by which it is applied, [those who accept traditional morality] must hold that a point has been reached beyond which only reasoning of the kind found at the second of Levi's stages is called for. (p. 68)

But why, if Levi is right, must acceptance of traditional morality consist in acceptance of a fundamental principle? Commitment to the tradition might simply involve standing squarely within the process of refinement and revision, ready to follow that process where it leads. Doubts about fundamental principles, even doubts about whether there are such principles, need not disqualify anyone. Moreover, why, given the doubts many philosophers have raised about the Kantian principle of respect, should we believe that we have become permanently ensconced in Levi's second stage?

As Levi sees it, the process he describes is likely to make some people "uncomfortable."

It runs contrary to the pretence of the system. It seems inevitable, therefore, that as matters of kind vanish into matters of degree and then entirely new meanings turn up, there will be the attempt to escape to some overall rule which can be said to have always operated and which will make the reasoning look deductive. The rule will be useless. It will have to operate on a level where it has no meaning.[5]

Levi is criticizing judges, lawyers, and philosophers of law. Perhaps the criticism has wider application. Is it fair to say that Donagan, caught up in the pretense of his own tradition and made somewhat uncomfortable by the never-ending spiral of reasoning that belies this pretense, has attempted to escape to an overall rule that can be said to have always operated and that makes all the reasoning of the tradition look comfortably deductive? Does the rule to which he escapes have to operate on a level where it has little or no meaning? If so, is the rule—and for that matter, any other so-called fundamental principle—entirely useless?

I shall not attempt the diagnosis of Donagan's motives necessary to answer the first of these questions. Yet it does seem fair to say that the systematic pretensions of the intellectual tradition that culminates in Kant have been a powerful historical force—one that has made acceptance of dialectical views of reasoning difficult. And it is comforting to think of oneself as finally beyond the need of the messy sorts of reasoning a tidy deductive framework cannot accommodate. So whatever Donagan's motives may be, we must all be careful not to be seduced by an image of stability and coherence merely because it seems so comforting or because it is sustained by a pretense of long standing.

On close examination, we find that Donagan's fundamental principle bears virtually no weight. Nothing in the system depends upon it alone. The entire system of precepts is said to derive from the fundamental principle, but each precept can be derived only with the help of an additional specificatory premise. The reason "virtually all the philosophical difficulties that are encountered . . have to do with establishing the specificatory premises" (p. 72) is that specificatory premises have been made to do virtually all the philosophical work the system has to do. The fundamental principle is treated as little more than a placeholder waiting to be filled with the content provided by specificatory premises. The crucial problem becomes that of selecting and justifying specificatory premises, and this cannot be done deductively.

What the specificatory premises specify, as I have said, is the concept of respect. "The problems that will occupy us in what follows," Donagan says in his second chapter, "all have to do with what falls under the concept of respecting a human being as rational, and what does not" (p. 66). The concept of love, Donagan already has said, is "desperately ambiguous" (p. 62). Now he avers, "The concept of respecting a human being as a rational creature is not usefully definable for our purposes" (p. 67). If we could usefully define the concept of respect, it might make sense to say that the remainder of the system can be derived from the fundamental principle. If the meaning of the concept of respect or the truth of the fundamental principle were self-evident or could be grasped without reference to the system of precepts and specificatory premises, it might make sense to say that the system is already implicit in the fundamental principle taken alone, needing only to be "unfolded in the specificatory premises" (p. 31) and deductively applied to cases. But I think Donagan is right to eschew appeals to self-evidence. And if we take Levi's remarks to heart, we shall be inclined to say that the concept of respect derives its meaning largely from the role it plays in the specificatory premises that connect it to cases.

That would mean, however, that the fundamental principle is not something whose truth can be established independently, apart from the rest of the system. The significance of its central concept depends upon the network of implications that constitute the system in its entirety. The meaning of respecting a human being as rational will depend upon other factors as well—such as the use of the word *respect* in nonmoral contexts and the theory of human nature given in Donagan's discussion of practical reason—and these factors will constrain the behavior of the concept within the system by ruling out some premises as obviously unsuitable specifications of respect. They will not, however, uniquely determine a concept of respect which need only be subjected to analysis to produce the results of the system.

If I am right, then, it is misleading to call the fundamental principle fundamental. The principle of respect is simply the most general substantive rule of the system. Nothing can be derived from it until its meaning has been determined, but the only way to determine its meaning is to know one's way around a system of precepts and premises already largely in place. We learn what the principle means by using the term *respect* in relation to cases, and it was in reasoning about cases in the manner of Levi's first stage that the concept took on the meaning it now has. That meaning continues to be refined and revised as we consider new cases and change our minds about old ones. The crucial point is this: at no stage does the rule function as something independently understood, awaiting only application to cases. To understand a rule is to have certain abilities with respect to it, abilities that already involve the capacity to deal with standard cases. To treat the rule as fundamental in any strong sense—as the basis on which the rest depends or as the essence from which the rest derives—is precisely to make it operate, as Levi would say, on a level where it has no meaning.

This is not to say that principles are useless. They do indeed have uses, and important ones at that. I believe they are best thought of, in Michael Oakeshott's phrase, as "abridgments" of tradition.[6] An abridgment does not precede that which it abridges. The latter cannot be derived from the former. An abridgment is not a foundation on which all the details can be built up, nor the essence that remains when all the details have been cleared away. If there is an essence, it resides in the details. Or rather, as Oakeshott puts it, "since a tradition of behavior is not susceptible of the distinction between essence and accident, knowledge of it is unavoidably knowledge of its detail: to know the gist is to know nothing."[7] It can be useful to abridge a tradition by formulating a highly abstract moral principle, but the dangers of misuse and abuse are great. They are the same dangers associated with a sophomore's use of abridged versions of great literary works.

Oakeshott sees all explicitly formulated moral ideals and rules as abridgments of, and abstractions from, customary forms of behavior. A highly abstract moral principle of the kind Donagan calls fundamental is, for Oakeshott, an abridgment of an abridgment. What's the use of that? None, in abstraction from the tradition it attempts to summarize. For those who understand the tradition at the level of detail, however, it may well be of use. I have already noted the use of general principles to organize and explain relatively specific rules and beliefs about cases. Schneewind, after criticizing a conception of classical first principles like the one I have tentatively ascribed to Donagan, happily grants general principles an important role in carrying out "a critical and explicit projection of our moral beliefs to new kinds of problems and new combinations of circumstances" and in articulating "what may be called the spirit of our morality."[8] Especially when used in connection with other elements of an ethos—such as myths about the origin of the cosmos, theories of human nature, and stories of exemplary lives—general principles help us to recognize, and to teach others to recognize, those features of cases that count for us as morally relevant.

My complaint, it should now be plain, does not concern moral principles as such but only the tendency to substitute abridgments of tradition for the genuine article. Just how far Donagan and I disagree on this matter I am not sure; his text allows several readings, depending on how much weight is given to the remarks on Levi and how much to the pervasive use of foundationalist imagery. What matters here is that this imagery, however little Donagan would have us make of it, offers temptations to self-deception. It can seduce us into thinking that because we have found some reason for accepting a highly abstract articulation of a tradition, we have somehow isolated that tradition's essence.

III

It might seem odd that someone who believes himself to have derived the fundamental principle of morality from a Kantian theory of practical reason could find any room in his ethical theory for the notion of tradition. Pure practical reason, made transparent to itself in transcendental reflection, would seem sufficient. The theory of practical reason, and the theory of morality it supports, will no doubt be transmitted through history by a tradition, but the tradition itself seems inessential. Pure practical reason, operating by itself, should in principle be enough to guarantee the desired result, and it is possessed by all rational agents, regardless of their access to the preferred tradition. Nonetheless, one may do well to check one's results against traditional materials. Anyone, after all, can make mistakes in the employment or trascendental analysis of practical reason. Familiarity with the tradition breeds contempt for these mistakes, as well as the critical capacity to recognize them—most of which have been both made and diagnosed before. But when tradition is consulted in this fashion, its function is to help us overcome our imperfections as rational creatures. Were we completely and perfectly rational, it would seem, our need of tradition would fall away.

Thus Kant, who took the notion of pure practical reason seriously if anybody did, treated the religious traditions as "vehicles" of pure rationality. They meet the needs of imperfect sensuous humanity by helping attain or maintain a certain stage of progress toward perfect rationality, but they are ultimately to be rendered obsolete or superfluous when moral progress is complete. He gave tradition more of a role than have many of his rationalist predecessors and successors, but the end was the same: we were meant to hope for the day when tradition had been left behind and reason could shine forth in all its purity. The idea that sensuous humanity is imperfect in various degrees at various times and places in its history allowed him to dismiss traditions that were sharply at odds with his own as relatively low on the ladder of moral progress and therefore not to be treated as potential counterevidence to his claims about the universality of reason as he understood it.

Donagan does not follow his mentor in this direction. Few recent heirs to the Kantian tradition have. Yet, unlike most neo-Kantian ethical theorists, Donagan recognizes the need to account for the existence of divergent traditions in a way that does not sacrifice Kantian claims about universality. If divergent traditions are not simply to be dismissed as so many signs of the sensuous side of human nature leading the morally imperfect astray, then their existence seems to become *prima facie* evidence against the conclusion that Kantian ethics flows straightforwardly from "our common rationality." In his preface, Donagan credits James Mackie with "forcibly pointing this out, in discussing a paper of mine read in Melbourne in 1968." Donagan poses the problem as follows:

> The moral tradition associated with the Jewish and Christian religions is incompatible in various respects with other venerable moral traditions, for example that of Hinduism. Hence a theory according to which that tradition was simply derivable from a theory of practical reason would imply that those who follow others, for example Hindus, are either deficient in practical reason or inept at exercising it. (p. xv)

Because he found this consequence unacceptable, Donagan felt required to abandon the Kantian idea that a theory of practical reason suffices to establish the morality of the Hebrew-Christian tradition. A theory of practical reason remains necessary, he now thinks, but certain additional presuppositions must also be brought in. All rational agents, whatever their tradition, employ the same practical reason. The conclusions they reach in employing their common rationality differ, however, insofar as the presuppositions they make differ, and these presuppositions vary from one tradition to another. The notion of tradition is therefore essential to the explanation of moral disagreement and assumes an importance it does not have in the greater part of the Kantian tradition. Equally significant, the theory of morality itself is made relative to traditional metaphysical presuppositions that are by no means universally shared.

For our purposes, the presuppositions that matter are the assumptions of "the Hebrew-Christian tradition about the nature of human beings and their world" (p. 33). The distinctiveness of these presuppositions can be "most economically ascertained" in a brief comparison with a "rich alien tradition" that reaches different conclusions about permissible human conduct—a tradition like Hinduism.[9] Two crucial presuppositions of the Hebrew-Christian tradition emerge from the comparison with Hinduism, according to Donagan: first, that human beings, considered as moral agents, are rational animals; and second, that the world inhabited by human beings is a system of nature, in which events occur according to morally neutral laws. We are animals, not souls transmigrating through a series of bodies. A human being is, moreover, rational in the sense spelled out in the theory of practical reason: autonomous, self-existent, an end-in-itself. We are not in essence members of this or that caste nor the product of decisions taken in previous lives as governed by the law of Karma. The consequences of our acts do indeed reverberate through history, but not because of their moral properties.

Hinduism provides only one of many relevant contrasting cases, of course, and one wonders what we might have learned about the presuppositions of Donagan's tradition if he had considered others. There are many possibilities to be confronted closer to home than India, which is to say, within a Western tradition that would make more room than Donagan does for the likes of Aristotle, Maimonides, and Ockham. Keeping such possibilities in view would, among other things, indicate how far Donagan's preferred theory of practical reason stresses the concept of negative freedom. Rational agency, for Donagan as for Kant, is determined by nothing other than itself: neither external causes, nor natural inclinations and desires. We are, in this sense, autonomous, and this is what makes human beings ends-in-themselves. "What this tells us about the principle of respect for human persons as ends-in-themselves," Margaret Farley has written in an excellent review of Donagan's book, "is that autonomy is the key to something's being an end-in-itself. Autonomy, in fact, is not only the reason why a person is intrinsically valuable, it is itself constitutive of what is valued in the person."[10] And this leads, according to Farley, to a fundamental principle that is essentially impoverished (p. 233).

Despite some recognition that there is more to being human than just possessing autonomy, Donagan makes autonomy "the sole aspect of the human person that is directly incorporated into the fundamental first principle. . . . The consequence of this is a moral system which gives priority to freedom and individuality." Farley concludes that Donagan's preoccupation with autonomy "gives us too 'thin' a theory of the human person on which to base a whole system of morality" (pp. 235–36). What we need, she suggests, is a view of ourselves that is rich enough to sustain both a healthy respect for autonomy and a genuine regard for the positive dimensions of well-being.

Persons are not just freedoms jostling about in the world. Freedom can do anything, so long as it does not violate itself or the freedom of another. But knowledge and love must deal with a reality in persons that is structurally complex, essentially interpersonal and social, existing in correlation with a world that is historical and that is constituted not only by other persons but by things and other living beings and institutions. (p. 237)

It seems clear that Farley would lead us back toward a tradition in which moral precepts take their place in a view of the good life—the kind of view in which the vocabulary of character and community have at least as much primacy as the concepts of individual conduct and moral impermissibility. Equally important, Farley's criticisms of Donagan help us see that it is precisely the thinness of Donagan's assumptions about what human beings are like and what is important about them that separates his (Kantian) strand of Western moral thinking from the rest. Serious confrontation with other strands of Western tradition would have required him to say why his selection of presuppositions from the tradition is the appropriate one. To amend or reject his presuppositions, or even to set them within the context of a richer theory, is to call his reconstruction of our moral inheritance into question.

I suspect that Donagan's account of his presuppositions follows from a desire to make the smallest adjustment in his theory that would respond adequately to Mackie's objection. He sought to retain as much of the standard Kantian picture as possible while replacing Kant's account of moral disagreement. The new account of moral disagreement, with its appeal to tradition-bound presuppositions, was then stitched into place to cover the flaw. The patch was meant to be minor. No presuppositions beyond those needed to handle Mackie were to be introduced.

Unfortunately, the seams show. There seems little reason to expect them to hold together. The repair significantly alters the structure of the theory. In the standard Kantian account, the appeal to pure practical reason as an ingredient of our common rationality is meant to explain, all by itself, why one system of mores is to be preferred to the alternatives. Thus, failure to reach the preferred conclusions must involve the intrusion of irrational or nonrational factors. Donagan's attempt to interpret disagreement more charitably, by making representatives of alien traditions rational relative to their own presuppositions, decisively shifts the explanatory burden. Practical reason loses its purity, and in so doing ceases to play a genuinely explanatory role in the theory. Moral conclusions are now justified not so much by our common rationality as by a network of presuppositions, precedents, and precepts embedded in a specific historical tradition.[11] To say why a particular precept counts as justified is to show that it can be tied into a coherent network including elements of all these kinds and to give a Levi-like story recounting the spiral of visions and revisions that reveal the current network as superior to its ancestors and competitors. If this is how justification works, however, we shall have to hear much more about presuppositions and also a much more elaborate and persuasive Levi-like story than Donagan has given us.

In short, the adjustment Donagan rightly makes in the standard Kantian theory is not minor at all. The new talk of traditions and presuppositions and virtuously circular reasoning not only fails to combine easily with the old talk of practical reason and common rationality, it also makes the old talk seem utterly vacuous. There are, in effect, two books here. One is Kantian in form, takes seriously the notion of universal reason, and stresses the notion of a fundamental principle on which all authentic moral precepts depend. The other is Hegelian in form, sees moral reasoning as essentially rooted in historical context, and requires completion in a spiraling narrative in which foundationalist imagery has no place. The two books are not compatible, but in *The Theory of Morality* we can see the first giving way, however partially and reluctantly, to the second.

That is why I see Donagan's book, like Nielsen's, as a work that, despite its author's intentions, shows moral philosophy in transition from one set of images and concerns to another. If we take the implicit trajectory of these books seriously, we shall have to devote far more energy than we have so far to the facts of moral diversity, to the impact of religious and other sorts of assumptions on moral conclusions, and to the shaping influence of traditions (religious and secular) on moral reasoning.

IV

My own sympathies obviously lie with Hegel, not with Kant, and my attempts to bring out the implicitly Hegelian tendencies in Donagan's explicitly Kantian writing is a classically Hegelian dialectical maneuver. What remains to be considered is Donagan's defense of Kant against Hegelian objections. Here we are brought face-to-face with some of the problems that ensue once we begin speaking of relativity to tradition or question the usefulness of appeals to a universal practical reason. In the second section of his book's first chapter, Donagan deploys two arguments. The first tries to refute Hegel's charge that Kantian morality (Moralität) ultimately reduces to "an empty formalism" that is "defective because it is purely abstract." The second aims to show that Hegel's own position, which claims to find content for the ethical life in the ethos (Sittlichkeit) of an actual community, itself proves empty in the sense that "any filling whatever" is allowed wherever the restrictions of practical reason are not in force. Let us now consider each argument in turn, while keeping in mind the tension between Kantian and non-Kantian elements in Donagan's work.

Donagan introduces his first argument by granting that Kant's first formulation of the categorical imperative, which invokes the requirement of universalizability (Act only according to that maxim by which you can at the same time will that it should become a universal law), "helped to create an impression that he took it to be empty," as did his claim that the fundamental principle is purely formal. "But," Donagan warns,

that impression cannot be sustained. In Kant's terminology, "formal" principles are contrasted with "material" ones, that is, with principles grounded in experience and interest. There is no implication that they are compatible with any content whatever. Moreover, he went on to maintain that his fundamental principle presupposes that action has an end prescribed by reason and not by interest or whim, to wit, rational nature itself; and that, accordingly, it has a second formula, equivalent to the first, namely, Act so that you treat human-

ity, whether in your own person or in that of another, always as an end and never as a means only. It is therefore evident that he did not think of the formal first principle of morality as devoid of content. (p. 13, italics in original)

So if Hegel was saying that Kant thought the fundamental principle of *Moralität* to be empty, the error was clearly Hegel's.

There is, of course, a more charitable interpretation of what Hegel was saying. We can imagine Hegel reasoning as follows. Let us take Kant at his word: the first formulation of the categorical imperative is fundamental; the others are all equivalent to it. If we grant this much, and the first formulation does not in fact yield a determinate content for morality, then it follows that Kant's system is, in the relevant sense, empty. It is merely formal in a sense more telling than Kant is prepared to allow.

Notice that Donagan is himself bound to accept this inference, given Kant's own assumptions, for Donagan rejects the first formulation of the categorical imperative as a candidate for fundamental principle precisely because it requires nothing more than impartiality and therefore fails to pick out a unique system of mores. This is why he favors the principle of respect or the version of the categorical imperative that requires us to treat ourselves and others as ends-in-themselves. It is also why he cannot treat all of Kant's formulations of the categorical imperative as equivalent. We can therefore view Donagan's system as a possible reformulation of Kant's, grounded in the admission that Hegel was right about universalizability.

The further question, however, is whether Hegel's objections have any force against a position like Donagan's, in which the principle of respect has been made fundamental and its equivalence to the principle of universalizability has been denied. Donagan admits that "the *onus probandi* lies upon those who assert that pure reason furnishes substantive moral principles," and that anyone who follows Kant's model "thereby undertakes to demonstrate" how the principles of morality "are required by pure reason" (pp. 13–14). But we have seen that Donagan demonstrates nothing of the kind, for in responding to Mackie's criticism he has had to grant that pure reason, by itself, does not suffice to generate a specific content for morality, that tradition-bound presuppositions turn out to be essential in exactly the way Hegel would have supposed. Hegel's point, I take it, was that reason is always parasitic on tradition in this way. Pure reason is an abstraction from which no unique content can be derived. When we think we have derived something determinate, close inspection will always reveal that this content actually derives from a previously unacknowledged tradition. It is Donagan's occasional (albeit reluctant) admission of this fact that constitutes the Hegelian tendency in his work. Had he taken this admission fully to heart, his heart would no longer belong to Kant.

So much for the first argument. What about the second? The worry behind Donagan's second argument against Hegel seems to be that, in the absence of fundamental principles established by pure reason, we would simply be left at the mercy of whatever our traditions happen to hold. We would be left, in other words, without the means to criticize. Rationality essentially relative to traditional presuppositions is not rationality at all but rather an exercise of unchecked prejudice.

We can see at once that if I am right about the Hegelian tendencies in Donagan's work, this argument causes as much trouble for Donagan as it does for Hegel. How much, then, does it cause? I shall return to this question in later chapters. For now, two comments from the Hegelian side of the debate will suffice. First, unless something substantial can be made of the appeal to pure reason without tacitly smuggling in the content donated by a tradition, we should not be tempted to think of our moral thought as somehow lacking simply because it has not been given a basis in pure reason. To have such a basis would not be to have anything more than we already have.

Second, it remains to be shown that tradition-bound thought is necessarily uncritical. We may have no power to transcend our traditional inheritance completely—for we are finite, historically situated beings—but we do not have to rise above history to call assumptions in question. The attempt to stand outside one's age, Hegel said in a famous phrase, is like trying to jump over Rhodes. You cannot do it. The danger comes when you think you have, for then you will be more likely than ever to set limits to criticism. You will view some of your assumptions as eternal deliverances of reason. It would be better to think of them as prejudices (in Gadamer's sense) —as prejudgments any one of which can in principle be placed in question provided most are kept in place at any given moment.

Donagan concedes that "Hegel's observations on morality contain much that is true. A moral life cannot be solely the conscious following of explicit moral precepts" (p. 10). It must also involve "what Michael Oakeshott has called 'a habit of affection and conduct.'" Moreover, "the tradition of such a disposition" can be capable of change. "The kind of change which belongs to it, as Oakeshott has remarked, 'is analogous to the change to which a living language is subject: nothing is more habitual or customary than our ways of speech, and nothing is more continuously invaded by change'" (p. 11). Nevertheless, Donagan charges,

Hegel did not perceive that a pure morality of affection and conduct—a morality the content of which is wholly a matter of sharing the unselfconscious mores of an actual community—is weak both internally and externally. Its internal movement, Oakeshott has observed, which "does not spring from reflection on moral principles, . . . does not amount to moral self-criticism." Hence it has little power of recovery if, as is probable, "it degenerates into superstition, or a crisis intervenes." (p. 14)

Perhaps Donagan's real worry, then, is that without something like Kant's transcendental perspective, we shall end up, sooner or later, relying upon traditions that have, through a "process of degeneration," allowed "the practice of self-criticism" to fall into disuse (pp. 14–15).

It is certainly possible for a tradition to degenerate in this way. We shall, later in this book, look closely at the claim that our tradition has degenerated to the point of leaving moral discourse in ruin. It remains doubtful, even so, whether pure reason can rescue us from the difficulty, for it remains doubtful whether pure reason can *do* anything. But is Hegel's position equally empty? Donagan is simply wrong when he charges Hegel with failing to recognize the weakness of completely unselfconscious *Sittlichkeit*. It was a major aim of the *Phenomenology of Spirit* to show, against one-sided Romanticism, that unselfconscious ethical life could not help breaking down. Nor did Hegel advise a return to unselfconsciousness, which he knew to be impossible. He hoped instead for the emergence of a genuinely self-conscious *Sittlichkeit*. Like Oakeshott, he sought to call attention to the fact that the moral life is—entirely in the first instance, but always in large measure—an unreflective habit of affection and conduct. Also like Oakeshott, he saw moralities of abstract ideals and principles as invitations to self-deception and concluded that moral reflection must find its roots in an actual way of life as a wholly immanent kind of rationality.

What might this immanent rationality be? Hegel's answer, to the extent that it depends on his metaphysics of Absolute Spirit, nowadays seems highly dubious. But what remains of his answer once the metaphysics has been filtered out, I submit, is simply Levi's spiraling process of innovation, criticism, and revision—the immanent rationality of a tradition in which habitual action and reflective thought are related dialectically. The philosophical interest of such a tradition, if it is our own, is that the problems we face, as well as the conceptual resources we have at our disposal for resolving them, are likely to belong to it. To fail to understand it is to fail to understand ourselves. But we shall never understand it by making all its diversity seem inessential or by reducing its richness to a single idea.

When we look at the full expanse of our moral history, we find that Donagan's language of respect is only one of many in which representatives of Jewish and Christian traditions and their more secular descendants have thought about moral matters. Another, ironically, is the language of consequentialist calculation favored by Nielsen, which can be seen in a relatively pure (if somewhat vulgar) form in the work of someone like Joseph Fletcher and in somewhat more subtle variations in the work of liberal Roman Catholics. As I have already noted, there are also those who speak primarily of obedience to divine command, like Adams, or pursuit of the good life through cultivation of the virtues, like Aquinas. But in the next chapter, I want to look at a rather more extreme example of the sort of moral language that tends to be neglected when we take some version of moral Esperanto as definitive of the field—namely, the language of abomination.

Why this example? I choose it precisely because it seems initially so resistant to philosophical reflection, so natural a candidate for simple dismissal as superstition, so radically "other," that philosophers have said almost nothing about it. It has been left entirely to the anthropologists (and the historians influenced by them), to specialists in exotica. If religious ethics has been in eclipse—the eclipse projected, as it were, by moral philosophy's own shadow—then the language of abomination can be said to occupy that shadow's darkest corner. If I want to dispel the shadow, that may be the best place to begin.

7

MORAL ABOMINATIONS

Suppose the action I am imagining is a harmless and highly pleasurable expression of loving respect between consenting adults bound to each other by public commitments of fidelity. Could such an action be an abomination on a par with cannibalism, bestiality, and intercourse with corpses? Evidently not, for in granting that the action brings about harmless pleasure, derives from the mutual commitment and informed consent of competent adults, and expresses loving respect, we seem to have excluded all possible grounds for a conclusion so extremely negative. Utility measures up well; no rights have been violated; both parties have been treated as ends in themselves. How could such an action be abominable? But add that the action in question is sodomy and that the adults in question are both males, and we see at once that many people would indeed view this action as an abomination.

How can this be so? The idea that such an action might be symptomatic of psychological traits we would not want to commend is perfectly intelligible, even to those liberals who would finally disagree. Yet to find such an action abominable seems like mere superstition or taboo—an attitude that cannot be explained by the presence of good reasons. Small wonder, then, that debates over homosexuality often degenerate quickly into ad hominem attacks. Each side considers the other either too irrational or too depraved to profit from reasoned argument.

Perhaps we can profit, however, from giving the notion of moral abomination more thought. We stand to learn something not only about the impasse just mentioned but also about ourselves. For most of us have experienced intense revulsion at the thought, the sight, or the artistic representation of some action Jerry Falwell would classify as an abomination. Many were the liberals who, sometime during the late 1960s, succumbed to nausea at the cinema after witnessing simulations of acts against which they had no principled objection. Where sacrilege and sodomy fail to offend, necrophilia, bestiality, and cannibalism often succeed. It behooves us to understand these reactions of ours and their possible relevance to ethical theory. We still, on occasion, use the language of abomination to express these reactions. Whatever distance we may feel from certain traditional judgments of abomination, talk of the abominable persists.

Yet recent ethical theory is virtually silent on the topic. Modern moral philosophers rarely invoke, much less systematically elucidate, the notion of abomination. When they do use the term to decry the deeds they most abhor, it seems to supply little more than rhetorical flourish. If a moral abomination is simply an especially serious violation of human rights, a particularly striking sign of disrespect for those who should never be treated as means only, or an act with unusually sweeping bad consequences, then such concepts as rights, respect, and utility, not the notion of abomination itself, will demand attention. I have already noted, however, that outside philosophy the notion of abomination sometimes plays a much more prominent role—one not always easily explained by means of the more familiar concepts of ethical theory. It belongs to a language that moral philosophers, *qua* moral philosophers, do not speak. The notion does, of course, appear prominently in the practical discourse of other cultures, including those that immediately precede our own in the history of the West. The concept is central to some strands of the biblical traditions, for example, and (as we shall see) ethical theorists working in close proximity to those traditions once felt bound to account for the specific judgments of abomination present in the biblical materials.

These thoughts raise interesting questions. Is it possible to make sense of the abominable at all? Is the notion finally unintelligible, or at best a vestige of primitive thought essentially unrelated to the realm of morality properly conceived? What explains the silence on the abominable in contemporary ethical theory? I propose to elucidate the notion of an abomination as I understand it, drawing on a theory that is by now old hat in anthropology although rarely discussed by ethical theorists. I have nothing new to add to the theory, but I do hope to show how it can be used to determine the kinds of social and cognitive contexts in which the language of abomination tends to take hold and also the kinds of contexts in which certain specific judgments of abomination are likely to be rendered. I shall then reflect briefly on the relevance of the theory to moral reflection in our context. My purpose will not be to revive the language of abomination but rather to come to grips with it philosophically. Let me begin, then, with a relatively unthreatening example of the repulsive from personal experience. This example possesses no moral interest of its own, but it will direct us toward salient features of cases that might.

I

Cabbits are said to be produced by crossbreeding. Take any cat and any rabbit meeting certain conditions of appropriateness and fecundity, subject them to the standard procedures, and (barring mishap) you will soon have a cabbit. Or so I heard one evening while watching television and read the next morning in a local tabloid. It was probably a single cabbit making the rounds. The hind parts were those of a rabbit, the head unmistakably feline. It may have been nothing more than a Manx cat with a rabbit's tail attached, but both the television producer and the newspaper editor knew that this combination would hold an audience. The televised version proved more effective because it conveyed the anomaly in more dimensions. It also afforded an opportunity to observe the responses of other observers. This cabbit was no mere object of quiet curiosity. The audience was clearly fascinated, at once attracted and repelled.

You may find all this unconvincing if the thought of a cabbit does not disconcert you. I doubt that the thought of a cabbit, by itself, would have bothered me. I have no objection in principle to cabbits. Yet the sight of a living cabbit did affect me. I found it revolting. Even the sight of a cabbit, of course, would not thus affect everyone. The question is how to explain the variation.

My daughter has never seen a cabbit. Yet I am certain she would not have found a cabbit revolting had she seen one just after her second birthday. In those days she regularly confused cats with rabbits. She had not yet learned to treat them as distinct kinds of thing, having only begun to master the requisite vocabulary. A person who lacks the concepts of cat and rabbit would not be fascinated by the anomalous combination: no distinction, no anomaly. So it is not the cabbit-in-itself or the cabbit as immediately given to the senses that offends. The offense one takes depends upon the concepts one brings to the scene.

It seems reasonable to suppose that my daughter and I then stood at opposite ends of the spectrum of attitudes toward cabbits. Unable to recognize the anomaly, those at her end of the spectrum would not be offended by cabbits. Those at my end, equipped with sharp distinctions between cats and rabbits, would be much more likely to be offended. I speculate that my daughter has moved closer to my end of the spectrum during the years since her second birthday. Sharpen someone's concepts, and they will be more likely to find the corresponding anomalies repulsive.

Repulsive perhaps, but not abominable. We need to look elsewhere for full-fledged abominations. Horror movies are full of them, as are ancient myths, folk tales, and side shows at circuses. Monsters and freaks make ideal abominations. There seems to be a recipe for constructing them—a procedure akin to crossbreeding. An abomination must be anomalous. Like the cabbit, it must combine characteristics uniquely identified with separate kinds of thing, or at least fail to fall unambiguously into any recognized class. But the recipe for abominations should include another injunction: if possible, load the anomaly with social significance. A combination of characteristics that straddles the line between *us* and *them* will be highly effective. Darwin's culture (or at least some classes within it) guarded the line between human and nonhuman. In such a culture the man-beast may well be an abomination. The elephant-man is famous; the cabbit is not. Where the line between masculine and feminine roles becomes accentuated and forms the basis of the division of labor or the rules of inheritance, we may see bearded women and hermaphrodites turning up in freak shows.

An abomination, then, is anomalous or ambiguous with respect to some system of concepts. And the repugnance it causes depends on such factors as the presence, sharpness, and social significance of conceptual distinctions. For a detailed defense and elaboration of these marks of the abominable, readers should consult the work of Mary Douglas, whose sociological reflections on the relevant ethnography inspired the approach I am taking here.[1] There is no need in this context to pursue the details of Douglas's theories or their application to specific anthropological cases. My present purposes require only a very thin conception of how the categories of someone's cosmology and social structure might render intelligible their attitudes toward abominations. I need just enough theory to stimulate reflection on how judgments of abomination might be related to what I have said in previous chapters about such matters as moral truth, justification, and the spectrum of relativity. We have thus far concentrated on monsters and freaks. The next task is to extend the account to abominable acts, where moral relevance may start to figure in. We should then be in a better position to address questions at the level of ethical theory.

Before going any further, however, I should enter one caveat. I have not claimed that *all* objects, events, or acts that seem anomalous or ambiguous relative to the categories of someone's cosmology and social structure will be treated by that person as abominable. Douglas and others have shown, to the contrary, that an entire range of phenomena demand explication in such terms. Leviticus proscribes eating the flesh of the pig and the hare, which fail to fit neatly into biblical cosmology. But the Lele revere the pangolin, which is similarly ambiguous relative to their concepts of natural kinds. Many sorts of defilement and even humor, according to Douglas, follow closely related patterns. Wayne Proudfoot has offered a similar explanation of mystical experience.[2]

So anomalous and ambiguous objects, events, and acts are often emotionally charged, but whether they make our eyes glaze over in rapture, our sides ache with laughter, or our stomachs turn with disgust requires further explanation. And while Douglas has much of interest to say about how these phenomena can be correlated with types of social significance, this too must be only partially developed here. All we need for my purposes is the vague notion that an anomalous or ambiguous act is more likely to seem abominable where it seems to pose, or becomes symbolic of, a threat to the established cosmological or social order. One form of humor owes its excitement to flirtation with the line between joking and obscenity or abomination. When we sense that playful inversion of the norms, which gives us the delight of momentary release from them, has given way to direct assault, we know that a comic has crossed the line.[3] Likewise, we might well revere an anomalous creature, as the Lele revere the pangolin, if its way of crossing conceptual boundaries becomes symbolic of some beneficial kind of boundary-crossing in our social life.[4] A great deal hangs, therefore, on whether the anomaly in question is viewed as a mediator between realms or as a transgressor across boundaries that guard cosmic and social order.

I shall henceforth confine the term *abomination* to transgressors (or transgressions) of this kind, ignoring any other types of abomination there might be. In a looser sense of the term, anything loathsome would count as an abomination. My (still rather loose) definition of the term is designed to abbreviate a theory in which reactions to such creatures as monsters and freaks and to such actions as cannibalism, bestiality, and homosexual sodomy are grouped together and explained along the same lines. The basic idea is this: in contexts where the anomalous or ambiguous character of an object, event, or act seems to threaten disruption of the natural-social order, rather than promising to knit that order together, the object, event, or act will be abominated. In such contexts, one should expect to find talk of abominations. To see what this idea comes to, let us now consider attitudes toward cannibalism, bestiality, and sodomy in turn.

II

A man enters a seaside restaurant, orders albatross, and is served. After a single taste of the bird, he removes a gun from his pocket, presses its barrel to his forehead, and pulls the trigger. Why? I first heard this question put while playing parlor games as a teenager. The riddler poses the problem. The audience, using only these scraps of evidence and whatever can be gleaned from the riddler's answers to yes-no questions, tries to piece together a plausible narrative making sense of the circumstances of the suicide.

Here is the solution. Three men were adrift at sea in a lifeboat. One died. The survivors had killed an albatross for food, but knew that at most one of them could stay alive until the rescue party arrived if they ate nothing but the albatross. The only other available food was the flesh of their dead comrade. Neither had ever eaten albatross before, let alone human flesh, and the thought of cannibalism appalled them. Hoping to avoid overwhelming guilt, they devised a method of culinary disguise. One would eat the albatross; the other, human flesh. But neither would know which he was eating. The disguise worked, at least for the time. By keeping them ignorant, it held their consciences at bay. After the rescue, however, our protagonist found a way to satisfy his curiosity. He went to the restaurant because he knew that a taste of albatross would tell him what he had eaten on the lifeboat. If the taste was unfamiliar, he must have been eating human flesh at sea. Otherwise, his conscience would be clear. As it turned out, the taste was unfamiliar, and he shot himself dead.

Notice that this puzzle would make sense only in a culture that treated cannibalism as utterly repulsive. If the audience cannot recognize the protagonist's discovery as a plausible reason for his suicide, the puzzle falls flat. The reason need not be compelling, yet it must be plausible. But what did our hero have to feel guilty about? He had not taken his comrade's life. He had, indeed, saved a life (his own) by taking his comrade's flesh for food. So the balance of utility was favorable. It is certainly not clear that he had violated anyone's rights. The puzzle remains plausible even if we stipulate that the dying comrade expressed the hope that the others would eat his remains rather than starve at sea. Why? Because our hero's sense of guilt is akin to defilement. His concern is not simply for his comrade but also for himself. His action has stained him. He is repulsed at the thought of himself. The abominable act has made him abominable.

My hypothesis is that cannibalism offends us for the same reason that the thought of becoming a werewolf does: it threatens our unambiguous status as human beings. A creature that usually resembles humans in all respects but, when the moon is full, becomes more wolflike than human has slipped into an ambiguous position between heretofore delimited classes. The same thing happens, in our culture, to cannibals. Being unambiguously human entails, for us, a kind of dietary restraint. Some objects in the environment count as food, others do not. Ingestion of the wrong objects threatens one's status as human. Eating dirt or feces is degrading in the straightforward sense that it puts you in a different (lower) class. Eating human flesh strays outside the normative diet in another direction, but the effect is the same—to render the diner's status as a human insecure. Nonhuman carnivores make no bones about eating human flesh. To eat human flesh is to become like them, to straddle the line between us and them, to become anomalous.

None of this applies in the same way, of course, where the line between us and them—between members of the community and outsiders—is drawn in a different place. Some vegetarians embrace a community that extends well beyond the confines of our species. Jain monks have been known to go further, including even most vegetables as members of the community. Jains abominate most human meals. I would be surprised if they singled out cannibalism for special disapprobation. At the other extreme, there are tribal societies whose moral community excludes most of humanity. The line between us and them is drawn tightly around the tribe itself, and no broader conception of the species appears to be present. If such a tribe were to practice cannibalism (whether such tribes actually exist is highly disputed in the scholarly literature), it would not surprise me if their victims were always strangers while making meals of one's kin was fully abominated.

I am tempted to generalize by inverting Feuerbach's dictum that you are what you eat. As far as social identity goes, what you eat is what you are not. Most societies define themselves in part by proscribing the use of their members as food. Violation of this proscription threatens the boundary of the social order. Not every society, however, defines its boundary with a sharp line. A society that does not will, if I am right, show relatively little concern over cannibalism. Its attitude toward cannibals will be like a toddler's attitude toward cabbits. It takes sharp lines to bring anomalies into focus. Most societies impose sexual as well as dietary constraints upon their members, and restraint in the use of sexual organs is often at least as important as proper habits of ingestion in maintaining identity as a member of the group. Sexual intercourse with beasts, like eating human flesh, is beastly. It calls into question one's social identity.

I have argued that the social identity of the cannibal is the basic issue at stake when a social group abominates cannibalism. Respect for the dead might be seen as the real issue: cannibalism is simply a kind of desecration of corpses. While cannibalism may be that as well, I want to insist on the centrality of the cannibal's social status. The parallel to bestiality strengthens my case, for bestiality is structurally similar to cannibalism but also simpler. To whom does bestiality show disrespect? Surely not the beast. When the shepherd's lust takes his flock as its object, it is the shepherd, not the flock, that we fear for. What we fear, I suggest, is that the shepherd has become too beastly to maintain a firm grip on his social identity. His abominable act has made him an abomination. The violated sheep, on the other hand, is not an end-in-itself and therefore makes no claim on the shepherd's respect for persons. If our shepherd has shown disrespect for anyone, it must be himself. What makes the action abominable is its degrading character—its capacity, within some social settings, to make the agent himself seem (or be) less human.

Sodomy,[5] like bestiality, involves a use of sexual organs that can render one's social identity anomalous or ambiguous, but, unlike both bestiality and cannibalism, it does not concern the line between human and nonhuman or the boundary of the social structure. On this score, sodomy is more like the bearded woman and the hermaphrodite in its relation to the distinction between masculine and feminine roles. The line that becomes crucial here is one internal to the social structure, not the external boundary. Once again, I assume that the line must be both sharp and socially significant if trespassing across it is to generate a sense of abomination. Attitudes toward homosexuality can be expected to vary accordingly. The sharper the line between masculine and feminine roles and the greater the importance of that line in determining matters such as the division of labor and the rules of inheritance, the more likely it is that sodomy will be abominated.

So once again, as with cannibalism and bestiality, social identity is at stake, although the issue is access to stereotypically defined roles, not membership in the group. If your society defines masculine and feminine roles, as many do, partly in reference to socially legitimated uses of sexual organs, then sexual activity of the wrong kind can threaten your claim to play a certain role. You become, in effect, a social anomaly—ambiguous with respect to the partition of available roles. You become, that is, the social equivalent of a monster—an object of abomination.

John Boswell has recently contrasted attitudes toward homosexuality in two general types of social organization, which he calls urban and rural.[6] According to Boswell, urban societies, which "are characteristically organized in political units which transcend kinship ties" (p. 34), tend to show more tolerance of homosexuality than do rural societies, in which kinship structures are the primary or sole elements of social organization. But Boswell is bothered by exceptions to the rule. He grants that the growth of intolerance of homosexuality in Catholic Europe during the late middle ages seems to have nothing to do with his distinction between urban and rural societies. In fact, urbanization was increasing along with intolerance. He also grants that some rural societies—in particular, nomadic societies such as bedouins and American Indians—"are generally favorable to gay people." Boswell therefore concludes that his "generalizations must be viewed with extreme caution." He even laments that the "complexity of human existence must inevitably frustrate efforts at logical analysis . . ." (p. 36).

That may well be true, but the problem with Boswell's analysis is that his contrasting types give only a crude description of the relevant features of social structure. What matters, if I am right, is the line between masculine and feminine roles: how sharply it is drawn, how much and what kind of social significance it has, and how stereotypical definitions of these roles harness sexual activity to socially legitimated purposes. Clearly, Boswell's distinction between urban and rural societies is insufficiently subtle to handle the crucial variables. A society in which political units transcend kinship ties might still display the very features that, on my view, tend to make homosexuality seem abominable. And a society in which kinship ties remain primary might lack these features. To transcend kinship ties in some respects by introducing political structures of a certain kind is not necessarily to supplant a sharp distinction between masculine and feminine roles stereotypically defined or to make such a distinction socially insignificant. By the same token, to place the entire burden of social organization on the structure of the extended family is not necessarily to make everything depend on an exhaustive and mutually exclusive distinction between masculine and feminine roles or to establish stereotypical conceptions of these roles that will make homosexual activity seem anomalous.

Boswell points out, when listing counterexamples to his generalizations, that some rural societies "recognize homosexual marriages, as long as one partner agrees to play the role of wife" (p. 34 n. 63). Such societies, on my account, maintain the line between male and female roles, although without defining these roles specifically in reference to the possession of male and female sexual organs. Male roles are not restricted to men; female roles are not restricted to women. In such societies, homosexuals will have clearly defined roles to play, so they will probably not seem utterly anomalous. Nor is this the only way of providing homosexuals with clearly defined roles. Some rural societies keep the distinction between masculine and feminine roles in place while setting aside additional roles specifically restricted to homosexuals.[7] The distinction between standard masculine and feminine roles need not be exhaustive. In such a social setting, homosexuals are marginal but not anomalous. They constitute an independent kind with its own defining traits. They are not likely to be abominated.

So much, then, for cannibalism, bestiality, and sodomy. The account could easily be extended to cover other acts often thought to be abominable, such as incest (which might be called the familial equivalent of cannibalism) and the pointless or sadistic murder of innocents (acts so gruesome, like the recent carving of crosses in the body of a nun, or so massively destructive, like those which set the holocaust in motion, that we hesitate to call them human). I leave speculation on such matters to my readers, assuming that my approach is relatively clear. The next task is to draw out some implications of the foregoing discussion for ethical theory.

III

I shall begin by making a couple of remarks reminiscent of points made before by Rodney Needham.[8] The first is that, given what I have said in Chapter 3 about the relativity of expressibility, we should not expect our terms for the various kind of prohibited acts we have been considering (such as *cannibalism, bestiality,* and *sodomy*) to have exact equivalents in every culture we wish to compare with our own. The significance of such a term, and of the proscriptions in which it appears, will depend on features of social and cognitive context that may well frustrate attempts at cross-cultural comparison. It is misleading to speak, say, of prohibitions of sodomy without making clear that these prohibitions do not necessarily comprise a definite class. Some cultures may lack the concept of sodomy altogether; others may possess only inexact equivalents of our term. Any responsible comparison must proceed cautiously and with all possible sensitivity to context. The same point would apply, as I hinted briefly in an earlier chapter, to a concept like slavery.

The second remark is related to the first. Part of the context in which prohibitions appear consists of permissions and prescriptions. As Needham says, it is "methodically defective" to consider only prohibitions.[9] Judgments of abomination are typically the reverse side of affirmative valuations and cannot be understood without keeping these in mind. This point bears on the relativity of justification. A table of abominations tends to appear pointless, and therefore especially lacking in justification, if it is considered apart from the positive value of a harmonious social and cosmic order.

Abominable acts sometimes overpower us with a sense of revulsion that does not lend itself readily to discursive elaboration. The reason should now be clear. We occasionally have trouble saying anything coherent about the abominable precisely because of its anomalous or ambiguous character. The more severe the anomaly or ambiguity at hand, the more paradoxical and mysterious our speech is apt to become. This helps explain not only the character of our revulsion, given the uneasiness that can be produced whenever coherent interpretation of experience is impossible, [10] but also the suspicion that the very notion of abomination is somehow beyond comprehension.

We need not conclude, however, that this notion is unintelligible. To treat the abominable as a cultural artifact and our sense of revulsion as a function of cognitive context is to make sense of them, to demystify, to render the repellent approachable. This does not mean, of course, that we cease to experience revulsion in the face of ambiguous or anomalous phenomena. I still find cannibalism repulsive, theory or no theory. But we are in a better position to ask dispassionately what status our sense of revulsion should have in moral deliberation.

Revulsion tends to be immediate in this sense: we do not normally arrive at revulsion as we arrive at the conclusion of an argument, by moving through a series of inferential steps. We may therefore be tempted to think of our responses to the abominable as a kind of prelinguistic given—an incorrigible datum to which any ethical theory must be held responsible. In fact we do, as noted in the previous two chapters, tend to demand that ethical theories account for our deepest moral feelings and hunches. Any theory that cannot explain what seem to be the paradigmatic cases of evil hardly deserves credence. Philosophers have often spoken of these deepest moral feelings and hunches as deliverances of the moral sense or as a species of intuitive cognition. Alternatively, the immediacy of the experience and its insusceptibility to discursive elaboration can be taken as grounds for suspicion. We may fear that sheer revulsion is too primitive to be trusted and too mute to be factored into deliberation. The experience of revulsion is to ethical theory as mystical experience is to philosophical theology. The same aspects of the experience that can make it seem foundational and revelatory can also make it seem nonsensical or superstitious, depending on one's philosophical leanings.

I happily grant that revulsion need not involve inference. It can, in that sense, be immediate. I also grant that we do (and should), in most cases at least, hold ethical theories accountable to our deepest feelings and hunches, including our sense of revulsion in the face of the abominable. But the other conclusions do not follow. We need not think of revulsion as prelinguistic or incorrigible, as a product of an unchanging moral sense, or as a species of intuitive cognition. Nor need we simply reject it out of hand as blind emotion that must remain forever unintelligible. Indeed, if my account is correct, these additional conclusions must be false, for they are incompatible with the context-dependence of responses to the abominable.

I said early on that it is not the prelinguistic cabbit that offends. Responses to cabbits are neither incorrigible intuitions nor blind emotions, however primitively noninferential they may seem. They depend, to the contrary, on a (usually unacknowledged) cognitive context. So too with responses to other abominations, including abominable acts. We can understand these responses if we set them in their context—the network of cosmological and social categories relative to which some phenomena are bound to seem anomalous or ambiguous. We see at once that the responses are hardly a matter of blind emotion. They are thoroughly informed by cognitive categories, the categories of a moral language infused with cosmological and sociological assumptions. Nor are the responses incorrigible. Change the relevant network of categories enough, and you will alter the list of abominable acts while redirecting the corresponding sense of revulsion.

The intuitionist and the theorist of moral sense leave us at the mercy of our feelings and hunches. The answer is not, however, to ignore feelings and hunches altogether. Without them, ethical theory loses contact with the data of moral experience. But we need not merely accept feelings and hunches as given. The myth of the given is as naive and misleading in morals as it is in science. Even the most immediate perception is, in either arena, deeply implicated in cognitive context. To recognize this is to begin to achieve critical distance from the data we employ to test the theories we inherit and devise.

Most of us in the modern West share roughly the same sense of revulsion to cannibalism. Those of us who do not share this sense typically lack any motive for opposing the popular conclusion that cannibalism is morally abominable. In such an instance, we have little reason to theorize. Deeply felt and widely shared revulsion is reason enough for the conclusion. Theorizing would not strengthen the case. Cannibalism would become significant to theory only if theories devised for other purposes could not account for it. We might then be forced to decide whether the theories should be emended or the revulsion should be taken less seriously.

The issue is quite different with homosexuality, where some of us feel deep revulsion and others feel none at all. Rational disputation breaks down quickly in circumstances where the moral data against which one group tests its theories are not even recognized by another. What we need in such instances is the critical leverage an explanatory theory can provide. We want to know where the intuitions in question come from and how they may be assessed. It is here that my account should prove useful.

The debate over homosexuality need not end in appeals to conflicting intuitions. What requires defense, if I am right, is the battery of categories that gives rise to an intuition in the first place. If the issue is genuinely in dispute, it is not enough to appeal to one's own sense of revulsion (or lack thereof) and leave it at that. For the revulsion itself derives from antecedent commitment to categories that are themselves subject to dispute. The question is not whether homosexuality is intrinsically abominable but rather what, all things considered, we should do with the relevant categories of our cosmology and social structure. Addressing this question at all places us squarely within what Levi identifies as the "circular motion" of a moral tradition. If we wish to address it self-consciously, we shall need an account of the forces at work in the reconfiguration of our tradition's moral languages over time.

Traditional Christian natural law theory may be viewed (in part) as an attempt to explain and justify specific judgments of moral abomination by explicitly defending the corresponding features of cosmology and social structure. Contrary to the standard interpretation of Aquinas's ethics, he rarely used natural-law categories to justify specific moral judgments.[11] But when he turned to "unnatural vice," including bestiality and sodomy, natural-law categories become central to his argument. Unnatural vice, he said, is especially ugly because it conflicts with "the natural pattern of sexuality for the benefit of the species":

Take any class of objects grouped together for comparison, and the worst of them all will be that which saps the basis on which all of them rest. The lines along which our minds work are those consonant with the nature of things; the fundamentals have been laid down for us by nature, we have to start with these, the presuppositions which our later development must respect. This is true of both theory and practice. A mistake in our thinking about the inborn principles of knowledge goes to the very bottom, and so does a practice opposed to the pattern set for us by nature.

Unnatural lust is the gravest kind of lust, then, because it "flouts nature by transgressing its basic principles of sexuality." Of the unnatural sins of lechery, "The greatest is that of bestiality, which does not observe the due species. . . . Afterwards comes sodomy, which does not observe the due sex."[12]

These are clearly the words of a man who recognized, and sought to explain, the connection between his table of abominations and a broader context of cosmological and social assumptions and categories. Whatever fault we find with the theory of natural law that Aquinas uses to frame his explanation—and I would be inclined to find much fault—it must be admitted that he is locating debate at the proper level. He does not merely appeal to an inarticulate sense of revulsion. He attempts to justify his revulsion in relation to his conception of the seams of the moral universe. If that conception can be sustained, the moral import of the revulsion would be established.

The social and cosmological categories of Aquinas's moral language have eroded greatly over the intervening centuries, and they were hardly unquestioned by his contemporaries. It would be hard for us to assume, as he did, that they are simply "laid down for us by nature" as "presuppositions which our later development must respect." My point, in any event, is not to defend Aquinas but rather to show that the notion of moral abomination does make sense when set within a context of assumptions and categories like his. If we wish to explain why the notion of abomination came to be neglected in ethical theory, the answer will surely lie, at least in part, in whatever makes our context different from his, in a story of the erosion, for example, of sharp lines between masculine and feminine roles.

Yet the erosion has not been complete—or, for that matter, uniform—and that is why the language of abomination is still with us and why it still repays philosophical scrutiny with morally relevant insight. If we dismiss it as entirely foreign, hoping to elevate ourselves above the "primitive" or "religious" thinkers of previous generations, we fail to come to terms with important features of our own moral experience. Most of us do abominate cannibalism, bestiality, and necrophilia. And even those of us who do not abominate homosexuality often interact with subcultures in which the language of unnatural vice and moral abomination survives as a primary means for appraising sexual activity. We had better try to understand them as well as ourselves.

Such subcultures, of course, are more prone to produce Jerry Falwells than academic ethical theorists. Ethical theorists of the kind I had in mind tend to hail, by the time they have become ethical theorists,

from communities and subcultures in which the line between masculine and feminine roles has become blurred or is self-consciously
viewed as provisional. Any such context is unlikely to prove hospitable
to the attitudes Aquinas felt obliged to account for. So we should not
find it surprising that the language in which modern moral philosophers frame their moral judgments differs from the languages in which
Aquinas, the author of Leviticus, and Jerry Falwell have framed theirs.

We can understand their concepts, if we put our minds to it and
learn enough about their use of words and their way of life. The notion
of abomination is not so foreign that we lack the needed linguistic
resources to translate their sentences. The relativity of expressibility is
no barrier. We can also sensibly say that specific judgments of abomination we would not be inclined to make were justified under the circumstances in which Aquinas and the author of Leviticus found themselves. So the relativity of justification can help us avoid charging such
people with irrationality by allowing us to understand the concepts and
reasons at their disposal. What, then, about truth and falsity? Can we
sensibly say of such people that their judgments about which acts or
agents count as abominable were false? Can we meaningfully criticize
people and actions in distant cultures or epochs as truly abominable,
intending by this something more than the idea that we find them
abominable or that they are revolting to us?

I do not see why not. At least some of the judgments of abomination
we make seem to fall roughly where judgments about evil do on the
spectrum of relativity.[13] When the Nazis made lampshades out of the
skins of their human victims, that was truly abominable. I would be
prepared to say the same thing about members of some more distant
culture if they engaged in similar practices. In saying so, I would be
doing more than simply reporting how things seem to me, although I
would of course be presupposing that the line between human and
nonhuman ought to have moral significance and that there are certain
ways in which human beings (and their remains) shouldn't be treated.
If members of a distant culture said that their (Nazi-like) treatment of
their victims wasn't abominable, I could surely judge them wrong. I
needn't simply call attention to differences in sensibility to explain why
a practice they find morally indifferent is abominable "for us" and leave
it at that, as if truth weren't at issue. And I wouldn't, unless judging
them wrong had no point.

Supposing that the notion of the abominable is less central to our moral language than it used to be, we still need to determine why it should be virtually absent from, and not merely a marginal concept within, present-day moral philosophy. Why doesn't it receive at least some attention from theorists like Nielsen and Donagan? The answer, if the previous chapters were on the right track, must have to do with the literary and argumentative means by which moral philosophers constitute their subject matter. But what made those means seem appropriate to so many philosophers throughout the modern period? To answer this question, we need to return to the issue of secularization raised in Chapter 3.

Rights, respect, and utility gained virtually exclusive priority in moral thought precisely when appeals to a wide range of assumptions and categories in the traditional ethos of our predecessor culture became more likely to generate conflict than agreement. Recoiling from Reformation polemics and the religious wars, modern ideologues and ethical theorists increasingly had good reason to favor a vocabulary whose sense did not depend on prior agreement about the nature of God and the structures of cosmos and society ordained by him. That the favored notions were abstracted from that same ethos should not surprise us. Neither should the fact that the resulting abstractions are ill-suited to interpret or explain much of the moral revulsion sustained by remnants of that ethos which still survive. But that these abstractions have powerfully influenced how many of us think and speak about morality can hardly be denied.

Early modern ethical theorists disagreed rather little about cannibalism, bestiality, and the like. But as religious discord grew, they found it necessary to devise a language in which highly contentious social and cosmological categories and assumptions would no longer be presupposed. Ethical theory, by sticking to this more austere language, drew a relatively tight circle around morality. That is, it gave itself a more narrowly delimited topic to be a theory of—a topic that looks more like the one Donagan tries to mark off than the one Aristotle discussed in his *Ethics* or Aquinas discussed in his *Summa*. With much of the old context no longer simply taken for granted, a notion like that of the morally abominable, which derives its intelligibility from features of a context in which certain lines are both sharp and socially significant, was bound to become less central. The sense that the abominable has something to do with morality came to seem paradoxical. The abominable and the moral now fell in distinct cultural spheres. Ethical theorists have consequently felt less and less comfortable about rendering judgments of abomination—especially, perhaps, in the area of sexual conduct, where the increasingly contested line between masculine and feminine roles assumes importance.

Kant, here as elsewhere, is the great transitional figure, the author who did more than anyone else to differentiate morality from other cultural domains. Like most of his immediate predecessors and contemporaries, he still experienced intense revulsion at the thought of bestiality and homosexuality, but the radical contraction of the moral sphere to which his own moral philosophy gave expression left him without the means to defend this revulsion convincingly or to explain it. A latter-day Kantian like Donagan, while granting that Kant had "put into words the horror of irregular sexual activity that appears to underlie both Jewish and Christian condemnations of it," concludes that his arguments "verge upon hysteria." Donagan finds Aquinas' arguments "more dispassionate," but "no more persuasive."[14]

My conjecture is that Aquinas, Kant, and Donagan represent, respectively, three crucial stages of the history of the abominable in ethical theory: an initial stage in which the abominable not only makes sense but occupies a central position in ethical theory; a transitional stage in which ethical theorists still largely share their gardeners' sense of revulsion at standard examples of the abominable but no longer find themselves able to defend this response except with raised voices; and a third stage in which much of the revulsion has come to seem alien and groundless, a datum even ethical theorists sympathetic to Jewish and Christian tradition are more concerned to explain away than to explain. To test this conjecture comprehensively would require a breadth of sociological and historical knowledge I lack. And it is surely possible that the ideas I have been borrowing from anthropology will have more trouble withstanding the scrutiny of comparative ethicists than I suppose. But if my hunches about the abominable are borne out by further inquiry, we will have clear confirmation of the need to make ethics more sensitive to its own history, the value of prying open the aperture through which we have been looking at that history, and the importance of tracing the fate and influence of religious assumptions and categories if we are to understand that history well.

8

THE VOICE OF THEOLOGY

Academic theology seems to have lost its voice, its ability to command attention as a distinctive contributor to public discourse in our culture. Can theology speak persuasively to an educated public without sacrificing its own integrity as a recognizable mode of utterance? This dilemma is by now a familiar one, much remarked upon by theologians themselves. To gain a hearing in our culture, theology has often assumed a voice not its own and found itself merely repeating the bromides of secular intellectuals in transparently figurative speech. Theologians with something distinctive to say are apt to be talking to themselves—or, at best, to a few other theologians of similar breeding. Can a theologian speak faithfully for a religious tradition, articulating its ethical and political implications, without withdrawing to the margins of public discourse, essentially unheard?

The worry that this question imposes an exclusive choice between two foci of loyalty, that one must turn one's back on tradition in order to be heard by the educated public at large (and vice versa), has turned many theologians into methodologists. But preoccupation with method is like clearing your throat: it can go on for only so long before you lose your audience. Theologians who dwell too long on matters of method can easily suffer both kinds of alienation they fear. They become increasingly isolated from the churches as well as from cultural forums such as the academy and the leading nonsectarian journals of opinion.

163

This isolation helps explain why the much-heralded religious resurgence in American culture lacks a theological (as opposed to a prophetic or evangelical) voice and also why theology has benefited little from the resurgence. The resurgent piety tends not to be disciplined by serious thought, just as academic theology tends not to be nourished by piety—at least not the kind of piety now enjoying resurgence.

Theologians find the intellectual vacuity and dogmatism of that piety every bit as troubling as other intellectuals do. But for them, it is embarrassing as well. To dissociate themselves from it, they identify with critical theory, the hermeneutics of suspicion, and religious movements in the Third World. Because theologians in the United States, unlike many of their European cousins, are primarily employed as professors at seminaries, where intellectually vacuous and dogmatic piety thrives among candidates for ministerial degrees, they are often placed on the defensive by their own students, not to mention the more official guardians of orthodoxy.

Meanwhile, secular intellectuals have largely stopped paying attention. They don't need to be told, by theologians, that Genesis is mythical, that nobody knows much about the historical Jesus, that it's morally imperative to side with the oppressed, or that birth control is morally permissible. The explanation for the eclipse of religious ethics in recent secular moral philosophy may therefore be rather more straightforward than I have suggested so far. It may be that academic theologians have increasingly given the impression of saying nothing atheists don't already know.

I

How, then, might theology rejoin the conversation under such circumstances? How can it initiate a dialogue not only with its own tradition but also with the several voices of secular culture? How might it provide some respectable intellectual orientation for educated clergy and laity who would like to be able to say why their equally educated secular neighbors should start paying attention to representatives of religious tradition again? One point is clear. No theology can today afford to be "prone to *superbia*, that is, an exclusive concern with its own utterance, which may result in its identifying the conversation with itself and its speaking as if it were speaking only to itself."[1] A voice in conversation, unlike the chorus that speaks for the new religious right, must take its place among the other voices, as often to be corrected as to correct. The time is past when theology can reign as queen of the sciences, putting each other voice in its place and articulating, with a conviction approaching certainty, the presuppositions all share. For if all voices indeed share some presuppositions, they would not nowadays be theological. The existence of a specific sort of God is no longer taken for granted on all sides. The language spoken in the public arena, while compatible with belief in God, does not presuppose it. In that arena, a hearing for theological ideas must be won, if they are to get a hearing at all.

A theology that hopes to converse on moral and other topics in a pluralistic setting like ours had better dispense with the quest for a method. There is no method for good argument and conversation save being conversant—that is, being well versed in one's own tradition and on speaking terms with others. David Tracy, the contemporary theologian most taken by the metaphor of conversation, nonetheless proposes what he calls a *fundamental theology*, defined by a "reasoned insistence on employing the approach and methods of some established academic discipline to explicate and adjudicate the truth-claims of the interpreted religious tradition and the truth-claims of the contemporary situation."[2] Fundamental theology draws a method from "philosophy or the 'philosophical' dimension of some other discipline" in order to establish "strictly public grounds that are open to all rational persons."[3] If I am right, however, a fully conversable theology will be skeptical that any such grounds can be found and suspicious that such a method, once in place, would succeed only in reducing all utterance to a single mode and thus in ending the conversation. There is no more certain way for theology to lose its voice than to imitate that of another.[4]

In practice, theologians seeking philosophical foundations for theology have turned, naturally enough, to foundationalist philosophy. Theological conclusions were often hard to defend on such a basis. But with the recent wave of attacks on foundationalist philosophy in philosophical circles, the basis of fundamental theology has come to seem very vulnerable indeed, leaving some theologians complaining that they have enough problems of their own without adding those of foundationalist philosophy besides.

Fundamental theology does not exhaust the discipline. Tracy also speaks of *systematic theology*, which essentially acknowledges a particular location in history and, from the perspective of that location, offers a normative interpretation and reappraisal of one's tradition and contemporary situation.[5] Systematic theology, according to Tracy, begins in "a profound acceptance of finitude and historicity" and progresses toward a kind of understanding found in "authentic conversation."[6] He sees systematic theology as one of theology's three basic forms. His *magnum opus* is projected as a trilogy that starts with a fundamental theology *(Blessed Rage for Order)*,[7] receives further development in a systematic theology *(The Analogical Imagination)*, and will achieve completion with the publication of a practical theology designed to draw out implications for ethics. In considering Tracy's work here, I want to raise three possibilities—that there may be a conflict or tension between the first two parts of the trilogy, that theology might usefully abandon its devotion to philosophical foundations, and that a conversable theology might better stress finitude and historicity from first to last.

Tracy's fundamental theology looks to a "hermeneutical phenomenology" of human experience as the basis on which Christian theological principles can be reinterpreted and seen as an intellectual necessity. Phenomenology is meant to set the basic criteria of all rational discourse, thereby grounding theology in the elemental structures of human experience. Other theologians look elsewhere for much the same thing. Dennis McCann and Charles Strain, for example, turn to Jürgen Habermas's theory of communicative competence in hope of establishing "the ground rules of public discourse." These ground rules are meant to provide "criteria for practical theology, criteria that will not prejudice the ideological questions disputed among practical theologians, but will make it possible to discuss those questions in a disciplined way and resolve them."[8] But this sort of ambition is bound to seem hopeless in all its forms to those of us who have given up on the quest for basic grounds rules of rationality or criteria for public discourse as such—those of us who suspect, for example, that Habermas's theory of communicative competence is yet another failed attempt to make the latest dialect of moral Esperanto seem necessary and universal, this time by decking it out in the fashionable idiom of speech-act theory.[9]

The "sad little joke" about universal languages, Mary Midgley once said, is that almost nobody speaks them.[10] Not all theologians, however, cast their lot with the Esperantists, and I want to devote most of this chapter to the work of one who does not—James Gustafson, Tracy's colleague at the University of Chicago Divinity School. Unlike Tracy's *magnum opus*, Gustafson's has only two parts: the first, a systematic theology in Tracy's sense; the second, a more explicitly practical theology.[11] Missing from Gustafson's project is anything analogous to Tracy's first volume—a fundamental theology. Gustafson sees theologians who share the foundationalist ambitions of their philosophical counterparts as actually trying to rid themselves of the essential markings of historically conditioned thought. Their failure, he thinks, has a moral as well as an intellectual aspect—a failure to consent to finitude as well as to acknowledge it. Like the tower of Babel, their project is a prideful attempt to escape the human condition itself.

Gustafson gently mocks the desire for a "propaedeutic to one's propaedeutic" (p. 64), eschews the "philosophy of theology," and proceeds directly to his interpretation of the theological situation. He writes in the conviction that methods are better seen as instruments for accomplishing a purpose than as foundations on which to secure one's arguments (p. 68). He speaks eloquently on behalf of his tradition, especially that strand of Calvinist piety in which the sense of dependence on God figures most centrally, although he forcibly denounces elements of the tradition that either conflict with the themes he deems most central or that cannot be given sufficient experiential warrant. His principal aim is to show what ethics looks like in the view of this tradition at its best.

Gustafson does not turn to philosophy as one would to a symposiarch or arbiter,[12] hoping to discover ground rules for rational discourse. He does not abandon his own idiom in favor of one that is more strictly philosophical. Hence, he is not faced with the difficulty of finding (or transforming) a philosophical system whose principles are either benign toward religious claims or already implicitly religious. His intent is not, however, to withdraw from dialogue with philosophy. One need not recognize philosophy as a kind of cultural symposiarch or adopt a specific philosophical idiom as one's own to converse with philosophy. Nor does one need to break off conversation with a given philosophy because one rejects its pretensions to the role of symposiarch. How, then, might theology proceed, if not by adopting a method from philosophy, if not by submitting to the verdicts of an arbiter?

II

Self-conscious reflection, Gustafson tells us, always begins in some place at some time. It is situated in a tradition at a given point in its history. It does not involve membership in the "fictive and illusory community of all rational persons" (p. 151) to which Kantian moral philosophers and fundamental theologians so often appeal. If reflection begins in a context, it had better begin by acknowledging what that context involves. But this acknowledgment will necessarily be an interpretation from a point of view. Like all understanding, it cannot be a matter merely of allowing reality to impress itself directly upon the mind. So acknowledgment of context is itself conditioned by context. It can always be deepened, and possibly significantly altered, by setting a preferred interpretation next to its competitors and by subjecting its assumptions to critical scrutiny. But never is the point reached where all assumptions have been examined or given independent support. The process could in principle go on forever.

Gustafson does not, however, use the relativity of justification or our inability to rise above history as an apologetic ploy to keep criticism at bay. He does not pull tradition over his head like a blanket, as so many other theologians and apologists for Tradition recently have. A tradition, used in that way, simply suffocates thought and very quickly becomes useless for anything, including blocking out the voices of those whom Friedrich Schleiermacher called the cultured despisers of religion. Gustafson acknowledges that a kind of circularity is intrinsic to all reflection (a kind like Levi's), but it becomes vicious, he thinks, only when it stops delving deeper into its own assumptions and answering objections from other perspectives.

It would be naive to expect a single argument to be equally compelling to everybody. Reasons belong to particular social and historical settings, and tend to vary somewhat from setting to setting. The apologist who aims for universal consent is courting frustration, whether the topic is religion, art, politics, or science. Theology, Gustafson thinks, had better expect to persuade only some while conversing with the rest. The theologian's arguments should not be deemed deficient simply because they do not, in Stanley Cavell's phrase, "work on people at random, like a ray."[13] Theology, Gustafson says, presupposes prereflective piety and brings such piety to reflective expression. What it says need not necessarily convince the impious. But this does not absolve theology from winning a hearing—from earning the respect, if not necessarily the consent, of other parties to the conversation. A conversable theology must have something distinctive, something recognizably theological, to say. It must at least make clear what difference theology makes and how an educated person could reasonably believe its distinctive claims.

Theological ethics develops, according to Gustafson, in a process of selective retrieval of tradition, recombination and reinterpretation of traditional elements, and innovation. It does not unfold an original essence (p. 144) or apply an unchanging inheritance to new situations. It works with different, and at times competing, sources of normative insight—biblical, philosophical, empirical, and broadly experiential. It must judge how and why these sources are relevant, how much weight a given source should carry in a specific area, precisely what elements drawn from these sources should be put to use or set aside, and how to interpret the significance of what is to be used. It must employ concepts, analogies, metaphors, and symbols to establish a coherent relation among the various elements to be used and between part and whole. Gustafson is, in short, a most self-conscious practitioner of what I call moral *bricolage*.[14] And, as we shall see, he is prepared to depart radically from his predecessors' tropes, emphases, and doctrines.

Gustafson comes by his stress on human finitude and historicity honestly. It is part and parcel of the ethical heritage of the Reformed tradition that culminates in Schleiermacher and reaches Gustafson through intermediaries such as Ernst Troeltsch and H. Richard Niebuhr. So Gustafson is hardly imitating the secular opponents of Kantian ethics when he satirizes its foundationalist pretensions or when he denounces its glorification of human freedom. For Gustafson, to be human is to be situated in nature, history, culture, and society—to have a particular location. It is to be embodied as a member of a species with certain traits and needs, to occupy a specific position in the cosmos, in one's own tradition, and in a personal history that stamps the self with whatever character it has. No one can simply think all of this away. We must, in the first instance, accept these facts about ourselves. In any event, we are wise not to ignore the many ways in which they limit us, shape us, and give us our identities. This is something we can learn from conversation with the Reformed tradition, whether or not we take on its theological commitments.

Yet, to affirm the importance of situating human agency in nature and history is not to deny freedom a place in human life. Gustafson favors what he calls an "interactional" view of freedom (pp. 187, 272, 293), according to which we act upon and to some extent alter our circumstances and our traits even as we are conditioned and constrained by them. Gustafson, like his mentor H. Richard Niebuhr, views freedom as essentially responsive: the central task of moral deliberation is to discern the fitting thing to do, given a conception of what we are like and an interpretation of our situation.[15] We are guided in the exercise of our freedom principally by our understanding of what human beings and the human condition, broadly construed, are like.

Theology is grounded, for Gustafson as for Schleiermacher, in the piety of a historical community, in the prereflective experience of religious feeling. Theology consists largely of reflection on the religious affections, and the persuasiveness of its arguments is relative to the piety it presupposes. Richard R. Niebuhr has said that on Schleiermacher's view, "thinking always starts in history" and proceeds "as we continually revise our initial idea against the new pattern of data that has become relevant in light of the revised idea."[16] It is precisely this dialectical process of revision that, for Gustafson, gives theology its claim to being a critical discipline and saves it from the vicious circularity to which vulgar relativism condemns all thought. Still, theology's "construal of the world" is derivative. It rests on piety and piety is its first evidence. Gustafson does not follow Schleiermacher in identifying the essence of piety with the sense of absolute dependence (p. 178), but he places this sense first on his list of the religious affections, the "aspects of piety" (p. 130). He aims for an account of piety both more nuanced than Schleiermacher's and more open to specifically ethical development.

One need not be religious, in any standard sense of that term, to recognize that we are finite, limited, and conditioned beings who owe our existence to forces beyond our own control and who exercise whatever freedom we have only under circumstances we have not authored ourselves. Any of us can testify to that (pp. 5–16). This recognition can give rise to a sense of awe in the face of the powers that bear down upon us; a sense of gratitude and obligation to that on which we depend for our existence, our identity, and the satisfaction of our desires; a sense of remorse and a need to repent when our gratitude ebbs or we fail to meet our obligations; a sense of the real possibilities that are left open by our circumstances, which despite the extent of our dependence, leave ample scope for the exercise of human agency and ground for the cultivation of realistic hope; and a sense of how, given the ordered relationships in which we find ourselves, one's life might have meaningful direction (pp. 130–34). These "senses," nurtured and articulated in the first-order language of a tradition, constitute that tradition's distinctive sensibility or piety.

The theologian's task, as Gustafson conceives it, is not merely to repeat the first-order language of a tradition but to reflect critically on that tradition and its piety. Gustafson commends the central themes of his tradition as the basic elements of a construal of the world to which he can consent as a critical thinker. He finds them faithful to experience as he knows it (while granting that his own construal is itself deeply conditioned by the presence of these themes in his tradition). They are to some extent confirmed by dimensions of experience to which secular thought can testify. But there are other tendencies in the tradition that a theologian has an obligation to criticize—either because they cannot be given sufficient warrant from human experience or because they conflict directly with what the central themes, rightly understood, entail.

Gustafson argues, for example, that anthropomorphic conceptions of the deity, while often unavoidable and harmless in the first-order language of worship and prayer, should be more carefully qualified in theology proper than most theologians have allowed (pp. 179–80). He rejects as excessive the idea "that God has intelligence, like but superior to our own, and that God has a will, a capacity to control events comparable to the more radical claims made for human beings . . ." (p. 270). He believes that we can meaningfully speak of divine purposes for creation, although he finds insufficient warrant for talk of divine intentions (p. 271) or for postulating a clear *telos* in God's creative and sustaining powers (p. 240). Gustafson says rather little to distinguish purposes from intentions, but he does illustrate what he has in mind: "A distinction has frequently been made between purpose and intention. Animals have purposes but, so far as we can determine, they do not have intentions; they cannot think about their ends and the means of fulfilling them in the way that human beings can" (p. 270). So Gustafson's desire to avoid anthropomorphic conceptions of the Deity leads him, in the end, to the view that in one important respect the Deity is more like a dog than like a human being. This is not the result one would expect from an attempt to avoid anthropomorphism in theology.

Gustafson's doctrine of God as redeemer does not depend upon the possibility of eternal life. His Christology has nothing to do with the resuscitation of a corpse. He thinks we have insufficient evidence to warrant such ideas. We may acknowledge them as part of our heritage. Christians may even cherish their symbolic import in the first-order language of piety. But concerning the literal truth of such ideas, theology should confess ignorance.

The problem, however, is not simply paucity of evidence. Many of the doctrines for which Gustafson finds insufficient evidential warrant "even in piety" (p. 271) are also, in his judgment, incompatible with full affirmation of the sovereignty and majesty of God. They conflict, directly or indirectly, with a central theme of the tradition, a theme that is warranted by a sense of dependence upon and grateful obligation to God. Fully to affirm God's sovereignty and majesty, in Gustafson's eyes, entails refusing to limit our conception of the Deity by ascribing anthropomorphic attributes, especially those that are really designed to flatter us and not God at all. Gustafson's book attempts to turn an austere doctrine of divine sovereignty derived from the Reformed tradition against everything in the tradition that in fact glorifies humanity rather than God.

Perry Miller, writing of "the Augustinian strain of piety" in Puritan New England, elucidates the theme that Gustafson places at the center of his own work. From the vantage point of the Puritans, according to Miller, theologians had long

endeavored to confine the unconfinable within artificial distinctions. . . . The various "Calvinist" groups started from a fresh realization that to fix too narrow limits or too explicit tendencies upon the principle of the cosmos was to court disaster. . . . Puritans reasserted the divine simplicity and warned men to guard their thinking lest they again identify God's essence with whichever of the attributes seemed most attractive to them.[17]

To Gustafson, the traditional doctrines of eternal life, of God as the one who redeems us from death, who loves us as a supremely intelligent agent would love his children, of human happiness as the chief end of creation, are all supremely attractive. They are all-too-attractive to us, for we are all too human, too eager to be consoled by wishful thinking, too willing to acquiesce in the narcissism that masquerades as worship of Another.[18]

Gustafson is an iconoclast, out to smash the idols of Christian narcissism in the name of God's sovereignty. The piety for which he speaks is not "piousness, that pretentious display of religion which offends me as much as it does anyone" (p. 164), "the kind of sanctimoniousness that lends itself to caricature" (p. 201). Nor is it at all consistent with the "instrumental pieties" and "superficial Easters" of much contemporary religion (p. 21). It does not seek "cheap grace" and "consolation" in the face of suffering and death. Genuine piety, according to Gustafson, places God not humanity at the center. While a kind of consolation does derive "from a deep spiritual consent to the divine governance" (p. 20), the desire for "some larger, more dramatic, ultimate meaning and perfection" expressed in "the biblical claim that all things are or will be made new in Christ" is greeted with suspicion. "Why," asks Gustafson, "do persons want a hope that is beyond the conditions of possibilities for them?" In part, because "we do not consent to our finitude properly." The good news of the Gospel, Gustafson seems to be saying, must be dismissed as "hyperbole" (p. 310).

To show how radically Gustafson's *bricolage* departs from traditional formulations would require extensive exegesis. The difficulty here is that Gustafson, who always writes with an eye toward possible objections, rarely misses an opportunity to qualify a thesis. The cumulative effect of this habit, which has served him well in the strictly analytical work that established his reputation as a leading living American interpreter of Christian ethics,[19] is to deprive his *magnum opus* of much of its lucidity. This is a jeremiad in the great tradition, but one written in the cramped hand of an excruciatingly careful scholar.

Consider the following sentence, in which Gustafson discusses the "revisions I make of the Christian theological tradition": "The principal one is that we cannot be as certain as the tradition has been that man is so centrally, so exclusively, the object of divine beneficence or divine providence" (p. 188). Is the point simply that we cannot be so certain as the tradition has been? May we be nearly as certain, or must we be not certain at all? Or should we deny outright what the tradition has so confidently asserted? Or, still more radically, can we be certain in denying the traditional assertion? Moreover, are we meant to qualify only our certainty that man is *centrally* and *exclusively* the object of divine beneficence, and even hope for salvation in the traditional sense, if God's beneficence is neither centrally nor exclusively directed at us?

Similar questions arise when we turn to this passage from Gustafson's discussion of the natural-law tradition:

What is not *well established*, in my judgment, is . . that there is a purpose inherent in nature which makes man the *chief* aspect of the creation in whose service *all* other aspects are properly placed, that the happy *coincidence* of the ordering of nature and what is beneficial to man can be sustained. . . . (p. 92, italics added)

Again, is the question simply whether such consequences are well established, or does Gustafson mean to deny them? Would it suffice merely to be less certain, or must we deny their truth? Would it suffice to question merely that *all* other aspects of creation are properly placed in man's service, or is that clause meant to be nonrestrictive? Is only *perfect* coincidence being questioned or any coincidence at all? When Gustafson goes on to say that "there is good reason to doubt" that "the Deity has so designed *all* things for man as the *chief* end of his creation" (p. 92, italics added), he seems to move closer to outright denial. But even outright denial of this conclusion is compatible with holding that man is the chief end of creation (if not the end for which God designed *all* things) or that man (while not the chief end of creation) is destined for salvation in the traditional sense, given *all* of God's purposes (not just the chief one).

Sometimes Gustafson qualifies his views of God's purposes in other ways, as in this passage:

The benevolence that we know and experience does not warrant the confidence that God's purposes are the fulfillment of my own best interests *as I conceive them*. . . . I reject the notion of trust as ultimate confidence that God intends my individual good *as the usually inflated and exaggerated terms portray that good*. (pp. 202–3, italics added)

These sentences are more definite but not more radical. They are entirely consistent with confidence that among God's purposes are the fulfillment of my own best interests (as they really are) or faith that God intends my individual good (as appropriately chosen terms portray that good). Likewise, when Gustafson raises the possibility that "the Deity is not bound to *our judgments* about what is in our interests" (p. 99, italics added), his words do not strictly imply that God does not have our interests at heart.

"Perhaps," writes Gustafson, "Jonathan Edwards was closer to the truth when he described the end for which God created the world as God's glorification of himself" (p. 272). Perhaps? Gustafson could not be proceeding with more caution. His main worry with Edwards's formulation is its anthropomorphic ascription of volition to God. But Edwards does move away from anthropocentrism. "What *might* be right about the direction of Edwards' argument . . . ," Gustafson continues, "is that the purposes of the divine governance are, *insofar as human beings can discern them*, not *exhausted* by its benefits for us" (pp. 272–73, italics added). Here Gustafson seems concerned at most to deny the notion that every natural event, such as an earthquake, can be interpreted as showing divine purposes toward the well-being of specific individuals and groups. Can anything more definite be said about his conception of how human well-being enters into divine purposes?

Fortunately, Gustafson does let some sentences get by without so much qualification. At one point, for instance, he asserts quite plainly, "The salvation of man is not the chief end of God; certainly it is not the exclusive end of God" (p. 110). He is not simply questioning or expressing uncertainty about the traditional view but denying it, although he still seems to leave open the possibility that our salvation or happiness is encompassed by God's purposes, if not as creation's chief or exclusive end. There is also a point at which he identifies as the "key" to his position the doctrine that "the chief end of man is to glorify God, to relate to all things in a manner appropriate to their relations to God" (p. 184). Again, however, this does not obviously exclude the possibility that true human happiness might be one of God's purposes for creation or even bound up with God's glorification. Nevertheless, Gustafson does state unequivocally that he intends to displace salvation "as the principal point of reference for religious piety and for the ordering of theological principles." We must do without "the assurance that regardless of how difficult and tragic human life is, God will make it right, at least for those who trust in him" (p. 112). We cannot, in other words, reasonably affirm the symbols of traditional eschatology (p. 268).

Is there any sense in which God is for us? "I do not say God is against man," writes Gustafson. "But the sense in which God is for man must be spelled out in a carefully qualified way" (p. 181). What might that be? "God is for man in the sense that the possibilities of any human flourishing are dependent upon what we have received and on forces that are not ultimately under our control" (p. 182). That is, whatever happiness we do have and whatever happiness we can plausibly hope for depend upon the beneficial consequences of forces beyond our control. Because Gustafson's piety identifies these forces as divine, he feels free to see their beneficial consequences for human beings as signs of the extent to which God is for us, as an indication of divine purposes.

Gustafson does not show, however, why—by parity of reasoning—we are not bound to conclude that God is ultimately against us, given the likelihood that human life will soon be snuffed out by the next major turn in cosmic history. Gustafson does speak of fear of and aversion from God as belonging to the religious affections. But if the more comforting consequences of the powers that bear down upon us are to be taken as evidence that God is for us, why should we not conclude that cosmic catastrophe for our species, which hangs like a dark cloud at the horizon of Gustafson's outlook, is not evidence that God is probably against us in the end? Why soften the blow by saying, mildly, that while God is (in a carefully qualified sense) for us, he also limits us? I am not sure how Gustafson would want to respond to these questions and I shall not pursue them here. But they do seem to lead directly to other questions of equally serious import for Gustafson's project. Why construe anything that happens to us as a result of the "powers that bear down upon us" as happening in any way on purpose? If we have already abandoned the idea that there are divine intentions, what might the notion of divine purposes mean? Why, for that matter, call such purposes "divine"?

III

Gustafson agrees with H. Richard Niebuhr that such questions as "What is going on?" and "What is being done to me?" are prior to the question, "What shall I do?"[20] But his rejection of the language of divine agency prevents him from accepting Niebuhr's doctrine: "God is acting in all actions upon you. So respond to all actions upon you as to his actions."[21] Gustafson's most general formulation of his ethics is this principle: "We are to conduct life so as to relate to all things in a manner appropriate to their relations to God" (p. 113). In his second volume, where he discusses specific moral issues, he amends this formulation slightly: "We, as participants, are to relate ourselves and all things in a manner appropriate to our and their relations to God" (p. 146). What matters, then, is how we interpret those relations and render judgments of appropriateness. Since we cannot be certain about divine purposes ordering and sustaining creation, neither can we be certain about our particular moral conclusions. Gustafson's treatment of moral issues is sensitive and exploratory, intended to take full account of the complexities and conflicts of the moral life, not to reach confidence in particular stands. There is no table of divine commands, historical revelation of divine intentions, or natural law from which a permanent casuistry might proceed. Nor is there any guarantee that moral tragedy can be avoided. What is good for some part of creation may not be good for another. Our task is to do our best to discern the relations between part and whole and then to conduct our lives accordingly (p. 342).[22]

If we can be certain of anything, as Gustafson sees it, we can be certain that we are finite, that we are not God (pp. 8–16). We should not, therefore, treat ourselves or humanity in general as if we were divine. That would be unfitting—the kind of inappropriateness known in religious language as idolatry. Idolatry may signal the corruption of our rational capacity to recognize the proper relations of one thing to another in the universe. It may also encourage wrongly ordered loves or a failure to recognize and meet our obligations. Such are the several dimensions of human fault, which go hand in hand with our finitude (pp. 191–92, 297–303). To be human is to be fallible in distributing one's confidence, to be prone to corruption of one's understanding, to be inclined to order one's loves wrongly, to be liable to do wrong. The most we can hope for is to be transformed—in thought, affection, and intention—by the recognition that God, not humanity, is the center of value. Only the infinite and sovereign Other can serve as an appropriate focus for our ultimate confidence, loyalty, hope, and love. This recognition may enlarge and correct our vision, although it does not make us infallible. Conversion of the religious affections helps us accept our finitude; it does not make us divine (pp. 307–17).

Those familiar with H. Richard Niebuhr's writings will see that Niebuhr's influence on Gustafson extends well beyond the theme of interactive freedom.[23] Indeed, the most enlightening way to view Gustafson's book is as a further radicalization of the main theme from Niebuhr's *Radical Monotheism:*

For radical monotheism the value-center is neither closed society nor the principle of such a society but the principle of being itself; its reference is to no one reality among the many but to the One beyond all the many, whence all the many derive their being. . . . Monotheism is less than radical if it makes a distinction between the principle of being and the principle of value; so that while all being is acknowledged as absolutely dependent for existence on the One, only some beings are valued as having worth for it. (p. 32)

Or, as Niebuhr says more polemically:

Dogma, doubtless, there must be. . . . But the dogma of a relativism which assumes the privileged position of one finite reality, such as man, is so narrow that it cuts off inquiry into great realms of value, and tends to confine the discussion of the good to an arbitrarily chosen field, for instance to that of the human good. (p. 112)

Gustafson wants to keep Niebuhr's radically theocentric orientation. What makes Gustafson's monotheism still more radical is the austerity of its God. We are simultaneously told that God's purposes should be the focal point of all ethical reflection and that we lack the means for bringing either God or his purposes into clear focus. Moreover, it remains unclear why, despite his stress on theocentrism, Gustafson insists on speaking of God or divine purposes at all?

To see why Gustafson ultimately needs to face this question, let us return to his relation to Schleiermacher. Gustafson is persuaded that a conversable theology will have to initiate a dialogue with science. Most theologians indebted to Schleiermacher have been more concerned to negotiate a truce with science than to carry on a conversation with it. The truce was to be a pact of nonaggression—what Schleiermacher called an "eternal covenant"—which was to allot science and theology separate realms of human experience to govern and then to prohibit all trespassing across boundaries as the intellectual equivalent of imperialism. Science was to govern the realm of cognition; it alone would have the authority to tell us what we know. Theology was to reign in the realm of religious affectivity; it alone would have the authority to tell us what piety implies.

This strategy can work, however, only if two conditions obtain. Science must turn out to have no knowledge, strictly speaking, concerning God's existence and attributes, whereas theology must somehow make sense of itself without claiming such knowledge either. In other words, the eternal covenant could be effective only as long as both parties remained silent on the issue in which both were once thought to have an interest—namely, knowledge of God. Far from initiating a dialogue, Schleiermacher's eternal covenant was an attempt to keep both parties eternally quiet at precisely the point where their interests have always seemed to overlap.

How could such silence be enforced? On the one hand, Schleiermacher endorsed Kantian arguments intended to show that science cannot, in principle, either prove or disprove anything about God. Theology was therefore supposed to be free to have its say about God without fearing contradiction from science. On the other hand, Schleiermacher used an apparently sharp distinction between knowing and feeling to mark out the sphere of religious experience. The doctrines of Christian theology he then described as "accounts of the Christian religious affections set forth in speech."[24] Theology is permitted to speak of "divine attributes and modes of action" and of "the constitution of the world," but only if it does not claim knowledge of such matters, least of all as they are *in themselves*. Theology must confine itself to saying how God and the world are *for piety*, which is a feeling and not a knowing. As Schleiermacher put it, "every formula for that feeling is a formula for a definite state of mind; and consequently all propositions of Dogmatics must be capable of being set up as such formulae."[25]

I have argued elsewhere that Schleiermacher's covenant breaks down if a sharp distinction between knowing and feeling cannot be maintained. I have also argued that the attempt to exclude cognitive claims from theology threatens to eliminate the reasons that made people care about defending theology from scientific criticism in the first place.[26] Schleiermacher, it seems, could not have it both ways. The scientific threat can be kept at bay only by making theology vacuous, a matter of feeling.

If you have trouble understanding the dilemma I am posing, imagine a follower of Sartre who sets out to do for nausea what Schleiermacher did for piety. She proposes a discipline which will offer accounts, analogous to theological doctrines, of the feeling of nausea set forth in speech. These accounts indicate how things are *for nausea* without entailing or presupposing knowledge of any kind. One doctrine might be that God is dead. The death of God will be proclaimed as the *Whence* of nausea.[27] Now, must we take our Sartrean seriously? If not, what gives her proposal less serious a claim on our attention than Schleiermacher's theology? If we must take her seriously, are we to take her doctrines as incompatible with the corresponding theological doctrines? It would seem not, for she and the theologian alike present themselves as refraining from making theoretical claims. Each is telling us how God and the world are *for* affectivity of a certain kind—existentialist *nausée* and Reformed *pietas*, respectively. But then how long can theology be taken seriously it if is not taken to be incompatible with what our antitheologian has to say? On what grounds might we explain the difference between these two expositions of doctrine or the depth of feeling they express if not by ascribing to their authors precisely the theoretical claims that each makes a point of eschewing?

Gustafson does not maintain the sharp distinction between knowing and feeling essential to Schleiermacher's strategy for dealing with science,[28] and that is why he is able to initiate a dialogue with science whereas Schleiermacher could not. He thus avoids some of the characteristic difficulties of Schleiermacher's theology, but only by undertaking the risk Schleiermacher was himself trying to avoid. For admitting that cognitive and emotive strands are thoroughly intertwined in religious affectivity implies that theoretical questions about the explanatory adequacy of theological doctrines cannot be ruled out in advance as irrelevant. It is because such questions must be deemed relevant that dialogue with science is necessary as well as possible.

When Gustafson says that piety is affective or prereflective, his point is not that it is noncognitive. To the contrary, he repeatedly insists that we should not draw overly sharp distinctions among the affective, cognitive, and volitional aspects of experience. Any such distinctions should be treated as abstractions from experience, useful perhaps for some specific purpose in a particular context, but not to be reified (pp. 116–17, 287). The point of saying that piety is affective is to resist a rationalistic or voluntaristic reduction of piety to a mere exercise of the intellect or the will, not to promote in turn an emotivist reduction of piety to sheer feeling. Similarly, the point of asserting that experience is prior to reflection is to portray theology as a second-order activity, not to deny the role of cognitive categories "in the ordering of even very primary experiences" (p. 116).

Piety is immediate only in the sense that it is not mediated by self-consciously intellectual activity. It is, however, thoroughly bound up with the cognitive categories implicit in what Gustafson calls the first-order language of piety. When Gustafson speaks of religious experience, he is not appealing to a kind of prelinguistic or nonpropositional awareness of God. Experience may be prior to reflection, but it is not prior to "the context of a religious community, with its first-order religious language, its liturgies and symbols, and its procedures for transmitting a heritage" (p. 318).[29] It follows, therefore, that the appeal to religious experience and affectivity is not, in Gustafson's work, an attempt to place the cognitive commitments of piety beyond the reach of criticism. Piety employs a language whose categories and presuppositions are corrigible in light of the rest of what we know and feel, including what we learn in dialogue with science.

What does its dialogue with science teach theology? Mainly, concludes Gustafson, that "we have a Ptolemaic religion in a Copernican universe" (p. 190). If theology is to be reasonable, it must cease to be Ptolemaic. If our universe is that described by Copernicus and his successors, if the prehistory of our species is that explained by Darwin and his heirs, then Herbert Butterfield was right in saying, "it is absurd to suppose that this colossal universe was created by God purely for the sake of men, purely to serve the purposes of the earth" (quoted on p. 98). Ernst Troeltsch was right to conclude, "As the beginning was without us, so will the end also be without us" (p. 98). Given the best science of our time, says Gustafson, it would be indefensibly Ptolemaic to hold that our happiness is the chief end of creation or that salvation awaits us at the end of time. Theology has not yet fully reoriented its vision to accommodate what the likes of Copernicus and Darwin have been saying. Truly to listen to the voice of science is to risk having one's vision transformed. Gustafson does not imitate the voice of science any more than he imitates the voice of philosophy, but he does subject his own theology to the kind of questioning that a dialogue with science necessarily entails.

Mine is not a theocentric vision. I do not postulate divine purposes, let alone divine intentions, in order to explain the data of modern science or to explicate the sense of dependence I feel. But there is room in my vision for wonder, awe, and even gratitude—a kind of piety, in short, for the powers that bear down upon us, for the majestic setting of our planet and its cosmos, and for the often marvelous company we keep here. I admire Mary Midgley's diagnosis of the existentialist angst of those who bewail their own alienation from the cosmos after the death of God: It is the reaction of emotional cripples. Antitheism like Kai Nielsen's has already lost its point. So has the radical theology that takes its cues from Nietzsche: if God is dead, asks Midgley, "why dress up in his clothes?" "If we know the house is empty, why ring the bell and run away?" And why, Midgley asks, should we feel alienated from the only sort of universe in which we are adapted to live, one that surrounds us with a sublimity we have only begun to explore?[30]

The affinity between Gustafson's outlook and my own may finally be as troubling as it is pleasing. It is pleasing in part because it helps me see my own secular piety as analogous to and even indebted to a central theme from the Reformed tradition. But Gustafson does not make clear why we shouldn't view the secular piety I share with Midgley as the natural successor to theocentric piety. Gustafson's criticisms of traditional religious doctrines create a momentum that seems bound to carry us beyond his own position to atheism—not the narcissistic antitheism by means of which Feuerbach and Nietzsche tried to put themselves in God's place, and not the obsessive atheism of existentialists who reeled and whined as they peered into the abyss, but something like Midgley's sane and sober vision of our place among the other species in a vast and largely unknown universe.

The problem is not that Gustafson and his secular conversation partners are setting out to say the same thing. Gustafson's perspective is theocentric; mine is not. Gustafson's piety is directed toward a single Other; mine is more diffuse. Gustafson does not hesitate to speak of the powers that bear down upon us as divine; I do. Worshipping such powers, once Gustafson has pruned away various traditional theological attributes that make the divinity seem worthy of worship, strikes me as unfitting and incongruous. Taking such powers as one's ultimate concern all too easily swerves towards the grotesque. When Gustafson goes beyond correcting the faults of anthropocentrism and uncharitably belittles the ordinary concerns and pleasures of human life, I find him too bleak and severe. I worry that he fails to find the mean between the intemperance of self-idolatry and a kind of distorted insensibity or abnegation. But these differences, while real enough, will for many readers only point to another question. Is not Gustafson's theology distinguishable from a humane and recognizably secular vision only at the points where he is also most elusive, where we have the most difficulty figuring out what he is saying and why he is saying it, where we have the most trouble discerning what the difference comes to and why he wants to maintain it?

A careful reading of Gustafson would show, I think, that he never explains clearly why one ought to speak of "the powers that bear down upon us" as divine or what this addition in fact adds. Nor does he explain why the powers, which he nearly always refers to as plural, should be construed *mono*theistically. And he leaves the sense in which his deity is supposed to have purposes shrouded in mystery, telling us only that divine purposes should not be understood as intentions. My concern is not that he has failed to offer compelling arguments—arguments so powerful that any reasonable intellect would be forced to lay down its objections and submit. (Do such arguments play a major role in any discipline?) Neither am I simply indicating that I have not yet been convinced. I am saying that Gustafson has not shown why he himself, "even in piety," might have reason to be convinced.

Gustafson would be a less interesting theologian and my questions would have much less point if his appeal to piety were designed to place his conclusions beyond the scope of critical scrutiny, if he held piety to involve a contact with the really Real totally innocent of cognitive categories and corrigible assumptions. To his credit, he does not evade hard questions in that way. Furthermore, it is by pressing hard questions about the meaningfulness and evidential warrant of theological claims that Gustafson builds his case against the less austere theologies of his predecessors. We can see why he concludes that his theology had better do without the doctrine of eternal life, the ascription of intentions and intellect to God, and so on. What remains entirely unclear is how the scruples that would lead to these conclusions would allow Gustafson to retain what little theological content he has at the end.

Gustafson's message, abstracted from its specifically theological context, is both clear and reasonable: to keep our confidence, loyalty, hope, and love proportioned to their objects; never to make the merely finite our ultimate concern. Midgley, the secular moral philosopher, could agree to that. I surely do. Why add, as Gustafson does, that there is an Ultimate Other who deserves our ultimate concern? What difference does it make for ethics to place a Mystery at the center once Humanity has been displaced? It is ironic that a theocentric ethics would conclude its exposition of theological doctrine without making its answers to such questions clear. Those of us who read theology from a distance, from the outside, need to be told why the moral impulse against idolatry, which began in the Near East several millenia ago and found fresh expression among the Calvinists who did much to shape the ethos of the modern world, shouldn't finally be turned against the last remnants of theistic metaphysics itself.

IV

Such questions bring us back to the theological dilemma with which this chapter started. Can theology retain its distinctiveness as a mode of utterance without ceasing to speak persuasively to the culture that it would like to influence? I have commented at length on Gustafson because I can think of no recent writer who has struggled more valiantly or more honestly with theology's dilemma. He is refreshingly free of the fundamental theologian's philosophical ambitions. Our culture would be a better place if it took his critique of narcissism seriously. His effort would not be exemplary—it would not teach us so much about the predicament of theology in contemporary culture—if these things could not truly be said of his accomplishment. Yet precisely because he presses his scrupulous questioning so much further than most theologians are willing to go, his theology illustrates with special clarity the difficulty posed by theology's current predicament. I think that this predicament, not Gustafson's rigor as a theologian, explains his failure to make plain the distinctively theological content of his proposal and his reasons for accepting it.[31] The question is whether he *can* make such things plain without violating the critical scruples that set him in motion away from orthodoxy. Can *anyone?*

Gustafson sometimes expresses annoyance at secular intellectuals who say that they wish theologians would be more orthodox—at those who imply, without undergoing any risk of their own, that what we have here (say, in the case of Hans Küng) is a failure of excommunication. But there may be more to such remarks than the cheap shot. Serious conversation with theology will be greatly limited if the voice of theology is not recognizably theological. Conversation partners must remain distinctive enough to be identified, to be needed. They must be able to clarify the difference their outlook makes and to say why they differ from the rest of us at the most crucial points. That is not the same thing as wanting them to stand still.

I do not mean to imply that Gustafson, or any other theologian, does not belong in the conversation. Gustafson is a remarkably courageous, honest, and learned man. Nor do I mean to question the authenticity of his debt to the Reformed tradition. But I am not surprised to find his critics within the religious community asking whether the Reformed tradition ceases, in Gustafson's discourse, to be primarily a matter of Christian theology at all. And he seems to wonder about this, too:

At what point are there beliefs and concepts the cost of whose abandonment would be the loss of identity and integrity of Christian theology itself? What degree of reformulation runs the risk of tipping the balance from a presumption in favor of the Christian tradition to a presumption against it? (p. 144)

He refers to the "agonizing honesty" with which Troeltsch faced the possibility that pursuit of theological inquiry might "lead unnoticed away from Christianity." "Such," comments Gustafson poignantly, "are the risks" (p. 230, cf. p. 274).

Gustafson is both more aware of these risks and more willing to undergo them than most theologians. By my lights, for better or for worse, he has already moved beyond the point at which reformulation tips the balance from a presumption in favor of the Christian tradition to a presumption against it. Judging by the reactions that have reached print so far, most of Gustafson's fellow theologians seem inclined to agree. But asking how theologians would have to move in order to resist conclusions as unorthodox as his can generate a useful map of the contemporary theological landscape.

Theologians can (1) try to show that something like Gustafson's critical scruples, rightly interpreted and applied, in fact support a more orthodox variety of theism. Most of Gustafson's theological critics, however, have responded differently. They assume that he is probably right about the direction in which those scruples lead, but they would rather junk the scruples than be moved toward a position like his. The desire to junk the scruples can itself lead in various directions: (2) to a kind of fundamental theology; (3) to something like Schleiermacher's pact of nonaggression with science, whether in its Kantian, Romantic, or existentialist forms; (4) to radical relativism of a sort designed to make orthodox theology a form of life that one can confess or describe from the inside but never, in principle, explain or criticize; (5) to a kind of dogmatic theology like Karl Barth's, which perseveres in valuing scripture over science and experience and rigorously avoids making a systematic apology for its acceptance of biblical authority; or (6) to political attempts, from the right or the left, to overthrow the entire epistemic context characteristic of pluralistic societies and, with it, the "secular humanism" or "scientism" from which scruples like Gustafson's are thought to derive.

All these options have takers. Each presents risks of its own. The influence of Kant, Schleiermacher, and the existentialists, especially among Protestant theologians, has meant that option (1) has received very little serious attention since the late eighteenth century.[32] Options

(2), (3), and (4), despite the best efforts of their proponents, have pretty much ceased producing effective responses to their critics. Anyone wanting to pursue those options now in an intellectually responsible way will have to face arguments like Gustafson's head-on. Much imaginative effort has recently gone into developing option (5), although it is too early to know whether its proponents will be able to address more than a quite narrow public.[33] Its critics, Gustafson included, view this option as an irresponsible willingness to abandon public discourse and critical thought altogether—a kind of fideism whose natural social expression is sectarianism.

Its defenders respond that proclamation and witness, carried on without overly ambitious apologetic support, need not preclude fruitful conversation and collaboration with nonbelievers on specific issues of common concern. They point to figures like Archbishop Tutu, who have made theological assumptions relevant to public discourse without assuming that their interlocutors either share or need systematic reasons for sharing their theological beliefs.[34] But whether academic theologians can win a wide hearing even within the academy depends in part, it seems to me, on whether religious resurgence produces dramatic change, independently of theology, in what most people, including intellectuals, take for granted about the nature and existence of God when they speak to matters of moral importance in public settings. Such a change would shift the burden of proof in a way that might make some kind of theology central to the culture again. That, of course, is precisely the outcome sought by the champions of option (6).

Nobody knows what the next turn in political and economic events will bring, and it is conceivable that social and epistemic circumstances will change in ways that will give new intellectual standing to theology. On the other hand, the possibility that epistemic circumstances will change is not yet an argument, either practical or theoretical, against scruples like Gustafson's—the same scruples, roughly, that led an earlier generation by stages from Latitudinarian theology, to Deism, to Hume, to Holbach. At any rate, we are wise to hold onto whatever scruples we've got until somebody gives us good reasons for discarding them. And it is by no means obvious that religious resurgence and political upheaval, even if they eventually displace the forms of thought and practice that have been inhospitable to theology in the modern world, will themselves prove hospitable to the kind of theological reflection proponents of options (5) and (6) have in mind.

Before turning, in the final part of this book, to some of the most interesting recent critics and defenders of pluralistic society, I want to clarify what I have been driving at in this chapter and throughout Part 2. First of all, I have not been trying to demonstrate that theologians are irrational or that they are unjustified in believing what they believe about God. It follows from what I said in Part 1 that people can be justified in believing something even if they are unable to produce positive justifying arguments for believing it or arguments that can justify that belief to others. It also follows that two people can be justified in believing quite different sets of propositions. So if I am right about such matters, the problem of public theology in our day should not be conflated with problems pertaining to the rationality of religious individuals or the justification of particular beliefs they hold.[35] I have been addressing the problem of public theology.

Furthermore, I have not claimed that any of the options—Gustafson's or any of the others just mentioned—has been permanently ruled out. Nothing I have said shows that theologians of genius will never find a way through the dilemma as it now stands. Nor, my own skepticism notwithstanding, have I implied that certain theological claims are either false or at fault. For all I have said here, some version of theology could be true and the theologian's position at the margins of modern intellectual culture could be evidence of the decadence of that culture. What I have tried to do in this chapter is to lay out the theological options as I see them while saying enough about their difficulties to help explain the marginality of theology in North American society today. This is meant to add more depth to my account of the fate of religious ethics and the nearly complete breakdown of fruitful dialogue between secular philosophical thought and the religious traditions. It is not simply that secular moral philosophers have adopted tropes and fetishes that virtually preclude rigorous investigation of religious assumptions and categories. It is also true that theology, from its side, has had trouble making such assumptions and categories seem worthy of an educated public's attention.

My own argument for putting the critical study of religious ethics back on the intellectual agenda is threefold. First, as I claimed early on in Part 2, we cannot understand even the most secularized forms of moral discourse in contemporary society without understanding how the fate of religious ethics has played a role in their formation. Second, even if we are not persuaded to accept theological conclusions, the study of religious traditions may still teach us something of moral importance, as I hope my reading of Gustafson's critique of narcissism and idolatry indicates.

And finally, the secularization of public moral discourse—which has meant that most attempts at moral persuasion presented under the aegis of certain public institutions do not presuppose the truth of specific theological beliefs, given the religiously plural nature of the audience being addressed—does not mean that religious assumptions and categories play no essential role either in what people actually say as participants in public discourse or in the moral deliberation of many people in our society. If we want to understand our fellow citizens— whether they be Dorothy Day, Martin Luther King, Jr., Jerry Falwell, the Roman Catholic Bishops, Mario Cuomo, or Elie Wiesel —we had better develop the means for understanding the moral languages, including the theological ones, in which they occasionally address us and in which their deliberation is couched.

3

MORAL DISCOURSE IN PLURALISTIC SOCIETY

9

VIRTUE AMONG THE RUINS

"We have reached the point," wrote Livy long ago in ancient Rome, "where we cannot bear either our vices or their cure." Livy's message may come from another epoch but, according to Robert Bellah and his coauthors in *Habits of the Heart*, it applies to us here and now. We speak not one moral language but several, and they serve us poorly, at least as they stand. The primary language in which we understand ourselves is shot through with individualism and is therefore ill-suited for public discourse on the common good or for shaping meaningful lives. Our secondary languages of morals, which hark back to older traditions, biblical and civic republican in outlook, have begun to wither away, to lose their power to hold public discourse together. As a result, "the time may be approaching when we will either reform our republic or fall into the hands of despotism, as many republics have done before us." [1]

As Alasdair MacIntyre sees it in *After Virtue*, that time has come: "the new dark ages . . . are already upon us." Our moral premises are like so many incommensurable fragments of lost languages. The moral concepts we use, deprived of the contexts in which they formerly made sense, have become merely means of expressing our feelings and manipulating others. Where once there was coherent discourse on the virtues and the common good, we now have the assertion of arbitrary wills, masked by moral fictions, managed by bureaucrats. The barbar-

191

ians, MacIntyre says, "are not waiting beyond the frontiers; they have already been governing us for quite some time. And it is our lack of consciousness of this that constitutes part of our predicament."[2]

Bellah and MacIntyre are not telling us to be nihilists, or skeptics, or radical relativists. Their doubts are not directed at morality as such, doubts of the kind explored in Part 1. Their doubts are about our particular predicament, the contemporary confusion of tongues we dignify with such names as liberalism and pluralism.[3] Rational moral discourse may be possible in principle, and it used to be actual, but that does not make it possible for us. Bellah and MacIntyre are concerned about the fate of rational moral discourse, community, and the virtues under specific historical conditions, those in which we find ourselves speaking all-too-many moral languages, sharing all-too-few common assumptions and ends, divided by disagreements of the deepest kind, but apparently lacking the means to resolve them rationally. The worry raised by these authors is one touched on briefly in the first two parts of this book. It now deserves our undivided attention: Has our own moral heritage in fact degenerated to the point that all is lost or nearly so? If so, how do we—indeed, how could we—know? If not, how can our situation be more aptly described and assessed? And either way, what is to be done?

These are the questions I wish to address in Part 3. My discussions of moral philosophy and religious ethics in Parts 1 and 2 will inform the answers I offer. The present chapter asks whether conclusions as dire as Bellah's and MacIntyre's can be justified by the kind of evidence presented in *Habits of the Heart* and *After Virtue*—two books that have reached a vast reading public, as academic writings go, and which pose a powerful challenge to our culture. I shall begin by raising doubts about some of the interview material used in *Habits of the Heart*, arguing that the grim picture Bellah and his colleagues paint of their informants may owe more to the authors' method of Socratic questioning and to their unstated assumptions about what healthy moral discourse would be like than it does to the way the informants themselves are inclined to speak about their lives. I shall then try to show that MacIntyre's account of moral disagreement and conceptual diversity, although more limited in scope than the one that gives rise to the forms of skepticism and nihilism discussed in Part 1, nonetheless suffers from similar deficiencies.

In Chapter 10, I'll explore alternatives to MacIntyre's position—not the standard ones, derived from Enlightenment philosophy and cast in some version of moral Esperanto, or the amoralist one inspired by Nietzsche as he is usually understood, which MacIntyre sees as the only real option for those who don't side with Aristotle, but rather non-standard ones to which he pays little heed. Some of these will be theological; another, represented by the recent writings of Richard Rorty, will not. Chapter 11 will ask whether the kind of pragmatic approach I have been advocating in this book, secular in orientation and eclectic in spirit, itself contributes to or unwittingly reflects the degeneration of our moral tradition. My answer to that question will clarify the relation between my position and Rorty's. Finally, in Chapter 12, I'll come back to MacIntyre, hoping to show how we might split the difference between his position and something like Rorty's pragmatic liberalism.

My conclusion will be that we are likely to profit less from sweeping pronouncements, either for or against "pluralistic society" and its characteristic forms of moral language, than from a determined effort to recast our self-descriptions and normative questions in more specific terms. This is a pragmatist's point in its own right, of course. But despite the criticism of MacIntyre I am about to give, it will turn out that some of the tools he offers can help us greatly with the important critical work remaining to be done—and do so all the better if we set aside labels like *liberal* and *communitarian*, as well as hyperbolic talk about the new dark ages.

I

Habits of the Heart portrays the American predicament as an impasse: "Modern individualism seems to be producing a way of life that is neither individually nor socially viable, yet a return to traditional forms would be to return to intolerable discrimination and oppression" (p. 144). Individualism is our "first language," the moral vocabulary Americans share (pp. 20, 161). But it feeds an illusory "quest for purely private fulfillment" that "often ends in emptiness." Moreover, it "often implies a negative view of public life" (p. 163) and lacks concepts we would need for addressing ourselves to the public good. Our only hope, then, lies in reclaiming and reforming the "second languages" of biblical and civic republican traditions. Doing so will work to keep our individualism in check, and our individualism will limit the tendencies of such languages toward discrimination and oppression.

This picture has considerable appeal, and it is anything but unfamiliar. We need to ask, however, what it might mean to say that individualism is our first language of self-understanding and why we should believe that this is so. Bellah and his colleagues do not answer these questions directly in *Habits of the Heart*, so we shall need to tease out answers from the use they make of their interviews with white middle-class Americans. Describing their methods, they write, "Though we did not seek to impose our ideas on those with whom we talked . . . , we did attempt to uncover assumptions, to make explicit what the person we were talking to might rather have left implicit. The interview as we employed it was active, Socratic" (p. 304).

There are good and bad senses in which the questioning of informants can be Socratic, depending on whether you think of Socrates as the inspiration of what Oakeshott and Gadamer call conversation or as an intellectual bully who used ill-formed queries to grind an axe for Platonic metaphysics and make people like Euthyphro look like fools.[4] A Socratic interview in the good sense would have interviewer and informant caught up in a conversation that leads to unexpected self-understanding. A Socratic interview in the bad sense has the interviewer keep saying "Why?" or "How do you know that?" until the informant either becomes confused or starts sounding suspiciously like a philosopher. *Habits of the Heart*, I think, uses Socratic interviews in both senses. For present purposes, I want to restrict the phrase to its bad sense in order to ask whether that kind of "Socratic questioning" might be at least partly responsible for the harsh judgments *Habits* sometimes makes of its subjects.

Consider an example of the Socratic interview in action. Ann Swidler, "trying to get Brian Palmer to clarify the basis of his moral judgments," was told that "lying is one of the things I want to regulate." "Why?" asked Swidler.

A: Well, it's a kind of thing that is a habit you get into. Kind of self-perpetuating. It's like digging a hole. You just keep digging and digging.
Q: So why is it wrong?
A: Why is integrity important and lying bad? I don't know. It just is. It's just so basic. I don't want to be bothered with challenging that. It's part of me. I don't know where it came from, but it's very important.
Q: When you think about what's right and what's wrong, are things bad because they are bad for people, or are they right or wrong in themselves, and if so how do you know?
A: Well some things are bad because . . . I guess I feel like everybody on

this planet is entitled to have a little bit of space, and things that detract from other people's space are kind of bad . . . (pp. 304-5, ellipses in original)

It is the final answer in this series, of course, that sounds to Swidler and her colleagues like the language of American individualism. Swidler, like Plato's Socrates at his mechanical worst, kept on probing—asking "Why?" and "How do you know?"—until Brian produced something resembling a moral principle. And this, presumably, is to be taken as "the basis for his moral judgments" about lying and perhaps therefore as evidence of what constitutes Brian's first language of self-understanding.

There is, however, another way to read this interview. Brian's first inclination is not to invoke a moral principle. In fact, he initially sounds downright Aristotelian. Why does he want to regulate lying? Because lying is a bad habit. Every act of lying reinforces the habit, makes things worse. "So why is it wrong?" Brian seems both puzzled and put off by the question. Aristotelian answers seem not to wash with this questioner. So he rephrases the question, as if searching for a real doubt to address. Finding none, he confesses that he doesn't know why lying is wrong. "It just is."

Evidently, like C. S. Peirce, Brian doesn't know how to answer questions that aren't connected to real doubts. When Brian says that the wrongness of lying is basic, I suggest a Wittgensteinian gloss reminiscent of *On Certainty*: he can't think of anything more certain than the wrongness of lying that might be introduced to support the idea that lying is wrong. He'd rather not be bothered with the sort of challenge the question implies. This, for Peirce and Wittgenstein, shows wholesomely pragmatic philosophical instincts. But his interviewer won't stop. Her next question is worthy of the *Euthyphro*, a question that would be hard to answer without invoking a principle for Socrates to pounce upon. And like poor Euthyphro, Brian plays along.

Habits of the Heart places Brian Palmer front and center. It is his case with which the book begins. Brian, we are told, "recalls a youth that included a fair amount of hell-raising, a lot of sex, and considerable devotion to making money" (p. 3). After marrying at twenty-four, he threw himself into his career, hoping to support his family and achieve success. Nearly fifteen years later, his wife left him, and Brian began to reexamine and reorient his life. He has since remarried. Here is Brian describing his second marriage:

To be able to receive affection freely and give affection and to give of myself and know it is a totally reciprocal type of thing. There's just almost a psychologically buoyant feeling of being able to be so much more involved and sharing. Sharing experiences of goals, sharing of feelings, working together to solve problems, etc. My viewpoint of a true love, husband-and-wife type of relationship is one that is founded on mutual respect, admiration, affection, the ability to give and receive freely. (p. 5)

This is how Brian talks when not interrupted by Socratic questions. Reciprocity, involvement, shared goals, and mutual respect define for him what makes his second marriage better than his first. Is this the language of individualism? Bellah and his colleagues would not deny that Brian has made some moral progress beyond individualism, at least in its crudest form; "Yet despite the personal triumph Brian's life represents, despite the fulfillment he seems to experience," our authors hasten to add, "there is still something uncertain, something poignantly unresolved about his story" (p. 5). For Brian has trouble, they say, explaining why his new life is better than his old one:

His description of his reasons for changing his life and of his current happiness seems to come down mainly to a shift in his notions of what would make him happy. His new goal—devotion to marriage and children—seems as arbitrary and unexamined as his earlier pursuit of material success. Both are justified as idiosyncratic preference rather than as representing a larger sense of the purpose of life. (p. 6)

Yet if Brian does not sound much like an individualist when he tells his story, neither does he seem to be appealing to arbitrary or unexamined preferences. The only evidence *Habits of the Heart* offers to support the conclusion that there is something uncertain or unresolved about his story comes not from his storytelling but rather from Swidler's Socratic questioning. Only at the end of a chain of Socratic questions does he produce what our authors redescribe as "the ultimate ethical rule . . . that individuals should pursue whatever they find rewarding, constrained only by the requirement that they not interfere with the 'value systems' of others" (p. 6). If anything, the language of individualism seems to be less his first language of self-understanding than his language of last resort—a set of slogans he reaches for (with obvious reluctance) when somebody won't take storytelling or unprincipled talk of habit and happiness as sufficient for the purposes of justification.

Brian's story takes shape as what MacIntyre would call a dramatic narrative.[5] He narrates the major transition of his life as an overcoming, not a tragedy. Only if character traits, actions, and outcomes are depicted, within the evaluative framework of the narrative, as good or bad, happy or unfortunate, can the plot take the dramatic form it does. The story implies moral judgments. If Brian were unable to render this sequence of events convincingly as a comic triumph, that would constitute powerful evidence against the judgments implicit in his narrative. The story does not portray Brian's conversion as arbitrary; it portrays it as a reasonable response to crisis. It shows us how Brian, when faced with an unhappy situation for which he can now recognize his own responsibility, reoriented himself in a way that made him happy.

When Swidler asks Brian why he finds the outcome happy, he says that he just finds "more personal satisfaction from choosing course B over course A" (p. 8). It makes him feel better about himself. Bellah and his coauthors treat these remarks as if Brian were advocating a moral principle of the form, "One ought always to choose the course that will maximize one's own satisfaction." Brian can, however, just as easily be read as offering his own experience as evidence for the claim that one course is objectively better than the other and therefore should be preferred to it. He may be saying, in effect, "I have lived in each of these ways. The first way made me miserable. The second way, with its shared goals and mutual respect, made me happy." He does not say that merely feeling happy makes that way right. And if Swidler had asked him whether somebody who derived "personal satisfaction" from cheating or raping people should be deemed morally upright, I suspect he would have said no. Then the interview would have become Socratic in the good sense, with Brian and questioner alike achieving insight into what he really believes and loves.

Brian reoriented his life not by appealing to principles but by identifying his problems and solving them. Bellah and his colleagues complain that within the context of Brian's life, "Solving conflicts becomes a matter of technical problem solving, not moral decision" (p. 7)—but "technical" is their word, not his, and he does not contrast his attempts to solve problems with *moral* decision making. He identifies the problems that brought about the crisis in his life by saying that he had disordered priorities. Reordered priorities solved his problems. Far from employing merely technical reason, in the sense that treats ends as morally indifferent or arbitrary and seeks only the most efficient and appropriate means, Brian seems to recognize the importance of re-ordered ends or loves in a quest for the good life.

I can sum up my doubts about the portrait of Brian Palmer in *Habits of the Heart* as follows. Brian's justification of his life does not, as the authors think, rest on "a fragile foundation" (p. 8), for it doesn't rest on a foundation at all. It rests in the details of his story. It is by telling his story and implicitly invoking its evaluative framework that Brian initially understands his life and justifies his current commitments as superior to his old ones. *Habits of the Heart* seems at times to assume, despite its own philosophical proclivities, that what Brian's life needs, to count as justified, is a philosophical foundation—a principle that will stop the regress of answers to Socratic questions—or perhaps a reflective view of "the purpose of life" spelled out in a philosophically coherent language. Only if we make this assumption does the material quoted from Swidler's interviews support the conclusion that Brian "lacks a language to explain what seem to be the real commitments that define his life" (p. 8).

Brian Palmer's case is one of many discussed in the book, and it would be tedious to go over all of them here. But I have similar doubts about other cases. When Margaret Oldham says, "I just sort of accept the way the world is and then don't think about it a whole lot," I take her to be showing resistance to her interviewer's method of questioning (p. 14). When she says that things will turn out well if she's the "best person" she knows how to be according to her "own lights," I don't take her to treating her values as given, "whatever they might happen to be" (p. 15). A Socratic questioner in the good sense would have said, "But suppose your 'own lights' were those of Nazism, would it still be right for you to follow them?" And Margaret would have said, "Of course not" or "I see what you mean." Then she wouldn't seem individualistic in quite the same way.

When Wayne Bauer has trouble defining, in response to Socratic questions, what a better society would be like, I find him predictably puzzled by the abstract turn of the dialogue or perhaps simply unprepared to offer a grand utopian vision, not "strangely inarticulate" (p. 19). Maybe his political reasoning takes its departure from specific instances of especially salient injustice, suffering, greed, or selfishness rather than first working up a blueprint of the future as it ideally ought to be. If so, we may have something to learn from him. When the authors characterize all these people as "confused about how to define for themselves such things as the nature of success, the meaning of freedom, and the requirements of justice," I recall Peter Geach's portrait of poor Euthyphro and wonder whether Socratic questions (in the bad sense) are bound to make nearly anybody from whatever time or place seem inarticulate.[6]

Am I saying that Brian Palmer, Margaret Oldham, and the rest are wholly admirable people, articulate in all the ways I would want them to be, or that the picture of them put forward in *Habits of the Heart* is without merit? No. In later chapters, I shall come back to Brian Palmer and try to say, in my own way, what still seems deficient about his life after he has reordered his priorities. In doing so, I rely on evidence from *Habits* that I haven't yet discussed.[7] My main point here is that the more reliable material comes when the interviewers don't press too hard with "philosophical" probes.[8] The question is how best to state what remains lacking in a life like Brian Palmer's and what the crucial evidence that something is lacking turns out to be. My complaint is that there seem to be various points in the book where the Socratic probing gets too heavy-handed, and these seem to be precisely the points most heavily relied upon in justifying conclusions about the "fragile foundations" or "strangely inarticulate" character of the lives being examined.

Robert Bellah takes me to be charging the book with "a foundationalism in moral philosophy" to which he and his fellow authors "are not in the least committed."[9] It may be worth noting that the metaphor of "fragile foundations" comes directly from the book, but that is not really the point. I would have been greatly surprised to find these authors, of all people, committed to foundationalism. I therefore find it somewhat ironic that *Habits* seems, at times, to make too little of its subjects' stories and too much of their stammering responses to the kind of questioning that made philosophers invent foundationalism. Postfoundationalists should be suspicious of what can be learned from repeatedly asking "Why?" The weight that *Habits* seems to place on answers to questions of this kind would make more sense if the authors were foundationalists (which they obviously are not). Evidently, intellectual habits change more slowly than intellectual commitments do.

I worry, therefore, that "Socratic questioning" (of a sort) is an interview procedure bound to make people sound either more like fifth-rate philosophers or less articulate than they ordinarily are. If, after a long

chain of Socratic questions, someone utters what seems like an especially vapid quasi-philosophical principle or is reduced to a blank stare,
I find this less a significant sign of the times than Bellah and his colleagues do.

II

Let us now turn to a book whose influence can be felt throughout
Habits of the Heart—namely, MacIntyre's *After Virtue*, which declares
that the disorder of our moral discourse leaves us "all already in a state
so disastrous that there are no large remedies for it" (p. 5). Since the
Victorian period our culture has flattered itself by contrasting its own
moral discourse with the "mere taboos" of eighteenth-century
Polynesia, and as early as Dickens's *Little Dorrit*, satirists have deflated
the self-flattery by hinting that there may be no comforting contrast
between ourselves and the "primitives" to be found.[10] MacIntyre, as if
some reader new to his work might miss the most effective bit of rhetoric in his repertoire, has made the point repeatedly over two decades.
Our use of the distinctively moral *ought*, he reminds us once again in
After Virtue, resembles the Polynesian use of *taboo* in all relevant respects.[11] Captain Cook and his sailors were puzzled by Polynesian taboos, MacIntyre suggests, for precisely the same reasons we should be
puzzled by our own "moral obligations." Our moral discourse is no
better off than theirs, he says, and it would be nice if we could do
something about it.

What, then, does MacIntyre's insistence upon the similarity of *ought*
and *taboo* involve, and what does his introduction of this comparison
achieve? Assume for the purposes of argument that H. A. Prichard's
analysis of our emphatic use of *ought* succeeded at least in isolating the
following three facts. First, when using the word *ought* in its moral
sense, one offers a special kind of reason. But, second, "this reason
cannot itself be supported by further reasons, unless the sentences
which express them also contain the Prichardian 'ought'" (*Self-Images*,
p. 165). And, finally, the word makes demands that seem to go beyond
expressions of personal preference. One central problem of moral philosophy in this century has been how to account for all three characteristics of the word. How, given the second characteristic, can moral
ought sentences express a kind of reason that transcends expressions of
personal preference?

Some philosophers have responded to this question by trying to show that some moral *ought* sentences are, in a strong sense, foundational. That is, the justification of such sentences derives not from further sentences we might adduce in their support but rather from their status as intuitively self-evident truths (as Prichard would have it) or as truths that simply must be accepted if practical reason is to function coherently (as Donagan wishes to claim). Foundational *oughts* would thus stop the regress of moral reasons short of infinity and endow such reasoning with an authority more compelling than appeals to personal preference. One difficulty with this strategy, as we have seen, has been that of explaining apparent disagreement over the various candidates for the role of foundations. Given the extent of moral disagreement—even among the proponents of this strategy—how can the foundations of moral reasoning be intuitively self-evident? Only, so most intuitionists have been forced to conclude, if these foundations consist of "vague generalizations almost nobody will deny."[12] But then it becomes difficult to use such platitudes to explain the disagreement that remains at other levels, and it becomes hard once again to distinguish reasoning on the basis of such foundations from the expression of merely personal preference. Nor does the difficulty dissolve if we replace the intuitionist's notion of self-evidence with something like Donagan's neo-Kantian account of practical reason, because the problem of accounting for moral disagreement remains basically the same.

These and other reasons have convinced some philosophers that, despite appearances to the contrary, moral *ought* sentences do not in fact express more than personal preference. If my moral reasoning proceeds from a foundation, that foundation must consist in my emotions, or attitudes, or essentially arbitrary decisions of principle. The foundation of my reasoning need not be identical to the foundation of yours. This would explain the possibility of widespread and deep-seated moral disagreement, although only by raising further questions about how to explain away or accommodate the fact that moral *ought* sentences make demands that seem (at least) to go beyond expressions of personal preference.

MacIntyre urges us to stand back from these puzzles and to notice that what Captain Cook and his sailors found so confusing about the Polynesian word *taboo* was that it shared the basic characteristics of Prichard's *ought*. His speculation about what Polynesians would have said about *taboo* had they "enjoyed the blessings of analytical philoso-phy" is splendid satire (*After Virtue*, p. 112; *Self-Images*, p. 166). What makes the Polynesian case different, MacIntyre suggests, is simply that we are more distant from it than from our own. If we are inclined to declare Polynesian talk of taboo incoherent, given the apparent inabil-ity of Captain Cook's informants to connect such talk with reasons in such a way that the emphatic force of the proscriptions makes sense, why not say that Prichard's *ought* is incoherent for the same sort of reason? And if we are prepared to speculate about how Polynesian moral discourse became incoherent, as the anthropologists do when they hypothesize about the circumstances in which Polynesian talk of taboos may have lost a coherence it once had, then why not formulate and test similar explanations of our own situation?

It must be admitted that MacIntyre's satire alone does not prove that our use of the term *ought* is incoherent. The stubborn moral philoso-pher is free to insist that, in point of fact, Captain Cook, his sailors, and the anthropologists have been puzzled by *taboo* only because they indeed have lacked the blessings of analytical philosophy, that the fa-vored analysis of *ought* can be extended to *taboo* as well. Or one might sidestep the satire by denying the parallel. These possibilities seem to shift attention back to the question of whether one of the standard ana-lyses of *ought* can be established, possible analogues notwithstanding. But the point of MacIntyre's references to Polynesia is not to nail down a conclusion; it is rather to set the competing analyses of *ought* in a much broader context and thus to increase the range of data with which any serious analyst would have to deal. After MacIntyre has had his say, it becomes more difficult to assume, without argument, that *ought* belongs to something called *the* language of morals, that it is a basic element of a conceptual framework whose basic elements do not change (*Short History*, p. 1). For it is hard to see how to hold one's own against MacIntyre's challenge, to look at ourselves as an alien anthro-pologist might, without entering his own broadly historical frame of reference, which is something those who received their training during the heyday of ahistorical conceptual analysis have been most reluctant to do.

Such reluctance may be understandable, but it can hardly be cited as a legitimate excuse for ignoring the possibilities raised by MacIntyre —that our own moral discourse may be largely incoherent, that it necessarily remains unintelligible as a social practice unless placed in a narrative of decline and fall. Philosophers sometimes dismiss MacIntyre's writings in this area as inconclusive or even careless. They talk as if he were simply moving around clumsily within the framework of analytic moral philosophy, displaying a disturbing tendency to bump into stationary objects. Rather, he is trying to assault that framework— admittedly, with contestable historical possibilities and comparisons. His satirical use of Polynesian parallels is just the opening attack, designed to take moral philosophy onto essentially contestable ground where historical learning and breadth of vision will come into play. The best thing to be said on behalf of a given analysis of a moral concept is that it explains the strengths and weaknesses of its predecessors and competitors more adequately than they can themselves. But to explain the strengths and weaknesses of MacIntyre's account of *ought* is necessarily to offer a historical narrative that competes with his story of conceptual survivals. For this reason, he has probably done more than anyone else to place historical and comparative questions on the agenda of analytic moral philosophy and to discourage naive assumptions about the uniformity of its subject matter.

How does MacIntyre purport to explain the strengths and weaknesses of competing analyses of *ought*? One of his characteristic strategies is to turn all other analyses against one another. Moral philosophers rarely have much trouble refuting one another. They have more trouble accounting for one another's strengths, and that is why the refutations do not silence the opposition. From MacIntyre's historical perspective, however, each analysis can be viewed not only as a failure to capture a supposedly unchanging conceptual truth but also as a potentially rich source of insight into the use of moral language under specific historical circumstances. Viewed in this way, the history of moral philosophy's quest for timeless analyses of moral concepts ironically reveals vast new evidence of conceptual change in morality itself. And by situating each moral philosophy in this history of conceptual and social change, the initial plausibility of the various analyses of moral concepts should become clear without weakening our case against them as purportedly universal claims about the conceptual framework of morality.

If, for example, our emphatic use of *ought* is a survival from an earlier form of discourse in which one's reasons for doing what one ought to do could be stated clearly in terms that transcend expressions of personal preference, that should help us see why each of the leading twentieth-century analyses of *ought* has been able to win a following, despite counterexamples raised against it. *Ought* sentences do indeed seem to express more than personal preferences in our discourse, just as the intuitionists insisted, and it is hard to imagine why moral discourse would be needed if it did not actually succeed in expressing something more, except perhaps for the purpose of perpetrating a hoax on the naive. But it is equally hard to avoid granting that, as a matter of historical fact, people now often use moral language to express their own personal preferences and nothing more. That is what makes emotivism (and the various grand attempts to unmask morality) seem plausible, at least in reference to how moral language is used in our period.

All of this becomes perfectly intelligible, according to MacIntyre, if and only if we view both intuitionism and emotivism, together with the linguistic phenomena that make each of these positions seem initially plausible, as products of moral and conceptual fragmentation. In an earlier form of discourse, *ought* signified the presence of statable reasons that transcended personal preference. Because these reasons were statable and widely accepted, the debate between intuitionism and emotivism could not yet have begun. When such reasons ceased to be available, the term *ought* retained its aura of authority but not any genuine claim to authority. Intuitionism, lacking any historical perspective on its situation, tried unsuccessfully to vindicate the aura, while emotivism, also with its nose to the ground, tried to explain the aura away. Neither was in position to treat the aura as the lingering ghost of a formerly real authority that had passed away.

What MacIntyre seemed to need, in order to confirm this line of speculation, was a historical account sufficiently persuasive at the level of detail to dispel the initial implausibility of its major thesis, that "we are in a condition which almost nobody recognizes and which perhaps nobody at all can recognize fully" but which nonetheless consists in the unrepaired fragmentation of an earlier moral scheme—a virtually invisible catastrophe (*After Virtue*, p. 4). In his *Short History of Ethics* and other writings spanning the period between 1959 and the early 1970s, MacIntyre undertook to supply such an account. We who speak the language of Prichard's *ought*, he concluded, live among the ruins of traditional morality, or rather, among the relics of various moralities developed at one point or another by one group or another in our past.

I quote now from the concluding pages of the *Short History of Ethics* (p. 266):

It follows that we are liable to find two kinds of people in our society: those who speak from within one of these surviving moralities, and those who stand outside all of them. Between the adherents of rival moralities and between the adherents of one morality and the adherents of none there exists no court of appeal, no impersonal neutral standard. For those who speak from within a given morality, the connection between fact and valuation is established in virtue of the meanings of the words they use. To those who speak from without, those who speak from within appear merely to be uttering imperatives which express their own liking and their private choices.

The debate over Prichard's *ought* therefore "expresses the fundamental moral situation of our own society," and because there is "no impersonal neutral standard" to appeal to when addressing that society on matters of moral importance, we inevitably speak in ways that make emotivism seem true. We are at best expressing or reporting how we feel and trying to cause others to feel likewise. Moral reasoning gives way to emotive manipulation and ejaculation.

III

What, then, are we to do? Each of us, MacIntyre wrote, must "choose both with whom we wish to be morally bound and by what ends, rules, and virtues we wish to be guided" (*Short History*, p. 268). But on what grounds? If the situation is as MacIntyre described it, is not any choice bound to be indefensible and self-defeating? From what vantage point in the situation described by the author is he himself speaking? What conceivable authority can attach to his own words? Does not his narrative of descent render both purposeful action and the hope that might sustain it impossible, issuing finally in incoherence?

In the preface to *After Virtue*, MacIntyre looks back on his earlier work with just such questions in mind:

at the same time as I was affirming the variety and heterogeneity of moral beliefs, practices and concepts, it became clear that I was committing myself to evaluations of different particular beliefs, practices and concepts. I gave, or tried to give, for example, accounts of the rise and decline of different moralities; and it was as clear to others as it ought to have been clear to me that my historical and sociological accounts were, and could not but be, informed by a distinctive evaluative standpoint. More particularly I seemed to be asserting that the nature of moral community and moral judgment in distinctively modern societies was such that it was no longer possible to appeal to moral criteria in a way that has been possible in other times and places—and that this was a moral calamity! But to *what* could I be appealing, if my own analysis was correct? (p. ix, italics in original)

MacIntyre had produced, in effect, a typically modernist authorship in his earlier work—although not, of course, an example of the optimistic modernism we find in Kantianism or utilitarianism. A historical deconstruction of ahistorical thought concludes by leaving its own point of view unsituated in the history it describes, thus raising doubts about its own right to speak. This result I shall call the paradox of point of view. A less interesting writer might have let the matter stand there, content to wallow in the paradox and despair we have all learned to expect from a certain kind of intellectual in our period, but MacIntyre set himself the task of recasting his narrative so as to make this paradox evitable. I read *After Virtue* as an attempt to do just that—without sacrificing, however, either the downward trajectory or the explanatory power of the original narrative.

Literary critics since Henry James have spoken of the problem of point of view in fiction—the problem of establishing a coherent and compelling relation among the author, the voice of the narrator, and the story.[13] MacIntyre's difficulty shows that historical writing encounters its own versions of this problem, although without the full range of options that writers of fiction have at their disposal for resolving it. Authors of realistic historical narrative are not free to tell their stories in other people's voices. If a narrative includes a rendering of the author's own situation, the point of view from which the story is told must itself be recognizable in the narrative as part of that situation. The information the author conveys and the standards the story invokes must be plausibly accessible to a historical agent thus situated. (The narrative cannot take omniscience as its point of view.) As an author, one can neither describe nor judge one's own situation from a distance without establishing a position at the margins of, but still belonging to, that situation. There is no rising above situation in its entirety. Any total condemnation of one's own age necessarily issues in incoherence.

A *Short History of Ethics* narrates the career of morality from Homer's Greece to Prichard's Britain. Morality itself is the protagonist. The tale is one of disintegration. The point of view of the narrative is that of the protagonist, recollecting the story as it is told and gradually achieving ironic distance from an original self-image of unchanging uniformity. Yet if the protagonist suffers disintegration, how can the story be told in that voice without falling apart? The narrative lacks a point of view from which the fragmentation might be judged and found wanting—a vantage point from which it would make sense even to speak of *fragmentation* as opposed to *richness* or *diversity*. Author and reader alike are left suspended in midair—disillusioned, perhaps, but unable to judge or to act. MacIntyre seems to have been looking down on his age from above, while also telling us that this cannot be done.

In *After Virtue* MacIntyre seeks to resolve the problem of point of view by finding a new leading character with which the narrator's voice can be identified. The protagonist of the new narrative is not morality *per se* but rather the tradition of the virtues. The narrator now speaks for this tradition and takes full responsibility for its point of view. This point of view belongs to the situation it describes, however marginally. Indeed its marginal status helps explain both the initial implausibility of its message and its capacity for achieving critical distance from the age to which it belongs.

In the new story, the protagonist suffers misfortune. It is rejected by modern culture, which suffers moral disintegration as a result. Its fate is to live, insofar as it is able, at the margins of a fragmented world in which the aesthete, the manipulative manager, and the therapist are central characters. But the protagonist must admit a causal relation between its fate and its faults or deficiencies—its excessive metaphysical commitments, its insufficiently developed sense of tragic conflict, and so on. Yet the protagonist, the tradition of the virtues for which Aristotle remains the foremost spokesperson, does not itself disintegrate—at least not completely. It lives to recognize its fate, correct its faults, and face the future with a renewed sense of value and hope. Its situation, however, is essentially a fragmented one, and this fact sets severe limits on what ends can be reasonably pursued, at least for the time being.

It is evident how MacIntyre's imaginative handling of the problem of point of view in *After Virtue* is meant to resolve the paradox posed by his earlier work. But even if MacIntyre's position no longer self-destructs, we still need to ask whether his story of decline and fall is the one we ought to accept. How to decide? Let a theory, in science or in ethics, be as systematic as you please. To be vindicated or justified, MacIntyre says, the theory will have to explain the history of theory-succession on the topic in question by accounting for the strengths and weaknesses of its predecessors and competitors. It follows that a theory must be judged not least in light of the historical narratives it makes possible. A successful theory, then, enables

> us to understand precisely why its predecessors have to be rejected or modified and also why, without and before its illumination, past theory could have remained credible. It introduces new standards for evaluating the past. It recasts the narrative which constitutes the continuous reconstruction of the . . . tradition.
>
> It is because and only because we can construct better and worse histories of this kind, histories which can be rationally compared with each other, that we can compare theories rationally too.[14]

When MacIntyre speaks of these histories as dramatic narratives, he means in part to draw attention to the necessity of "an evaluative framework in which good or bad character helps to produce unfortunate or happy outcomes."[15] Self-conscious commitment to such an evaluative framework was what he had found lacking in his early attempt to narrate the history of ethics. His inquiry into the epistemological significance of dramatic narrative may be viewed as an attempt to correct the deficiency. He now maintains explicitly that both character and outcomes must be judged, for only if they are depicted in the evaluative framework of the narrative as good or bad, unfortunate or happy, can the narrative fulfill its purpose—in the case of scientific or ethical theory, that of explaining what made earlier theories plausible (under the conditions in which they were originally proposed) but (when viewed from a more adequate perspective) deficient in some significant respect.

In short, the narrative must be dramatic. Like Brian Palmer's life story, it must depict the interaction of character and circumstance from a point of view that is not morally neutral. It must render this interaction in a plot whose dramatic form (comic, tragic, or whatever) already involves an evaluative judgment. Because the evaluative judgment implies a history of a certain dramatic form, our inability to render the relevant historical sequence convincingly in the form implied by a given evaluative judgment constitutes a disconfirmation of the judgment—insofar as the inability cannot be overcome, a decisive disconfirmation.

It should be obvious that *After Virtue* is precisely the kind of book that someone underscoring the epistemological significance of dramatic narrative should want to write. The book is itself a dramatic narrative designed to explain the strengths and weaknesses of its predecessors and competitors in ethical theory, written in the hope of superceding them. If we are to judge MacIntyre on his own terms, we must ask how well his dramatic narrative performs this task.

I am happy to grant, indeed to affirm, that MacIntyre's narrative is to be preferred to the self-congratulatory stories the Enlightenment told about itself—the Kantian's essentially uniform story of modest progress toward perfect rationality, for example, or the standard utilitarian story of triumph over traditional superstition. As we saw in Part 2, contemporary reformulations of these stories tend either to gloss over evidence of moral diversity and conceptual change or to make our ancestors and distant cultures look unduly irrational. MacIntyre, in contrast, is able to take evidence of moral diversity and conceptual change seriously. He endeavors to portray the leading figures of the Enlightenment as reasonable people who had every good reason to seek an ahistorical foundation for morality but who, for reasons not readily accessible to them, were bound to fail. To place their project in its context is to treat them charitably—not, of course, in the narrow sense of maximizing the overlap between their beliefs and ours but rather in the broader sense of making them out to be reasonable yet finite human beings. MacIntyre is hardly the first to declare the Enlightenment project a failure, but he takes pains to show how reasonable human agents, under such circumstances, could have found that project a plausible response to the problems at hand.[16] They were right, for instance, in finding faults with received Aristotelian tradition, and MacIntyre feels compelled to correct those faults, in his own selective retrieval and reconfiguration of traditional concepts and arguments, before he can lay claim to that tradition as a living legacy.

Grant, then, that MacIntyre's verdict on the Enlightenment's foundationalist project is correct. Grant, as well, that his explanation of the Enlightenment's failure to secure an ahistorical foundation for morality is neither unduly reductive nor uncharitable. We still need to know whether other explanations, coupled with somewhat more subtle retellings of our moral history, are finally to be judged preferable. In the following chapter, I shall consider possible alternatives to MacIntyre's moral history, alternatives that do not trade on the Enlightenment's epistemological ambitions. In the remainder of this chapter, I shall consider a more limited question. Does MacIntyre offer persuasive evidence for his claim that our moral discourse has suffered virtually complete breakdown? If he does not, then a narrative of decline and fall may not be necessary to explain our fate after all.

IV

MacIntyre begins his defense of the catastrophe hypothesis by inviting us to notice, "The most striking feature of contemporary moral utterance is that so much of it is used to express disagreements" (p. 6). No doubt, moral language in our period is often used to express disagreements. Why, however, should this seem striking or surprising? We do not debate whether it is just to torture people for fun. The matter is hardly trivial, but it is not something we disagree over or entertain serious doubts about, and we therefore have little reason to mention it unless it can be made relevant to the resolution of some disagreement. Public discourse, at least under conditions of relative freedom, tends to concentrate on controversial matters, the better to resolve them, leaving platitudes to one side. It would be more striking, and perhaps even disturbing, if this ceased to be so and moral language came to be used in public settings largely for the ceremonial expression of widespread moral agreement.

Moral platitudes do play a role in our use of moral language outside of public ceremonial expressions of consensus, but one must look in the right places to find them. As I have suggested in previous chapters, one such place is the nursery, where we begin to initiate our children into the moral consensus we share, such as it is. MacIntyre's attention is fixed, however, on those points at which we most obviously lack consensus, and he cites our public debates over warfare, abortion, and the tensions between equality and freedom. He finds, moreover, that "the most striking feature" of these debates is "their interminable character." "There seems," he says, "to be no rational way of securing moral agreement in our culture" (p. 6).

The reason we have so much trouble securing moral agreement on such issues, MacIntyre suggests, is that the various premises from which people argue are conceptually incommensurable. The premises from which argument proceeds employ concepts originally at home in quite different moral languages. We know how to construct valid arguments using one set of premises or another, but we don't know how to appraise the significance of the concepts used in any given argument without begging the question. "From our rival conclusions we can argue back to our rival premises; but when we do arrive at our premises argument ceases and the invocation of one premise against another becomes a matter of pure assertion and counter-assertion" (p. 8). As a result, our public discourse becomes "an unharmonious melange of ill-assorted fragments" (p. 10). We speak as if we were appealing to impersonal criteria, but we each in fact typically fail to do more than express our unreasoned decision to adopt some set of premises as a starting point. Nor have the philosophers fared any better. They too have failed "to provide a shared, public rational justification for morality" (p. 50).

MacIntyre does not conclude from this failure that in principle there can be no such thing as moral knowledge. He holds, to the contrary, that in earlier stages of our history, stages in which there was widespread agreement on "man-as-he-could-be-if-he-realized-his-*telos*" (p. 54), people were capable of engaging in rational public discourse on conduct, character, and community. It is only by recovering something like an Aristotelian teleological framework and tailoring our inherited moral languages to fit, he thinks, that we shall be able to render moral discourse rational again. Hence MacIntyre's program of *bricolage*.

Any such recovery is not, however, a merely philosophical undertaking. It cannot succeed, according to MacIntyre, without being embodied in the habits, dispositions, shared assumptions, and goals of a living community dedicated to the common good. Since our society is not such a community and is not likely to become one in our lifetimes, the only hope for moral rationality is the "construction of local forms of community within which civility and the intellectual and moral life can be sustained" (p. 263). The most salient characteristic of our society, on this view, is that it is not unified by a *telos*, an end or system of ends widely believed to be worth striving for together, the common good. Liberal institutions attempt to manage collective life in the absence of agreement on the good. In such institutions, politics cannot help being "civil war carried on by other means" (p. 253).

I am prepared to agree that complete absence of agreement on the good would render rational moral discourse impossible. I am also prepared to grant that our agreement on the good falls well short of perfect harmony. Furthermore, liberal institutions are plausibly viewed as an attempt to manage collective life in the absence of perfect agreement on "man-as-he-would-be-if-he-realized-his-*telos*." But MacIntyre does not exclude, it seems to me, the possibility that moral discourse in our society can itself be understood as held together by a relatively limited but nonetheless real and significant agreement on the good.

We are not united in consensus around a particular theory of human nature or man's ultimate *telos*, and so our disagreements about certain moral issues have proved especially difficult to resolve, but our disagreement about what human beings are like and what is good for us does not go all the way down. In fact, it is hard to see how it could. As I argue in Part 1, if you push disagreement about some matters down too far, it tends to disappear by becoming merely verbal. Complete disagreement about something leaves us unable to identify a common matter to disagree over. It therefore makes sense to speak of disagreement, in morals as much as elsewhere, only if we are prepared to recognize a background of agreement. It would be a mistake, then, to think that our disagreement on the good is total or that the areas of apparently intractable moral disagreement to which MacIntyre calls attention could be the whole story.[17]

This line of reasoning suggests a picture of our society both more complicated and less dismal than MacIntyre's. Even though we no longer share a single theory of human nature (when did we exactly?) and despite the fact that Aristotelian teleology has long since passed out of philosophical fashion, most of us do agree on the essentials of what might be called the provisional *telos* of our society. What made the creation of liberal institutions necessary, in large part, was the manifest failure of religious groups of various sorts to establish rational agreement on their competing detailed visions of the good. It was partly because people recognized putting an end to religious warfare and intolerance as morally good—as rationally preferable to continued attempts at imposing a more nearly complete vision of the good by force—that liberal institutions have been able to get a foothold here and there around the globe.

In other words, certain features of our society can be seen as justified by a self-limiting consensus on the good—an agreement consisting partly in the realization that it would be a bad thing, that it would make life worse for us all, to press too hard or too far for agreement on all details in a given vision of the good. We can define our shared conception of the good as the set of all platitudinous judgments employing such terms as *good, better than,* and the like. We can define a platitude, echoing David Lewis, as a judgment that only the philosophers (and the morally incompetent or utterly vicious) among us would think of denying. The set of all such platitudes would include far too many to mention.

Admittedly, it does not extend far enough to eliminate disagreement on many matters of importance. Where we do disagree on such matters, that is where we should expect the complexity of our conceptual heritage to show itself, both as a resource and as a problem. And, clearly, not everyone who participates in the consensus would offer the same sorts of reasons for the particular judgments we in fact share.[18] But that does not make the consensus ineffective or insignificant. Furthermore, while there are times when, in response to Socratic questioning or an especially knotty dilemma, we're unsure how to carry on with our reason-giving, there are vast regions of moral terrain in which we carry on perfectly well. Such was the main point of my argument in Chapter 1. It applies here as well.

If something like this alternative picture could be sustained, we should be less tempted to see moral discourse in our culture as simply incapable of supporting rational argumentation. Our failure to provide philosophical foundations for the premises we use in arguing long-disputed points will be less likely to elicit far-reaching doubts.[19] If we rarely give compelling reasons for our preferences when we weigh conflicting considerations in a specific controversial case, that is because controversial cases are the ones where conflicting considerations frustrate the search for clear answers. We could resolve all or most such cases only if a more nearly complete conception of the good were already in place—that is, only if we already agreed on more judgments at the level of detail than we do. Strict consensus on the good would, in some respects, be very good to have. Overlapping consensus, however, remains substantial enough to do a lot of ordinary justificatory work that MacIntyre tends not to mention—the sort of work we tend to undervalue precisely because it provides a background against which our disagreements occur.[20]

No form of discourse, in order to be deemed fully respectable, need exhibit either philosophical foundations or means for resolving our most intractable disputes. Any criterion of respectability that implies otherwise deserves rejection. The irony is that MacIntyre, like Bellah and his coauthors, seems implicitly to adopt a criterion of respectability suspiciously similar to the one his foundationalist opponents share with skeptics and nihilists. He seems bound to find our moral discourse wanting, just as Bellah finds Brian Palmer's answers to Swidler's questions wanting, for the simple reason that his criterion can be satisfied only under exceptional circumstances, if at all.

Only very rarely, if ever, are human societies of any size and complexity united in perfect agreement on the common good. Ours certainly is not. But it is still possible for us to recognize the unfortunate effects of religious warfare, invent ways of talking and living with one another that make such effects less likely, and tell stories to justify those ways to one another, just as it is still possible for us to carry on with our moal reasoning in many other ways, relying throughout on agreements we do have. What might these agreements be? We all agree that nuclear destruction would be bad, that Charles Manson shouldn't be held up as a model to the young, and that torturing innocents for the fun of it would be abhorent. Most of us agree that extending legal protection to peaceful fellow citizens who disagree with us religiously is better than starting the religious wars up again. These are very important things to agree on, as would quickly become evident if we stopped agreeing on them. Then we would indeed find ourselves in the dark ages. But we do agree on these things. Anyone who didn't would be recognized in the community at large as morally incompetent.

If the Davidsonian considerations introduced in Chapter 1 are correct, the judgments I have just mentioned barely scratch the suface of a vast body of platitudes. We have no choice but to treat them as justified, as ways in which we construe ourselves and our world, at least until we come up with something clearly better. Without some such platitudes in place, we could not even make sense of the doubts we have about this or that detail. Global doubt, as MacIntyre says in another context, "is an invitation not to philosophy, but to mental breakdown, or rather to philosophy as a means of mental breakdown."[21]

How much disagreement must we be able to resolve, how far must our language resemble that of a coherent systematic moral philosophy, for us to be enaged in rational discourse? Few people, if any, whatever the time and place, could go on supplying reasons for their premises in a moral dispute without running dry before long. That includes philosophers. It also includes ancient Greeks and medieval Christians. Are our contemporaries less articulate and more prone to protracted disagreement than other people have been? That depends, I suppose, on which of our contemporaries we select and to whom in ancient or medieval society we choose to compare them. To be fair, we will have to take comparable samples from each. The comparision will then confront us, as *After Virtue* does not confront us, with the exclusivity of ancient and medieval elites, as well as the means they employed to establish agreement.

Even fair samples, however, will leave us with another problem. How, exactly, should we measure a given population's relative powers of articulation or the depth of their disagreements? Here we must take care, lest our philosophical preconceptions set the standard of rational discourse unreasonably high, thereby putting our contemporaries in a bad light whenever they don't measure up to Aristotle. By the same token, we will be tempted to write off our discourse as essentially groundless or arbitrary in the absence of nearly perfect means for resolving disputes. Some disagreements linger. This should hardly be surprising, especially when large numbers of people influenced by widely disparate traditions are crowded together in the same areas or linked together across vast distances by modern media of communication. Precisely how deep do our disagreements go, as compared to those of other societies? *After Virtue* does not tell us what sort of evidence to use in answering this question or how to assess that evidence. It relies, at this crucial point, on little more than a "disquieting suggestion."

Human societies have always shown great diversity in moral belief, language, and practice. Whatever the extent of present-day diversity, however, modern conditions confront us with it close up every day. We must either devise means for living with this fact of modern life or be at each other's throats. We don't always know what to say next to each other, how to keep the argument going in the face of someone else's bewildered stare or persistent objections. At times, there seems no alternative to coercion. All this seems clear. But I worry that MacIntyre, although no skeptic himself, mirrors the skeptic's hasty passage from examples of protracted disagreement to an excessively bleak prognosis concerning the possibility of rational moral discourse. I suspect that, in reaching his conclusions, he both underestimates the level of agreement on the good actually exhibited by our society and overestimates the level required for us to reason coherently with each other on most matters of common concern.

MacIntyre could respond to this line of criticism, of course, by granting that our moral disagreements don't go all the way down and that our moral discourse does get along tolerably well in certain limited areas, thanks to the accidents of overlapping consensus. He might then add, however, that we nonetheless lack agreement of the kind needed to support rational moral discourse outside those limited areas. Having enough agreement to identify a common subject matter—such as the question whether abortions are morally permissible—might still leave us without the means to resolve debate on that matter rationally. Davidsonian reassurances about the limits of disagreement don't address the real problem. At most, they undermine greatly exaggerated descriptions of our predicament.

True enough, but the point of introducing Davidsonian reassurances is that the opening chapters of *After Virtue*, like most versions of moral skepticism and nihilism, do rely on greatly exaggerated descriptions of our predicament. Even if we take those chapters as hyperbole, designed to pull us back from excessive confidence in "contemporary moral utterance," we shall eventually require a less hyperbolic mode of description. And it will be hard to supply that, as long as levels of agreement and conceptual incommensurability remain the central issue, unless we at least soften the distinction between our predicament and that of our premodern ancestors. That, however, would threaten the dramatic structure of MacIntyre's narrative.

In a recent essay, "Relativism, Power, and Philosophy," MacIntyre contrasts two types of moral languages.[22] The first type—think of the imaginary Corleone dialect presented in Chapter 3—is such that

to share in its use is to presuppose one cosmology rather than another, one relationship of local law and custom to cosmic order rather than another, one justification of particular relationships of individual to community and of both to land and to landscape rather than another. In such a language even the use of proper names may on occasion have such presuppositions. (p.405)

The users of such a language will typically be able to refer and allude to a shared canon of texts that presents agreed-upon exemplars of moral reasoning and models of the process of criticism and revision. Such an ability, MacIntyre claims, is the *sine qua non* of rational moral discourse. It is what allows users of the first type of moral language to identify areas of disagreement without losing their capacity to discriminate, in accordance with publicly recognized criteria, between justified and unjustified moral beliefs or good and bad moral arguments.

The second type of language—namely, ours—is one whose use is "free from such commitments" (p. 405). Its use surely involves some presuppositions, but not presuppositions of this kind. Thus, as I have stressed at various points throughout this book, we do not, in our public discourse, presuppose the existence of a specific sort of God, related to us and our land in a certain fashion. Nor do we share a single, essentially unitary canon of texts, exemplars, and models to serve as a rational constraint on what can count, for us, as justified or true in ethics. MacIntyre thinks we are therefore unable, despite whatever agreements we may have about the whiteness of snow or the evil of pointless cruelty, to engage in rational moral disputation on the issues that really divide us. Our moral language allows us to identify and describe our disagreements. But, says MacIntyre, "the culture that is able to make such a language available is so only because it is a culture offering, for the relevant kinds of controversial subject matter, all too many heterogeneous and incompatible schemes of rational justification" (p. 405).

This account of our predicament is, I think, better than the one offered in *After Virtue*. It allows us, for example, to acknowledge the force of Davidsonian reassurances concerning vast regions of agreement. Once again, however, there is room to doubt that MacIntyre has made his case. His contrast between two types of moral language may be too sharp to do justice either to the diversity of certain premodern cultures, where established canons were often actively contested over time, or to the resources offered by our own culture for resolving moral disputes. Moreover, he has not shown that rational moral discourse requires an established canon. Nor has he clarified just how unified a cultural inheritance would have to be to qualify as a canon. Don't we in fact muddle through much of the time, quite reasonably, by appealing to areas of agreement with fellow citizens, by practicing immanent criticism on our opponents or on ourselves, by coming to terms with unfamiliar vocabularies in conversation, by using our creative powers, by confronting the moral imagination with instances of injustice and suffering, and by, in countless other ways, exploiting a culture too rich and complicated to be confined to a canon?

Even MacIntyre's revised account, then, does not ring entirely true. Perhaps his remarks about dialogue across the boundaries of communities using distinct moral languages will help us see where the problem lies. Consider a comment he makes about two communities whose languages would belong to the first type defined a moment ago: "It is not that the beliefs of each such community cannot be represented in any way at all in the language of the other; it is rather that the outcome in each case of rendering those beliefs sufficiently intelligible to be evaluated by a member of the other community involves characterizing those beliefs in such a way that they are bound to be rejected" (p. 390). *Bound* to be rejected? Here MacIntyre takes insufficient heed of what I have called a language's capacity for hermeneutical enrichment. He is treating the two languages as static systems, not (despite his protestations to the contrary) as "natural-languages-in-use," and this leads him to underestimate the capacity of members of premodern cultures to change their minds, for good reasons, in dialogue with strangers.

What has this to do with us? If MacIntyre is right, the conceptual incommensurability of the various fragments of our own moral language places us constantly in a position analogous to premodern dialogue crossing the boundaries of communal agreement. Because we possess a relatively presuppositionless language in which we can describe disagreements with considerable ease and precision, we have an advantage often lacked by premodern dialogue with strangers from abroad. But because our language achieves this advantage by ridding itself of a level of presuppositions that would make rational discourse possible, we too are bound to reject the conclusions of fellow citizens whose preferred language of deliberation and criteria of justification differ from our own. For us, even most neighbors will be strangers. Since we cannot appeal to an established canon, MacIntyre assumes that we are *bound* to fail in our attempts at rational moral discourse.

If, however, MacIntyre has underestimated the premodern language-user's capacity to enrich a language hermeneutically or to embrace new moral possibilities for good reason, perhaps he has underestimated ours as well—and for much the same reason. He may be thinking of the various fragments of our moral language as static systems that could only make sense in their original settings. He seems not to consider the possibility that the coherent moral languages of earlier generations were themselves products of eclectic *bricolage*, on the one hand, and conceptual adaptation to new circumstances, on the other. New Testament Greek brought several moral languages together, transforming the significance of each. Thomistic Latin was made entirely of borrowed parts, designed to insert Aristotle into a canon intent on excluding him. These examples suggest that our predicament may not be as distinctive or as bleak as MacIntyre thinks. If premodern language-users have been able to converse across cultural boundaries, change their minds in dialogue with strangers, and invent new moral languages out of apparently incompatible fragments, perhaps we can too.

Moral languages, our own included, are not static systems. We need a kinematics to understand their changing presuppositions, an evolutionary history to understand how old concepts, originally at home in one environment, might find their niche in a new one, combining with others in unanticipated ways to form a viable linguistic ecosystem. For all that, MacIntyre could be on to something. I have not demonstrated that our linguistic ecosystem is viable. Even if we do have sufficient agreement and conceptual wherewithal to support rational moral discourse, we could still be too vicious and our institutions too corrupted to live well. My point is not that everything is fine, that we should just carry on, confident that because disagreement never goes all the way down, we needn't worry about becoming barbarians. But neither do I think that the evidence surveyed in this chapter gives us reason to conclude that the new dark ages are upon us, that any adequate account of our history will necessarily trace a downward spiral toward ruin, or that our only hope is to gather in small cells with the truly virtuous until a new age dawns.

What alternatives do we have? One alternative, to which I shall return, is that other arguments and themes from MacIntyre and Bellah will provide a better view of our predicament than we have been able to achieve so far. MacIntyre, however, thinks our options are severely limited. He says that once we join with Nietzsche in seeing through the Enlightenment's philosophical pretensions, we can only choose between an amoralist's glorification of the arbitrary will and something like *After Virtue*'s narrative of decline and fall. Let us now see whether he is right.

10

LIBERAL APOLOGETICS AND
TERMINAL WISTFULNESS

MacIntyre sees our society as an expression of Enlightenment philosophical ideas gone wrong. If he is right, and the Enlightenment project was bound to fail, then our way of life was bound to fail too, and we should not be surprised to find it in ruin. On MacIntyre's view, our society is as radically individualistic and unconcerned with the common good as liberal philosophers have always wanted it to be, and this is the clue to its moral downfall. It embodies emotivism to perfection.

I remain unconvinced. To explain why, I must explore alternatives to MacIntyre's position. But in the end I shall not simply side with either MacIntyre or his opponents. I want rather to move altogether beyond the debate between those called communitarians and liberals.

I

Why, exactly, was the Enlightenment project bound to fail? The received moral tradition, according to MacIntyre, involved three elements: a conception of human nature as it is, a notion of what we would be like if we realized our proper end or essence, and a set of virtues and rules that enable us to make progress from one state to the other. "But the joint effect of the secular rejection of both Protestant and Catholic theology and the scientific rejection of Aristotelianism was to eliminate any notion of man-as-he-would-be-if-he-realised-his-telos" (*After Virtue*, p. 54). So the Enlightenment was trying to ground a set of precepts whose very point had been lost. The attempt to use untutored human nature as a foundation for inherited moral injunctions could hardly succeed, for these two elements of the old scheme "had been expressly designed to be discrepant with each other" (p. 55). Nor would it prove any easier to divorce the injunctions from our sensuous nature altogether while seeking a foundation for them in pure practical reason.

Even if something like this explanation is correct, it is by no means clear, from what MacIntyre says here, why we shouldn't try to revive specifically theological elements of the inherited moral tradition. If our emphatic use of *ought* is a conceptual survival, a residue of an earlier theological morality in which one was obliged to do what one ought by the commands of God, why not turn this fact into a sort of moral argument for theism? MacIntyre, following G. E. M. Anscombe,[1] would have us drop the so-called emphatic *ought*, at least for the purposes of secular moral philosophy, precisely to avoid what he takes to be its necessary theological presuppositions. All *ought* sentences that remain are to be construed functionally or conditionally. But other philosophers less interested in preserving a strictly secular moral philosophy, such as Robert Merrihew Adams, would argue that we should simply accept the theological presuppositions of the emphatic *ought* we have.[2]

In fact, Basil Mitchell has used similar arguments while constructing something much like MacIntyre's story of conceptual survival. The moral of his story, however, is that we should revive the theological presuppositions of the "traditional conscience" still visible in otherwise secular authors like Iris Murdoch and Stuart Hampshire. Mitchell's book,[3] given as the Gifford Lectures of 1974–75, opens with a chapter entitled, "Our Contemporary Moral Confusion." There Mitchell invites us to reflect, in a manner similar to *After Virtue*'s second chapter, on familiar examples of moral disagreement. The respective parties, writes Mitchell on p. 3 of his book, "are divided not only in their opinions but in their vocabulary. They inhabit different worlds of discourse, and are perpetually arguing at cross purposes—when, that is, they bother to argue at all." Mitchell then surveys the leading types of modern ethical theory, tracing their roots and diagnosing their difficulties. Finally, he presents his case for the theological vindication of the "traditional conscience," adding, "Of course there is another alternative altogether open to modern man. He may abandon the traditional conscience and rejoice with Nietzsche in his consequent liberation" (p. 120).

For MacIntyre, our choice is either Nietzsche or Aristotle; for Mitchell, Nietzsche or some form of traditional theism. I raise Mitchell's alternative not because I think we can or should resuscitate our public moral discourse by his means. Nor am I simply calling attention to the irony produced by juxtaposing Mitchell's disjunction with MacIntyre's. The point is rather that MacIntyre's story suffers because it neglects the role that theological ideas and religious conflict played in bringing about the modern world.[4] A more adequate treatment of these themes would, I think, make evident the risks of reshaping public discourse according to the dictates of a set of theological ideas. It would be one thing if we had already resolved our religious differences and settled rationally on a common public theology. But even if we agree with Mitchell that some theology or other would lend coherence to our discourse, this doesn't tell us which theology to adopt. And anyone who is dubious about our making much progress on that question in the foreseeable future may be inclined to conclude that the social and political arrangements MacIntyre so vehemently abhors have something going for them after all.

MacIntyre's reviewers have raised many interesting objections to the details of his narrative.[5] I am suggesting the need for a relatively sweeping revision. Suppose we render the polemics and warfare of the Reformation and Counter-Reformation as a contest between two (or more) fully articulated conceptions of the good, fleshed out in competing schemes of the virtues. Might it be that theology got into trouble with the intellectuals largely because it was unable to provide a vocabulary for debating and deciding matters pertaining to the common good without resort to violence? Could it be that the distinctive vocabularies of modern politics and ethics—the languages of human rights, of Benthamite utility, of respect for persons, and so on—owe their existence in part to a complicated history of attempts to minimize the unhappy consequences of religious conflict? If so, if my sketchy speculations about the emergence of a secularized form of public discourse can be developed and withstand scrutiny, then several implications ensue.

To begin with, as I argued in Part 2, we cannot disconnect the history of Western ethics from the history of religions without risk of radical distortion. Furthermore, until theism proves able to gather a reasonably broad rational consensus around a specific conception of the good, an eventuality that now seems remote, we probably should not follow advice like Mitchell's. The risks of reviving religious conflict like that of early modern Europe are too great. It would indeed be fortunate for all of us, including atheistic fellow travelers, if people like Robert Bellah got their wish and a form of biblical tradition essentially continuous with republican virtues began to flourish and enrich public life. But since the murder of Martin Luther King, Jr., religious traditions of other sorts seem to be the ones making inroads. Much contemporary evidence—from Belfast to Beirut, from Teheran to Lynchburg, Virginia—gives ample reason for concern.

From MacIntyre's point of view, of course, this could be taken as support for his own metaphysically austere, "sociological" teleology against its explicitly theological competitors. Note well, however, that MacIntyre's attempt to disconnect an Aristotelian conception of the virtues and the good from Aristotle's "metaphysical biology" does not by itself yield a specific conception of the good. It does place meaningful constraints on what a fully acceptable conception of the good must involve, constraints that determine a minimal interpretation of the virtues required for living well. But more specificity in a conception of the good can come, by his own reckoning, only from particular practices and traditions. Here the "tradition of the virtues" is too amorphous to help, and it would be useful to know where MacIntyre would have us turn for details and why.

Instead, he issues a frustratingly vague call for "the construction of local forms of community within which civility and the intellectual and moral life can be sustained through the new dark ages which are already upon us" (*After Virtue*, p. 263). He fails, in the end, to clarify either his indictment of our society or the practical implications of his position. In fact, it is hard to know where he locates himself in social and political space, despite his attempt to identify himself with Aristotle's legacy. Is MacIntyre the Thomas Münzer of contemporary moral philosophy, intent on withdrawing into a sect until the time is ripe for virtue to triumph over vice? Or does he see some meaningful role for the relatively virtuous to play within a social and political world that leaves much to be desired?

There are passages in *After Virtue* to support each reading. At times MacIntyre seems to recognize significant residues of the tradition of the virtues in contemporary society, residues one might reasonably hope to draw upon and nuture while participating in that society, misgivings notwithstanding. This suggests a picture of our society quite unlike the one typically given in liberal theory, offering some ground for the hope that our society contains resources for its self-transformation. (I shall try to fill out this picture in more detail in Chapter 12.) More often, however, MacIntyre seems much more dualistic and sectarian, dedicating himself strictly to local forms of community, denouncing the new dark ages, and grounding his hope only in the thought that things have been this bad before.[6]

If the favored forms of community must be local, then broad rational agreement on a full-fledged conception of the good, religious or not, must now be beyond reach. Yet if this is true, is it not one-sided, even shrill, to denounce our society as the new dark ages? Suppose we say that modern politics is "civil war carried on by other means." This idea still seems to underestimate the extent and significance of our moral consensus, but it does tie in nicely with my account of modern moral and political discourse as the outcome of a kind of social contract for minimizing the undesirable effects of discord among competing conceptions of the good. Let us, however, be clear about one thing: even civil war carried on by other means is preferable to plain old civil war—the kind you get when one fully developed conception of the good, unable to achieve rational consensus, comes crashing down upon another, bringing about rather little good but much bloodshed, tyranny, and terror.

We can all dream of what life would be like in a world united in perfect rational consensus on the good, but this dream represents no accessible alternative to what we have now. What I find lacking in *After Virtue* is a sufficient recognition of what our society has going for it as a form of life. The most visible global alternatives to our society, the ones most likely to be instantiated if our provisional and self-limiting consensus on the good were to be scrapped, are obviously far worse. One risks a sort of vice by condemning our society too flatly and then leaving it to its own devices.

We need to free ourselves from seeing our past, especially our immediate past, through the eyes of Enlightenment philosophy, and until we do so we shall continue to oscillate between overestimating and underestimating the merits of the kind of society that Enlightenment philosophers sought to defend. MacIntyre belittles what our early-modern ancestors accomplished, in part, because he interprets their work largely in the philosophers' terms, as if liberal society were as individualist and as dependent on philosophical foundations as the philosophers thought. Might it be that the Enlightenment project was doomed to fail chiefly because foundationalism (in the relevant sense) is false as an account of epistemic justification?[7] Might not our society seem more defensible without the foundations?

Our society and its distinctive modes of public discourse are best viewed, I would argue, as the result of a manifest failure to achieve agreement on a fully detailed conception of the good—as the arrangements and conventions of people who contracted, in effect, to limit the damage of that failure by settling for a thinner conception of the good that more people could agree to, given the alternatives and until something better came along. The language of human rights and respect for persons can be seen as a conceptual outgrowth of institutions and compromises pragmatically justified under historical circumstances where a relatively thin conception of the good is the most that people can secure rational agreement on. I support MacIntyre's verdict on standard philosophical defenses of this language. I share his desire to rehabilitate talk about the virtues and the common good. But I am less suspicious than he is of the language of rights and respect itself. I am also less disposed to assume that talk about rights and respect cannot live in harmony with talk about virtues and the good.

Am I saying that human rights are mere "fictions" after all, just as MacIntyre charges? Not if that implies that our rights are any less real than our virtues and vices. My position has little to do with the ontology of moral properties. I grant that the language used to refer to human rights is a human invention, created only recently. It does not follow, however, that rights are unreal in any worrisome sense or that we are incapable of uttering truths when we use the language of rights invented by our ancestors. It is our ancestors' philosophical justifications I have trouble with, not their idea that we members of the constitutional democracies really do have rights like the right not to be enslaved or the right to religious freedom.

I hold that everybody possesses certain rights—including the right not to be enslaved. I take this to mean neither more nor less than that enslaving people does them an injustice. Slavery violates justice and did so even in societies that didn't realize it. There is good reason to think of the right not to be enslaved as a real property we all have. There is equally good reason to be thankful that our ancestors invented a language in which this truth could both be expressed and inscribed at the center of our moral consensus. I can say this because I am confident that the various beliefs which once seemed to justify slavery are false.

Some other rights, including the right to religious freedom, although real enough, obtain only under particular social-historical conditions. If it could be shown by modes of reasoning commonly recognized that belief in a specific sort of God were both justified and essential for realization of the common good, we ought not to go on showing liberal tolerance to religious dissenters. It is precisely because we fall so far short of rational agreement or objective certainty in religious matters that the right to religious freedom obtains in our society. Religious liberty is justified by conditions of discord and uncertainty that might not always obtain. Let us say that the right to religious freedom is real but relative, in the sense David Wong discusses under the heading, "environmental relativity."[8]

The various rights we recognize can be justified teleologically—that is, by reference to a widely shared conception of the good. But the *telos* that matters is one actually achievable under our social-historical circumstances by acceptable means, not the highest conceivable good derived from philosophical or theological reflection on the "function" or "ultimate purpose" of humanity.[9] And, as I argued in the previous chapter, such a *telos*, although it needs to be widely shared to perform its justificatory function, need not be embodied in a strict or complete consensus. An overlapping consensus will do. We need not agree on all matters of moral importance to agree on many, and where our judgments happen to coincide, we need not reach them for the same reasons. The judgments we share about the achievable good are ample enough to justfiy our practice of ascribing rights. They allow us to offer a pragmatic defense of certain liberal arrangements and concepts as justified, here and now, given that we can not presuppose, nor bring about by acceptable means, a more nearly perfect meeting of minds.

II

Standard philosophical defenses of liberal society take for granted the need for something like what MacIntyre calls the Enlightenment project. As Richard Rorty points out in a recent essay, "The Priority of Democracy to Philosophy," this strategy plays right into the hands of the communitarian critic.[10] For, as MacIntyre never tires of pointing out, the various proponents of foundations for liberal society are very good at wrecking one another's proposals. They don't need help from communitarian critics. And the disputes they are trying to resolve prove every bit as intractable after a new proposal is made as before.

Rorty's recent writings defend liberal society in a nonstandard, pragmatic way.[11] Rorty does not begin by trying to establish a philosophical foundation, like an individualist theory of human nature or a Kantian critique of practical reason, and then construct upon it an apparatus for resolving disputes by cranking out liberal conclusions. He is apt to be as suspicious of such attempts as any communitarian. But he does not see liberal society as dependent on foundations. Rorty defends liberal society in part by deflecting the demand for foundations and in part by pointing out contingent features of liberal society that make it the best available set of arrangements we can get under the circumstances, at least by our lights.

Much of Rorty's argument in "The Priority of Democracy" is an attempt to reinterpret John Rawls's *A Theory of Justice* as the great contemporary expression of pragmatic liberalism, thereby defending that book against those like Michael Sandel, who see Rawls as founding a liberal theory of justice on an incoherent metaphysics of the self.[12] Actually, I think this struggle over *A Theory of Justice* is beside the point. Both Rorty and Sandel probably make the book seem more coherent and self-conscious than it was. Rorty reads it backward, from the vantage point of Rawls's subsequent, consistently pragmatic and antimetaphysical writings. He has little trouble finding passages in Rawls's book that prefigure the later, Deweyan Rawls of the Dewey Lectures and related essays.[13] But Sandel would have equally little trouble finding passages in *A Theory of Justice* to support a more metaphysical reading. My own view is that Rawls hadn't yet worked out all the implications of his pragmatic conception of justification when he wrote the book that made him famous: as a result, his book was fundamentally ambiguous.[14] He got clear, and achieved his true greatness as a philosopher, only later.

The irony of Rorty's reading of Rawls, as he himself seems to realize, is that it is hard to see why Rawls would have spent so much time elaborating on the technical details of the original position—the feature of the book for which it is best known—if he had started out with a fully consistent version of the pragmatism clearly expressed in his recent essays. As Rorty says, "It is tempting to suggest that one could eliminate all reference to the original position from *A Theory of Justice* without loss, but this is as daring a suggestion as that one might rewrite (as many have wished to do) Kant's *Critique of Pure Reason* without reference to the thing-in-itself" (p. 19). If Rawls had started out as a Rortian, he would have written a much shorter book memorable mainly for the ideas of "reflective equilibrium" and "overlapping consensus." Or perhaps he would have written something more like Michael Walzer's *Spheres of Justice*.[15]

Actually, Walzer's book strikes me as not only a clearer example of pragmatic moral philosophy than Rawls's but also in some ways a more helpful one. Rawls gave us a valuable trope for saying what liberal justice is all about but, with the help of his many followers, immediately pressed it too hard in hope of finding something sophisticated and technical for liberal moral philosophers to do. The resulting rigor was almost entirely misplaced. Walzer, who has been criticized for being impressionistic, gives us something more useful. He helps us see moral philosophy as reflexive ethnography. The anthropologist's thick descriptions discern the difference between a wink and a blink in some foreign culture. Walzer's thick descriptions discern the difference between an apt application of a principle and an application that takes a principle outside its proper sphere. The culture in question is ours, and if interpreting "to one's fellow citizens the world of meanings that we share" is impressionistic, that is because it has to be.[16]

In any event, we can easily defer considering what to make of Rawls's book and take Rorty's main point to be that we should shift attention away from "the claim that the social theory of the liberal state rests on false philosophical presuppositions."[17] When we follow this advice, he thinks, our attention naturally shifts toward questions such as whether liberal institutions can be "combined with the sense of common purpose which pre-democratic societies enjoyed" (p. 40) and whether "the sort of human being who is produced by liberal institutions and culture is undesirable" (p. 6). These are better questions, in no small measure because they are more concrete, but Rorty has thus far done little to answer them (although he has usefully insisted that no one such question must be viewed as prior to all the others that might occur to us).

If communitarian critics of liberalism stuck to questions like these and stayed clear of questions about the putative philosophical foundations of liberalism, Rorty says, they would at least "avoid the sort of terminal wistfulness with which their books typically end" (p. 40). He cites the conclusion of *After Virtue*, with its talk of the new dark ages and its call for another St. Benedict, as an example of such wistfulness. But the terminal wistfulness, I think, has little to do with concentration on questions about philosophical foundations. It is rather a function of everybody's inability to imagine a full-blown alternative to our society that would be both achievable by acceptable means and clearly better than what we have now.[18] No one has trouble imagining a way of life that, by their lights, would qualify as an improvement on the current order. But it always turns out to be a way of life in which everybody, or nearly everybody, comes to see the light—that is, comes to see things by my lights, by light of my conception of the good in all its detail. If imagined utopias are to generate more than terminal wistfulness, we'll need also to be able to imagine realistically how to achieve them by acceptable means, how to make them nonutopian.

The main problem with communitarian criticism of liberal society, then, is its implicitly utopian character. The critics do succeed, at times, in articulating quite reasonable misgivings many of us feel concerning life in our society. Yet they very rarely give us any clear sense of what to do about our misgivings aside from yearning pensively for conditions we are either unwilling or unable to bring about. When you unwrap the utopia, the batteries aren't included. Liberal responses to communitarian criticism, on the other hand, often show what seems to be smug insensitivity.

Rorty acknowledges the force of the misgivings that make some people become communitarians, but only rarely and in passing. For instance, in a passage meant to extol the liberalizing changes that increased "people's sense of themselves as free citizens of free countries," he adds as an aside, "Weber was of course right in saying that some of these changes have also worked the other way (to increase our sense of being controlled by 'them')."[19] And he speaks of the "sort of 'shock' we get when, reading Foucault, we realize that the jargon we liberal intellectuals developed has played into the hands of the bureaucrats."[20] But these concessions must be developed before they will lessen the impression of smugness.

Elsewhere Rorty says, "We should be more willing than we are to celebrate bourgeois capitalist society as the best polity actualized so far, while regretting that it is irrelevant to most of the problems of most of the population of the planet."[21] If the concession tagged onto the end of this sentence were intended only to say that bourgeois capitalist society is unlikely to solve most of the problems of most of the population of the planet, Rorty is certainly right. But it is hard to see how bourgeois capitalist society could be deemed irrelevant to most of those problems, at least as a source of dramatically important unintended consequences, many of them bad enough to make celebration seem the wrong tack to take. With no more than asides like this to go on, we are left with what seems a dangerously myopic moral vision, apparently blind to relations of interdependence and dominance within the economic world-system from which we derive our wealth, a vision compatible with gross insensitivity to that system's sorrows, injustices, and corrupting influences.

My point is not that Rorty is himself a myopic, smug, or insensitive man. I am talking about the impression created by his writings, an impression I believe he regrets but has had trouble disowning or undoing. In fact, when Hilary Putnam says that it would be "facile" to accuse Rorty of "conservatism," I wholeheartedly agree. "Rorty," Putnam writes, "is as 'wet' a liberal as they come." And yet, Putnam goes on to say, "If Rorty is not conservative, he does, at times, seem ever so slightly decadent."[22] Thus, in Putnam's view, whatever Rorty's voting habits and privately held political convictions may be, his writings have created the impression that he cares more about the conversation of Western intellectuals as an end in itself than he does about anything else—including, for example, justice for the poor or throwing out the Reaganites. Rorty has confessed finding the charge that he is "treating democratic societies as existing for the sake of intellectuals" the "most disturbing" objection to his position.[23] He clearly wants to show solidarity with people who aren't intellectuals or poets, but like most of us he seems unable to think of much to say beyond the familiar clichés.

It should therefore not be surprising to find some of Rorty's fellow Deweyans[24] complaining that he has thus far done little to satisfy Dewey's hope for a philosophy that would speak in detail about the problems we confront as a society. He helps us clear away certain philosophical interpretations of those problems. He holds that we must locate our problems in society and history, accepting the contingency of our ways. But he does not show us how to locate our problems or even say much about what they are. Perhaps he doesn't think he's the right person for the job. Maybe he is saying that philosophers like himself are trained only to satirize other philosophers and that when the satire is complete or becoming tedious they should stand aside, deferring to poets, novelists, and people who actually know something about the empirical workings of our society. If so, then we can hardly fault him for having the courage of his modesty.

But he seems at times to be saying more, if only this: Our institutions are the best invented so far. Fear the secret police beyond our borders. Abhor Stalinists of every stripe, including those in sheep's clothing. Be thankful for the blessings of capitalism and bureaucracy, not least the leisure they make possible for intellectuals. Cherish the liberty to think and speak freely. Use it to keep the conversation of Western intellectuals going. Let philosophers stay in the conversation, but satirize them whenever they cannot resist the temptation to impose their modes of discourse on everybody else. Tolerate the superstitious, but only if they agree to hold their fanatical tendencies in check. Do not speak lightly of revolution; someone might take you seriously and disturb the peace. Beware of intellectuals who "hate the bourgeoisie more than [they] love anything else."[25] Be not alarmed about a culture dominated by the rich aesthete, the manager, and the therapist, "so long as *everybody* who wants to gets to be an aesthete (and, if not rich, as comfortably off as most—as rich as the Managers can manage, guided by Rawls's Difference Principle)."[26]

I have no objection to most of this as far as it goes, especially as satirical counterpoint to philosophers' pretensions, on the one hand, and the currently popular sport of bashing the West, on the other. Whatever we make of Rorty's possible motives for being cryptic, however, such remarks do not take us very far toward understanding our situation. And without being supplemented by detailed social and political reflection, they are apt to have the effect of encouraging everybody to share the rich aesthete's complacency and insensitivity. At his worst, Rorty seems to be working within something like MacIntyre's dualistic vision, content merely to take the opposite side, making liberals out to be the children of light and their critics the children of darkness, as if all we needed to address our problems well were less regard for communitarian wistfulness and more loyalty to fellow members of the bourgeoisie. His way of sloughing off worries about the kind of people we are becoming does little justice to the predicament we face. He is too quick to say, for example, that a sense of common purpose may just have to be given up if we want to enjoy the benefits of our society, or "that even if the typical character-types of liberal democracies *are* bland, calculating, petty and unheroic, the prevalence of such people may nevertheless be a reasonable price to pay for political freedom."[27]

We do not confront a choice between a society in which political freedom reigns but the people are lousy and one in which somewhat better people would emerge if we were only willing to sacrifice political freedom. We do, however, live in a society where economic and other forces seem increasingly to produce people who lack the virtues needed to use their freedom well—whether in the political arena, in the workplace, at home, or elsewhere. Bellah and his colleagues are right to worry about what will become of our society, including the very freedom we cherish, if we cease to produce people who can make a republic work. They are right to wonder how to improve the situation. Terminal wistfulness doesn't help, but neither does the idea that liberal freedom is worth the price of bad people. The latter is as far removed from our actual choices as the former.

What we need to discover, it seems to me, is the mean between smug approval of the *status quo* and wistful alienation from it—the mean between liberal apologetics and implicitly utopian criticism. I think that all the authors I have been discussing would like to find this mean, but this has proven to be no easy task. Wistful alienation enjoys the comforts of distance from evil. It takes consolation in the moral and epistemic privilege of marginality while denying itself the necessities of engagement and action. Its characteristic tone betokens a failure of generosity, an inability to transcend the limits of its own outrage. Denouncing its age, it implicitly announces its own impotence, escaping despair, if at all, only by gesturing weakly toward the future or the past. But it is very hard to distance oneself from this sort of posture without allowing oneself false consolations and self-deceptions of another kind. It is all too easy to lose one's moral balance, falling back into complicity and complacency, giving comfort to the wrong people and reinforcing the wrong tendencies in our common life.

Perhaps this impasse cannot be broken just now. The moral task of social criticism, however, is to press against the limits of contemporary thought, trying to break the impasse if it can be broken. I'm convinced that we won't get very far until we set aside such polar oppositions as "liberal vs. communitarian" and invent more detailed ways to flesh out reasonable misgivings about our predicament. Liberal apologetics papers over misgivings most of us genuinely feel, misgivings that give communitarians an audience, a claim on our attention. But a misgiving counts as more than merely wistful, and thus worth being fleshed out, only if it can be connected with something more than vague yearning, some relatively concrete proposal about what to do. We need, somehow, to maintain the courage of our misgivings without sacrificing our capacity to act in concert with fellow members of our society or to show generosity, as well as critical intent, in describing them.

III

Pragmatic liberalism is not the only nonstandard defense of liberal society. Like Richard Rorty, Gilbert Meilaender defends liberal arrangements as the best—or rather, the least bad—available and dissociates himself from the typically individualist premises found in standard forms of philosophical liberalism. Also like Rorty, he is wary of communitarian proposals. Yet his reasons come not from Dewey's pragmatism but from Augustine's theology. [28]

The most we can hope for from the earthly kingdom at its best, according to Meilaender, is a measure of order that can secure private space in which we can form friendships and families and voluntary associations. In these spheres, not in the sphere of political doings, we find the closest thing to true happiness available in this life—analogues to the forms of association the blessed enjoy in God's Kingdom. Politics at its best makes room for such happiness and such associations. It also opens up the space in which individuals can pursue the spiritual life as they understand it. Politics is no substitute for that and always goes sour the moment we begin thinking of an earthly political community, whether actual or potential, as our real home.

Meilaender defends the liberal state, then, not because he considers its arrangements truly just, for there is no truly just state in this life, but rather because it is the form of political life best suited to proper recognition of the limits of politics. Communitarians are to be distrusted because they call us into a kind of solidarity with others in public life that would be disastrously totalitarian, threatening our private bonds and spiritual freedom. Much of what they say in criticism of liberal society is true enough, from Meilaender's point of view, but this should not be surprising. Liberal society is not the Kingdom of God. So, like all forms of political association in this life, it is radically imperfect. It is to be preferred not because it approximates the ideal but because its recognition of the limits of politics makes it not quite so bad as the other forms.

Meilaender in fact goes out of his way to call attention to what he sees as liberal society's limitations and dangers—in particular, its tendency to allow the language of the capitalist marketplace or the ethos of minimal decency to seep into the parts of our lives where they don't belong:

> When enshrined at the center of our public consciousness is the minimal virtue which asks only civility, when our common life acknowledges a plurality of forms of the good life and the need for freedom to pursue our private visions of the good life—when these are the beliefs upon which our community is founded—it will be difficult to prevent a belief in the primacy of private interests from seeping down into and dominating our understanding of virtue. Serious moral education, serious training in virtue, may then become difficult to sustain. We may even have difficulty sustaining the common life of smaller groups upon which we are relying to transmit those "higher" elements of our moral vision. (p. 7)

Meilaender can sound like *Habits of the Heart* when he says that "the individualism of our world often seems destructive, that we demonstrate little willingness to sacrifice private desires for public ends" (p. 5). He readily grants that the liberal state is not a true home for its citizens.

But things would be much worse, according to Meilaender, if we overthrew the liberal state and replaced it by an earthly political community, of our own making, meant to be our home. What we need, instead, is "a Chalcedonian politics":

> a form of the liberal tradition which does not attempt to overcome the tension between ethics and politics, yet does recognize that there is indeed a tension. This form of the tradition claims that the public realm—the political—exists *not* just to support and make possible individual pursuit of private goals and projects, *nor* to foster fraternal solidarity. Rather, the political realm exists to foster *private, social* bonds—to make space in life for families, friendships, clubs, faiths, neighborhoods. (p. 9, italics in original)

Meilaender is saying that the Chalcedonian public realm exists to create space for families, friendships, and so on, not *just* to serve the "individual pursuit of private goals and projects." The term "just" is meant to leave some room for the language and values of individualism, while the term "not" puts unrestricted individualism in question.

Meilaender's Chalcedonian public realm aims to protect private *bonds*, and thus forms of association in which the virtues might flourish and be taught, not merely the "individual pursuit of private goals and projects." It seems not at all concerned to promote fraternal solidarity among the citizenry. Meilaender does not say, "nor *just* to foster fraternal solidarity," but simply: "nor to foster fraternal solidarity." Suppose, however, we seek out a middle way between Meilaender's Augustinian vision and the totalitarian tendencies he fears in communitarian politics as follows: first, by granting that the political sphere ought to leave room for both private bonds and the individual pursuit of private goals and projects; and second, by adding that yet another legitimate purpose of politics is to foster a sort of public life in which members find some part of their identity as citizens of a republic directed to the common good.

By slipping between the Augustinians and the totalitarians in this way, we can avoid seeing complete identification of oneself with one's political roles as the only alternative to Meilaender's virtually exclusive emphasis on the private sphere. The truth in Augustinian liberalism can then be reformulated as the idea that every sphere of earthly human life, from the most public to the most private, has its temptations and dangers. No sphere can rightly occupy the position of be-all-and-end-all in our lives without throwing the rest out of proper proportion—neither vocation, nor family, nor voluntary association, nor private projects, nor politics.

This allows us to say, at last, what remained deficient about Brian Palmer's life after he remarried. He has, we sense, simply traded one disproportionate preoccupation, his dedication to his career, for another, his dedication to his family. His life is better than it used to be, somewhat less narrow in orientation. He has recognized the limitations and miseries of a life dedicated wholly to the individual pursuit of private goals and projects. And he has found considerably more happiness, not merely greater subjective satisfaction, in private bonds. But in a sense, his life remains narrowly focused, a sense in which one aspect of life has acquired a disproportionate importance. (This is what I take the authors of *Habits of the Heart* to be trying to get at in discussing his case, but it has little to do with his stammering in response to Socratic questions or his apparent commitment to individualism as an ultimate principle.)

Meilaender has not established a special deficiency in political life that would disqualify it as a realm in which we might, and perhaps should, seek some measure of our fulfillment as people. He has simply drawn attention to features of communitarian solidarity that, if allowed to take over our entire lives, would make things much worse than they are now. Atomistic individualism and totalitarian solidarity do not exhaust our options. They are more like obviously undesirable extremes than like options anyway, and none of the authors I have been discussing is proposing either. My question at this point is not exactly Rorty's, whether liberal institutions and practices can be "combined with the sense of common purpose which pre-democratic societies enjoyed," but rather how we might enhance the sense of common purpose and civic virtue we already have, limited as it may be, without acting unjustly or making things worse.

I introduce Rorty and Meilaender partly to show that liberalism comes in forms, both pragmatic and Augustinian, that owe little to individualism as a metaphysics of the self or as an unrestricted philosophy of life. Nor are these forms of liberalism recent historical developments. They can be traced well back into early stages of liberal thought. The picture of liberalism as dependent upon radically individualist philosophical foundations does justice to neither liberal society nor liberal thought. This should give communitarian critics pause. But my aim is not to advocate a nonstandard form of liberalism. My aim, instead, is to describe our situation in such a way that "liberal" and "communitarian" no longer seem like meaningful options.

IV

Communitarians and liberals alike tend to view liberal society as centered in the idea that we can get along without what Cicero called "an agreement with respect to justice and a partnership for the common good." Meilaender sees this idea as rooted in good Augustinian theology, suspicious of any this-worldly attempt to instantiate a truly excellent form of political community. Pragmatic liberals see the same idea as rooted in contingent features of modern societies where diverse populations will either coexist at close quarters or kill each other off and no group succeeds in imposing its own fully detailed conception of the good. Communitarians see the same idea as an especially telling expression of what is wrong with the liberal order. I wish now to raise the possibility that this picture of our society, so widely shared by its defenders and its critics, is seriously misleading.

My reasons for thinking so were already implicit in the treatment of MacIntyre offered in the previous chapter. There I suggested that while people in our society obviously fall well short of complete agreement about matters pertaining to justice and the common good, it doesn't follow that they don't agree at all about such matters. If my argument was correct, their disagreement on such matters could not be total. We should therefore be less impressed by the opposition between Cicero and Augustine or by overly sharp contrasts between societies that agree on such matters and societies that do not. If we think of our society as oriented, by virtue of shared intentions and a self-limiting consensus on the good, toward a provisional *telos*, we should be able to avoid thinking of the question, "individual freedom or common purpose?" as presenting an exclusive choice. We have so little sense of common purpose in part because we have become so accustomed to a picture that hides the actual extent of our commonality from view. We need also to remember that preserving a healthy degree of individual freedom inheres in our common purpose and helps define our conception of justice.

It follows that something resembling MacIntyre's metaphysically austere and historically informed teleological framework—Aristotelian in inspiration but without the "metaphysical biology"—can be used not only to describe radical alternatives to the *status quo* but also to describe so-called liberal society itself. It is important to see that MacIntyre takes full cognizance of the necessity for a provisional and corrigible conception of "the good."[29] His *telos*, despite the impression one might get from the first half of his book, is not a fixed conception of the good, derived once and for all from a philosophical view of the human essence.

Consider the following passage, in which MacIntyre explains the sense in which pursuit of the good is a quest:

It is in the course of the quest and only through encountering and coping with the various particular harms, dangers, temptations and distractions which provide any quest with its episodes and incidents that the goal of the quest is finally understood. A quest is always an education both as to the character of that which is sought and in self-knowledge. (*After Virtue*, p. 219)

Later on the same page, he offers a tentative definition of the good life: "the good life for man is the life spent in seeking for the good life for man, and the virtues necessary for the seeking are those which will enable us to understand what more and what else the good life for man is."

Many readers have, I suspect, found this definition exasperating. They have wanted MacIntyre to supply an antecendently known, yet substantive and detailed, conception of the good—a fixed goal we can get clearly in our sights before starting our journey toward it, a *telos* that defines a single way of life fit for all human beings no matter where and when they live. Instead he refuses, insisting that the good is not something we first know, capture in a theory, and then pursue. Rather, we always find ourselves, at any moment in our history, already committed to pursuing a cluster of interrelated ends, our conception of which changes as we pursue them. As MacIntyre has put it in a recent essay, "there is not one kind of life the living out of which is the *telos* for all human beings in all times and places."[30] Still, there is a truth of the matter about what constitutes our *telos*, given our time and place. And the good life for us is one in which the necessity of a self-consciously provisional, contextually sensitive, conception of the good life is recognized. We have discovered that a life worth pursuing will be one in which we possess the virtues that allow us to alter our conception of the good in light of experience. One such virtue, of course, is practical wisdom *(phronesis)*.

If so, however, it becomes imperative to ask what the experience of the religious wars and related facts of modern history have taught us about the good life as appropriately conceived in our time and place. Does not our society embody the recognition, born of *phronesis* and forged in the religious strife of early modern Europe, that the good life for us must make allowances for our inability to achieve perfect agreement on the good life? I believe it does. Where MacIntyre sees the social embodiment of emotivism, I see implicit commitment to a provisional, self-limiting conception of the good. This commitment helps explain, as MacIntyre's view does not, why people of various philosophical and religious persuasions are so reluctant to discard the arrangements, institutions, and vocabularies we have.

MacIntyre rejects modern politics because he sees it as expressing "in its institutional forms a systematic rejection" of Aristotelian tradition (p. 255). What makes him see it in this way? I believe there are at least two problems here. First, as I have already argued, he neglects the extent to which our society is, despite the claims of liberal philosophers, held together by shared beliefs and common ends. I grant, of course, that liberal philosophers have characteristically rejected Aristotelian tradition. It is by no means as clear, however, that the practice of modern politics is itself anti-Aristotelian in the relevant sense. So MacIntyre, in effect, accepts a picture of our predicament excessively indebted to the forms of liberal philosophy he otherwise dismisses. Second, if Bernard Yack is right,[31] MacIntyre (like most contemporary interpreters) overlooks the complexity of Aristotle's own conception of political community—in particular, its balanced and realistic account of political conflict.

To be sure, for Aristotle all forms of community involve something held in common. The individuals who make up political communities come together out of need, but, in Yack's words, "their human capacity for reasoned speech compels them in some way to share in something more than need, to share something to do with the just and unjust."[32] What they share, however, is neither perfect agreement nor the bond that we, in contemporary English, call friendship. Otherwise, they wouldn't spend so much time using reasoned speech to argue about justice. Nor would they be as prone as Aristotle thinks they are to fall into conflict and mutual suspicion. To be members of a political community, according to Yack's reading of Aristotle, they need only share enough agreement about standards to make argument about justice possible. If we accepted this reading of Aristotle, we would have all the more reason for thinking that our politics, far from implicitly rejecting Aristotle's conception of community, in fact conforms to that conception rather closely.

Rorty, for his part, often seems simply to reject teleological understandings of our society. Yet he also sometimes places a notion of shared intentions (borrowed from Wilfrid Sellars) at the center of his conception of morality.[33] I fail to see, however, why a group's shared intentions, subject to critical assessment and change over time, should be thought to differ significantly from what MacIntyre would call a group's provisional and corrigible *telos*. Rorty has not yet explained with any clarity why we shouldn't take his own view to be teleological in roughly the same sense as MacIntyre's. Ignore for the moment the separable issue, to which I shall return in the next chapter, of whether we ought to banish all mention of essences or human nature, as Rorty would seem to prefer. One can be teleological in the relevant sense without deriving a *telos* from a philosophical theory of the human essence.[34] One can also be teleological in the relevant sense without supposing that we need to generate religious or philosophical agreement on anything so grand as the meaning of life or the ultimate purpose of human existence.[35]

The question is whether our society should be understood in reference to, among other things, common ends (or shared intentions) and deeply entrenched platitudes of the form, "Other things equal, X is a state of affairs worth pursuing" or "X, morally speaking, is better than Y." The claim that it should can be supported by Davidsonian arguments which Rorty himself employs for other purposes but which also, it now seems clear, make it easier than one might have thought to split the difference between MacIntyre and Rorty, between a suitably revised Aristotle and a pragmatic liberal.

In a nicely turned footnote, Rorty abets my "splitting the difference" strategy by softening up MacIntyre's "Nietzsche or Aristotle?" partition:

It is tempting to say that I would accept MacIntyre's claim that the only real choice is between Aristotle and Nietzsche, and then side with Nietzsche. But the choice is too dramatic and too simple. By the time MacIntyre gets rid of the nonsense in Aristotle (e.g., what he calls the "metaphysical biology"), Aristotle doesn't look much like himself. By the time I would finish discarding the bits of Nietzsche I do not want (e.g., his lapses into metaphysical biology, his distrust of Hegel, his *ressentiment*, etc.) he would not look much like Nietzsche. [36]

But Rorty does not take advantage of the opening toward Aristotelian vocabulary provided by this passage. If MacIntyre has, at least in his better moments, transcended the nonsense in Aristotle, why not experiment, as an eclectic and pragmatic moral *bricoleur*, with his new and improved language of the virtues and the common good, seeing how far it can take us toward an understanding of our society?

Instead, Rorty himself sticks with oversimplified contrasts between Aristotelian and anti-Aristotelian concepts, saying that he wants to make our discourse coherent "by discarding the last vestiges" of Aristotelian ways of thinking. I, too, would like our discourse to be coherent, but I think MacIntyre and Rorty are both too hasty in deciding that because Aristotelian vocabularies and modern moral vocabularies are incompatible, one or the other must be discarded. The matter is both more complicated and more promising than that. Creative *bricolage* knows how to make apparently incompatible vocabularies work in concert, cutting out and filling in as need be. If we take Aristotle to be saying what Yack thinks he is saying about political community and conflict, and carefully remove the outmoded metaphysics, recognizably Aristotelian habits of speech may prove surprisingly adaptable to our environment. On the other hand, remembering the example of

Aquinas, whose *bricolage* baptized the same pagan vocabularies for use in Christian ethics, perhaps we shouldn't be surprised at all.

We also can see oversimplification at work in Rorty's repeated use of a distinction borrowed from Michael Oakeshott between *universitas* and *societas.*[37] In *Philosophy and the Mirror of Nature,*[38] for example, he defines an *universitas* as "a group united by mutual interests in achieving a common end" and a *societas* as a group of "persons whose paths through life have fallen together, united by civility rather than by a common goal, much less by a common ground." He urges us to think of our society as an instance of the latter type. As he has put it in his most recent reflection on Oakeshott's distinction, we should think of ourselves as a "band of eccentrics" collaborating merely for "purposes of self-protection," not a "band of fellow-spirits" bound together by comprehensive agreement on all aspects of where we want to be headed.[39] I say we should think of ourselves as neither, that the distinction is simply too coarse to do anything but distort our situation. In Rorty's writings on epistemology, no rigid dualism is allowed to stand. In his remarks on politics, however, apparently rigid dualisms abound. Universal distaste for dualisms would serve us better.

Having "an agreement with respect to justice and a partnership for the common good" is hardly an all-or-nothing affair. We need not be a band of fellow-spirits, united in perfect agreement, partnership, and camaraderie to benefit from a Davidsonian consensus. And it is not merely the purpose of self-protection or the virtue of civility that holds us together. Despite our liberal philosophical rhetoric, we are more Aristotelian than we tend to think.

Most of us would be happy to expand our agreement with respect to justice and enhance our sense of common purpose provided we could do so without unacceptably displacing private bonds, curtailing our freedom to pursue private projects and goals, or imposing our preferences by force. If someone asks where we should draw the line between acceptable and unacceptable displacement of private bonds, curtailment of freedom, or imposition of preferences, we can say nothing that is both highly general and highly illuminating. We can say "Imagine yourself needing to agree with others while meeting behind a veil of ignorance . . ." or "Count as acceptable whatever can be justified to others on grounds they could not reasonably reject" or "Suppose yourself to be conversing under conditions of undistorted communication

. . . ."[40] Yet no such saying helps very much in abstraction from what Dewey called the meaning of the daily detail.[41]

We determine our fate in the end not by choosing for or against liberal society, nor by finding the right general principle of acceptability, but by drawing the line here or there in countless particular cases, given our sense of the daily detail. If we do it well, it will be because we have the virtue of practical wisdom—just as Aristotle (and Dewey) would insist. So we had better strive to maintain and strengthen whatever it is about our society that makes this and other virtues possible. Failure to exhibit the virtues, to concern ourselves with the sort of people we are becoming, is bound to create conditions under which the virtues themselves will be harder to acquire and thus all the more difficult to exhibit. Here, as so often, wisdom begins in a refusal to let oversimplified, excessively abstract contrasts define our options. But it cannot rest before descending to significant details and forging a language in which they can be understood and assessed.

11

THE MORAL CONSEQUENCES OF PRAGMATISM

Without minimizing the discontents that turn some of us into communitarians, I have portrayed use of the language of rights as pragmatically justified under the circumstances (provided we view it as a creole that has gradually been absorbed into our moral language, not as an all-purpose Esperanto). I have also expressed doubts, reminiscent of pragmatists like Dewey and James, about the explanatory value of saying that true moral propositions correspond to the Moral Law and about the usefulness of saying that moral knowledge rests on foundational principles. And I have been referring to creative moral thought as *bricolage*, thereby underlining its eclectic and pragmatic character. In these and various other ways, I have flirted with the appellation *pragmatism* without quite embracing it. The reason for my reluctance is simple. Pragmatism stands for many things, only some of which I find congenial. Using the label too freely or too early in the game would have invited premature dismissal of what I want to say. Before going any further, however, I must clarify my relation to some of the things that might be meant by pragmatism, not only to avoid confusion but also to answer an important class of objections.

For pragmatism, so its critics say, leads to unwelcome consequences in ethics and may even contribute to the collapse of all we hold dear — not least the virtue of tolerance, dedication to justice, and respect for rights. Is not pragmatism itself an expression of modernist decadence, what a MacIntyre might call emotivism American style? Doesn't it induce in its adherents a kind of moral aphasia, an inability to talk back in the face of generalized tyranny? Can any moral language worthy of use survive for more than a moment if defended primarily in pragmatic terms?

I

Edmund Santurri has taken me to task for advocating a pragmatic theory of justification, most fully developed in the writings of Richard Rorty, according to which: (1) "to say that we know x is to say that belief in x is warranted by criteria that form part of some largely useful, social institution," (2) "our knowledge of, for instance, the wrongness of torturing innocents is simply a belief we have that is justified by some expedient social convention," and (3) "the wrongness of torturing innocents is merely to be regarded as a fact socially contrived." [1] Once this much is granted, Santurri says, nihilism ensues, whether I want it to or not.

I plead not guilty. [2] In *The Flight from Authority*, which Santurri was criticizing, I carefully avoided committing myself to a theory of this kind. I saw this careful avoidance as part of my contribution. Evidently, this was not enough. It was still too easy to interpret my silences on certain topics as implicit assent to a reductive analysis of "S knows that *p*" in terms of nonepistemic expressions about the position of a proposition in expedient social conventions. So in this book, especially its first two chapters, I have taken pains to deny, as explicitly as possible, the theory Santurri ascribes to me. I offer *no* "analysis" of knowledge in terms of necessary and sufficient conditions, let alone a reduction of "S knows that *p*" to nonepistemic expressions.

I would say that justification and cognition are distorted when viewed in abstraction from such characteristically human activities as the attempt to solve problems. But saying this much, by itself, does not elevate usefulness and expediency in the manner suggested, for it does not propose any criterion of justification. Some people who call themselves pragmatists speak of usefulness, expediency, and cash value in ways that make them sound suspiciously like consequentialists. I am not proposing consequentialism applied to mental acts—the idea that one ought to believe whatever maximizes utility in the consequences of one's believings. Nor am I saying that cost-benefit calculation is the ultimate language of commensuration—the basic vocabulary of all rational thought because it is the vocabulary in which we weigh the costs and benefits of vocabularies. The language of cost-benefit calculation is just one language among others. It enjoys no special privilege.

I have said that being justified in believing something depends on features of one's epistemic context, some of which may well be facts about conventions and institutions native to that context. This claim does not, however, entail nihilism. It would entail nihilism or related heresies only if, contrary to the doctrine defended in Part 1, I went on to say things like "Truth is warranted assertibility" and "Justification is what your peers will let you get away with," intending these dicta as reductive analyses.

I deny that the wrongness of torturing innocents is simply a belief we have that is justified by some expedient social convention. Knowingly and willingly torturing innocents is wrong, impermissible, unjust. It always has been. It would still be unjust if, after the general collapse of civilization, everybody was justified in believing it permissible, given the expedient conventions of the day. Some rights—including some that extend protections of tolerance unique to liberal states—are best viewed as properties assigned to persons by institutions justified relative to the highest achievable good under the circumstances. But knowingly and willingly torturing innocents, on my view, simply fails to give the victims their due, whatever the circumstances. That is the moral truth of the matter, whether we recognize it or not— a truth I deem more certain than any explanation I could give of it or any argument I could make on its behalf.[3] It is a "fact socially contrived" only in the sense that the proposition "Knowingly and willingly torturing innocents is unjust" is itself cast in a particular vocabulary, invented by human beings. Propositions are interpreted sentences in human languages and thus cultural artifacts, socially contrived. Which propositions you can believe or entertain depends on what "that-clauses" (or their cognates) can name in the languages you know. But that the proposition in question is true is not socially contrived at all.

To what extent does this line of response to Santurri put me at odds with Rorty, whom Santurri rightly identifies as the leading contemporary pragmatist? That depends on how Rorty should be taken—hardly an uncomplicated issue in its own right (and perhaps one we shouldn't try to resolve beyond a certain point). Without attempting to nail down a definitive reading of his work, however, we can profit from considering some of the passages that worry his critics, as well as some other passages that make him seem much less radical. In the remainder of this chapter, then, I shall try to clarify my own position by relating it to various possible readings of various things Rorty has said.

In an essay on Jacques Derrida, Rorty quotes J. L. Austin's witticism, "There's the bit where you say it and the bit where you take it back." He then praises Derrida for not taking back the seemingly radical dicta that enrage the defenders of common sense.[4] But Rorty almost always gets around to taking back his own seemingly radical dicta. That is, he usually shows us how to read them not as reductive analyses or inherently paradoxical attempts, on the part of an anti-essentialist, to capture the essence of something but rather as "pithy little formulae." Such formulae, though useful for rhetorical purposes in assaulting an orthodox position, are typically wrong about what they seem to be asserting. They are right only about what they implicitly deny. Using them can make you sound unprofessional, slightly naughty, or downright absurd, depending on the context. And yet, Rorty assures us, they are rarely meant to mean what they seem to say. They are the philosophical ironist's stock in trade, tools for troping.[5]

In fact, by the end of the very paragraph in which he praises Derrida for refusing to take it back, Rorty tells us:

James, when he said that "the true is what is good in the way of belief" was simply trying to debunk epistemology; he was not offering a "theory of truth." So Derrida, when he says "il n'y a pas de hors-texte," is not putting forward an ontological view; he is trying to debunk Kantian philosophy generally.

You get a charitable reading of Rorty's pragmatism if you stress "take it back" passages like this over the "pithy little formulae." Play down the former while taking the latter literally and you get the kind of pragmatism Hilary Putnam has criticized as a form of "epistemic reductionism." On this reading, which is now widely held among professional philosophers, Rorty becomes a radical relativist, one of the undertakers philosophy always ultimately buries, a convenient symbol of what can happen even to the best of us if we spend too much time reading Derrida and associating with literary theorists.

I remain inclined toward a charitable reading of Rorty's writings on justification and truth. I therefore find it frustrating when Rorty relies excessively on pithy little formulae, thus giving hostages to the opposition. What concerns me here, however, is not which reading is right but what we can learn about the dialectical terrain from the interplay between the two sorts of passages just mentioned. Consider, for example, several pages from *Philosophy and the Mirror of Nature*, in which Rorty poses the following question:

Shall we take "S knows that *p*" (or "S knows non-inferentially that *p*," or "S believes incorrigibly that *p*," or "S's knowledge that *p* is certain") as a remark about the status of S's reports among his peers, or shall we take it as a remark about the relation between subject and object, between nature and its mirror?[6]

The first alternative, which Rorty prefers, "leads to a pragmatic view of truth," among other things. The second, on the other hand,

leads to "ontological" explanations of the relations between minds and meanings, minds and immediate data of awareness, universals and particulars, thought and language, consciousness and brains, and so on. . . . The aim of all such explanations is to make truth something more than what Dewey called "warranted assertability": more than what one's peers will, *ceteris paribus*, let one get away with saying. (pp. 175–176)

Now this seems to place Rorty pretty squarely in a position I rejected in Chapter 1. He seems to be offering his own theory of truth, according to which truth is merely warranted assertibility, and a theory of justification, here called "epistemic behaviorism," according to which epistemic warrant can be reduced to nonepistemic sociological facts. A paragraph later, however, he says something quite different:

The question is not whether necessary and sufficient behavioral conditions for "S knows that *p*" can be offered; no one any longer dreams they can. Nor is the question whether such conditions can be offered for "S sees that *p*," or "It looks to S as if *p*," or "S is having the thought that *p*." To be behaviorist in the large sense . . . is not to offer reductionist analyses, but to refuse to attempt a certain sort of explanation . . . . (p. 176)

As he puts it on another page, what he wants to preserve from his pragmatic mentors

is not the attempt to substitute one sort of account of human knowledge for another, but an attempt to get away from the notion of "an account of human knowledge." It amounts to a protest against an archetypal philosophical problem: the problem of how to reduce norms, rules, and justifications to facts, generalizations, and explanations. (p. 180)

Passages like the last two seem a far cry from "epistemic reductionism." But before long Rorty begins sounding like a reductionist again. In an article that includes all the passages just quoted from *Philosophy and the Mirror of Nature*,[7] for example, he eventually backslides into applauding Quine and Sellars for helping make William James's "pragmatic notion of truth" respectable. According to Rorty's paraphrase of James's pithy little formula, the true sentence is "the sentence asserted by the man who knows how to get what he wants." Truth thus becomes "something inherently relative, inherently temporary" (p. 109). This remark seems to collapse the distinctions between truth and justification that I have been insisting upon, leading directly to the kind of reductionism and relativism Putnam rightly rejects. Surely, it would have been better simply to eschew pithy little formulae and seemingly reductionist dicta altogether.

Similar problems appear in Rorty's more recent work. To take one example, in an essay called "Solidarity or Objectivity?" he defines pragmatists like himself as "those who wish to reduce objectivity to solidarity," in contrast to realists, "who wish to ground solidarity in objectivity."[8] But why should resistance to traditional attempts to ground objectivity in a relation of correspondence to undescribed reality be thought to involve the idea that objectivity needs to be reduced to something? Rorty does not say. He does, however, go on to say quite helpful things about how little actually separates Rorty the pragmatist from Putnam the "internalist"—showing, in particular, why his own position is not usefully called relativism and why Putnam's "limit-concept of ideal truth" actually reverts to the notion of a "God's eye" point of view which Putnam elsewhere argues effectively against. Indeed nothing Rorty goes on to say in "Solidarity or Objectivity?"—except the slogan-length summaries of his position—needs to be glossed as a form of epistemic reductionism. And in a review of the third volume of Putnam's *Philosophical Papers*, he praises Putnam's critique of epistemic reductionism while adding that "many of the people whom Putnam criticises," presumably including Rorty himself, "would not think of themselves as giving a reductive account of anything."[9] But toward the end of "Solidarity or Objectivity?" (p. 11), he again employs the slogan of "reducing objectivity to solidarity" as a way to sum up his position, thus making it inevitable that critics like Putnam will continue taking him to be a reductionist.

Rorty is sometimes much more careful. In an essay from the mid-1970s, perhaps too technical for inclusion in *Consequences of Pragmatism*,[10] he keeps pithy little formulae to a minimum, rigorously separates justification from truth, and steers clear of relativistic theories of the latter. "Although justification is relative to time and place, and truth is not," he says, "this is not because truth is a relation to something unchanging out there."

There is no special relation between justification and truth. We are bound to treat our present views on nature and morals as true, for we know no better. But the invidious distinctions we draw between ourselves and the Trobrianders, or between our chemists and those who believed in phlogiston, are to be backed up in the detailed and humdrum ways in which we explain the advantages of the rule of law, or of thermodynamics, over any alternatives so far canvassed. There is nothing *philosophical* to be said. (p. 323, italics in original)

He goes on to give a subtle commentary on recent debates over realism and reference, employing arguments similar in structure to those in his more famous essay "The World Well Lost" (which was reprinted in *Consequences*), though in this reformulation the arguments are less likely to be misread as advocating "idealism." He concludes not by offering his own snappy, seemingly reductive, definition of truth, but rather by cautioning against the temptation to do so:

But if the temptation to offer a definition of truth (the temptation to be epistemological) is resisted, then one can catch the pragmatists' intent in such mild-mannered platitudes as "We always judge other ages and cultures by our own." One can catch the realists' in such wry remarks as "Our remote descendants may view us as we view our primitive ancestors." (p. 336)[11]

If this be pragmatism, we need not fear its consequences for ethics. For it does not, thus formulated, imply a reductionist or relativist theory of truth. It therefore does not entail a reductionist or relativistic conception of moral truth. Neither does it drive us toward moral nihilism, the view that there are no moral truths, or toward emotivism, the view that moral propositions are, at most, reports of or attempts to evoke certain emotions, and not to be taken at face value. To the contrary, it allows us to put moral propositions on a par with propositions of other kinds, taking them all at face value unless special reason arises in a specific context for extraordinary interpretive measures.

A modest pragmatism, which stops short of the temptation to define truth, seems to remove the most familiar means for drawing invidious, philosophically motivated distinctions among kinds of apparently propositional statements—distinctions of the sort that have led philosophers to think of "moral truth" as second-rate in comparison with "scientific truth" or as so problematic when taken at face value as to require emotivist interpretation. Such a pragmatism is an expression neither of nihilistic decadence nor of emotivism American style, because it maintains, in Rorty's words, "that there is no epistemological difference between truth about what ought to be and truth about what is, nor any metaphysical difference between facts and values, nor any methodological difference between morality and science." [12] In the eyes of a modest pragmatism, true moral propositions correspond to the moral facts in the same (epistemologically trivial) sense that true scientific propositions correspond to the scientific facts.

According to a modest pragmatism, saying that a proposition (of any type) corresponds to the facts is (at best) just another way of saying that the proposition is true, not a way of explaining its truth. Since modest pragmatism finds the idea of correspondence to undescribed reality incoherent when pressed into epistemological service, it allows us to upgrade moral truth to philosophical respectability without inventing what J. L. Mackie called "queer" entities (like "values") with which moral propositions might correspond. And because it avoids putting a reductive or relativistic substitute in place of the old definition of truth as correspondence, it achieves its leveling of moral and scientific truth without downgrading the latter—without, for example, reducing the truth of scientific propositions to mere assertibility. [13]

II

In one of the essays collected in *Consequences of Pragmatism*, Rorty characterized pragmatism as "anti-essentialism applied to notions like 'truth,' 'knowledge,' 'language', 'morality,' and similar objects of philosophical theorizing" (p. 162). But when pragmatists succumb to temptation and offer their own definitions of truth and justification, they seem to contradict themselves at the crucial moment by offering essentialist analyses. For what does the new and improved definition purport to capture if not the real essence of truth or justification? By the time he wrote the introduction to *Consequences*, Rorty had pretty much left "truth as warranted assertibility" behind and was content to say simply that, according to pragmatism, "truth is not the sort of thing one should expect to have a philosophically interesting theory about" (p. xiii). [14] This aphorism gave him a slogan-length summary of his position not subject to demolition by either counterexample or a tendency to self-destruct. He was now able to identify pragmatism not with a new and improved definition but rather with an unwillingness to commit to any.

But isn't that just a refusal to do philosophy? And isn't there something phony about Rorty's claim that he has no desire to substitute one account of truth or justification for another? Isn't he relying on one all the while, using it to press his case against the opposition, and then slyly trying to repress its more noxious implications by leaving it unstated? To answer these objections, we need to see what Rorty means (or should mean) by "anti-essentialism," and the best way to do that, I think, is to go back to a passage from the introduction he wrote for another book, *The Linguistic Turn*.[15] There he defines *methodological nominalism* as the view that

all the questions which philosophers have asked about concepts, subsistent universals, or "natures" which (a) cannot be answered by empirical inquiry concerning the behavior or properties of particulars subsumed under such concepts, universals, or natures, and which (b) can be answered in *some* way, can be answered by answering questions about the use of linguistic expressions, and in no other way. (p. 11)

Notice what happens when we take this definition as the key to what Rorty means by "anti-essentialism."

In the first place, methodological nominalism does not rule out the possibility that empirical inquiry into the "nature" of reason-giving as a social practice might tell us a great deal about what justification is like. We might learn, with Thomas Kuhn, that scientific reasoning conforms to something like the philosopher's foundationalist model only in some fields and there only for limited periods of time. Or we might learn, with Levi or Schneewind, that normative reasoning typically involves a dialectical interplay between general principles and intuitions about specific cases.

Second, methodological nominalism does not rule out the possibility that we might learn something philosophically interesting about the concepts of truth and justification from detailed study of our use of the relevant expressions in ordinary language. We might learn, with Putnam, that justification is relative in ways that truth is not. We might learn, with Davidson, that seeing how the expression *is true* functions in sentences of the form "'Snow is white' is true if and only if snow is white" gets us further in the philosophy of language than we might have thought. Or we might learn, with J. L. Austin, how *true* contributes to the force of certain speech-acts.

Moreover, as some of these examples make clear, what we learn from empirical inquiry and from studying our use of expressions like *is true* and *is justified* might give us reason for doubting traditional philosophical theories of truth and justification. The methodological nominalist is free to have views about truth or justification, beliefs useful in arguing against traditional philosophical theories, provided they do not go beyond the kinds of claims that can be warranted by empirical inquiry and linguistic reflection.

When Rorty objects to philosophical accounts of these topics, I believe he means accounts that make claims about the nature or essence of truth or justification, where these claims cannot be warranted by empirical inquiry and reflection on the use of words alone—accounts that claim to provide a special kind of insight into a special kind of problem only philosophy has the tools to investigate. To be an anti-essentialist with respect to truth is not to offer a quasi-metaphysical thesis—namely, that truth has no essence. It is to hold that once we have learned everything Davidson, Austin, and others like them have to teach us about the behavior of *is true* and cognate expressions, there is nothing remaining to be told about the concept or essence of truth. To be an anti-essentialist with respect to justification is not to empty one's mind of all beliefs of a certain type—namely, those about what justification is like. It is to hold that social-scientific and historical insight into the character of justificatory practices plus Wittgensteinian insight into the use of epistemic terminology give all the insight into justification we know how to get.

The only way to defend such methodological nominalism consistently, of course, is to provide enough piecemeal "immanent" criticism of one's philosophical opponents that the burden of proof eventually shifts to their side. A transcendental, knock-down, drag-out argument demonstrating the impossibility of securing philosophical accounts of truth and justification in the grand style would itself be an example of philosophy in the grand style. Nothing prevents the opponents from clinging to their hopes in the face of the pragmatist's criticism of this or that instance of philosophy in the grand style. After all, nobody any longer supposes that it will be easy to achieve traditional philosophical goals. And as Santurri has said, "recognition of the project's difficulty is not in itself reason for abandoning the task" (p. 338). But the pragmatist's immanent criticism aims for a cumulative effect: unless somebody succeeds one of these days in showing how to get past the usual pattern of pragmatic counterargument, sooner or later almost everybody will cease believing that it can be done and stop paying attention to the remaining diehards who keep trying.

Rorty sometimes says, quite misleadingly, that he has no argument to offer against the hope for distinctively philosophical accounts of truth and justification.[16] By this I take him to mean that he has no compelling argument cast in a neutral vocabulary to support a blanket rejection of the tradition. He does, however, supply a lot of effective immanent criticism by starting within traditional philosophical vocabularies, granting certain traditional premises for purposes of argument, and then getting traditional arguments to deconstruct, usually by exposing confusion (such as between justifying and explaining a belief) or equivocation (such as between two senses of *world* or *reference*). The danger of argument by immanent criticism is that by using a vocabulary he wants to displace, he risks seeming to favor substantive theses within its dialectical space, which is not his intention. Pithy little formulae are the most obvious symptoms of getting trapped within the vocabulary one is trying to overcome.

Immanent criticism is unlikely to snare many converts for pragmatism unless the need for distinctively philosophical accounts of truth and justification ceases to be felt. Anybody who, after witnessing the latest round of pragmatic deconstructions, nonetheless shares Santurri's conviction that "the quest for rational groundings seems as needful as ever" (p. 338) will be inclined to keep up the good fight. Needful for what purpose? I suspect that Santurri fears that without help from a philosophical picture—a picture according to which we are valuable because a special something glows within the human breast, or because a transcendent Moral Law replete with propositions about human rights is "out there" to be corresponded to—we shall begin to lose faith in the values of Western civilization. The habitual activities through which we express our respect for justice and love of other people will wither away for want of grounding.

It is doubtful, however, that very many people use such a picture to hold up their first-order moral beliefs and dispositions. To suppose otherwise is to make the entire populace out to be philosophers. Our fellow citizens are not nervously awaiting vindications of philosophical pictures before proceeding to hold each other valuable. A modest pragmatism, fully understood, would encourage us to view most of our first-order moral beliefs as more certain, and most of our dispositions as more worthy of confidence, than any of the pictures philosophers have introduced in hope of explaining and grounding them.

Pragmatists need not desire to banish such pictures from the culture.

The problem is not with the pictures themselves but, first, with the distinctively philosophical purposes they are sometimes meant to serve, and, second, with the misguided fear that our ethos depends as a matter of empirical fact upon having those philosophical purposes fulfilled. I have no wish to oppose the metaphor of an inner something-or-other as the locus of human dignity, or the idea of a Moral Law as such. Both can be tolerated as picturesque, if well-worn, images cast up by our ethos. Because I believe philosophers have been wrong to suppose that these pictures can be made to perform the epistemological functions often intended for them, however, I see only harm coming from the repeated assertion that they are essential to the survival of our ethos. People who are persuaded that our ethos cannot survive unless philosophers can show how these pictures ground or explain our first-order moral beliefs and dispositions are, from my point of view, all too likely to give up on our ethos when they read the relevant philosophy and find the arguments wanting.

Suppose, however, that Santurri became convinced that such arguments will never be successful. He might still become what Timothy Jackson has described as a *skeptical realist*, admitting that we will never apprehend reality as it is in itself (since apprehension always takes reality under a description) but hoping against hope that our beliefs correspond to that reality and wishing all the while that immediate apprehension of the real were possible.[17] Why not take the upshot of Rorty's immanent criticism to be skeptical realism?

Once the significance of pragmatic counterarguments sinks in, Rorty thinks, they make the hope of apprehending undescribed reality seem incoherent. The realist's situation is not like having good chances for promotion and then having hope dashed by a nasty departmental chairman. Having a coherent hope dashed might give me good reason for being disconsolate. The skeptical realist is more like someone who wants to be his own father and then has the nature of that desire brought to light in therapy. He might be unhappy, perhaps even very hard to console, upon realizing that he will never be his own father, but it's hard to see how he could have good reason for wallowing in the disappointment of such an incoherent desire. What fuels the unhappiness, it seems safe to suppose, is still half-thinking that maybe the desire does make sense.

The inconsolable skeptical realist seems to agree on almost all matters of substance with the pragmatist who says that "correspondence to undescribed reality" can play no role in justification and should therefore be banned from epistemology. They disagree only about whether it is reasonable to wallow in disappointment once a long-held goal comes to seem unattainable in principle. Pragmatists can refuse metaphysical comfort because they adopt a Buddhist-like attitude toward incoherent desires that add nothing but disappointment to life. That is, they try to extinguish such desires. The skeptical realist sees this as sour grapes and portrays pragmatists as using a program of adaptive preference to deny a desire built into the nature of human beings or their rationality. Pragmatists, in turn, see this move as the skeptical realists' attempt to foist off their incoherent desires on everybody else. The skeptical realist, on this view, is marked by the obsessions of a half-successful cure.

So another part of the pragmatist's strategy is to show that the need for something deeper than empirical or Wittgensteinian insight into truth and justification is something you have good reason to feel only if you adopt a certain vocabulary and accept certain assumptions. This Rorty tries to accomplish mainly in two ways. First, he tries to establish that recognition of the problems we are tempted to regard as perennial and eternal—problems alleged to arise as soon as any rational being reflects—cannot be found in the historical record before this or that particular vocabulary took hold among the intellectuals at a certain date. He thus intends to cast doubt on the claim that the problems are really perennial and eternal. In this respect, his use of historiography resembles MacIntyre's, minus MacIntyre's desire to retrieve premodern concepts and habits. If a set of problems came on the scene as a result of the adoption of a vocabulary, Rorty thinks we should be able to leave those problems behind if we can bring ourselves to abandon the vocabulary.

Second, Rorty tries to show by the example of his own overcomings that we can get by rather nicely without either using traditional philosophical vocabularies or solving the problems that arise within them. We can get along with our lives even better, he is telling us, if we learn how to disregard such problems while attending instead to problems of other sorts.

III

This, however, is where the moral consequences of pragmatism begin to get more interesting. For the opponents of pragmatism, Santurri and

Jackson among them, charge that it deprives us of moral resources we need if we want to get along with our lives in any reasonable continuity with the best in Western civilization. Pragmatism, the critics conclude, fails its own pragmatic test. As we saw in the previous chapter, Rorty's pragmatism is meant to serve liberal society and the conversation of the West by saving them from their philosophical critics and defenders alike. Our way of life, he says, looks better without the philosophical foundations that its defenders try to supply for it, and its critics' success in demolishing those foundations is therefore beside the point. Rorty's pragmatic deconstructions have a moral purpose. He realizes, nevertheless, that there remains a gnawing moral concern to be addressed, a concern about "the issue between lovers of conversation and lovers of self-deceptive rhetoric" or between lovers of justice and champions of tyranny.[18]

The concern is whether we can be pragmatists without, as a practical matter, ultimately betraying the very ends that pragmatic liberalism is meant to serve by having too little to say in the face of tyranny or by losing access to our own culture's reservoir of moral reasons. It is this concern more than anything else that makes people today feel that the Enlightenment "quest for rational groundings seems as needful as ever." As Rorty himself says:

Our tyrants write philosophy in the morning and torture in the afternoon; our bandits alternately read Hölderlin and bomb people into bloody scraps. So our culture clings, more than ever, to the hope of the Enlightenment. . . . We hope that by formulating the *right* conceptions of reason, of science, of thought, of knowledge, of morality, the conceptions which express their *essence*, we shall have a shield against irrationalist resentment and hatred.[19]

What, then, can the pragmatist say when the torturers come? What reasons could a society of pragmatists have for holding out against the tyrants?

They will, I suspect, be reasons of a familiar sort, reasons having to do with the viciousness of certain kinds of people, the consequences of certain kinds of acts, the violation of certain rights, the relative advantages of one way of life over another. Modest pragmatists will see such reasons as making some claim to truth. They need not shrink from the notion that one conception of reason or of morality is right and another wrong. They will be anti-essentialists in the sense of denying that there are any privileged forms of insight into the essence of reason or the nature of morality over and above what empirical inquiry and Wittgensteinian investigations (or ordinary moral reflection) can teach us. But they will not hesitate to allow their moral conclusions to be informed by their justified beliefs about what human beings are like, what has transpired in history, and what the likely consequences of tyranny will be. There is, then, a strong sense in which they can have a "theory of human nature" and appeal to it in their moral reasoning.[20] How far such an appeal will go in dissuading tyrants from tyranny or providing a shield against irrationalist resentment and hatred is, however, another question.

To answer it, we need to consider a passage widely thought to prove that decadence and moral aphasia are the chief moral consequences of pragmatism, a passage near the end of the introduction to *Consequences*:

Suppose that Socrates was wrong, that we have *not* once seen the Truth, and so will not, intuitively, recognize it when we see it again. This means that when the secret police come, when the torturers violate the innocent, there is nothing to be said to them of the form "There is something within you which you are betraying. Though you embody the practices of a totalitarian society which will endure forever, there is something beyond those practices which condemns you." (p. xlii, italics in original)

Rorty grants that this thought "is hard to live with." So, he says, is Jean-Paul Sartre's remark that someday the fascists may triumph, that "the others may be cowardly or miserable enough to let them get away with it," and that when such a time comes, if it comes, "fascism will be the truth of man."

Such thoughts may be hard to live with, Rorty implies, but live with them we must. Pragmatism holds out no metaphysical comfort. That much is clear. But it also seems to provide no moral response to the Terror. Can morality itself survive widespread acceptance of such thoughts? Or will the dissemination of pragmatism lead, in practice, to the demise of morality? Before answering these questions, we need to determine exactly what Rorty has said in this passage, what can possibly be said on his behalf, and whether the source of any remaining difficulty in the passage can be traced to his pragmatic approach to truth and justification.

The whole passage is framed by the supposition that Socrates was wrong, "we have not once seen the Truth, and so will not, intuitively, recognize it when we see it again." If I understand this much, I am prepared to go along. Almost nobody accepts a Platonic view of memory anymore, nor do most of us think that we can recognize the Truth as such by intuition.[21] But nothing much follows from denying that Socrates was right about these things. You could grant that Socrates was wrong and still say to the secret police that they are violating rights. You could even say, in perfect sincerity and consistency, precisely what Rorty says you're logically prohibited from saying. You could, for example, be a Kantian. So the consequences of this particular supposition can't be the real issue. The real issue, at least as far as I am concerned, is what follows from the supposition that pragmatism is true—the kind of pragmatism that avoids reductionism and radical relativism, the kind I've associated with a modest methodological nominalism. If we accept pragmatism in this sense, what can we say to the secret police?

First of all, whatever you say to the secret police will be unlikely to convince them. There won't be time for that, and they'll probably be too vicious to listen, let alone to be persuaded. This is a very important point, not to be belittled. When the tyrants have taken over and send their thugs to call upon you at midnight, arguments from Kant and Donagan aren't going to help. This is clearly a situation in which pragmatists would be no worse off than traditional philosophers. As Bernard Williams put it, "What will the professor's justification do, when they break down the door, smash his spectacles, take him away?"[22]

But suppose that isn't the issue. Suppose a secret policeman and I are stranded in a cave together (with food and without weapons) for a year, and I have a lot of time to work on him. Can I, while remaining true to my kind of pragmatism, appeal to something within him which he is betraying? On the assumption that Socrates was wrong about memory, I won't be able to appeal to some Truth he must have already seen and forgotten. More to the point, if my pragmatism is right, I shouldn't assume in advance that he will already possess reasons and habits essentially identical to mine. He might even be justified in believing various things I know to be false. And the environment in which he has been trained has undoubtedly engrained in him deeply vicious habits likely to lessen the effects of any arguments I might offer.

Nothing prevents me, however, from practicing immanent criticism in hope of finding a contradiction that might convince the fascist to change his mind. I can try to exploit whatever vocabularies and patterns of reasoning we have in common, using them toward the end of bringing him around. If I am successful, though, it will probably be because he has observed me long enough to be taken, despite himself, by the way I live, to find his loves gradually shifting, irrespective of argument, in the direction of mine, to become, through unconscious modeling more than argumentative persuasion, a less vicious person. Then, and only then, are the arguments likely to make a difference. He might, of course, be too far gone, too bitter or hateful or narrow-minded to reach. It is, moreover, quite conceivable that a whole society could suffer moral atrophy in this way. As Rorty puts it, "The pragmatist must avoid saying . . . that the truth is *fated* to win."[23]

Rorty seems to go further, immediately after quoting the remark from Sartre, when he says that "there is nothing deep down inside us except what we have put there ourselves." I'm not sure what this comment means. It seems a negative ontological thesis, a view about what there isn't. No such thesis follows from pragmatism in the carefully delimited sense I have been defending. Is Rorty denying that human beings are innately valuable? Perhaps. But again, no such denial follows from what I have been saying about truth and justification. I do have doubts about the idea that being valuable, having rights, and related notions can be explained by "something" that's inside of you. Where is that something? Under the left nipple? Why would something inside you make you valuable? Such pictures lack the power to explain. Doubting the explanatory value of such pictures, however, need not commit me to doubting that people are worth caring about and caring for.

Now consider Rorty's suggestion concerning something else not to be said to the torturer: "Though you embody the practices of a totalitarian society which will endure forever, there is something beyond those practices which condemns you." That suggestion seems false, on the first reading that occurs to me, even according to Rorty's own view. There is something beyond totalitarian practices that condemns the torturer. There's me. There's my (better) set of practices. There's the example of every remaining virtuous person, as well as whatever exemplary lives we can keep alive in memory. But Rorty would grant that, so I'm led to wonder whether he could have meant something else.

Maybe he meant that the difference between a good practice and a bad one isn't to be explained by reference to some transcendent third thing "beyond" both of them. Perhaps he meant, even more modestly, that the conflict between a good practice and a bad one isn't to be settled by reference to a neutral standard of goodness "beyond" all particular ways of life. Neither of these claims need imply that the one way of life isn't really worse than the other, that there is no moral truth of the matter. The pragmatist's doubts should be confined here to the question of how to explain the difference or how to adjudicate the conflict between good and bad practices. The pragmatist need only be saying that the Moral Law, as it is in itself, explains nothing and is powerless to adjudicate conflicts. For those purposes, we have only practical wisdom and our own justified beliefs about the moral truth to go on.

So far, we've seen that on some readings, parts of Rorty's secret-police passage simply don't follow from the doctrines I have isolated and described as a fittingly modest pragmatism. On other readings, those parts of the passage seem more innocuous. At best, then, the passage succeeds mainly in muddying the waters. But the part of the passage I most regret is the remark quoted favorably from Sartre. Why should we be tempted, if we are good pragmatists, to describe the possible future triumph of the fascists as a situation in which "fascism will be the truth of man"? Surely, if we are going to avoid the temptation to define truth as warranted assertibility, if we grant (as Rorty does on p. xxv, several pages before mentioning the secret police) that "Putnam is right that no such analysis will work," then Sartre is wrong to say that fascism, if triumphant, would be the truth of man. It might be something people would believe to be true. It might even be something they would be justified in believing to be true, given the sorry state of their epistemic and evaluative practices. But it would still be false. The triumph of fascism presents such a terrible prospect, after all, largely because it would be the triumph of falsehood over truth.

IV

From my vantage point, I usually take it as a sign of backsliding or an invitation to misreading when favorable references to Sartre and existentialism appear in Rorty's work. For as I read Sartre's existentialism, it does spell trouble for ethics. And it does so precisely by accepting the forms of moral nihilism, epistemic reductionism, and radical relativism that a fittingly modest pragmatism shuns.

I am put at ease when I find Rorty saying in *Philosophy and the Mirror of Nature* that we might "in an imaginary age in which consensus in these areas was almost complete, view morality, physics, and psychology as equally 'objective'" (p. 335). Similarly, I am pleased to find him rejecting the idea "that once 'all the facts are in' nothing remains except the 'noncognitive' adoption of an attitude—a choice which is not rationally discussable" (p. 363). He adds, again entirely to my liking, that we should not

pretend that we can split ourselves up into knowers of true sentences on the one hand and choosers of lives or actions or works of art on the other. These artificial diremptions make it impossible to get the notion of edification into focus. Or, more exactly, they tempt us to think of edification as having nothing to do with the rational faculties which are employed in normal discourse. (p. 364)

He goes on, if I interpret his intentions correctly, to praise Gadamer for trying to "get rid of the distinction between fact and value" and for trying to break down "the distinctions which Kant made among cognition, morality, and aesthetic judgment."

At his best, then, Rorty shows us how to blur metaphysical distinctions between morality and science, subjectivity and objectivity, making and finding—distinctions the existentialist merely inverts by glorifying subjectivity, renouncing the desire for objectivity in ethics as a form of bad faith, and encouraging us to stare bravely into the abyss while inventing our own values. But it must be admitted that Rorty often seems merely to invert such distinctions himself. I grow uneasy, for example, when he introduces his own "'existentialist' distinction between people as empirical selves and as moral agents"—all the more so when he explicates this distinction in a way that makes "questions of moral choice or of edification" seem essentially separate from the "search for objective truth" (pp. 382–383). And many passages in his published writings seem not so much to blur the line between making and finding as to express a Romantic preference for making over finding.

Is Rorty guilty of inconsistency? Is he a modest pragmatist who occasionally backslides into existentialist modernism, or is he simply, like the rest of us, the author of some sentences that require further gloss to be redeemed from misinterpretation? I shall not try to answer these questions. My concern instead is to see what these passages can teach us about ourselves and our situation. What they bring out, I think, is the importance of moving beyond modernism in all its forms—not only the optimistic modernism of the moral Esperantists, but also the existentialist modernism that reacts to the disappointment of Enlightenment hopes by glorying in the creation of meaning and value *ex nihilo*.[24]

Rorty keeps alive existentialist modernism—and MacIntyre's concerns about pragmatism as an expression of an emotivist culture—when he says such things as this:

> We need an apologetics for liberalism which revolves around the hope that culture as a whole can be 'aestheticised' rather than around the Enlightenment hope that it might be 'scientised'. Liberal politics is best suited to a culture whose hero is the strong poet rather than the truth-seeking, 'logical', 'objective' scientist.[25]

Such a culture, Rorty says, would "slough off" Enlightenment vocabulary and thereby cease to be "haunted by spectres called 'relativism' and 'irrationalism'." It should be clear, however, that this passage hardly succeeds in sloughing off Enlightenment oppositions between the aesthetic and the scientific, the strong poet and the objective scientist, making and finding, free exercise of one's subjectivity and constraint by objective reality. It merely inverts the oppositions, letting the positive valuation fall with Romantic rather than Enlightenment emphasis; because it does no more than that, it makes the spectres of "relativism" and "irrationalism" inevitable.

Like Rorty, I want to slough off Enlightenment metaphors and to be freed from the spectres of irrationalism and radical relativism. My claim is that the only way to succeed in fully overcoming Enlightenment modernism, thereby exorcizing the spectres of relativism and irrationalism, is to avoid opposing making to finding, strong poet to objective scientist. That means adopting a language in which it makes sense to say that making and finding are equally present in the work of the poet, the scientist, and the moralist. In such a language, we would know how to say that poetry and science and ethics lay claim to truth and objectivity while also saying that their objective discovery of truth depends upon and is inseparable from the invention of linguistic artifacts that bring into being new tropes—and eventually new truths, truths that pay their way by serving as rules for action. To speak such a language is to resist the temptation to single out either the strong poet or the objective scientist as a cultural hero.[26] It is also to put the social critic or the activist on equal footing with both. It is to see each as engaged in a kind of art that manages, much of the time, to ensnare truth while informing action, a kind of *praxis* in which poetic means and objective constraints have a place, a kind of seeking after truth that remains on intimate terms with delight in beauty and the life well lived.

Kant was not wrong to distinguish cognitive, practical, and aesthetic dimensions of human life. He was wrong, however, to distinguish them sharply—in effect, handing over each to an essentially separate domain of culture with its own conceptual framework and constitutive rules. Philosophers overreact to Kant's lines of demarcation, and give pragmatism a bad name, when they seem bent on reducing the cognitive to the merely practical or the merely aesthetic. A modest pragmatism needs to publicize its antireductive intent. It needs to display the cognitive, practical, and aesthetic dimensions of human life diffused throughout the culture, inseparably interrelated and not parcelled out as the special responsibilities of the scientist, the moralist, and the strong poet. That is why Gadamer's attempt to show that truth-seeking and practical wisdom play a role in aesthetic endeavors and Kuhn's attempt to show that practical and aesthetic judgments figure heavily in scientific revolutions each serve the purposes of the modest pragmatist. It is also why a modest pragmatism insists on reclaiming, in its own way, the cognitive as well as the aesthetic aspects of morals.

Rorty is suspicious of Habermas's "universal pragmatics" because

it seems to promise just what Sartre tells us we are not going to have—a way of seeing freedom as nature (or, less cryptically, a way of seeing our creation of, and choice between, vocabularies in the same "normal" way as we see ourselves *within* one of those vocabularies).[27]

I, too, am suspicious of Habermas's "universal pragmatics." As I hinted in an earlier chapter, I wish he had been content with immanent criticism and hadn't gone transcendental, trying to perform an essentially Kantian service for our culture without using outmoded Kantian means. Yet I am also suspicious of Rorty's apparent suggestion that freedom—the creation of, and choice between, vocabularies—is something we exhibit outside one of those vocabularies. Whatever Rorty means to suggest in this passage, I suggest that our inability to secure an ultimate language of rational commensuration shouldn't induce us to think of our decisions to invent or employ a vocabulary as ultimately unconstrained, as taking place, by necessity, outside of and epistemically prior to the adoption of any vocabulary.

On the picture I call existentialist, beneath all our "normal" choices,

which are carried out within the logical space of one or another vocabulary and governed by its "objective" constraints, lie our ultimate
choices, which are carried out, perhaps unconsciously, in the terrible
vacuum of perfect freedom, where unconstrained will is governed by
nothing but its own inner movement. Anyone who accepts this existentialist picture in the name of pragmatism will finally be unable to reclaim ethics as a full-fledged cognitive endeavor. "Truth" and "objectivity" in ethics will remain but a mask for arbitrary will. Vulgar
pragmatism resists this picture by saying that there is an ultimate language of rational commensuration after all—the language of instrumental reason, in which one weighs the costs and benefits of adopting
vocabularies, the better to maximize utility in the consequences of
one's mental acts.

A modest pragmatism, however, says no such thing. It abandons the
optimistic modernist's hopes for an ultimate language of rational commensuration, for it views the language of instrumental reason as just
another language—a useful one, to be sure, but not one that enjoys
the privileges which would derive from being prior to all the rest. It
insists that the creation of new vocabularies always begins with existing
linguistic patterns, making something new out of something found.
And it insists that choice between or among vocabularies itself always
takes place within some vocabulary or other, although not always the
same one, governed by entrenched standards and assumptions, as well
as the perceived needs of the moment.

The existentialist's freedom is too sublime and vacuous to be worth
having. Thinking that such freedom lies beneath our "normal" choices
misdescribes the moral life as we know it. So, at any rate, says the
modest pragmatist, for whom the choice of a language for choosing
itself must be couched in some language. It may not necessarily be a
language we choose, of course, and it is perhaps only rarely a language
we employ self-consciously. It may simply be one we find ourselves
speaking, the only language at our disposal under the circumstances,
or the only one a sane person could use for present purposes. And
while we do not choose the circumstances in which we initially find
ourselves—the age in which we live, the conceptual resources at hand,
the traditions and problems impinging on us in our particular time and
place—we can, if we have the requisite virtues and avoid being
crushed by the secret police, choose to criticize received doctrines, re-
pudiate specific authorities, and foment change in hope of serving jus-

tice and making things better. If we do not so choose, if we allow the discovery of our particularity to insulate the established order from criticism, what began as unchosen contingency becomes complicity in that order's injustice.[28]

Modest pragmatism, by itself, holds no brief for conservativism in politics and morals.[29] Nor, for that matter, does it incline toward revolution. It merely confronts us with the contingency of our location in society and history while pointing out that selective retrieval and creative *bricolage* have long been the lot of conservative and revolutionary alike. It deprives us, to be sure, of metaphysical comforts and epistemological guarantees but not of the need to judge moral propositions true or false, justified or unjustified, and to act accordingly. Its doubts about philosophical theories leave the notions of moral truth and justified moral belief intact, ready for use, just as always. No such doubts, properly construed, are likely to endanger the moral inheritance of Western civilization, although they may of course endanger somebody's favorite philosophical interpretation of that inheritance. What you make of what you find in the moral traditions at hand will depend upon what those traditions are like as well as the extent to which you possess the virtues needed to judge them wisely and justly. If you lack those virtues or if the conceptual resources within your reach have disintegrated beyond repair, no exercise of existential freedom, no invention of value, will make things better.

What, then, is to be said about the established order, insofar as we can make it out clearly at all? In what terms might we describe and assess pluralistic society, consistent with the best in contemporary pragmatism, if we find the most familiar forms of apologetics for and criticism of liberal society equally distorted by philosophical assumptions? With this question, as I have said, Rorty helps us little. In the final chapter, I shall return to MacIntyre, borrow some terms from him, disconnect them from his story of decline and fall, and try to show how they might contribute to a more perceptive account of our society than he himself provides.

12

SOCIAL CRITICISM WITH
BOTH EYES OPEN

The early chapters of *After Virtue* portray pluralistic society as too fragmented by fundamental disagreement and conceptual diversity to sustain rational discourse. I have criticized that picture for reasons similar
to the ones adduced against nihilism and skepticism in Part 1, and I
have expressed doubts about both the details and the general trajectory
of MacIntyre's historical narrative. Yet I have also hinted that Mac-
Intyre's book does offer some of the conceptual tools needed to correct
that picture. What could they be?

The most valuable part of MacIntyre's book, to my mind, is the
explication of the virtues found in chapters 14 and 15. If we take up
the idiom he develops there, dissociating it from other aspects of the
book, we shall possess a vocabulary of moral description and assessment
in which a powerful and penetrating critique of our society can be
carried out. Such an account will not follow *After Virtue's* premises
about the extent of moral disagreement and conceptual incommensurability to its forebodings of moral catastrophe and the new dark ages. It
will rather move, as does MacIntyre's explication of the virtues,
through three stages: a first stage that concerns "the goods internal to
social practices," a second that concerns "the good of a whole human
life," and a third that concerns the concept of "an ongoing tradition." If
we want to know what the fate of the virtues has been in our society,
and we take our cue from the structure of MacIntyre's own explication,

the first task will be something *After Virtue*, oddly enough, barely begins—namely, a detailed investigation of our actual social practices. In this concluding chapter of an already wide-ranging book on the languages of morals, I obviously cannot go much further than he does, but I do want to say enough to suggest what such an analysis might look like. This should at least indicate why I think MacIntyre's vocabulary could prove fruitful as a language of perspicuous contrast and why it makes possible an account of social criticism unlike the one he offers elsewhere in his book.

I

By "social practices," MacIntyre means something quite particular. It is the same thing Bellah and his colleagues mean by the phrase "practices of commitment." A social practice, says MacIntyre, is

any coherent and complex form of socially established cooperative human activity through which goods internal to that form of activity are realized in the course of trying to achieve those standards of excellence which are appropriate to, and partially definitive of, that form of activity, with the result that human powers to achieve excellence, and human conceptions of the ends and goods involved, are systematically extended. *(After Virtue, p. 187)*

The crucial notion here, for my purposes, is that of goods internal to a form of activity, as distinct from goods external to it. Internal goods are those that can be realized only by participating in the activity well, as judged by its standards of excellence. External goods, in contrast, include prestige, status, and money—which can be achieved for reasons having little to do with excellence in the activity. One can know little about internal goods without acquiring experience and linguistic competence in the relevant activity. I would say that the requisite experience and competence can, in some instances, come at second-hand, through a skillful reporter's thick descriptions, although MacIntyre seems skeptical of this.

You can of course win prestige, status, and money by participating well in a genuine social practice like chess. But you can also achieve such goods by cheating at chess (if you don't get caught) or by participating in some other form of activity. Such goods are therefore external to chess. The goods internal to chess, goods that Kasparov has achieved and I have not, cannot be identified without employing the language of chess. Kasparov couldn't have achieved them by cheating at chess, and he couldn't have achieved them by becoming an excellent architect. The prestige Kasparov has won by playing chess can be won in other ways. Kasparov could not have achieved goods internal to chess, however, without playing chess, subjecting himself to its rules, and eventually acquiring qualities that enable him to satisfy its standards of performance. Kasparov's performance, needless to say, goes beyond competence. True masters go beyond the highest standards of excellence known to their contemporaries. They extend those standards, thereby establishing their own authority as master practitioners and enriching the goods that can be pursued and achieved by their successors.

Chess is only one of MacIntyre's examples of a social practice, a useful one for illustrative purposes if not a practice central to our society. It clearly exhibits all the traits indicated in the definition. But MacIntyre wants the term "social practice" to have quite broad application: "arts, sciences, games, politics in the Aristotelian sense, the making and sustaining of family life, all fall under the concept" (p. 188). Yet not all forms of activity do. Taking long showers does not. Nor, according to MacIntyre, do tic-tac-toe, bricklaying, and planting turnips, although he doesn't explain why. Presumably, he finds them insufficiently complex or cooperative, their standards of excellence insufficiently developed, and the ends and goods involved insufficiently capable of systematic extension for them to be grouped with activities like chess, architecture, and farming.

Take tic-tac-toe. It doesn't take long for an average child to acquire the skills needed to end every game of tic-tac-toe in nothing worse than a draw. Nothing within the rules of the game is going to make the activity more complicated, its standards of excellence more demanding, or its goods more worthwhile. So it makes some sense to exclude tic-tac-toe from the class of social practices that includes chess.

Some of MacIntyre's critics have complained that his line distinguishing activities like tic-tac-toe from activities like chess is imprecise. So it is. Bricklaying, for example, is harder to exclude from the class of social practices than tic-tac-toe is. But for my purposes, the fuzziness of the border matters little. We could just as easily count bricklaying as a relatively uncomplicated or undeveloped social practice as exclude it from the class altogether, provided bricklayers in fact pursue internal goods in the relevant sense and need to acquire certain qualities if they want to achieve those goods. What matters more than degree of complication and development is the tolerably clear distinction between internal and external goods. A virtue, as MacIntyre initially defines it in this context (before introducing further qualifications later), is "an acquired human quality the possession and exercise of which tends to enable us to achieve those goods which are *internal* to practices and the lack of which effectively prevents us from achieving any such goods" (p. 191, my emphasis).

Medical care is a social practice in MacIntyre's sense. Doctors and nurses pursue goods internal to the practice of medical care, goods that cannot be achieved in any other practice or by any other means than by being a good doctor or nurse, acquiring and exhibiting the qualities, forms of excellence, or virtues peculiar to those roles. Medical care requires the cultivation of various technical skills. But it also requires the cultivation of qualities that might be called the cardinal virtues of medicine—that is to say, the principal moral virtues as they appear when ordered toward the goods of medical care: *practical wisdom*, the ability to exercise sound medical judgment and discernment; *justice*, the capacity to give everyone involved in or affected by the practice their due, whether they be patients, their families, one's assistants, one's students, one's peers, those who have earned the right to speak and act with authority within the practice (whatever their relation to positions of power), other members of the community, or future generations; *courage*, the strength of character required to risk danger, embarrassment, alienation from one's cohort, loss of income, threats to one's career, and so on in order to pursue goods internal to the practice (as by opening a clinic in a high-crime area, admitting error in the treatment of a patient, or testifying against an incompetent colleague); and *temperance*, a trait that keeps one pursuing goods internal to the practice, undeflected by goods of other kinds (as when a surgeon leaves a dinner early on the night before operating or a nurse spends evenings learning new diagnostic skills instead of out on the town).

The virtues of medical care are still acquired, for the most part, the old-fashioned way—through imitation of role models. Moral philosophy is not often a formal part of the process. Few doctors or nurses would break into discourse about the four cardinal virtues if asked to speak about their professional lives, but this does not mean that their training and early years on the job leave them without some measure of practical wisdom, justice, courage, and temperance. Nurses may not say that a doctor exhibits the vice of imprudence, but they do castigate doctors for showing poor judgment. Dr. Dimsdale's patients complain that he is insensitive, Dr. Kildare's say that she knows how to talk to

you. A new resident on the floor, undergoing apprenticeship in obstet-
rics, who repeatedly fails to do a fair share of the work or to submit to
the genuine authority of experience may not be described as unjust but
will surely be found wanting by fellow practitioners. The same fate
awaits wimps and drunks.

A systematic vocabulary of the virtues does help us reflect on a practice like medical care and compare it with other practices; it may even
do some good to teach prospective doctors and nurses to speak and
think in such a language. It would be foolish, however, to overlook the
extent to which a practice like medical care already employs a nuanced
and supple language of character assessment, ordered toward goods internal to the practice itself but analogous to, and perhaps parasitic
upon, languages embedded in other practices ordered toward other
goods. To understand that language, one need only listen in patiently
as doctors and nurses talk about their lives, their patients, and each
other, uninterrupted by Socratic questions. Probing that talk for foundational principles doesn't help much. Its significance is all on the
surface, reflecting on goods to be sought, evils to be avoided, the do's
and don'ts of ends and means, the joys and sorrows of unintended
consequences, good and bad traits of character, and agents who deserve
praise or blame, each bit of discourse bearing some intelligible relation
to other bits and to the practice as a whole, ordered toward its distinctive goods.

The idiom of contemporary American medicine is not anybody's
first moral language, temporally speaking. But then neither is the language Bellah and his associates call individualism. True, most Americans have acquired a stock of shopworn individualistic sayings by the
time they reach adolescence (at which point the sayings often come
back to haunt the parents and teachers who transmitted them). I have
heard few such sayings during the time I have spent in my children's
nursery-school classes, where they tend to be uttered, if my experience
is any guide, mainly to discourage the development of excessive depen-
dency in children, not to enunciate underlying principles. How can
we discover the first moral language of America? Only, I think, by
participant-observation in the middle-class home, in the classroom,
on the playground, on ghetto streets, and so on. Brief consideration of
events in these settings already tells us something of interest. American
parents devote long hours (and at times great expense) to conscripting
young people into social practices. Tic-tac-toe, dolls, toy guns, and

jungle gyms are followed by chess, ballet, piano lessons, and baseball gloves. One function of the educational system is to recruit and train for the arts and sciences, all of which clearly qualify as social practices in MacIntyre's sense. So too do the forms of music, dance, and sport that thrive on urban streets.

Our society, in short, is richly endowed with widely valued social practices and goes to remarkable lengths to initiate new generations into them. So if MacIntyre is right about the relation between the virtues and social practices, we should find that the first moral language learned by Americans—the language in which we first learn to assess character and conduct—is as varied and as supple as those social practices. The more we learn about the social practices around us (whether by participation, observation, or hearsay), the more variegated our conception of human excellence and our vocabulary of appraisal can become. Virtues and vices of one practice invite comparison with virtues and vices of others, lending significance to each other through analogy. A young doctor summoning up courage for the first time in the pursuit of goods internal to medicine doesn't start from scratch. Experience in other practices where other kinds of courage are required should make the going easier.

We may parrot individualistic sayings on occasion, but we also acquire the qualities needed to achieve, at least to some degree, the goods internal to the practices in which we participate, goods that are nobody's private possession and that must be sought, if sought at all, for their own sake. In acquiring these qualities, we submit to the authority of people experienced in the practices by taking their advice and imitating their actions. Think of any high-school orchestra, class play, or ballet association. How much room for unbridled individualism do you find? Rather little. The scene is likely to be dominated by a single figure of authority and strict requirements determined by cooperative pursuit of common ends. Or think of any popular sport. My daughter, Little Leaguer and Yankee fan that she is, aims to run, hit, and field not simply by the rules but as her favorite Yankee does. She studies him with the dedication of someone who needs no convincing that the goods internal to baseball are worth pursuing or that imitating excellence is the only way to achieve them. She takes instruction from her coaches and understands the meaning of their criticisms and prescriptions. If she were a third-rate basketball player like her father, she would still know, without assistance from a theory of the cardinal virtues, how to recognize instances of imprudent judgment, injustice, cowardice, and intemperance. In describing such instances, she would employ a nonphilosophical vernacular. She would speak of "poor judgment on the break," of "hogging the ball," of "chickening out," and of "dogging it" on defense. She would also listen up when a veteran player explained why teams tend to play poorly if they lack athletic analogues of the theological virtues: hope (the mean between despair and presumption), faith (trust in genuine authorities, willingness to assent to truths they teach or reveal), and love of the good (properly ordered desire for goods internal to the practice, sought for their own sake).

II

The relation between goods internal to a practice and goods external to it tends to be morally problematic—a source of temptations that test our courage and temperance, as well as a source of difficulties that require wise and just resolution. Goods can be external to a practice in more than one way. Some goods, like the satisfaction of hunger, thirst, or sexual desire, belong to no particular social practice. One can seek and achieve them without engaging in any of the complex, cooperative, virtue-dependent forms of activity MacIntyre means to single out. Other goods are external to one social practice while internal to another. Goods internal to football may be external to the practice of preventive medicine, and vice versa. The goods of medical care overlap but sometimes conflict with the goods of biomedical research.

A courageous baseball player is capable of placing of one kind of good, such as the external good of unbruised fingers, at risk in the reasonable hope of sliding safely into home with the winning run. But to risk bruised fingers without reason would be merely rash, not courageous. This is something good players know. External goods are indeed goods. It is precisely because the absence of pain in my fingers is a good and I recognize it as such that I may be inclined to avoid the catcher's shin-guards as I begin my slide into home. Similarly, it is precisely because the pleasure of satisfying my hunger, thirst, or sexual desire is a good and I recognize it as such that I may be inclined, when offered an opportunity, to seek such pleasure, even when it might incapacitate me or distract me from the pursuit of goods that would make my life better on the whole. Temperance, like courage, often is concerned with the subordination of external to internal goods.

Justice is concerned, among other things, with the distribution of goods. Within each social practice, it gives full weight, as it goes about distributing goods, to considerations intrinsic to the practice itself. It looks upon considerations derived from other practices or from the pursuit of goods like fame and wealth as inappropriate reasons for distributing internal goods. Having achieved goods internal to the practice of football gives one no legitimate claim to glowing praise for one's work as a scholar. Justice requires that a student's scholarship be assessed for its own sake, as it relates to internal goods of the scholarly practice, not for some other reason, internal to some other practice or external to all. It also requires of your physician that your care not be subordinated to the goals of biomedical research without your informed consent.

If I may borrow a phrase from Michael Walzer's discussion of "complex equality," justice entails that we must "search for principles internal to each distributive sphere," allowing no one's standing in a given social practice to be undercut by their standing in some other practice or in the power structure of an institution.[1] It also mandates that certain external goods, such as honor and prestige, be distributed in accordance with merit as judged by impersonal standards within practices, thereby constraining the behavior of institutions and those who act as their officers. And justice demands that institutional power be distributed along lines set by genuine authority within practices, not merely by accidents of birth, economic fortunes, or ability to manipulate bureaucratic forces.

So there is more to justice, as we tacitly understand it in our society, than the kind of fairness usually emphasized in liberal theory, which eschews considerations of merit and builds procedural protections around individual liberty. But again, our actual moral language is more variegated than the theorists typically suppose. Justice as fairness has its own proper sphere of moral relevance—for example, in institutional settings where imposing reasonable limits on competition among conflicting conceptions of the good serves widely shared and justifiable ends. Yet fairness must leave room for other considerations, including desert, where the ends sought within a particular social practice matter more.

To search for principles of justice internal to the various spheres is in part to determine limits for acceptable behavior—limits justified at the first stage of reflection by a view of the goods sought within a given sphere and justified at further stages of reflection by a view of how such goods would best fit together with goods of other kinds from other spheres, both in a given human life and in a given society over time. Practical wisdom, in its attempt to determine such limits, must call upon detailed familiarity with specific social practices. The general principle, "Never commit injustice, either as an end in itself or as a means to some other end," expresses the importance of such limits, as well as the spirit of a way of life that depends upon their observance. The limits themselves, however, vary from sphere to sphere. The general principle abridges them; it does not, in abstraction from actual social practices, possess enough content to be their foundation.

Social practices are often embodied in institutions. In our society, the practice of medical care is embodied in institutions such as professional associations, medical schools, partnerships, independent hospitals, and increasingly powerful commercial hospital chains. It is also closely related to broader institutions such as the capitalist market and governmental agencies. Without some sort of sustaining institutions, the practice would change dramatically for the worse, if not collapse altogether. But that is only the happier half of the story. Institutions, as MacIntyre says, necessarily trade heavily in external goods: "They are involved in acquiring money and other material goods; they are structured in terms of power and status, and they distribute money, power and status as rewards. Nor could they do otherwise if they are to sustain not only themselves, but also the practices of which they are the bearer" (p. 194). MacIntyre also points out that institutions typically pose significant moral threats to the social practices they make possible. Goods like money and power and status, which have no internal relation to a social practice like medical care, can compete with and even engulf goods internal to the practice.

We are right to worry about a system in which the proliferation and distribution of external goods makes doctors and prospective doctors lose sight of the goods internal to medical care. That the distributive system is unjust becomes clear the moment we consider the standing of nurses, many of whom might have been trained as physicians had they not been women, and virtually none of whom receives external goods like money, prestige, and institutional power in anything like just proportion to their contribution to the practice of medical care. This injustice is important and merits scrutiny. For now, however, I wish to focus on the related fact that medical care in our society tends increasingly to be dominated by the modes of interaction and patterns of thought characteristic of the market and the bureaucracies, where goods external to medical care reign. Without the marketplace and the bureaucracies, the practice would undoubtedly suffer terribly. With them, it tends to be overwhelmed by goods and roles alien to its own *telos* of caring for the sick.

My maternal grandfather, for all his traditional skill in carrying out his own dying, did not die in his bedroom at home. Like the vast majority of Americans today, he died in a hospital, which he experienced as a sprawling bureaucracy, run by managers, staffed by technical experts, and clogged with advanced technology he could neither understand nor do without. Before long, he was calling his general practitioner a mere messenger boy from unseen experts. After days of frustration, he finally called a couple of doctors into his room and vented his moral outrage.

Did the doctors care for my grandfather? In a sense, yes, although for the most part they charged nurses with the tasks of caring. The physicians saw their principal task as curing, not caring. Scholars see this as part of a broad historical change in the practice of medicine. The doctor, according to William F. May, has for the most part ceased being caretaker of the sick and has become the enemy of death. "The patient," he says, "is like Poland lying helpless between two rival powers [death and medicine] that fight out their battle across relatively defenseless terrain."[2] That image sums up rather well my grandfather's last encounter with the medical system.

When I lecture on the problems of contemporary medicine, students often come to the podium afterward to swap stories worthy of Kafka, stories about how their relatives and friends have been lost in the maze of a medical bureaucracy. We've all heard enough such stories to sense the depth of the problem. Our disquiet doesn't mean that we yearn nostalgically for the past. Few of us would care to do without life-saving technology. Without the experts, the technology would not exist or be put to use. Without some sort of bureaucracy, the people who need the technology would never get together with the people who operate it. All of this is true and worth remembering, but it is equally evident that the social practice of medical care has been placed at grave risk by its own institutional setting and related social practices, and this risk is something we need to understand systematically.

It is in the uneasy relation between our social practices and our institutions that many of the most deeply felt problems of our society lie. The same pattern shows up nearly everywhere—not only in medicine but also in other practices that have managed to find a place for themselves in the economic and political institutional structure.[3] Sports, the other sort of social practice I have been exploiting for illustrative purposes, are hardly an exception to the rule. Indeed, it has become tiresome to hear complaints about how drugs, money, and status now threaten to dominate goods internal to the practice of sports at all levels of participation. The moral clichés of sports columnists, however, may tell as much about our society as protracted debates over abortion and nuclear weapons. They, too, belong to our ordinary moral language, and they express a kind of shared concern pertinent to goods and practices of many kinds.

I figure that few things could better prepare my children for the realities of life in our society than being baseball fans, for every month offers them new lessons about the troubled relations between internal and external goods in the age of advanced capitalism. They learn about vicious owners who show no appreciation for the goods of the sport and who manipulate and humiliate their employees. They learn about managers, commissioners, bureaucrats, superstars, agents, markets, racial prejudice, sexist exclusion from a social practice, the intemperance of drug use, corruption by fame, and insanely unjust salaries. Meanwhile, they also learn to love the way Don Mattingly swings a bat, to retell stories of moral heroes like Jackie Robinson, to savor the drama of a close game well played, to lose their sense of passing time, and to understand the pleasure that supervenes upon the realization of goals sought for their own sake through long and arduous effort.

III

The foregoing reflections may seem too ambivalent to lead to a clear appraisal of our predicament. I may seem to have affirmed the health of pluralistic society and the richness of its moral vocabularies at one moment while pointing out signs of rapidly advancing disease the next. I may be thought to have offered a less than fully candid apology for the established order, or perhaps, a radical critique blunted by failure of nerve. I may seem simply confused in trying to wed communitarian misgivings to liberal hopes. But I think this appearance of ambivalence derives more from the one-sidedness of the usual options in our political debate than from anything I have said.

Debate often functions as a centrifuge. The force it exerts rapidly transforms an untidy mixture of appreciations and misgivings into distinct and determinate theoretical possibilities, each of uniform density and purity, waiting only for the familiar labels. We then ask—all too confidently, as if our political options had to be described in this way—whether a given contribution to the debate is really a variety of optimism or pessimism, liberalism or communitarianism, a call for conservation of the established order or a call to replace it. That established, we rapidly send it to its appointed position on the shelf, grouped with others of its kind. Any contribution that resists the process of separation seems essentially impure, so we either discard it or label it an imperfect instance of its kind.

At its best, social criticism is more crucible than centrifuge. It holds together all the appreciations and misgivings that reasonable people in our society feel. It needs to be radical to account for their misgivings, generous in spirit to account for their appreciations, and nonutopian to sustain reasonable hope and cooperative political action among them. In aspiring to such criticism, must I waver unsteadily between the liberals and the communitarians? Not if I can shift debate to a level of specificity where the familiar labels will be pointless. We shall transform our social practices and institutions in quite particular ways, exerting some humane control over change that is already underway, or we shall simply find ourselves out of the action. The familiar labels reflect a failure of imagination. They also frustrate the effort to build consensus for specific projects of political experimentation and social amelioration. Yet we go on pinning them on one another or ourselves, in part because it is easier to strike moral poses than come up with morally balanced descriptions and concrete political proposals, and in part because the moral poses of our opponents seem to call out so urgently for censure or satire (just as ours do to them).

Consider Richard Rorty, who describes himself as liberal, and two authors sometimes described as communitarians: Cornel West, who identifies with both Afro-American Christianity and humanistic Marxism, and Robert Bellah, who aims to revive biblical and civic republican traditions. West and Bellah detest Stalinism and intolerance of religious diversity no less than Rorty does. Rorty detests racism, sexism, the behavior of multinational corporations in the Third World, and insensitivity to the plight of the underclass no less than West and Bellah do. All three favor some form of mixed economy, more nearly socialist than we have now, and would rejoice if the neoconservatives and Reaganites were deposed by a new wave of egalitarian social democrats.

These men, of course, have significant differences, but surely we further political paralysis rather than understanding when we use terms such as "liberal" and "communitarian" to divide them.

Now recall Alasdair MacIntyre, perhaps the last one here who would be expected to join an unruly assembly of social democrats in political experimentation and social amelioration. Yet, despite his distinctive arguments and preferred terminology, does he not in fact share most or all of the sentiments listed in the preceding paragraph? No doubt, his utopia would be unlike Rorty's or West's. But just how different would his political practice be, since he must live in this time and not some other? I cannot say. His writings, as I noted several chapters back, show divergent tendencies. He is not merely wistful; he sometimes makes concrete proposals. When he does so, he can sound like a pragmatic ameliorist *malgré lui*. It interests me that in his own discussion of medical care as a social practice, he sees the best available course of action open to us as defending the autonomy of patients. Declaring that "there is no longer in our culture any moral authority to whom we can hand over judgment" concerning how the goods of "health, preservation of life, and freedom from pain" are to be pursued, he concludes that each patient needs "to be given the autonomy which will enable him or her to decide where he or she stands on such issues as euthanasia and abortion." Furthermore, "We should establish means by which someone else—parent or child or designated friend—can assume responsibility in an emergency; we should make it easy and perhaps obligatory for all adults of sound mind to indicate what they want done to and for them if they cease to be able to exercise responsibility."[4]

It is hard to avoid the impression, when reading passages like these, that MacIntyre's "terminal wistfulness" makes less difference in practice than one would have thought. He too, it turns out, warms to the possibility of working "with those with whom one does share sufficient beliefs to rescue and to recreate authority" within social practices, trying one's best to mitigate the bad effects of disagreement and the threats posed by external goods. And in the medical sphere, "this means working for a variety of new forms of medical community, each with its own shared moral allegiance."[5] So he does not preclude searching out interim agreements and alliances that would make possible experimentation and amelioration, at least on a modest scale.

What, then, makes my account of medicine different from MacIntyre's, aside from tone? In the first place, I do not suppose, as he does throughout, that "what makes the problems of medical ethics unresolvable in our culture is the lack of any shared background of beliefs which could provide a context for moral reasoning by providing a view of human nature and society."[6] Indeed, I am persuaded to discard this supposition, among other reasons, by the very persuasiveness of MacIntyre's practical proposals and the moral importance of his distinction between internal and external goods. In putting these proposals forward, he is implicitly assuming three things: first, that his readers possess a rich enough "shared background of beliefs" to find his practical proposals plausible; second, that the *telos* which matters most in such practical affairs is the highest achievable good, not the ultimate good that might be achieved if everybody shared all his hopes and dreams; and third, that despite our disagreements, we can recognize certain features of "human nature" and of our society as he describes them and even determine the bearing his distinctions ought to have on action.

The advantage of MacIntyre's distinctions is that they make possible a stereoscopic social criticism, one which brings social practices and institutions, internal and external goods, into focus at the same time. We know how to describe a clinic or an academic profession in the idiom of reductionist sociology, but somehow we make everything look like a system of external goods in which people are moved only by the desire for status, money, and power. The standard way to compensate for this deficiency is to concentrate attention narrowly on the pursuit of internal goods, trying to get descriptions that are "thicker," "warmer," or "less dry" than the other approach can provide. This is done by showing "empathy" for participants in the practice, aiming to "understand" their *mentalité* or their "social world" rather than trying to "explain" what they are doing as a "function" or "reflection" of institutional structure.

Yet neither of these tacks proves entirely satisfactory. The first accounts best for the marketplace and the bureaucracy, where people are for the most part pursuing external goods or merely procedural justice and are not surprised to be told so. We may be slightly surprised, however, to be shown that the kindly old physician who took himself to be pursuing only the health and comfort of his patients was in fact unwittingly engaged throughout his life in a power struggle with his colleagues. Results like these can still occasionally take us aback morally, although they have now become unshockingly familiar. What makes people vaguely uneasy or downright suspicious of such results, of course, is that too much seems to have been explained away too quickly. Was not the kindly old physician in fact striving for the health and comfort of his patients when he engaged in hospital politics? Aren't we pursuing enlightenment when we try to account for him? Is our pursuit or his nothing more than a mask worn by motives different in kind, an epiphenomenon of institutional functions and structures? What can we do with our disillusionment, what program of action could be more than a bare assertion of arbitrary will, once a picture like this gains widespread acceptance?

The second tack, intended to compensate for deficiencies in the other, often has the effect of Romanticizing a social practice by screening external goods and institutional realities from view. It takes a more generous view of human motivation and thus grants to others the kind of charity we normally show to ourselves. It allows us to stave off a merely cynical view of people and thus to affirm our own interpretive practices. Too often, however, it seems simply to be wishing away the realities of power and the power of self-deception. And one of two things tends to happen to categories like "social world" or the principled avoidance of "explanation" when they are pressed with hard questions. They turn into mush, or they reveal underlying philosophical distinctions that few of us really want to own up to anymore.[7]

Attempts to overcome the deficiencies in both approaches have been going on for some time now, most often by means of awkward juxtaposition. A stereoscopic social criticism should help us do better. It affords a vantage point from which the strengths and weaknesses of each approach can be explained, and it enables us to enjoy the benefits of each approach without simply switching back and forth from one to the other. It brings social practices and institutions, internal and external goods, into a single frame rather than relying on *montage* to create an overall effect of unity.

A stereoscopic social criticism would make someone like the kindly physician intelligible by situating his actions within a network of social practices and institutions. Goods internal to social practices in which he participates, like the health and comfort of his patients or fellowship with his wife as they raise their children, actually motivate him and lend meaning to his life. They are not, however, the only goods he pursues, and the social practices in which he engages are embedded in institutions. He desires the well-being of his patients, yes, but also enough institutional power to influence his professional association and his hospital. Perhaps he desires fame and wealth for their own sake and not simply as a just reward, fittingly tailored to his contribution to the common good. Perhaps his desire for power seeps into other spheres of his life, reinforced by role models transmitted through institutional channels, until it overrides his desire for fellowship with his wife, reducing their relationship to an exercise of domination. Then again, perhaps not. In any event, we shall understand him poorly if either social practices or institutions, internal or external goods, are lost from view. To understand him well, we shall need a dramatic narrative—replete with moral appraisals, a coherent interpretation of his moral language, and a rendering of the mutual determination of character and circumstance.

MacIntyre's distinctions, then, make possible a stereoscopic account of our society. Such an account can show generosity in its construals of individual lives and motivations precisely because it keeps one eye trained on goods internal to social practices. If MacIntyre's own construals lack such generosity, it is only because he rushes past precisely the features of our society that make people care about it, the features that hold out some hope of transformation from within. He is convinced that, in a society not bound together by agreement on a full-fledged conception of the good, a social practice like medical care necessarily disintegrates in such a way that no genuine authority can be recognized and exercised within it.

This is so, he thinks, because without such an agreement, we won't be able to specify in a sufficiently determinate fashion the *telos* of the social practice itself. When this happens, the social practice—medicine, in this case—is reduced to a mere collection of techniques, its practitioners to technical experts for hire, its standards of excellence to the rules and regulations of a bureaucracy. That, he says, is why patients now require the protections of autonomy—as a last resort under conditions in which the social practice of medicine has disintegrated. On my account, however, we do agree on many aspects of the good life. We also mostly agree on what goods medical practice serves. We want our doctors and nurses to care for us when we are sick, to ease our suffering and cure us when they can, to inform us about how to prevent illness, to learn whatever they need to learn to do all of these things, and to receive just monetary compensation and prestige (no more, no less) in return. We are prepared, if at times reluctantly, to submit to their authority, to put our lives in their hands, even when they are strangers to us. Despite our concerns about their fallibility, the corruptions of prestige and wealth, and the facelessness of modern medical bureaucracies, we still pay tribute to the virtues and worth of medical practitioners. Few of them are saints, but most are more than technicians. Most of the cases they treat in our hospitals and clinics raise no serious moral problems for us.

It would therefore be mean-spirited or grossly hyperbolic to deny that medical care survives in our day as a valued and valuable social practice with much of its authority intact.[8] It happens, of course, that the various goods medical practitioners serve sometimes conflict. Improved technology creates new occasions for conflict among goods, occasions in which one good, like the prolongation of a life, may have to be sacrificed to another, like the easing of suffering. If we had a complete conception of the good in place, agreed upon by all, maybe we would know how to resolve such conflicts without protracted debate. If we suddenly came to religious and philosophical agreement, we might know how much or what kind of moral standing to ascribe to the unborn. These would be good things to know, but the survival of medical care as a social practice does not depend on knowing them.

IV

It follows that stereoscopic social criticism, making full use of MacIntyre's distinctions, could be much more generous in its interpretations than he tends to be. Could it also be radical? Could it give us more than trivial commentary on prevailing norms? Have I not said, in effect, that social critics can at most propose local folk-remedies for minor ailments—remedies that are more likely to mask the symptoms of moral decay than to cure them? In the final analysis, don't we need something more than immanent criticism?

The previous chapters make clear, I hope, that immanent criticism can take full advantage of all the conceptual resources available to any kind of criticism. It can burrow deep into its own culture's past in search of forgotten truths, learn enough about an alien culture to put our practices and institutions in fresh perspective, and imagine ways of life that have never been. It is immanent only in claiming no privileged vantage point above the fray. Only a tower of Babel would pretend to offer something like a God's-eye view. So if I am right, we lose nothing by confining ourselves to immanent criticism except the illusions and pretensions of philosophical transcendence. Even the critical work of those who have claimed such transcendence can be put to use. Kant is a brilliant *bricoleur,* Habermas a profound social critic.

Stereoscopic social criticism admits its own immanence, but it also helps us see why immanence can be critical. If our society consists of many social practices and institutions, oriented toward various goods, as I have suggested, it will not be so monolithic that social critics can find no opening for justifying their misgivings. In the first place, we have seen that within a social practice like medical care one can make effective use of established standards to appraise the conduct, character, and communal relations of actual medical practitioners. Second, we have seen that tensions arise not only among the goods internal to a given practice but also among goods internal to different practices and between the goods internal to a practice and goods such as physical pleasure, fame, money, and power. Stereoscopic social criticism finds much of its subject matter in such tensions and borrows much of its critical vocabulary from the social practices themselves. As the tensions become severe, the criticism can become radical.

Often enough, the social critic seeks to defend the internal goods of one social practice against encroachment by goods of other kinds. This may involve criticizing individuals for exhibiting some vice, such as greed, that allows an external good, such as money, to interfere with the pursuit or distribution of an internal good, such as the health of a patient. Criticizing individuals in this manner can be radical in one sense of the term, and it can certainly be dangerous if the individuals in question command power. But criticism needs to become radical in another, more germane sense when the troubled relations between one kind of good and another have far-reaching effects throughout the society. For then the trouble is systemic, and only a systematic account of the relevant social practices and institutions can get at its root.

A systematic account of this sort need not be hampered, nor its force lessened, by being carried out on native soil. We in the West do, I submit, face systemic problems. That was the point of calling attention, in the second section of this chapter, not only to the goods, habits of thought, and modes of interaction of the capitalist market and the bureaucracies but also to their tendency to engulf goods, habits of thought, and modes of interaction of other kinds. Goods internal to social practices are threatened in our society, but the trouble does not stem primarily from moral diversity and disagreement. It rather results from what Habermas calls "the rise to dominance of cognitive-instrumental aspects, which results in everything else being driven into the realm of apparent irrationality." Habermas defines socialism as the attempt to overcome this tendency in our culture—a definition, by the way, that Rorty cites in explaining why he takes himself to be a social democrat.[9]

Habermas's definition of socialism strikes the same note as the following passage from R. H. Tawney, which Cornel West has used as the epigraph of an article devoted largely to criticizing *After Virtue*:

> The burden of our civilization is not merely, as many suppose, that the product of industry is ill-distributed, or its conduct tyrannical, or its operation interrupted by embittered disagreements. It is that industry itself has come to hold a position of exclusive predominance among human interests, which no single interest, and least of all the provision of the material means of existence, is fit to occupy. That obsession by economic issues is as local and transitory as it is repulsive and disturbing.[10]

Much the same concern was eloquently expressed by John Dewey, who, although very much a creature of the modern world and hardly indisposed to value "cognitive-instrumental aspects," nonetheless feared for the well-being of a "society saturated with industrialism" and denounced its tendency to produce a "mental poverty that comes from one-sided distortion of mind."[11] "The virtues that are supposed to attend rugged individualism may be vocally proclaimed," he wrote, "but it takes no great insight to see that what is cherished is measured by its connection with those activities that make for success in business conducted for personal gain."[12] Richard Bernstein has recently underlined the contemporary importance of Dewey's claim that the corporate mentality has its own "language, its own interests, its own intimate groupings in which men of this mind, in their collective capacity, determine the tone of society at large as well as the government of industrial society."[13]

Surely, Habermas, Rorty, West, Tawney, Dewey, and Bernstein are all addressing the same problem, one echoed in Bellah's discussion of Brian Palmer's individualism, Meilaender's talk of "seepage," and Walzer's desire to fortify each of the various spheres of justice against incursions from other spheres. It looks as if it is possible, after all, for people with diverging conceptions of the good to identify the same moral problems and collaborate in common concern. It also looks as if our various moral languages, far from being what MacIntyre calls "an unharmonious melange of ill-assorted fragments" (*After Virtue*, p. 10), can actually be seen, from the vantage point of stereoscopic social criticism, as the languages of specific social practices and institutions. These languages have legitimate roles to play in our society's division of conceptual labor, but they also cause severe systemic problems when the habits of thought they embody and modes of interaction they promote seep into spheres of life they can only threaten or destroy.[14]

How do the languages of morals that have found a niche in pluralistic society correlate with specific social practices and institutions? I have already commented on how practices like medical care and baseball are animated by talk of particular virtues and vices, of role-specific duties and the rights that correspond to them, of standards of excellence, and of goods or ends to be pursued in common. I have also suggested that the language of abomination finds use wherever distinctions between "us" and "them" or between masculine and feminine roles remain sharp and acquire a certain kind of social significance. The religious languages of morals, which used to be presupposed by everyone participating in the practice and institutions of politics, now play a more limited role there, and the religious practices in which they remain central, including theological inquiry, have moved to the margins of public life. The language of human rights, respect for persons, and justice as fairness gains a foothold in those institutions—most notably the governmental bureaucracies, the public education system, and the secular forums of political debate—where participants cannot presuppose agreement on religious issues or full theories of the good yet still need some way to make reasoned appeals to each other. The language of cost-benefit analysis rules principally in the marketplace but in other spheres as well, wherever a course of action requires calculation and comparison of external goods and evils.

Each of these languages has its proper place in the pluralistic scheme of practices and institutions. Each serves goods of a specific sort. For the most part, we all can recognize the various goods as genuinely worthy, at least in a cool hour. (An exception would be goods defined in somebody else's religious terms, which presuppose metaphysical beliefs we deem false.) Systemic problems can arise when the pursuit of goods of one kind conflicts or interferes with the pursuit of goods of another kind. Such problems can be vexing. To be certain about how to resolve them, we would have to know more truths than we now know about what sort of God, if any, actually exists, what people are like, and what long-range consequences would result from changing the current configuration of practices and institutions. Lacking such certainty, we can only call upon the available knowledge and agreement and promote the best configuration of practices and institutions obtainable under the circumstances. Given the knowledge and agreement available to us, it seems unwise to join the religious right and some neoconservatives in their attempt to restore religious practices and vocabularies to a central position within our political institutions. It does seem wise, however, to try to protect practices like medical care, baseball, humanistic inquiry, family life, and democratic self-government from being swallowed up by the languages of cost-benefit calculation and human rights.

We are now in a position to see why the moral Esperantists, of either major type, are unlikely to help us identify one of the most pressing systemic problems we face: each type of Esperanto is itself a symptom of that problem. Consequentialism invites us all to speak the language of the marketplace all the time. It thus aides and abets the tyranny of external goods. Internal goods, when they are recognized at all, must be flattened out into units of pleasure and pain, satisfaction and dissatisfaction, so that they can be absorbed into the calculus of utility.

The Kantian form of Esperanto is both more modest and less harmful. It still characteristically aims to occupy the entire moral landscape, but it achieves this result by excluding most assessment of conduct, character, and community from view. Minimal decency, not the good life, is its concern. By excluding so much from view, however, it provides no means for surveying the dangers that ensue when its central concepts begin to pervade the entire culture, eroding not only the capacity to acquire virtues that go beyond minimal decency but also the ability to understand a kind of justice that does not consist in procedural fairness.

MacIntyre might respond, at this point in the argument, by saying that systemic problems like the one I have tried to identify are exactly the ones most difficult to resolve by rational means in a society like ours. Stereoscopic social criticism might allow us to say where the tensions are and which goods or languages threaten to dominate which. Its descriptions, even if complete, would not tell us how to ease those tensions or which goods and languages to protect. For that, MacIntyre might say, we would need to move beyond the first stage of his analysis, which concerns particular social practices and their institutional settings, to the second and third stages, which concern the good of a whole human life and the concept of a tradition. Even if we can secure rational agreement within a relatively wide circle on how to describe our social practices and institutions, such agreement will certainly break down completely by the time we get to stages two and three.

Here too I remain unconvinced, but not because I fail to appreciate the importance of moving on to those stages of analysis, nor because I gainsay the difficulty of securing agreement on certain issues once we get there. Take, first of all, the good of a whole human life. We are unlikely to secure perfect agreement on this topic in our lifetimes. Still, as I argued earlier, we needn't profess belief in the God of Moses and Calvin to be persuaded that our loves ought to be ordered toward genuine goods, each in proper proportion. From our various points of view, we can in fact recognize many genuine goods as such, including goods internal to such social practices as medical care and democratic self-government. We can also see that a life dedicated entirely to the pursuit of external goods degenerates into narcissism and idolatry, often ending in meaninglessness and despair. Finally, we can grasp that certain internal goods and the practices in which they are pursued deserve protection from the tyranny of external goods.

So we have reason to suppose that a good human life is not likely to flourish under conditions where the tyranny of external goods goes unchecked—reason, in other words, to protect such social practices as medical care, baseball, family life, and democratic government from being overwhelmed and corrupted. If this were not so, it would be hard to explain why the several authors I have been discussing, despite their religious and philosophical differences and their distinctive turns of phrase, seem to be articulating the same basic concern.

Moral discourse in pluralistic society is not threatened, then, by disagreement among its members about the good. Neither is it threatened by the confusion of tongues manifested in its various moral languages. It is threatened by the acids of injustice, which eat away at the moral fibre of privileged and victimized alike, and by the possibility of nuclear war, which would destroy much more than the prospects for rational moral debate. And it is also threatened by the corruption our lives have already suffered from idolizing external goods and the erosion of our most valuable practices by habits of mind and heart appropriate to the marketplace and the bureaucracies. About this, MacIntyre and Bellah are surely right to be concerned.

This brings me, at long last, to MacIntyre's third stage. Can pluralistic society achieve sufficient continuity over time to be called an "on-going tradition"? I believe it already has. This is perhaps hard to see because liberal theorists have devoted so much energy to transcending tradition that they have obscured their own position in one, as well as their own active borrowing from the past.[15] But whether pluralistic society survives much longer, in any recognizable form, depends not least on our ability and willingness to criticize it and transform it both reasonably and radically from within. If it is too late for that, too bad for us.

V

I shall now bring this final chapter to a close by bringing together some of themes I have been discussing in Part 3. Here follow fourteen points.

1. Rorty's shock, upon reading Foucault, that our vocabularies are playing into the hands of the bureaucrats, Meilaender's talk about "seepage," MacIntyre's descriptions of merely manipulative modes of interaction, the widespread dissatisfaction with technical rationality echoed in *Habits of the Heart* and in Habermas's critical theory, and related concerns expressed by Bernstein, Dewey, Tawney, Walzer, and West—all tie into this problem: the uneasy relation between social practices and such institutions as the capitalist marketplace and large-scale bureaucracies.

2. We do not need help from Rorty's light-mindedness toward traditional philosophical problems to help make "the world's inhabitants . . . more receptive to the appeal of instrumental rationality"—at least if we take instrumental rationality to be the kind of reasoning we use in the pursuit of external goods.[16] If that is what is meant by instrumental rationality, the world's inhabitants are already all too receptive to its appeal. Light-mindedness toward traditional philosophical problems might do us some good, however, if it helps us stop judging our moral discourse by the ultimate principles we utter in response to Socratic questions.

3. Our predicament tends to remain out of focus largely because we view it with one eye shut. A stereoscopic view of our society would bring both social practices and institutions into the line of vision. Our social theorists know how to talk about the marketplace and the bureaucracy. They also know how to talk about sectarian and revolutionary protests coming from the margins. Yet they have long had trouble bringing into focus the resources that liberal society makes available for

its own transformation. They have tended either to leave such resources out of the picture altogether or to romanticize them. We need a vocabulary in which to talk about both dimensions at once.[17]

4. MacIntyre goes wrong in part because he is diverted from putting his own most valuable vocabulary to use. The diversion comes from a picture suggested by emotivist moral philosophy, which he sees as an adequate reflection of moral discourse in pluralistic society. But emotivism was bad moral philosophy, driven to its paradoxical conclusions by unduly limited examples and by unjustified assumptions about the levels of agreement and conceptual uniformity required to make a given linguistic domain hospitable to objective and rational debate. Stereoscopic social criticism, assisted by MacIntyre's best philosophical insights, allows us to double back and notice how abstract and unrepresentative the linguistic data studied by analytic moral philosophers have tended to be.

5. A stereoscopic social critic would be inclined to concentrate on factors like these: the tendency of the capitalist marketplace and large-scale bureaucracies to provide material conditions that permit social practices to flourish, while at the same time they undermine the moral conditions needed to achieve goods internal to such practices; the tendency of professionalization and bureaucratic enforcement of rights, in some instances, to mitigate the bad effects of the marketplace on specific social practices and the people participating in them; the tendency of particular social practices, especially within the professions, to become all-consuming, thus making it increasingly difficult to be both a full-fledged participant in the practice and a good anything else[18]; the partial and ever-vulnerable secularization of linguistic transactions taking place under the aegis of certain institutions; and the inability of religious practices to serve as a unifying ideological center around which whole societies could order various goods, practices, and institutions.

6. It would be mere wistfulness to wish for a world in which we had only social practices and no institutions, a world in which external goods posed no temptations, because there can be no such world. As MacIntyre says, "no practices survive for any length of time unsustained by institutions" (*After Virtue*, p. 194). Nor can we reasonably hope for a world in which nothing like our current institutions had a place, for such a world would also have little or no place for many of the social practices we find most enriching and meaningful.

7. We can, nonetheless, reasonably hope for a world in which the proliferation, distribution, and merchandizing of external goods is subject to just political control and in which goods internal to worthy social practices, including the practice of self-government, are granted the right to life and given room to flourish. The hope that social practices, not simply private bonds and the individual pursuit of external goods, will be protected is not an expression of terminal wistfulness, for it is neither nostalgic nor utopian. There are in fact countless specific things one could do to improve the prospects of a particular social practice or to set particular internal and external goods in just relation. In the area of medicine, this might include organizing a hospice, reinstituting the rituals of the deathbed, socializing the delivery of health care, opposing the multihospital system, resisting biomedical researchers who experiment on patients without their informed consent, reforming the curricula and admissions requirements of medical schools, giving interns and residents shorter hours, and raising the prestige and wages of nurses.

8. Protection of goods internal to social practices need not, indeed should not, be extended indiscriminately. As MacIntyre puts it, "That the virtues need initially to be defined and explained with reference to the notion of a practice . . . in no way entails approval of all practices in all circumstances" (*After Virtue*, p. 200). Hence the importance of moving beyond the first stage of MacIntyre's analysis, which pertains to social practices and institutions, to the second and third stages, which pertain to the possibility of living a good human life within the extant configuration of practices and institutions, and the possibility of sustaining communities over time.

9. What sort of configuration of practices and institutions should we strive for? It must, in the first place, be one we can realistically hope to achieve. That sets an upper limit on relevant conceptions of the good society and, for us at any rate, places constraints on the possible role of religious practices. The sought-for configuration of practices and institutions must also, however, be one we can imagine wanting to live with. It must be both a sociocultural system in which individuals can, without too much hindrance and suffering, work out lives they can reasonably call good and one capable of achieving the temporal continuities and internal coherence of a tradition that maintains and extends acceptable forms of human interrelation. The virtues we need are not merely qualities essential to a given social practice, chosen at random.

We also need the virtues required to live out our lives well from beginning to end and to leave the next generation with a network of practices and institutions worth inheriting and continuing. Some social practices, institutions, and configurations thereof may simply be incompatible with the goods of a whole human life or with traditions to which we ought to be committed.

10. Anxiety over the language of individualism as a corrosive element in our lives, as expressed in *Habits of the Heart,* can be reinterpreted as the reasonable fear that our thought and speech are more and more dominated by external goods. A life lived merely in pursuit of external goods, a life like the one Brian Palmer used to lead, is morally empty. A society of people living such lives, a society in which people did not learn the virtues in social practices, would be morally corrupt. That such people would be idolatrous, that their loves would be distributed unjustly, is a truth we need not be Augustinians to recognize. A good human life is, at a minimum, one oriented toward goods worthy of our love, each in proper proportion.

11. The idea that liberal society lacks any shared conception of the good is false, but this doesn't mean that all is well. It could still be the case that politics, as the social practice of self-governance directed toward the common good, has begun to give way to merely bureaucratic management of competition for external goods. It could also be the case that we derive the benefits of our society for ourselves only by treating our underclass, as well as populations beyond our borders (especially to the south), with cruel injustice and indifference.[19] It is therefore right to worry about becoming despots and barbarians. The social practice of politics is, of course, always being threatened in some such way. All genuine republics, not just our kind, are fragile, susceptible to corruption by external goods and unjust acts. So there is no permanent, utopian solution to be sought. This is not an excuse for inaction and insensitivity but a reason for unflagging vigilance.

12. The languages of morals in our discourse are many, and they have remarkably diverse historical origins, but they do not float in free air, and their name is not chaos. They are embedded in specific social practices and institutions—religious, political, artistic, scientific, athletic, economic, and so on. We need many different moral concepts because there are many different linguistic threads woven into any fabric of practices and institutions as rich as ours. It is a motley: not a building in need of new foundations but a coat of many colors, one

constantly in need of mending and patching, sometimes even recutting and restyling.

13. We can make good use of Aristotelian and civic republican talk about the virtues and politics as a social practice directed toward the common good without supposing that this sort of moral language requires us to jettison talk of rights and tolerance. We can use this talk by thinking of liberal political institutions as oriented toward a provisional *telos*—a widely shared but self-limiting consensus on the highest good achievable under circumstances like ours. But this *telos* justifies a kind of tolerance foreign to the classical teleological tradition. And it rightly directs our moral attention to something our ancestors often neglected, namely, the injustice of excluding people from social practices because of their race, gender, religion, or place of birth.[20]

14. Our task, like Thomas Aquinas's, Thomas Jefferson's, or Martin Luther King's, is to take the many parts of a complicated social and conceptual inheritance and stitch them together into a pattern that meets the needs of the moment.[21] It has never been otherwise. The creative intellectual task of every generation, in other words, involves moral *bricolage*. It is no accident that Aquinas, Jefferson, and King were as eclectic as they were in using moral languages—and no shame either.

LEXICON

Optimistic modernism: What connects "Carnap's belief in Esperanto, socialism, and ideal languages . . . with Le Corbusier's 'radiant cities'" (Putnam,
Realism and Reason, p. 181); the desire, shared by architects and philosophers, to build "a machine to live in"; "the great hope that by rejecting the
tradition we would make possible . . . a utopian future for man" (*Realism
and Reason,* p. 303).

Existentialist modernism: The hope that by rejecting the tradition we would
make possible "a final recognition of the grandeur and terror of life, a final
immediacy which scientism and progressivism robbed us of" (*Realism and
Reason,* p. 303); the attitude that Midgley (*Beast and Man,* pp. 198–199)
describes as like "the fantasy of a child who, because he is disappointed in
his actual parents, decides to view himself as a kidnapped and disinherited
prince."

Abyss: Where existentialists thought they were when choosing basic criteria
or inventing values; the imaginary vacuum between conceptual schemes.

Bricoleur (bad sense): A French term, given currency by Claude Lévi-Strauss,
for someone who does odd jobs, drawing on a collection of available odds
and ends kept on hand on the chance they might someday prove useful;
someone whose mental habits contrast sharply with those of the engineer,
thus a symbol of the primitive, as opposed to modern, thought.

Bricoleur (good sense): An engineer without a degree; a term used here, as in
the writings of Jacques Derrida, partly to soften up Lévi-Strauss's contrast
between primitives and ourselves; an apt symbol of every moralist's need to
engage in selective retrieval and eclectic reconfiguration of traditional linguistic elements in hope of solving problems at hand.

Bricolage: What *bricoleurs* do with their collection of assorted odds and ends, namely, put some of them together to serve the purposes of the moment.

Moral bricolage: The process in which one begins with bits and pieces of received linguistic material, arranges some of them into a structured whole, leaves others to the side, and ends up with a moral language one proposes to use.

Postmodernism: What Venturi buildings and Rorty essays have in common; ironic eclecticism; the sense of belatedness expressed by Putnam as the feeling that the "great rejection of everything 'traditional'" and the hopes of both types of modernists are "beginning to look very tired" (*Realism and Reason,* p. 303); the realization that all creative ethical thought, not just the primitive kind, involves *bricolage;* the conviction that big problems in the philosophical tradition need "to be replaced by lots of little pragmatic questions about which bits of that tradition might be used for some current purpose."[1]

Moral Esperanto: What optimistic modernism strives for in ethics; an artificial moral language invented in the (unrealistic) hope that everyone will want to speak it.

Moral pidgin: Any simplified moral language developed as a bridge dialect to facilitate communication among communities otherwise unconnected by a common moral tongue.

Moral creole: A moral language that starts as a pidgin but eventually gets rich enough for use as a language of moral reflection (e.g., the language of human rights).

Kinematics of presupposition: David Lewis's term for the laws governing change in what parties to a conversation can take for granted.

Moral tropes: Any of the various literary or rhetorical means of arranging fragments of moral language in relation to one another and to the whole of which they are parts; see any good handbook of literary terms on the master tropes of metonymy, metaphor, synecdoche, and irony.

Normal discourse: What happens when a single vocabulary settles in and dominates discussion in some domain, thereby making all contributions to discourse in that domain commensurable; a kind of discourse possible, in principle, in theology, ethics, and aesthetics as well as in science.

Abnormal discourse: What happens when no single vocabulary achieves dominance: either the conversational interplay of vocabularies or the war of all against all, depending on how much civility the participants can muster.

Rational commensuration: The attempt to show that all contributions to a discourse share the same basic ground rules, which can be used to determine "how rational agreement can be reached on what would settle the issue on every point where statements seem to conflict" (Rorty, *Philosophy and the Mirror of Nature,* p. 316).

Incommensurability (Rorty's sense): What obtains, under conditions of abnormal discourse, when nobody has yet thought up a way to achieve rational commensuration; not necessarily a bad thing, depending on how important it is to achieve agreement by rational means under the circumstances.

Incommensurability (bad sense): What obtains when two or more groups assign different meanings to words, thereby (allegedly) causing their sentences to be about different worlds and opening an abyss between their respective conceptual schemes (in the bad sense defined below); a concept, supposedly introduced by Kuhn and Feyerabend, which once made philosophers nervous about the implications of conceptual diversity and change in science; recently revived by MacIntyre in an attempt to promote similar worries about contemporary morality.

Rational, objective, etc. (good senses): What you're being when you take all relevant considerations into account and exhibit all the appropriate intellectual virtues; what you become, if you're lucky, after being exposed to exemplars of excellence and acquiring extensive experience in a truth-oriented social practice.

Rational, objective, etc. (bad senses): What you're aiming for when you try, *per impossibile,* to have your judgment determined purely by the matter under consideration and by reason itself without relying on anything inherited, assumed, or habitual.

Superpower view of defense: Bernard Williams's name for the view that you have adequately defended a position "only if you can annihilate the other side" (*Ethics and the Limits of Philosophy,* p. 84); compare Robert Nozick (*Philosophical Explanations,* pp. 4–5) on the philosopher's hope for "arguments so powerful they set up reverberations in the brain: if the person refuses to accept the conclusion, he dies."

Romanticism (good sense): "The thesis that what is most important for human life is not what propositions we believe but what vocabulary we use" (Rorty, *Consequences,* p. 142).

Romanticism (bad sense): An obsessive preference for abnormal discourse; the exaggerated sense of liberation from normality to which some philosophers succumb when they rebel against their training in analytic philosophy.

Epistemology (innocuous sense): Reflection of any sort about knowledge; what one finds in books by Foucault and Kuhn; what Rorty (*pace* Ian Hacking) isn't opposed to; also, taking the currently entrenched vocabulary for granted for purposes of normal discourse or education of the young.

Epistemology (bad sense): The quest for the essence of knowledge; the type of philosophy dedicated singlemindedly to rational commensuration; what you're doing when you take the currently entrenched vocabulary as a permanent deposit of reason; the temptation of thinking that all discourse is or needs to be normal; related to what Donald Davidson (*Inquiries,* p. 31) calls "adventitious philosophical puritanism."

Immediate knowledge, intuitive knowledge (unproblematic senses): Knowledge unassisted by reflection or inference; true beliefs one is justified in accepting but wouldn't know how to argue for.

Immediate knowledge, intuitive knowledge (problematic senses): Justified true beliefs that are (allegedly) incorrigible, indubitable, infallible, immediately demonstrable, self-justifying, prelinguistic, or possible in the absence of extensive training; that belief in which constitutes the Myth of the Given.

Phronesis: Practical wisdom; a cardinal moral virtue.

Prudence (bad sense): Essentially self-interested technical reason; contrasts sharply with morality.

Prudence (good sense): Same as *phronesis*.

Method (bad sense): A self-sufficient set of rules for performing some task; what the rest of the academy would like to discover by reading philosophy; see hermeneutics (bad sense); perfectly captured in this sentence from Camus: "Quand on n'a pas de caractère, il faut bien se donner une méthode."

Method (innocuous sense): Rules of thumb for performing some task; not a substitute for *phronesis* and tact; see Oakeshott on "abridgments of tradition."

Philosophy (bad sense): Love of *scientia*; same as epistemology (bad sense).

Philosophy (innocuous sense): Love of *phronesis*; a kind of writing that includes, in MacIntyre's phrase, "ineliminable backward reference to Plato's dialogues"[2] and which is delimited, in Rorty's phrase, "not by form or matter, but by tradition—a family romance involving, e.g., Father Parmenides, honest old Uncle Kant, and bad brother Derrida" (*Consequences*, p. 92); also, a reflective view about how everything hangs together.

Analytic philosophy: Love of technical reason; what philosophy became under the pressures of professionalization and modernist ideology in English-speaking universities; underwent three stages of development: (1) a debate over the merits of positivism held together by commitment to logical analysis; (2) the gradual dissolution of that debate, in which the "notion of 'logical analysis' turned in upon itself, and committed slow suicide" (Rorty, *Consequences*, p. 227); and (3) the eventual loss of "shape as a tendency with the disappearance of a strong ideological current at its center" (Putnam, *Realism and Reason*, p. 303); recently referred to wistfully by Putnam as a phrase used by philosophy professors to excuse their students from reading books by Hegel and Foucault.

Ontology, metaphysics (innocuous senses): A view about what there is; also, a branch of philosophy in which one considers views about what there is.

Ontology, metaphysics (bad senses): What you're doing when you fix up your view of what there is in order to solve problems in epistemology (bad sense).

Idealism (technical philosophical sense): An implausible position in ontology, the view that only ideas exist; also, the related epistemological view, associated with Kant, that the only reality we can know is mental or spiritual in nature.

Idealism (moralist's sense): Any moral outlook shaped by unrealistically optimistic assumptions about what human beings are like; excessive preoccupation with moral ideals or with utopian wishful thinking; "the pursuit of perfection as the crow flies" (Oakeshott, *Rationalism in Politics*, p. 59).

"Esse est percipi": To be is to be perceived; summary of idealism (in the tech-

nical philosophical sense); also, a maxim used by deans for deciding tenure cases.

Consequentialism: One of two major forms of optimistic modernism in ethical theory, recently come upon hard times; roughly, the view that for any act D, the rightness or wrongness of D depends solely upon the overall value of the state of affairs D brings about; a machine for practical reason to live in.

Teleological ethics (first narrow sense): Same as consequentialism.

Teleological ethics (second narrow sense): Any ethical outlook in which all assessment of conduct, character, and community depends upon a *telos* or goal which is both built into the human essence and knowable once and for all through distinctively philosophical or theological understanding; what MacIntyre, despite initial appearances, isn't committed to.

Teleological ethics (loose sense): Any ethical outlook in which goals, ends, or intentions play a central role in the assessment of conduct, character, and community; a class of ethical theories of which consequentialism is only one member; applies to *Nichomachean Ethics, Summa Theologiae,* and *After Virtue,* as well as to books by Bentham and Mill.

Pragmatism (bad senses): Also called "vulgar" pragmatism; consequentialism applied to mental acts; the view that cost-benefit calculation is the ultimate language of rational commensuration, the highest court of appeal for the choice of a vocabulary; the doctrine that the essence of knowledge is problem-solving capability; an epistemological position (bad sense).

Pragmatism (good sense): Never having to say you're certain; "anti-essentialism applied to notions like 'truth,' 'knowledge' . . . and similar objects of philosophical theorizing" (Rorty, *Consequences,* p. 162); the notion that "there is no epistemological difference between truth about what ought to be and truth about what is, nor any metaphysical difference between morality and science" (*Consequences,* p. 163); the view that *phronesis* is a virtue as important to science as it is to textual interpretation or to ethical discernment.

Antipragmatism: The tendency to confuse the good and the bad senses of all the terms defined in this lexicon.

Methodological nominalism: Roughly, the view that "essences," "concepts," and "natures," if they exist, can be known about only by two means, namely: (1) empirical investigation of, or moral reflection upon, the objects to which the relevant terms apply and (2) the kinds of reflection on language use found in works by Ludwig Wittgenstein, J. L. Austin, and Donald Davidson; not equivalent to the negative ontological thesis that "essences" do not exist.

Essentialism: An ontological view holding that there are such things as "essences" or "natures."

Anti-essentialism (potentially troublesome sense): Denial of essentialism; an ontological view (bad sense).

Anti-essentialism (good sense): Same as "methodological nominalism."

Ontological realism: The noncontroversial view that objects of a given sort, such as rocks and trees, really exist and would have existed even if we had never come along to perceive them or apply language to them; an ontological view compatible with pragmatism (good sense).

Correspondence to reality (noncontroversial sense): The perfectly intelligible evidential relation of correspondence between theoretical statements and the facts as they are described in the vocabulary of a background theory.

Correspondence to reality (unfathomable sense): The relation between our true beliefs and things as they are in themselves, independent of our descriptions of them; a leading cause of mental cramps.

Epistemological realism: The hopeless attempt to make correspondence to undescribed reality serve as a criterion or explanation of truth (hopeless because criteria and explanations need to place reality under a description if they are to serve any purpose whatsoever); the tendency to confuse the noncontroversial and unfathomable senses of "correspondence to reality."

Skeptical realist: Someone who agrees that it is impossible to apprehend reality without describing it but who greets this result with inconsolable despair instead of Buddhist-like detachment.

Truth: One among many values we want our theories to have; what we don't need an epistemological theory of; a concept concerning which we learn all we need to know by reading J. L. Austin on the use of *true* in speech-acts and Davidson on the function of *true* in sentences of the form "'Murder is unjust' is true if and only if murder is unjust."

"Truth is warranted assertibility": A false theory of truth, associated with pragmatism (bad sense) and refuted by familiar cases in which we are warranted in asserting a proposition at a given time but later discover the proposition to have been false; also a snappy but misleading way of summing up the idea, characteristic of pragmatism (good sense), that seeking warranted assertibility for our sentences is the only way to seek truth; see following entry.

Pithy little formulae: What Rorty calls slogan-length sayings which are typically right about what they implicitly deny but wrong about what they explicitly assert; a means of expression to which Nietzsche, Derrida, Dewey, James, and Rorty are prone, especially when they make their points in their opponents' vocabularies or want to sound outrageous; a major cause of the misunderstandings that make this lexicon necessary.

Hermeneutics (bad sense): Epistemology (bad sense) imported by the humanities; the first science of the human sciences; the quest for *the* method (bad sense) of interpretation.

Hermeneutics (good sense): The art of enriching our language in conversation with others; also, reflection designed to raise this art to consciousness without reducing it to a set of rules.

Conceptual scheme (innocuous sense): A metaphor for a person's or group's favored vocabularies, background theories, normative commitments, and modes of reasoning.

Conceptual scheme (bad sense): That which stands over against uninterpreted reality and provides a structure for the perception of phenomena or for moral or aesthetic judgment; sharply contrasts with content; that without which intuitions are blind; something the very idea of which is said to constitute the third dogma of empiricism (Davidson, *Inquiries*, p. 198).

Relativism (bad senses): Also called "vulgar" or "radical" relativism; the idea that any theory is as good as any other; the idea that the same proposition can be true relative to one conceptual scheme and false relative to another; that to which Alan Garfinkel responds by saying, "I know where you're coming from, but, you know, Relativism isn't *true-for-me*" (Putnam, *Realism and Reason*, p. 288).

Relativism (good senses): The idea that what you are justified in believing or warranted in asserting or able to treat as a candidate for your assent depends upon what concepts and modes of reasoning are available to you; the idea that what makes a theory or an interpretation good or bad depends upon the purposes you might reasonably want it to serve.

Environmental relativity: David Wong's term for the relatively unexciting kind of relativity involved when a given practice (such as polygamy) is evil under some social-historical circumstances but not under others; the kind of relativity that helps us explain why dissenters wouldn't have a right to liberal tolerance if nearly all of us could reach rational agreement on all details of the good life.

Relativism of distance: The kind of relativism that obtains, according to Bernard Williams, when another moral system offers no "real option" for us and thus (supposedly) causes (at least much of) our evaluative vocabulary· to "break down" if we try to say whether that system is good or bad, right or wrong, and so forth.

Davidsonian antirelativism: The view that postulating conceptual schemes (bad sense) serves no explanatory purpose; the idea that by adjusting our assumptions about foreigners' beliefs and desires, revising our interpretations of their sentences accordingly, and enriching our own language in dialogue with them, we can always, in principle, make their languages translatable.

Indexicals: Expressions whose extension varies from context to context; example: the expression, *I*, which denotes me when I say it but you when you say it; a class of expressions to which, according to Wong, the phrase "adequate moral system" belongs.

Epistemic reductionism: The hopeless attempt to reduce epistemic notions (like *knowledge* and *rationality*) to nonepistemic ones; see following two entries.

Logical positivism: One type of epistemic reductionism; the attempt to reduce knowledge and rationality to syntactical notions.

Historicism (one of many bad senses): Another type of epistemic reductionism; the attempt to reduce knowledge and rationality to anthropological ideas, as in the proposition, "Knowledge is what your peers will let you get away with"; see "pragmatism" (bad sense); the only sort of historicism Putnam had in mind when he said, "I am not a fan of any sort of historicism" (*Reason, Truth and History*, p. 183).

Historicism (good sense): Acceptance of the historical contingency of one's vocabulary and styles of reasoning; the view that historical narratives of the right sort not only bring this contingency to light but also contribute to self-understanding; the only sort of historicism defended in *The Flight from Authority*.

Kant, Immanuel: Transitional figure between Hume and Hegel.

Kantian ethical theory: The second major type of optimistic modernism in ethics; what Kant's followers invented after reading his *Groundwork* out of context and ignoring the rest of his writings; *Sittlichkeit* evaporated into subjectivity; see "philosophical liberalism."

Sittlichkeit (Hegelian sense): The ethos or ethical life of a community either before too much alienation sets in, thereby giving rise to Kantian ethical theory, or after such alienation is overcome, thus allowing intellectuals to identify with their community again; contrasts with *Moralität*.

Moral nihilism: The view that there is no such thing as truth in ethics; widely feared to be among the moral consequences of pragmatism; actually a consequence not of pragmatism (good sense) but of existentialist modernism; the spectre raised whenever Rorty backslides into existentialist motifs and refers to Sartre in his discussions of morality.

Moral skepticism: The view that if there are moral truths, we do not have justified beliefs about them.

Moral aphasia: An inability to speak out in the face of generalized tyranny; a tendency sometimes said to be promoted by acceptance of pragmatism.

Moral realism (good technical philosophical sense): The view that moral propositions have truth value; the view that moral statements do not suffer in epistemological standing when compared with scientific statements.

Moral realism (bad technical philosophical sense): The idea that we need to explain the truth of a moral proposition by saying that it corresponds to something; the tendency to postulate entities called "values," a term recently exported to moral philosophy from economics, so that moral propositions would have something to correspond to; epistemological or skeptical realism applied to ethics.

Moral realism (moralist's sense): Negation of idealism (moralist's sense); the kind of moral realism at issue between Reinhold Niebuhr and the Fellowship of Reconciliation, not the kind at issue between Sabina Lovibond and J. L. Mackie.

Emotivism: The view that moral statements are essentially either mere expressions of, reports on, or attempts to evoke emotional states of some sort (such as "pro-attitudes") and thus not what they seem to be (namely, truth-claims about something beyond such emotional states); an ethical theory that, according to MacIntyre, was wrong about the meaning of moral language as such but is basically right if reinterpreted as a theory about how moral language is used in our culture (namely, to express one's feelings and manipulate the feelings of others).

The moral law, natural law, realm of values, etc. (relatively innocuous senses):

Usually not written in upper case; fancy names for all the moral truths, known and unknown, that can be formulated in all the possible moral vocabularies.

The moral law, natural law, realm of values, etc. (bad senses): Often written in upper case; that correspondence to which is sometimes thought to explain what makes true moral propositions true; see "moral realism" (bad sense).

Fundamental moral principle, foundational moral criterion, etc. (bad senses): According to some philosophers, a moral rule one could know, and would need to know, before one could be justified in believing less fundamental moral truths; that from which all nonfoundational moral knowledge is thought to derive and by which all systems of mores can (supposedly) be judged.

Fundamental moral principle, foundational moral criterion, etc. (innocuous senses): A highly general moral belief that sums up the spirit of one's morality, perhaps one you would be especially reluctant to give up; something you could know to be true and acceptable only by acquiring experience in a moral tradition and by knowing a lot about a lot of different things, including the moral truth about various specific cases.

Secularization (dubious sense): The irreversible tendency of modern societies to produce atheists, make religion utterly irrelevant, and cause existential despair; what Harvey Cox used to believe in.

Secularization (sense discussed in this book): What happens to the discourse produced under the aegis of an institution when speakers no longer presuppose the existence of a specific sort of divinity; not something that happens in the heads and hearts of individuals but rather something that happens to some of the linguistic transactions taking place between them; a phenomenon compatible with increases in levels of religious belief and feeling.

Radical theology: The last (and lowest) stage of existentialist modernism in theology; the attempt to keep the wake after the death of God going on forever; atheism in drag; John 1:1–3 meets Derrida.

Liberal theology: Letting theoretical reason live in the optimistic modernist's machine while finding another home for reflective piety; post-Kantian epistemology (bad sense) or hermeneutics (bad sense) applied to theology; compare "philosophical liberalism."

Fundamental theology: The branch of theology in which one uses epistemological findings to constrain and justify the task of apologetics; what most liberal theology is based upon.

Postmodern theology: Also called "postliberal theology"; the quest, initiated in recent years by the most interesting American followers of Karl Barth, to get beyond all forms of modernism in theology; either a *cul de sac* or the harbinger of a new theological age (too soon to tell).

Socratic questioning (bad sense): Asking "Why do you believe that?" over and over again until the person you're talking to either falls silent, gets confused, or gives up and utters what looks like a fundamental moral principle;

what Socrates at his worst, at least as interpreted by Peter Geach, did to his interlocutors in certain Platonic dialogues; what moral philosophers at their worst do to freshmen; what ethnographers at their worst do to the natives.

Socratic questioning (good sense): A kind of dialogue or reflective self-inventory in which one asks many different sorts of questions and eventually "remembers" what one had been committed to, without quite realizing it, all along; what Socrates, moral philosophers, and ethnographers have been able to do at their Gadamerian best.

Liberal society, pluralistic society (loaded senses): Any social system in which it is impossible to enjoy community, share common ends, or make politics intelligible as the collective pursuit of the common good; either a very good or a very bad thing, depending upon one's political and philosophical leanings; a kind of society that may not exist.

Liberal society, pluralisitc society (neutral senses): Names for the system of practices and institutions invented by the North Atlantic bourgeoisie; any society whose members show considerable diversity in religious or philosophical outlook and whose institutions tolerate such diversity by ascribing certain rights to citizens.

Pragmatic liberalism, postmodernist bourgeois liberalism: The view that institutions created by the North Atlantic bourgeoisie "give us the best polity actualized so far" even though it lacks philosophical foundations and is (regrettably) "irrelevant to most of the problems of most of the population of the planet" (Rorty, *Consequences,* p. 210); liberal apologetics without help from epistemology (bad sense).

Philosophical liberalism: A set of (mainly Kantian) philosophical arguments and principles thought to justify the hopes of the North Atlantic bourgeoisie; philosophy (bad sense) in the service of liberal society.

Communitarianism: Philosophical antiliberalism; the view that philosophical liberalism is right in thinking that liberal institutions and liberal philosophy stand or fall together but wrong in thinking that liberal philosophy stands; the view that because "liberal society" (loaded sense) adequately describes our lot, we had better dismantle, dissociate ourselves from, or radically reform our practices and institutions if community and the virtues are to have any hope of surviving; see *After Virtue, Habits of the Heart.*

Common good (misleading sense): The ultimate goal of political life, according to teleological ethics (second narrow sense); what we ought to strive for in the sphere of secular morality and politics if we want to achieve the *telos* built into the human essence.

Common good (good sense): The ultimate goal of political life, according to teleological ethics (loose sense); what we would strive for in the sphere of secular morality and politics if our shared intentions were perfectly transformed by love of justice and ideally well informed by realistic understanding of human beings and the world they live in; something that our conception of changes over time, as we change our minds about how best to describe human beings and the world they inhabit.

Individualism (good sense): The idea that the well-being of each human being, no matter how powerless or wretched or distant, should carry weight in our moral deliberation, with the burden of proof falling heavily on anyone proposing differential treatment of a sort that might place the well-being of one over that of another.

Individualism (bad sense): Preoccupation with acquiring such goods as physical pleasure, fame, money, and power for oneself; best described in old-fashioned terms as vicious and self-idolatrous.

Human nature (innocuous sense): What common sense, extended and corrected by historical inquiry, science, and artistic imagination, tells us about what human beings are like; a long list of facts about us which are relevant to moral reflection, including facts about our need for food and water, the unlikelihood of producing a generation of saints by tinkering with institutions and child-rearing practices, and the effects of suffering and injustice on our ability to live happily together.

Human nature (questionable sense): Facts about human beings that could be contemplated only by an essentialist, and therefore a particular kind of philosopher or theologian.

Social practice (MacIntyre's sense): "Any coherent and complex form of socially established cooperative human activity through which goods internal to that form of activity are realized in the course of trying to achieve those standards of excellence which are appropriate to, and partially definitive of, that form of activity, with the result that human powers to achieve excellence, and human conceptions of the ends and goods involved, are systematically extended" (*After Virtue*, p. 187); what baseball is and taking long showers isn't.

Goods internal to a practice: Those goods which can be realized only by participating in a given social practice (in MacIntyre's sense) and satisfying, at least to some significant degree, its standards of excellence; contrasts with "goods external to a practice," which are either internal to some other practice or external to all; in baseball, what Mattingly achieves, Red Smith appreciated, and Steinbrenner violates.

NOTES

INTRODUCTION

1. For a discussion of Kafka and Borges on this theme, see George Steiner, *After Babel: Aspects of Language and Translation* (Oxford: Oxford University Press, 1975), pp. 65–73.

2. Stanley Hauerwas, *The Peaceable Kingdom* (Notre Dame, Ind.: University of Notre Dame Press, 1983), ch. 1; Alasdair MacIntyre, *After Virtue*, 2d. ed. (Notre Dame, Ind.: University of Notre Dame Press, 1984), ch. 1; Basil Mitchell, *Morality: Religious and Secular* (Oxford: Oxford University Press, 1980), ch. 1.

3. Jacques Derrida, "Des Tours de Babel," in *Difference in Translation*, ed. Joseph F. Graham (Ithaca: Cornell University Press, 1985), pp. 165–207, esp. p. 165; Derrida, *The Ear of the Other*, ed. Christie V. McDonald (New York: Schocken, 1985), esp. pp. 98–110, 149.

4. Michael Oakeshott, "The Tower of Babel," in *Rationalism in Politics* (London: Methuen, 1962), pp. 59–79.

5. Irving Howe, *Politics and the Novel* (New York: Meridian, 1987), p. 21.

6. See Iris Murdoch, "Against Dryness: A Polemical Sketch," in *Revisions*, ed. Stanley Hauerwas and Alasdair MacIntyre (Notre Dame, Ind.: University of Notre Dame Press, 1983), pp. 43–50.

7. Howe, *Politics and the Novel*, pp. 21–22.

8. Ibid., pp. 22–23.

CHAPTER ONE

1. Stanley Hauerwas, *The Peaceable Kingdom* (Notre Dame, Ind.: University of Notre Dame Press, 1983), esp. chs. 1–4. C. S. Lewis, *Mere Christianity* (New York: Macmillan, 1960), esp. pp. 17–30.

2. Alasdair MacIntyre, *After Virtue*, 2d ed. (Notre Dame, Ind.: University of Notre Dame Press, 1984), pp. 192–193.

3. Colin Turnbull, *The Mountain People* (New York: Simon and Schuster, 1972).

4. Donald Davidson, "On the Very Idea of a Conceptual Scheme," in his *Inquiries into Truth and Interpretation* (Oxford: Oxford University Press, 1984), ch. 13. See also David E. Cooper, "Moral Relativism," in *Midwest Studies in Philosophy* 3/1978, ed. P. French, T. Uehling, and H. Wettstein (Minneapolis: University of Minnesota Press, 1980), pp. 97–108; and R. W. Beardsmore, *Moral Reasoning* (New York: Schocken, 1969), p. 35.

5. Davidson draws more dramatic conclusions than this, conclusions about the limits of conceptual diversity, but I postpone discussion of that topic until the next chapter.

6. Beardsmore, *Moral Reasoning*, p. 35.

7. Stanley Hauerwas, "The Church as God's New Language," in *Scriptural Authority and Narrative Interpretation*, ed. Garrett Green (Philadelphia: Fortress Press, 1987), p. 180.

8. By *proposition*, I shall mean a sentence paired with an interpretation—an *interpreted* sentence. By assigning a looser interpretation to the term *slavery*, as some Marxists would prefer, we could of course use the English sentence "Slavery is evil" to condemn a wider class of practices than I have in mind here. But then we would have a somewhat different proposition before us, a proposition whose truth we might go on to affirm or deny as we see fit. I ask you to grant, for present purposes, that the many ambiguities and vagaries associated with the term *slavery* are not at issue once the interpretation has been specified. We can then say that Hauerwas, in accepting the English sentence "Slavery is evil" under the presupposed interpretation, believes that the proposition under consideration is true. We can say this without denying that he might, in his capacity as a moralist or comparativist, wish to entertain other propositions in which the extension of the term *slavery* will be expanded, contracted, or shifted. Needless to say, interpreting a term of this sort will sometimes require careful attention and generate controversy. What I need now, however, is an interpretation of the term designed to yield a relatively clear proposition that Hauerwas and most of my readers would be inclined to accept without controversy.

9. I am ignoring exceptions to the rule, such as the self-referential proposition, "I believe this proposition is true," which of course becomes true if I believe it. No doubt there are also moral propositions that are exceptions to the rule—for example, where believing that I have a certain obligation actually obligates me.

10. When Sabina Lovibond, in perhaps the best discussion of these matters in recent moral philosophy, writes of "our lack of access to any distinction between those of our beliefs which are *actually true*, and those which are merely *held true by us*," I take her to be making essentially this sort of point. See her *Realism and Imagination in Ethics* (Minneapolis: University of Minnesota Press, 1983), p. 37.

11. I discuss the problems posed by excessive resort to such dicta in a later chapter and (somewhat more playfully) in the lexicon.

12. Lovibond, *Realism and Imagination in Ethics*, p. 148.

13. Ibid.

14. For an excellent treatment of "epistemic reductionism," see Hilary Putnam, *Realism and Reason: Philosophical Papers, Vol. 3* (Cambridge: Cambridge University Press, 1983), pp. 287–303. But do not assume that everyone who occasionally reaches for dicta of the sort just discussed is an epistemic reductionist. Do not assume, either, that historicism of the kind Putnam condemns as a type of epistemic reductionism is the only kind.

15. To borrow a phrase from Robert Nozick, a judgment can be true without necessarily *tracking* the truth. See Nozick's *Philosophical Explanations* (Cambridge: Harvard University Press, 1981).

16. See Jon Elster, "Belief, Bias and Ideology," in *Rationality and Relativism*, ed. Martin Hollis and Steven Lukes (Cambridge: MIT Press, 1982), pp. 123–48.

17. See Graham MacDonald and Philip Pettit, *Semantics and Social Science* (London: Routledge & Kegan Paul, 1981), p. 37.

CHAPTER TWO

1. This objection has been raised against my position by Timothy P. Jackson.

2. Gilbert Harman, *The Nature of Morality* (New York: Oxford University Press, 1977), ch. 1.

3. He also goes on to argue that ethics isn't as problematic as it initially seems to be, once we recognize his own reduction of moral *ought*-statements to relational facts about reasons. I postpone discussion of this matter until the fourth chapter.

4. See John McDowell's discussion of related matters in his paper, "Values and Secondary Qualities," in *Morality and Objectivity: A Tribute to J. L. Mackie*, ed. Ted Honderich (London: Routledge & Kegan Paul), pp. 110–29, esp. pp. 120 f.

5. See my *Flight from Authority* (Notre Dame, Ind.: University of Notre Dame Press, 1981), pp. 28 ff. For an excellent discussion of these matters, see Sabina Lovibond, *Realism and Imagination in Ethics* (Minneapolis: University of Minnesota Press, 1983), esp. pp. 110–16. Unfortunately, Lovibond sometimes seems to imply that all moral judgments are noninferential (see, e.g., p. 50). Whether this is her actual view, I am not sure. It is not mine.

6. For a similar point, see Renford Bambrough, *Moral Scepticism and Moral Knowledge* (London: Routledge & Kegan Paul, 1979), p. 18.

7. That is why we sometimes need Socratic questioning, in the good sense to be discussed in Part 3, in order to "remember" a moral truth to which we are already tacitly committed.

8. Ibid., pp. 95–96.

9. Hilary Putnam, *Reason, Truth and History* (Cambridge: Cambridge University Press, 1981).

10. See William Frankena, *Ethics*, 2d ed. (Englewood Cliffs, N.J.: Prentice Hall, 1973), p. 110.

11. For the arguments, see John McDowell, "Are Moral Requirements Hypothetical Imperatives?" *The Aristotelian Society*, suppl. vol. 52 (1978):13–29. Pursuing this topic would take me too far into virtue-theory and too far into Aristotle and Aquinas for present purposes.

12. Williams introduced this notion in his book, *Descartes: The Project of Pure Inquiry* (Harmondsworth, Middlesex: Penguin, 1978). For something like the argument made in this objection, see his *Ethics and the Limits of Philosophy* (Cambridge: Harvard University Press, 1985), pp. 135–40.

13. As I see it, this abstraction is achieved by acquiring virtuous habits, by becoming a particular sort of person and looking at the world as that sort of person would, not by looking at the world from some universal point of view, the view from nowhere. The virtuous person's moral principles and habits of judgment filter out morally irrelevant and "merely subjective" considerations. For a brief account of moral principles as information filters, see the editors' introduction to *Utilitarianism and Beyond*, ed. Amartya Sen and Bernard Williams (Cambridge: Cambridge University Press, 1981), pp. 4–5. For an account of moral objectivity as a kind of abstraction more like that achieved by the absolute conception, see Thomas Nagel, *The View from Nowhere* (New York: Oxford University Press, 1986).

CHAPTER THREE

1. R. M. Hare, *The Language of Morals* (Oxford: Oxford University Press, 1952).

2. Chris Swoyer, "True For," in *Relativism: Cognitive and Moral*, ed. Michael Krausz and Jack W. Meiland (Notre Dame, Ind.: University of Notre Dame Press, 1982), p. 102, 105, italics in original.

3. See Gilbert Harman, *Thought* (Princeton: Princeton University Press, 1973), chs. 4-6.

4. Hilary Putnam, *Meaning and the Moral Sciences* (London: Routledge & Kegan Paul, 1978), p. 99.

5. Or it might become richer in the relevant ways without help from hermeneutical innovators. Imagine, for example, that the Corleones begin to modernize on their own and develop a moral language analogous to Modernese. Now, as they turn back to Modernese, they suddenly find it much easier to understand.

6. On this danger, see Edward Said, *Orientalism* (New York: Vintage, 1979).

7. There might, of course, be practical difficulties. Suppose, for example, that Corleones won't initiate Modernist ethnographers into Corleone moral discourse beyond a certain point unless they are prepared to demonstrate commitment to various moral beliefs that any Modernist would find noxious. (Maybe a particular rite of initiation consists of rubbing out a few enemies of the family.) In such a case, it might be impossible, in practice, to understand the secrets of Corleone moral discourse without acting out Corleone beliefs.

But what if all merely practical difficulties were excluded? Imagine that the ethnographers had a complete supply of high-tech surveillance gadgetry and could spy on the Corleones' every word and movement? Then, I submit, they could come to understand Corleone discourse without adopting Corleone beliefs.

8. This paragraph bears on the position sometimes called vulgar Wittgensteinianism, which confuses the link between understanding a language and knowing one's way around in a form of life with the idea that forms of life are incorrigible. See Charles Taylor's criticisms of this confusion in "Understanding and Explanation in the *Geisteswissenschaften*," in *Wittgenstein: To Follow a Rule*, ed. Steven Holtzman and Christopher Leich (London: Routledge & Kegan Paul, 1981), pp. 191–210.

9. Ian Hacking, "Language, Truth and Reason," in *Rationality and Relativism*, ed. Martin Hollis and Steven Lukes (Cambridge: MIT Press, 1982), pp. 49–50. For a slightly different version of the same paper, including some interesting comments on parallels to Michel Foucault's notions of *episteme* and *discourse*, see "Styles of Scientific Reasoning," in *Post-Analytic Philosophy*, ed. John Rajchman and Cornel West (New York: Columbia University Press, 1985), pp. 145–64.

10. See David Lewis, *Philosophical Papers*, Vol. 1 (Oxford: Oxford University Press, 1983), p. 186.

11. They are also Wittgensteinian considerations. For a treatment of these issues that explicitly connects the relevant passages from Wittgenstein and Davidson, see S. L. Hurley, "Objectivity and Disagreement," in *Morality and Objectivity*, ed. Ted Honderich (London: Routledge & Kegan Paul, 1985), pp. 54–97. I must add, at this point, that my argument here does not trade on Davidson's strong claims about the limits of conceptual contrast as such.

12. At that point, Modernist translators of Corleone may be going out of their way to render in "nonmoral" terms what we take to be the central expressions of Corleone moral discourse. Our direct translations of Corleone may be quite unlike our translations of the expressions Modernists use in their translations of Corleone. This phenomenon resembles a case discussed by Hilary Putnam, in which two cultures with dissimilar interests are translating the same jungle language. One culture is ours, the other is Martian. The jungle language includes the term *gavagai*, which we translate as "rabbit." Putnam asks us to suppose that the Martians have "short expressions for 'undetached rabbit-part' and 'detached rabbit-part' (assuming *our* translation manual for Martian, of course) and parts are of great *interest* to Martians (perhaps they are very *small*, and rabbit-parts, tree-parts, etc., are much more perspicuous for Martians than whole trees and rabbits, of which they have little conception) but there is no short expression for whole rabbits, and whole rabbits, cats, dogs, etc., are not of much interest to Martians in everyday life. Then the Martians might well find the most 'natural' translation of 'gavagai' to be the Martian expression that *we* translate as 'undetached rabbit-part'." *Meaning and the Moral Sciences*, p. 45, Putnam's italics.

13. Taylor, pp. 205 f. Taylor goes on to say that his "notion of a language

of perspicuous contrast is obviously very close to Gadamer's conception of the 'fusion of horizons' and owes a great deal to it." Broadened horizons can bring horizons together.

14. Mary Midgley, *Beast and Man: The Roots of Human Nature* (New York: Meridian, 1980), p. 295.

15. Claude Lévi-Strauss, *The Savage Mind* (Chicago: University of Chicago Press, 1966), esp. pp. 16–36.

16. My use of the term is therefore closer to that of G. Genette and Jacques Derrida than to that of Lévi-Strauss. After reporting Genette's assertion that the analysis of *bricolage* could "be applied almost word for word" to criticism itself, Derrida has this to say: "If one calls *bricolage* the necessity of borrowing one's concepts from the text of a heritage which is more or less coherent or ruined, it must be said that every discourse is *bricoleur*. The engineer, whom Lévi-Strauss opposes to the *bricoleur*, should be the one to construct the totality of his language, syntax, and lexicon. In this sense the engineer is a myth. . . . As soon as we cease to believe in such an engineer and in a discourse which breaks with the received historical discourse, and as soon as we admit that every finite discourse is bound by a certain *bricolage* and that the engineer and the scientist are also species of *bricoleurs*, then the very idea of *bricolage* is menaced and the difference in which it took its meaning breaks down." I would prefer to say that the idea as Lévi-Strauss intended it is menaced, the difference in which he tried to establish its meaning breaks down. I propose to use the term, for my own purposes, on the assumption that Genette was right in seeking to broaden its extension. See Jacques Derrida, *Writing and Difference*, trans. Alan Bass (Chicago: University of Chicago Press, 1978), p. 285.

17. Cf. Nelson Goodman, *Ways of Worldmaking* (Indianapolis: Hackett, 1978), pp. 7–17.

18. For an introduction to the notion of tropes and definitions of terms like *metonymy, metaphor, synecdoche,* and *irony,* see Hayden White, *Metahistory: The Historical Imagination in Nineteenth-Century Europe* (Baltimore: Johns Hopkins University Press, 1973), esp. pp. 31–38. See also his *Tropics of Discourse: Essays in Cultural Criticism* (Baltimore: Johns Hopkins University Press, 1978), esp. ch. 2 and the useful discussion of Michel Foucault in ch. 11.

19. Ibid., p. 37.

20. I will discuss the perils of Socratic questioning in relation to a specific example in Part 3.

21. See Goodman, p. 19.

22. Richard Rorty, "The Contingency of Language," *London Review of Books* 8/7 (17 April 1986):3. Rorty isn't discussing ethics in this context. He is trying to capture the truth in the Romantic notion that truth is made rather than found. "What is true about this claim is just that *languages* are made rather than found, and that truth is a property of linguistic entities, of sentences."

23. Ibid., italics in original.

24. For a brief description of some of the ways in which moral systems can fail under new sorts of social circumstances, see J. B. Schneewind, "Moral Knowledge and Moral Principles," in *Revisions*, ed. Stanley Hauerwas and Alasdair MacIntyre (Notre Dame, Ind.: University of Notre Dame Press, 1983), pp. 122–24.

25. I borrow this phrase from David Lewis, *Papers*, Vol. 1, pp. 233–49.

26. "The Contingency of Language," p. 6. I reserve detailed analysis of Rorty's views until Part 3 below. For a full-scale development of the analogy to evolution, see Stephen Toulmin, *Human Understanding*, Vol. 1 (Princeton: Princeton University Press, 1972).

CHAPTER FOUR

1. Cf. Chris Swoyer, "True For," in *Relativism: Cognitive and Moral*, ed. Michael Krausz and Jack W. Meiland (Notre Dame, Ind.: University of Notre Dame Press, 1982), pp. 91–92.

2. For accounts of conditions-clauses, see Roger Wertheimer, *The Significance of Sense* (Ithaca: Cornell University Press, 1972); Gilbert Harman, "Moral Relativism Defended," in *Relativism: Cognitive and Moral*, pp. 189–204; G. H. Von Wright, "A Note on Deontic Logic and Moral Obligation," *Mind* 65 (1956):507–9; and David B. Wong, *Moral Relativity* (Berkeley and Los Angeles: University of California Press, 1984), esp. pp. 40–42.

3. See Alan Donagan, *The Theory of Morality* (Chicago: University of Chicago Press, Phoenix ed., 1979), pp. 100-108; and Hector-Neri Castaneda, *The Structure of Morality* (Springfield: Charles C. Thomas, 1974), p. 17.

4. Wong, *Moral Relativity*, esp. p. 66.

5. Gilbert Harman, *The Nature of Morality* (New York: Oxford University Press, 1977), p. 98, italics in original.

6. Wong makes a similar argument against Harman when he points out that "many of us recognize some basic moral duties that would survive a situation in which there were no implicit agreements. Suppose that in the next Great Depression, the fabric of society unravels into a Hobbesian war of all against all. Many of us think we would still have the elementary duty not to kill each other for amusement, even if we know that others had no intention of reciprocating. Under Harman's theory, this belief is false, and involves a misapprehension of the nature of morality. But in the absence of a good explanation of how so many of us came to be mistaken, we had better look for another conception of morality" (pp. 24–25). I will suggest below that similar arguments work effectively against Wong's version of relativism.

7. Harman, "Moral Relativism Defended," pp. 196, 190.

8. Ibid., p. 191.

9. Ibid., p. 190.

10. Harman, *The Nature of Morality*, pp. 107–10.

11. In addition to the works already cited, see Gilbert Harman, *Change in View* (Cambridge: MIT Press, 1986), pp. 129–37.

12. Despite the arguments, given in the first chapter of *The Nature of Morality* and discussed in my second chapter, that were meant to say why ethics

seems problematic when compared with science, later in the book Harman uses his account of "ought" to show that some moral judgments, at any rate, aren't so problematic as they might seem (see esp. p. 132). For an account of scientific explanation as a three-term, context-dependent relation, see Bas C. van Fraassen, *The Scientific Image* (Oxford: Clarendon Press, 1980), ch. 5.

13. Denying that there are moral truths would make you a moral nihilist, not a relativist. Denying that there are good moral arguments, in the sense of good reasons for believing any particular moral propositions, would make you a moral skeptic, leaving you free to be relativistic or not in your view of moral truth.

14. In this case, semantic ascent bogs things down.

15. I am assuming that true moral propositions cannot contradict one another. A full discussion of the matter would have to include a treatment of so-called tragic conflicts. I hold that moral tragedy is best viewed as the conflict of good with good or *prima facie* right with *prima facie* right, not as the conflict of true "all things considered" propositions about what is right, just, or obligatory. Absolutists who want to reject my view of tragedy would need a way of saying that there is a single true morality without granting that "the moral truth is one" in the straightforward sense that there are no true moral contradictions.

16. Bernard Williams, "The Truth in Relativism," in *Relativism: Cognitive and Moral*, pp. 175–88.

17. See Williams, *Ethics and the Limits of Philosophy* (Cambridge: Harvard University Press, 1985), ch. 9.

18. Ibid., p. 166.

19. The idiom of consequentialism has become more complicated since the days of Bentham and Mill, when all intrinsic value was held reducible to utility. Many consequentialists now recognize more than one intrinsic value to be maximized. In contrast, the idiom of the real Kant was actually much richer than the one his followers have typically drawn from his *Groundwork for the Metaphysics of Morals*, as may be seen from recent developments in Kant scholarship.

CHAPTER FIVE

1. Kai Nielsen, *Ethics without God* (Buffalo: Prometheus Books, 1973).

2. Glenn C. Graber, "In Defense of a Divine Command Theory of Ethics," *Journal of the American Academy of Religion* 43 (1975):62–69. This article includes a helpful discussion of unpleasant dilemmas.

3. J. B. Schneewind, "Moral Knowledge and Moral Principles," in *Revisions*, ed. Stanley Hauerwas and Alasdair MacIntyre (Notre Dame, Ind.: University of Notre Dame Press, 1983), pp. 118–19.

4. Philip Quinn, *Divine Commands and Moral Requirements* (Oxford: Clarendon Press, 1978). For Quinn's diagnoses of the stock arguments against divine-command theories, see pp. 1-65, 130–64. For his formalizations of such theories, see pp. 66-129.

5. Robert Merrihew Adams, "A Modified Divine Command Theory of

Ethical Wrongness," in *Religion and Morality*, ed. Gene Outka and John P. Reeder, Jr. (Garden City, N.Y.: Anchor, 1973), pp. 318–47.

6. For a defense of this conclusion and an extended response to the original version of Adams's theory, see my article, "Metaethics and the Death of Meaning," *Journal of Religious Ethics* 6/1 (1978): 1-18.

7. Robert Merrihew Adams, "Divine Command Metaethics Modified Again," *Journal of Religious Ethics* 7/1 (1979): 66–79.

8. For an interesting account of these problems, see Scott Davis, "Ethical Properties and Divine Commands," *Journal of Religious Ethics* 11/2 (1983): 280–300.

9. Adams makes this argument in the first section of his paper "Moral Arguments for Theistic Belief," in *Rationality and Religious Belief*, ed. C. F. Delaney (Notre Dame, Ind.: University of Notre Dame Press, 1979), pp. 116–40.

10. Adams's most interesting moral argument for the existence of God is actually of another sort altogether. It is a practical argument of Kantian lineage, which concludes that there is a moral advantage in accepting theism. If theism provides the most adequate theory of a moral order of the universe, if faith in such an order is necessary to avoid demoralization, and if demoralization is a bad thing, we would seem to have a strong moral reason for accepting theism (or trying to, anyway). See sections 2–4 of "Moral Arguments for Theistic Belief." I do not, however, find the argument persuasive, even on the assumption that we ought to (try to) adjust our beliefs so as to avoid demoralization. In the first place, the most adequate theory of a moral order of the universe would be part of the most adequate total view. That means other issues—including, for one, the problem of evil—will have to be factored in. So it would be very hard to show that theism does provide the most adequate theory of a moral order. Furthermore, as Adams grants in his remarks about tragedy, some people may be capable of sustaining moral motivation in the face of continuous frustration. What about the rest of us? All we need to avoid demoralization, to put it very roughly, is the conviction that moral striving can make a difference, that it can make things better than they would be without moral striving—that is, sufficiently better to motivate moral striving. For some of us, this need not be much difference at all. Think of Camus' *The Plague*. All that Dr. Rieux, the novel's protagonist, needs is the idea that he is making some difference; and even under the extreme conditions of the plague, he believes that he is doing so. Less heroic figures will need more than that to keep them going. But for any of us, it should be enough that the highest achievable good, given whatever causal powers we have independent reason to believe in, seem worth pursuing. Perhaps we would need to believe in God if we supposed that only the highest conceivable good would be worth pursuing. But why suppose that? Why take an all-or-nothing attitude in morality by not striving at all if we can't have virtue crowned with perfect happiness in heaven by and by? Adams's argument would be stronger if it could be shown that our moral motivation depends on belief in a causal power capable of bringing

about a specific sort of moral order—the highest conceivable good. Maybe only God would have the capacity to bring that about. But focusing on the highest conceivable good and then trying to believe in whatever causal powers could bring it about would be, it seems to me, unadulterated wishful thinking.

CHAPTER SIX

1. These tendencies in religious ethics are discussed in my book, *The Flight from Authority* (Notre Dame, Ind.: University of Notre Dame Press, 1981), ch. 10.

2. Alan Donagan, *The Theory of Morality* (Chicago: University of Chicago Press, Phoenix ed., 1979).

3. See Richard Rorty, *Philosophy and the Mirror of Nature* (Princeton: Princeton University Press, 1979), pp. 132–33, 148–49.

4. Edward H. Levi, *An Introduction to Legal Reasoning* (Chicago: University of Chicago Press, 1949), p. 8.

5. Ibid., p. 9.

6. Michael Oakeshott, *Rationalism in Politics* (New York: Barnes and Noble, 1962), pp. 91–92, 97–98, 108, 135.

7. Ibid., pp. 128–29.

8. J. B. Schneewind, "Moral Knowledge and Moral Principles," in *Revisions*, ed. Stanley Hauerwas and Alasdair MacIntyre (Notre Dame, Ind.: University of Notre Dame Press, 1983), p. 121.

9. Donagan's interpretation of Hinduism and his appeal to traditional presuppositions as an explanation of moral disagreement both can be traced to the influence of Arthur Danto, *Mysticism and Morality: Oriental Thought and Moral Philosophy* (New York: Basic Books, 1972).

10. Margaret Farley, review of Alan Donagan, *The Theory of Morality*, in *Religious Studies Review* 7/3 (1981): 235.

11. Kantians have always held that the maxims to be tested by the categorical imperative depend on inclinations and that because inclinations vary from one person, community, or historical period to the next, maxims may vary as well. But whatever their source, maxims that pass the test of the categorical imperative could not, from an orthodox Kantian point of view, conflict with each other. Donagan's appeal to tradition-bound presuppositions, if I am right, is an attempt to account for the fact that the conclusions of venerable moral traditions conflict. He is not simply repeating the standard Kantian view of the variability of maxims: he is trying to explain why practical reason's testing procedure itself seems to vary in ways that introduce the possibility of conflicting results.

CHAPTER SEVEN

1. Mary Douglas, *Purity and Danger* (London: Routledge & Kegan Paul, 1966); *Natural Symbols* (New York: Vintage Books, 1973), esp. ch. 3; and *Implicit Meanings* (London: Routledge & Kegan Paul, 1975).

2. Wayne Proudfoot, *Religious Experience* (Berkeley and Los Angeles: University of California Press, 1985).

3. See Douglas, *Implicit Meanings*, ch. 7.

4. Ibid., ch. 17.

5. For a discussion of the ambiguity of the term *sodomy*, see John Boswell, *Christianity, Social Tolerance, and Homosexuality* (Chicago: University of Chicago Press, 1980), p. 93 n. 2. I shall use the term to refer only to homosexual anal intercourse.

6. Ibid., pp. 31–36, 91, 119–21, 169–70, 208–9, 270.

7. See Boswell's reference (p. 34 n. 63) to the institution of the *berdache* among American Indians.

8. Rodney Needham, *Remarks and Inventions* (London: Tavistock, 1974), pp. 61–71. I owe this reference to Alasdair MacIntyre.

9. Ibid., p. 68.

10. See Proudfoot's development of this theme in *Religious Experience, passim*.

11. My interpretation of Aquinas is influenced by many conversations with my colleague, Victor Preller.

12. St. Thomas Aquinas, *Summa Theologica*, trans. Blackfriars (New York: McGraw Hill, 1968), 2a2ae.154, 11.

13. I claim only that some such judgments fall there. Others might fall elsewhere on the spectrum. Some, for example, might presuppose what Harman calls inner judgments, thereby partaking in their relativity to an agent's reasons. Moreover, the issue might be complicated in other ways, for example by what Wong calls environmental relativity.

14. Alan Donagan, *The Theory of Morality* (Chicago: University of Chicago Press, Phoenix ed., 1979), p. 105.

CHAPTER EIGHT

1. Michael Oakeshott, *Rationalism in Politics* (London: Methuen, 1962), p. 261.

2. David Tracy, *The Analogical Imagination: Christian Theology and the Culture of Pluralism* (New York: Crossroad, 1981), p. 52.

3. Ibid., pp. 62, 64.

4. Oakeshott, in a discussion of the dangers that ensue when one or two voices establish a monopoly on conversation, warns, "An excluded voice . . . may gain a hearing by imitating the monopolists; but it will be a hearing for only a counterfeit utterance" (*Rationalism*, p. 202).

5. See *Analogical Imagination*, esp. ch. 3.

6. Ibid., pp. 100–101, and *passim*.

7. David Tracy, *Blessed Rage for Order* (New York: Seabury, 1975). For a powerful criticism of Tracy's fundamental theology, see Van A. Harvey, "The Pathos of Liberal Theology," *Journal of Religion* 56 (1976):382–91. Tracy dismisses Harvey's criticism without argument in *Analogical Imagination*, p. 185, n. 32.

8. See Dennis P. McCann and Charles R. Strain, *Polity and Praxis: A Program for American Practical Theology* (New York: Winston Press, 1985), pp. 13, 3.

9. The reasons for this suspicion are stated elegantly by Raymond Geuss in *The Idea of a Critical Theory: Habermas and the Frankfurt School* (Cambridge: Cambridge University Press, 1981), ch. 3. The most memorable line from Geuss's argument is this: "I find it quite hard to burden pre-dynastic Egyptians, ninth-century French serfs and early-twentieth-century Yanomamo tribesmen with the view that they are acting correctly if their action is based on a norm on which there would be universal consensus in an ideal speech situation" (p. 66). Geuss's argument is meant to undermine not critical theory as such but rather the transcendental ambitions that made Habermas turn away from the contextualism he shared with Adorno in his earliest writings and toward the work of Chomsky and Searle. McCann and Strain are aware of arguments like these but deal with them ineffectively and dismissively (see *Polity and Praxis*, p. 83). I admire the passages in which they favor immanent criticism and those in which they disdain thinkers who claim hermeneutical privilege for a moral, political, or theological position, but their use of Habermas's anticontextualist writings, in the service of a doctrine about what *the* norms and procedures of public discourse are, seems to me yet another claim of hermeneutical privilege—on behalf of neo-Kantian philosophy. If they take some of Habermas's most recent work to show that he wants to drop the transcendental ambitions criticized by Geuss, they would still need to show that a thoroughly empirical, nontranscendental Habermas could establish what *the* norms and procedures of public discourse are in a sense that would constrain how the rest of us ought to speak. For an interesting discussion of recent developments in Habermas's position as they relate to criticisms (not unlike Geuss's) made by Richard Rorty, see Richard J. Bernstein, *Philosophical Profiles: Essays in a Pragmatic Mode* (Philadelphia: University of Pennsylvania Press, 1986), esp. ch. 2.

10. Mary Midgley, *Beast and Man* (New York: Meridian, 1980), p. 306.

11. James M. Gustafson, *Ethics from a Theocentric Perspective*, 2 vols. (Chicago: University of Chicago Press, 1981, 1984). Page references here, unless otherwise noted, will be to vol. 1.

12. See Oakeshott, *Rationalism*, p. 198.

13. Stanley Cavell, *The Claim of Reason* (New York: Oxford University Press, 1979), p. 326.

14. See vol. 2, ch. 4, for Gustafson's clearest statement of his procedure. See also vol. 1, pp. 141ff., for his discussion of selective retrieval, and Gustafson's earlier book, *Protestant and Roman Catholic Ethics* (Chicago: University of Chicago Press, 1978), for a comparative study of how different authors make quite different uses of biblical and philosophical sources. My colleague Paul Ramsey has criticized Gustafson for taking over a nominalist theory of traditions from Ernst Troeltsch, adding that "Jeffrey Stout and others under the influence of Richard Rorty appear to hold much the same notions of particular traditions and how they work." See Ramsey, "A Letter to James Gustafson," *Journal of Religious Ethics* 13/1 (1985):96. Ramsey does not explain what

Rorty has to do with the issue. I suspect he would have trouble citing passages in which Rorty puts forward the "generalized tradition-theory" by which I have supposedly been influenced. Rorty makes little mention of tradition. It would be easier to find relevant passages in someone like Alasdair MacIntyre. In fact, however, I read, and was influenced by, both Troeltsch and Gustafson before I had ever heard of Rorty or MacIntyre.

15. H. Richard Niebuhr, *The Responsible Self* (New York: Harper & Row, 1963).

16. Richard R. Niebuhr, *Schleiermacher on Christ and Religion* (New York: Scribner's, 1964), pp. 46, 48.

17. Perry Miller, *The New England Mind: The Seventeenth Century* (New York: Macmillan, 1939), p. 13.

18. See H. Richard Niebuhr, *Radical Monotheism and Western Culture* (New York: Harper Torchbooks, 1970), p. 119.

19. Paul Ramsey is the only American scholar of comparable distinction in the field, but Ramsey is now famous primarily as a polemicist and casuist, whereas Gustafson has concentrated on analytical and interpretive studies throughout most of his career. Gustafson accords Ramsey a remarkable honor by including him along with Karl Barth, Thomas Aquinas, and Karl Rahner as benchmarks against which his own theological ethics must be judged (vol. 2, ch. 2). For Ramsey's response to Gustafson, see his "Letter to James Gustafson"; then read Gustafson's "A Response to Critics," *Journal of Religious Ethics* 13/2 (1985):185–209.

20. *Responsible Self*, p. 63.

21. Ibid., p. 216.

22. Gustafson gives prominence to the imagery of part and whole in the concluding paragraph of his first volume, and he returns to it repeatedly throughout his second volume. The same imagery is deeply ingrained, of course, in the hermeneutical tradition represented by such contemporary philosophers as Charles Taylor and Hans-Georg Gadamer. It is also, as Gustafson points out, appropriated by Mary Midgley, whose work (as we shall see) has close affinity with his. Unfortunately, Gustafson criticizes Midgley for suggesting that we replace the language of means and ends with that of part and whole. Midgley does say this: "What we need *here* is to get rid of the language of means and ends" (*Beast and Man*, p. 359, italics added). I take it that she proposes elimination of this language only in the limited context of what she is "here" discussing—the question, "Why does man exist?" She is specifically concerned to dismiss the application of cost-benefit analysis to that one question, and her argument pivots on a distinction between cases in which such analysis is applicable and cases in which it is not.

23. See, for example, H. Richard Niebuhr's *Christ and Culture* (New York: Harper & Row, 1951), ch. 6, where he develops the theme of transformation and conversion that becomes crucial for Gustafson.

24. *The Christian Faith*, ed. H. R. Mackintosh and J. S. Stewart (Philadelphia: Fortress Press, 1928), p. 76, italics deleted.

25. Ibid., p. 125.

26. Jeffrey Stout, *The Flight from Authority* (Notre Dame, Ind: University of Notre Dame Press, 1981), ch. 7.

27. Compare Schleiermacher: "As regards the identification of absolute dependence with 'relation to God' in our proposition: this is to be understood in the sense that the *Whence* of our receptive and active existence, as implied in this self-consciousness, is to be designated by the word 'God,' and that this is for us the really original signification of that word" *(The Christian Faith*, p. 16).

28. I say that maintaining a sharp distinction between knowing and feeling is essential to Schleiermacher's strategy, not that Schleiermacher himself always keeps the distinction sharp.

29. For confirmation of my interpretation of Gustafson on immediacy, see his book *Can Ethics Be Christian?* (Chicago: University of Chicago Press, 1975), pp. 68, 183 n.14; his 1975 Père Marquette Theology Lecture, *The Contributions of Theology to Medical Ethics* (Milwaukee: Marquette University Press, 1975), pp. 5–6, 97–98 n.4; and John E. Smith, *Experience and God* (New York: Oxford University Press, 1968), pp. 52–53, a passage Gustafson cites as influential for his own thinking and in which Smith favors a notion of interpreted experience over a conception of experience as not mediated by language. As for Gustafson's relation to Schleiermacher on this issue, I have trouble saying anything definite, mainly because of the exceedingly imprecise explication of feeling as "immediate self-consciousness" offered in *The Christian Faith*, pp. 6–7.

30. Mary Midgley, *Beast and Man*, pp. 198–99, 388, 363.

31. Stephen Toulmin, Gustafson's most sympathetic philosophical critic, says about the "substantial intellectual burden" that Gustafson has undertaken: "Like the Stoics before him, he faces the task of explaining how we can infer the nature of the *logos*—or God's purposes for the *cosmos*—from the observable orderliness of our experience. In the two present volumes, he does little more than present these issues as a problem, but, if he addresses them more explicitly in future writings, they may take him further afield than he has yet fully explored." Stephen Toulmin, "Nature and Nature's God," *Journal of Religious Ethics* 13/1 (1985):47–48.

32. Philosophers of religion are showing an interest in reopening the case. The most impressive recent attempt is that of R. G. Swinburne in *The Coherence of Theism* (Oxford: Oxford University Press, 1977) and *The Existence of God* (Oxford: Oxford University Press, 1979). For powerful counterarguments, see J. L. Mackie, *The Miracle of Theism* (Oxford: Oxford University Press, 1982).

33. See Hans W. Frei, *The Eclipse of Biblical Narrative* (New Haven: Yale University Press, 1974); George Lindbeck, *The Nature of Doctrine: Religion and Theology in a Postliberal Age* (Philadelphia: Westminster Press, 1984); and Ronald Thiemann, *Revelation and Theology: The Gospel as Narrated Promise* (Notre Dame: University of Notre Dame Press, 1985). See also the essays collected in *Faith and Rationality: Reason and Belief in God*, ed. Alvin Plantinga and Nicholas Wolterstorff (Notre Dame, Ind.: University of Notre Dame

Press, 1983). Contributors to the latter volume would side with Gustafson against fundamental theologians and foundationalist philosophers but they would criticize him for accepting what they call "the evidentialist challenge." They would hold further that they, not Gustafson, retain the crucial epistemological insights of the Reformed tradition.

34. See, for example, Ronald F. Thiemann, "Response to George Lindbeck," *Theology Today* 43/3 (1986):382.

35. I have conflated these topics myself in previous writings. For a useful corrective, see Nicholas Wolterstorff, "Can Belief in God Be Rational If It Has No Foundations?" in *Faith and Rationality*, pp. 135–86; and his book, *Reason within the Bounds of Religion* (Grand Rapids, Mich.: Eerdmans, 1976). The extent of my agreement with Wolterstorff in epistemological matters allows me to accept most of what the best proponents of option (5) have been saying recently about the rationality of religious belief (for some people) without accepting their religious assumptions.

CHAPTER NINE

1. Robert N. Bellah, Richard Madsen, William M. Sullivan, Ann Swidler, and Steven M. Tipton, *Habits of the Heart: Individualism and Commitment in American Life* (Berkeley and Los Angeles: University of California Press, 1985), p. 294.

2. Alasdair MacIntyre, *After Virtue*, 2d ed. (Notre Dame, Ind.: University of Notre Dame Press, 1984), p. 263.

3. I resort to such unhappy terms as *liberal society* and *pluralistic society* merely because they call attention to societies like ours in two respects: their populations are similarly diverse in religious belief or philosophical outlook and their institutions are similarly disposed to tolerate such diversity. Beyond that, I want to leave open for now how our society ought to be described and what relation it has to *liberalism* and *pluralism*—a family of ideas invented by ideologues and philosophers. In fact I think our society is poorly understood and the main obstacle to understanding it well is the dominant form of liberalism, whose picture of our society is often accepted by both its friends and its foes. So I would prefer not to be described as attempting "to reconcile communitarianism with liberalism." See Christopher Lasch, "The Communitarian Critique of Liberalism," *Soundings* 69/1–2 (1986): 60–76, esp. 75. I am rather trying to move beyond the debate between communitarianism and liberalism by rejecting something both sides have in common—namely, a picture of so-called liberal society. See also Robert N. Bellah, "A Response: The Idea of Practices in *Habits*," *Soundings* 69/1–2 (1986): 181–87. Bellah says, "It is incorrect to call our society so confidently as Stout does a 'liberal society'" (p. 182). He wonders what my conception of liberalism could be, given the influence of Hobbes and Locke in the Anglo-Saxon world. But, as the following chapters should make clear, I'm actually trying to drive a wedge between the philosophical theorists of liberalism and the society those theorists were trying to defend. I shall be happy, in the end, if people find some new tag to replace *liberal*. *Pluralistic* may be slightly better, but it too tends to be assimi-

lated to an ideology I don't like, called plural*ism* and expressed in such odious notions as "values clarification" and a "laissez faire" approach to "the market-place of ideas."

4. For a portrait of Socrates as intellectual bully, see P. T. Geach, "Plato's *Euthyphro*: An Analysis and Commentary," *The Monist* 50 (1966):369–82.

5. Alasdair MacIntyre, "Epistemological Crises, Dramatic Narrative and the Philosophy of Science," *The Monist* (1977): 453–72.

6. I discuss related difficulties caused by the "structural similarity between the questioning of informants in the field and Socratic probing in philosophy" in *The Flight from Authority* (Notre Dame, Ind.: University of Notre Dame Press, 1981), pp. 212–13.

7. I therefore fully agree with Steven M. Tipton when he says, in response to the paper in which I first published these criticisms of *Habits*, that Socratic questioning (in the narrow sense under consideration here) hardly exhausts the ethnographic method employed by the research team. See his paper, "A Response: Moral Languages and the Good Society," *Soundings* 69 (1986):165–80, esp. 171–76. I do not intend any blanket indictment of the book or its method.

8. I am also trying to explain what it is about the book that makes many readers, in conversation, refer to some of the interview material as wooden or contrast the book unfavorably with the work of Robert Coles.

9. Robert M. Bellah, "A Response: The Idea of Practices in *Habits*," p. 182.

10. See Jonathan Arac, *Commissioned Spirits* (New Brunswick: Rutgers University Press, 1978), pp. 39–40.

11. *After Virtue*, pp. 111–13. See also his *Against the Self-Images of the Age* (Notre Dame, Ind.: University of Notre Dame Press, rpt. 1978), p. 167, and *A Short History of Ethics* (New York: Macmillan, 1966), p. 86. Hereafter, these works will be cited as *Self-Images* and *Short History*.

12. Alan Donagan, *The Theory of Morality* (Chicago: University of Chicago Press, Phoenix ed., 1979), p. 22.

13. For an introduction to the notion of point of view in literary theory, see Wayne C. Booth, "Distance and Point-of-View: An Essay in Classification," and Norman Friedman, "Point of View in Fiction: The Development of a Critical Concept," both in *The Theory of the Novel*, ed. Philip Stevick (New York: Free Press, 1967), pp. 87–107, 108–37.

14. "Epistemological Crises," pp. 460, 470. This, I believe, is the heart of the account of rationality presupposed by *After Virtue*, the account MacIntyre has promised to make fully explicit in the forthcoming sequel to that book. See also his essay, "The Relationship of Philosophy to Its Past," in *Philosophy in History*, ed. Richard Rorty, J. B. Schneewind, and Quentin Skinner (Cambridge: Cambridge University Press, 1984), pp. 31–48.

15. "Epistemological Crises," p. 456.

16. Whether MacIntyre is able to extend such charity to his own contemporaries is, as we shall see, another question.

17. For related criticisms of MacIntyre, see my paper "Virtue among the

Ruins: An Essay on MacIntyre," *Neue Zeitschrift für Systematische Theologie und Religionsphilosophie* 26 (1984):256–73; and J. B. Schneewind, "Moral Crisis and the History of Ethics," in *Midwest Studies in Philosophy 8/1983,* ed. P. French, T. Uehling, and H. Wettstein (Minneapolis: University of Minnesota Press, 1983), pp. 525–39.

18. The idea that we have an "overlapping," as opposed to "strict," consensus is raised by John Rawls in *A Theory of Justice* (Cambridge: The Belknap Press of Harvard University Press, 1971), pp. 387–88, and it is related to his attempt to achieve "reflective equilibrium" between our moral principles and widely shared conviction or intuitions. Since working out my own notion of a self-limiting consensus on the good (in previously published essays on MacIntyre and Bellah, as well as in drafts of this book), I have come across unpublished works in which Rawls develops his conception of overlapping consensus in a direction I find congenial, although his terminology and mine differ somewhat. One way of interpreting what I am doing here is to say that I am trying to make use of something like Rawls's notions of overlapping consensus and reflective equilibrium while disconnecting them from other elements of Rawls's theory such as his critique of justice as desert, his references to the vantage point "from which noumenal selves see the world," his use of the term *teleological,* and his elaboration of the "original position."

19. This picture also enables us to explain why both emotivism and intuitionism have struck some ethical theorists as plausible. Each of these theories concentrates on a different diet of examples: emotivism on how we use moral language to express our most recalcitrant disagreements, intuitionism on the vast body of platitudes we share. MacIntyre is able to portray emotivism as *the* ethical theory of our age only by underemphasizing data that have drawn theorists to intuitionism (and other varieties of cognitivism). From the vantage point of MacIntyre's narrative of decline and fall, it becomes too difficult to account for why most theorists in our century have turned their backs on emotivism.

20. Cf. Schneewind, "Moral Crisis." pp. 537–38.

21. "Epistemological Crises," p. 462.

22. Alasdair MacIntyre, "Relativism, Power, and Philosophy," in *After Philosophy,* ed. Kenneth Baynes, James Bohman, and Thomas McCarthy (Cambridge: MIT Press, 1987), pp. 385–411.

CHAPTER TEN

1. G. E. M. Anscombe, "Modern Moral Philosophy," originally published in 1956 and recently reprinted in the third volume of her collected papers, *Ethics, Religion and Politics* (Minneapolis: University of Minnesota Press, 1981), ch. 4. This essay forms an important part of the background essential for understanding the development of MacIntyre's moral philosophy.

2. We have already come across Adams's argument in Part 2. See his essay, "Moral Arguments for Theistic Belief," in *Rationality and Religious Belief,* ed. C. F. Delaney (Notre Dame, Ind.: University of Notre Dame Press, 1979), pp. 116–40. I should add that MacIntyre may have unexpressed theological

reasons for wanting to preserve a strictly secular moral philosophy, reasons Anscombe would share.

3. Basil Mitchell, *Morality: Religious and Secular* (Oxford: Oxford University Press, 1980).

4. MacIntyre has acknowledged the importance of this criticism and promised to do something about it in his next major book. See especially the final page of the postscript to the second edition of *After Virtue*.

5. See especially Bernard Yack, "Community and Conflict in Aristotle's Political Philosophy," *The Review of Politics* 47/1 (1985):92–112, on MacIntyre's interpretation of Aristotle; Richard J. Mouw, "Alasdair MacIntyre on Reformation Ethics," *Journal of Religious Ethics* 13/2 (1985):243–57, on his apparent assumptions about Luther and Calvin; Annette Baier, *Postures of the Mind* (Minneapolis: University of Minnesota Press, 1985), chs. 11–13, on his reading of Hume; and Richard J. Bernstein, *Philosophical Profiles: Essays in a Pragmatic Mode* (Philadelphia: University of Pennsylvania Press, 1986), ch. 4, on his failure to acknowledge his indebtedness to the Enlightenment and to Hegel. I add my own reservations about his treatment of Aquinas. These reservations bear on the importance of natural law, moral tragedy, and the unity of the virtues. The following pieces by J. B. Schneewind, if taken together, not only press specific objections against *After Virtue* but also begin to show what a fully developed alternative to MacIntyre's reading of modern moral philosophy might look like, a reading in which figures like Grotius and Pufendorf would play central roles: "Moral Crisis and the History of Ethics," in *Midwest Studies in Philosophy 8*, ed. Peter French, et al. (Minneapolis: University of Minnesota Press, 1983), pp. 525–39; "The Divine Corporation and the History of Ethics," in *Philosophy in History*, ed. Richard Rorty, J. B. Schneewind, and Quentin Skinner (Cambridge: Cambridge University Press, 1984), pp. 173–92; "The Use of Autonomy in Ethical Theory," in *Reconstructing Individualism*, ed. Thomas C. Heller, Morton Sosna, and David Wellbery (Stanford: Stanford University Press, 1986), pp. 64–75.

6. My interpretation is influenced by MacIntyre's response to an earlier version of my criticisms, when we participated along with Annette Baier in a philosophy colloquium on his book at the University of Houston in April 1983. On that occasion, I offered him the choice between these two strands in his work, and he seemed to come down clearly on the sectarian side—to my disappointment.

7. For a similar criticism of MacIntyre, see Schneewind, "Moral Crisis and the History of Ethics," pp. 525–39.

8. See the first and third sections of Chapter 4 above.

9. There is another reason for being careful not to be misled by the term, *teleological*. It is often used interchangeably with the term *consequentialist*. But when MacIntyre refers to his own view as teleological, he does not mean to side with the consequentialists. His moral philosophy involves essential reference to a *telos*, but it does not conceive of the good to be pursued as a state of affairs in which the greatest aggregate value has been achieved, irrespective of constraints on means. The *telos* he has in mind is itself defined in terms of

the virtues. The virtues are traits simultaneously needed in order to pursue the good and partly definitive of the good life sought. So the good, thus defined, places strict limits on acceptable means. We can construe the provisional *telos* of our society in much the same way. It ties into a rationally justified system of shared ends already implicitly informed by a conception of justice and by constraints on the means we may employ in pursuing either the common good itself or our own individual projects. Because justice and the good are inter-defined, because the good we seek is a shared life in which justice constrains action, it is misleading to say either, with the consequentialist, that the good is prior to the right or, with Rawls, that the right is prior to the good. See John Rawls, *A Theory of Justice* (Cambridge: Belknap Press of Harvard University Press, 1971), esp. p. 31.

10. Richard Rorty, "The Priority of Democracy to Philosophy," unpublished manuscript.

11. I have in mind, in addition to "The Priority of Democracy to Philosophy," especially these essays: "Method, Social Science, and Social Hope," in Rorty's *Consequences of Pragmatism* (Minneapolis: University of Minnesota Press, 1982), pp. 191–210; "Solidarity or Objectivity?" in *Post-Analytic Philosophy*, ed. John Rajchman and Cornel West (New York: Columbia University Press, 1985), pp. 3–19; "Habermas and Lyotard on Postmodernity," in *Habermas and Modernity*, ed. Richard J. Bernstein (Cambridge: MIT Press, 1985), pp. 161–75; "Postmodernist Bourgeois Liberalism," in *Hermeneutics and Praxis*, ed. Robert Hollinger (Notre Dame, Ind.: University of Notre Dame Press, 1985), pp. 214–21; "Freud and Moral Reflection," in *Pragmatism's Freud*, ed. Joseph H. Smith and William Kerrigan (Baltimore: Johns Hopkins University Press, 1986), pp. 1–27; and three pieces based on Rorty's Northcliffe Lectures at University College, London, published in the *London Review of Books*: "The Contingency of Language" 8/7 (17 April 1986):3–6, "The Contingency of Selfhood" 8/8 (8 May 1986):11–15, and "The Contingency of Community" 8/13 (24 July 1986):10–14.

12. Michael Sandel, *Liberalism and the Limits of Justice* (Cambridge: Cambridge University Press, 1982).

13. See, for example, John Rawls, "Justice as Fairness: Political not Metaphysical, *Philosophy and Public Affairs* 14 (1985):223–51.

14. Hence my reluctance to choose between "two concepts of Rawls" in *The Flight from Authority*, pp. 222 ff., 232–41, and my decision to focus my criticisms not on Rawls himself but rather on authors like David A. J. Richards and Ronald Green, who seem to take Rawlsian ideas in precisely the direction criticized by Sandel. It is in part because the metaphysical Rawls caught on with a significant reading public that Sandel's criticisms remain valuable even if Rorty is right about how to read *A Theory of Justice*. The most important point at which I agree with Sandel against even the pragmatic Rawls has to do with Rawls's criticisms of the concept of justice as desert.

15. Michael Walzer, *Spheres of Justice* (New York: Basic Books, 1983).

16. Walzer, p. xiv. On the same page, Walzer writes: "I don't claim to have achieved any great distance from the social world in which I live. One way to

begin the philosophical enterprise—perhaps the original way—is to walk out of the cave, leave the city, climb the mountain, fashion for oneself (what can never be fashioned for ordinary men and women) an objective and universal standpoint. Then one describes the terrain of everyday life from far away, so that it loses its particular contours and takes on a general shape. But I mean to stand in the cave, in the city, on the ground."

17. "The Priority of Democracy," p. 40. Rorty implies that "philosophical presuppositions" in this context should be taken to mean assumptions "about the nature of human beings" and about "whether there is such a thing as 'human nature'" (p. 17). But this explication can be seriously misleading, given the ambiguity of the expression "human nature." I shall return to this and related ambiguities in the next chapter, when I discuss Rorty's view of essentialism and "methodological nominalism." But I do want to ask what is left of Rorty's point if we take him to be denying only the idea that liberal society needs grounding in an *essentialist* view of human nature. He obviously wants to leave open the possibility that it might be desirable for liberal society to receive "articulation" in a conception of the self. Furthermore, I suspect he wouldn't want to deny that our continued commitment to particular liberal practices or institutions might depend on our ability to "justify" them in response to specific doubts. And those doubts might well take the form of questions like, "Do we really want to carry on with this practice if such-and-such a view of what people are like is false?" I wonder how many people, philosophers included, are committed to an essentialist view of what people are like. I therefore wonder whether Rorty's animus toward "philosophical presuppositions" is nearly as radical as it initially seems.

18. Irving Howe has shown how this inability has affected the political novel in recent years. See the epilogue to the new edition of *Politics and the Novel* (New York: Meridian, 1987), pp. 252–73, which includes perceptive commentary on Nadine Gordimer, Gabriel Garcia-Márquez, Milan Kundera, V. S. Naipaul, and A. Solzhenitsyn.

19. "Habermas and Lyotard on Postmodernity," p. 169.

20. Ibid., p. 173.

21. *Consequences of Pragmatism*, p. 210.

22. Hilary Putnam, "Liberation Philosophy," *London Review of Books* 8/5 (March 1986): 5.

23. "The Contingency of Community," p. 14.

24. See, for example, Cornel West, "The Politics of American Neo-Pragmatism," in *Post-Analytic Philosophy*, pp. 259–75; and Richard J. Bernstein, *Philosophical Profiles*, chs. 1, 2, 10.

25. Richard Rorty, "Beyond Nietzsche and Marx," *London Review of Books* (19 February–4 March 1981): 6.

26. Richard Rorty, "Freud and Moral Reflection," p. 16.

27. "The Priority of Democracy to Philosophy," p. 33.

28. Gilbert C. Meilaender, Jr., "Individuals in Community: An Augustinian Vision," *The Cresset* (November 1983):5–10.

29. See Bernstein, *Philosophical Profiles*, pp. 130–31.

30. Alasdair MacIntyre, "Bernstein's Distorting Mirrors: A Rejoinder," *Soundings* 67/1 (1984): 38.

31. Bernard Yack, "Community and Conflict in Aristotle's Political Philosophy," *The Review of Politics* 47/1 (1985): 92–112. As Yack observes, most recent interpreters of Aristotle, whether friends or foes of liberal society, "have disconnected Aristotle's analysis of political community from his analysis of political conflict" (p. 93). They therefore exaggerate the extent of commonality Aristotle takes to be necessary for political community, thus creating a distorted caricature to be contrasted with liberal individualism. Yack diagnoses the problem as follows: "The tendency of most contemporary readers to ignore the connections Aristotle makes between political community and political conflict may result from their familiarity with liberal political theories. In the light of liberal justifications of political institutions in terms of individual calculation of interest and obligation, Aristotle's statements about the logical priority of the community to the individual in book 1 of the *Politics* stand out and attract the great attention. Likewise, the analyses of political argument and conflict in the later books generally receive less attention since they do not contrast as sharply with widely accepted principles of liberal thought. Such a perspective distorts our understanding of Aristotle's concept of political community by making political community seem to be a form of identity and political conflict a divergence from political community. This may be the way in which some of Aristotle's antiliberal admirers understand political community. But it is not . . . the understanding of political community developed in the *Politics*" (p. 93).

32. Ibid., p. 97.

33. See "Postmodernist Bourgeois Liberalism," p. 218, and "The Contingency of Community." For Sellars's most extensive discussion of shared intentions, see Wilfrid Sellars, *Science and Metaphysics* (New York: Humanities Press, 1968), pp. 175–229.

34. MacIntyre says that "it is not the case that *first* I must decide whether some theory of human nature or cosmology is true and only *secondly* pass a verdict upon an account of the virtues which is 'based' upon it" ("Bernstein's Distorting Mirrors," p. 39).

35. Saying this does not put me at odds with Rawls. When Rawls refers to "conceptions of the good," he usually seems to have in mind religious or philosophical views of the meaning or ultimate purpose of human life. He is not denying that the citizens of a liberal society share common aims or ends. Nor is he denying that his own liberal theory of justice as fairness needs to make certain "thin" assumptions about the good, assumptions that fall well short of a full-blown view of the meaning, value, or purpose of life. When he expresses opposition to "teleological theories," he means what I mean by "consequentialist theories." I, too, oppose consequentialism. So I am much closer to Rawls than I may seem at first blush.

36. "Freud and Moral Reflection," p. 25 n.24.

37. See Michael Oakeshott, *On Human Conduct* (Oxford: Oxford University Press, 1975), pp. 185–326.

38. Richard Rorty, *Philosophy and the Mirror of Nature* (Princeton: Princeton University Press, 1979), p. 318.

39. The quoted phrases come from Rorty, "The Contingency of Community," p. 13.

40. These formulae allude, respectively, to John Rawls, T. M. Scanlon, and Jürgen Habermas.

41. John Dewey, *Reconstruction in Philosophy* (Boston: Beacon Press, 1957), p. 212. See Rorty, "Habermas and Lyotard on Postmodernity," p. 174.

CHAPTER ELEVEN

1. Edmund N. Santurri, "The Flight to Pragmatism," *Religious Studies Review* 9/4 (1983):330–38. The quoted phrases are on p. 337.

2. I shall confine myself here to rebutting only the aspects of Santurri's criticisms most directly relevant to the concerns of this chapter. But I maintain that Santurri has not established his case against me at any significant point, and I consider his interpretation of my views seriously mistaken throughout.

3. I grant, by the way, that some people in our society find this judgment either uncertain, in need of qualification, or downright wrong. They typically have in mind imaginary cases in which catastrophic consequences would ensue if an injustice of this sort were not committed. Such cases do not sway me, but this is not the place to argue the point. I also grant that there is ample room for debate over which activities ought to count as torture and which people ought, in a given context, to count as innocent in the relevant sense. Yet I am prepared to assert that knowingly and willingly torturing the innocent is unjust, leaving uncertainties af application and interpretation to the prudent casuist. If my concern were to show that most members of our society share certain moral judgments—a concern more relevant to previous chapters than to this one—I would select somewhat different examples. Torturing people merely for fun, I have said, is recognized as unjust by all morally competent members of our society. The same would hold for the judgment that torturing innocents is, other things being equal, morally wrong.

4. Richard Rorty, *Consequences of Pragmatism* (Minneapolis: University of Minnesota Press, 1982), p. 97.

5. Ibid., p. 154.

6. Richard Rorty, *Philosophy and the Mirror of Nature* (Princeton: Princeton University Press, 1979), p. 175.

7. Richard Rorty, "Epistemological Behaviorism and the De-Transcendentalization of Analytic Philosophy," in *Hermeneutics and Praxis*, ed. Robert Hollinger (Notre Dame, Ind.: University of Notre Dame Press, 1985), pp. 89–121.

8. Richard Rorty, "Solidarity or Objectivity?" in *Post-Analytic Philosophy*, ed. John Rajchman and Cornel West (New York: Columbia University Press, 1985), p. 5.

9. Richard Rorty, "Life at the End of Inquiry," *London Review of Books* (2 August–6 September 1984):6.

10. Richard Rorty, "Realism and Reference," *The Monist* 59/3 (1976): 321–40.

11. I do not mean to leave the impression that "Realism and Reference" was the last time Rorty demonstrated the willingness to abide by such caution. He has, in a series of recent essays, shown similar care in avoiding troublesome dicta. See, in particular, "Beyond Realism and Anti-Realism" (forthcoming); "Pragmatism, Davidson and Truth," in *Truth and Interpretation: Perspectives on the Philosophy of Donald Davidson*, ed. Ernest LePore (Oxford: Blackwell's, 1986), pp. 333–55; and "Is Natural Science a Natural Kind?" (forthcoming). The point of concentrating here on "Realism and Reference," instead of Rorty's more recent work—aside from its availability when I first drafted this chapter—is to show that he has known how to transcend the limitations of pithy little formulae for a long time now.

12. *Consequences*, p. 163.

13. See Sabina Lovibond, *Realism and Imagination in Ethics* (Minneapolis: University of Minnesota Press, 1983), p. 42.

14. In a recent essay he has even granted that *Philosophy and the Mirror of Nature* should be criticized for trying to offer a substitute for the realist's definition of truth. See Richard Rorty, "Beyond Realism and Anti-Realism," (forthcoming).

15. Richard Rorty, ed., *The Linguistic Turn: Recent Essays in Philosophical Method* (Chicago: University of Chicago Press, 1967). Rorty's introduction to the volume is called "Metaphilosophical Difficulties of Linguistic Philosophy" (pp. 1–41).

16. Keep in mind here that Rorty is opposing the idea of distinctively philosophical accounts, the kind of philosophy that violates the strictures of methodological nominalism, not anything else that might go by the name of philosophy. His problem with "truth as correspondence to undescribed reality" lies in its role in epistemology, where *epistemology* is defined as an attempt to supply a distinctively philosophical account of truth and justification. At one point in *Philosophy and the Mirror of Nature* Rorty endorses the view that "truth as correspondence" ought to be eliminated, and then adds: "or, more mildly, it requires separation from epistemology and relegation to semantics" (p. 179 n. 12). Also keep in mind that he has no complaint with *epistemology* either, provided the term means nothing more than empirical inquiry into knowing or Wittgensteinian inquiry into the grammar of the words we use in appraising beliefs.

17. Jackson defines and defends skeptical realism in a forthcoming paper, "The Varieties of Scepticisms." He finds Rorty's pragmatism wanting on moral grounds in another paper, "The Theory and Practice of Discomfort," forthcoming in *The Thomist*.

18. *Consequences*, p. 169.

19. Ibid., p. 171, italics in original.

20. See "The Priority of Democracy," p. 17, where Rorty affirms that his opposition to the idea of appealing to "human nature" employs that phrase "in

the traditional philosophical sense in which Sartre denied that there was such a thing, rather than in the rather unusual one which Rawls gives it." In Rawls's usage, he goes on to explain, a theory of human nature is "provided by, roughly, common sense plus the social sciences." Rorty makes clear that he has no objection to a theory of human nature in Rawls's sense—a point which vindicates my interpreting Rorty's anti-essentialism as what he once called methodological nominalism. I doubt, however, that Rawls's usage is all that unusual.

21. Unless, of course, we take *intuition* to mean something innocuous, like "noninferentially known but still dependent upon enculturation."

22. Bernard Williams, *Ethics and the Limits of Philosophy* (Cambridge: Harvard University Press, 1985), p. 23.

23. *Consequences*, p. 173.

24. See Hilary Putnam on the distinction between optimistic and pessimistic forms of modernism in the third volume of his *Philosophical Papers: Realism and Reason* (Cambridge: Cambridge University Press, 1983), pp. 180–83, 303.

25. "The Contingency of Community," p. 11.

26. In "The Contingency of Selfhood," Rorty seems prepared to follow Freud by dropping the idea that the strong poet has better claim to the title of paradigmatic human being than either the scientist in search of truth or the "dutiful fulfiller of universal obligations." Freud, he suggests, shows us how to see these people as so many "forms of adaptation . . . strategies for coping with the contingencies of one's upbringing, of coming to terms with a blind impress." In fact, he seems to applaud Freud for eschewing "the very idea of a paradigm human being" (p. 12). Why he returns to the idea of strong poet as "hero" for the purposes of liberal apologetics in "The Contingency of Community," I do not know.

27. *Philosophy and the Mirror of Nature*, p. 380.

28. See Lovibond, *Realism and Imagination in Ethics*, esp. pp. 117–36.

29. Ibid., pp. 165-219.

CHAPTER TWELVE

1. Michael Walzer, *Spheres of Justice* (New York: Basic Books, 1983), p. 19. See also MacIntyre, *After Virtue*, 2d ed. (Notre Dame, Ind.: University of Notre Dame Press, 1984), p. 192.

2. William F. May, "The Right to Die and the Obligation to Care: Allowing to Die, Killing for Mercy, and Suicide," in *Moral Dilemmas*, ed. Richard Purtill (Belmont, Ca.: Wadsworth, 1985), p. 104.

3. I hope to write at length elsewhere on the relation between the practice of humanistic inquiry and such institutions as colleges, universities, and professional associations.

4. Alasdair MacIntyre, "Patients as Agents," in *Philosophical Medical Ethics*, ed. H. T. Engelhardt, Jr., and S. F. Spicker (Dordrecht, Holland: Reidel, 1977), p. 210–11.

5. Ibid., p. 212.

6. Ibid., p. 211.

7. Careful analysis the notion of "social world," for example, sometimes discloses commitment to neo-Kantian distinctions between undescribed reality and socially projected phenomenal worlds. And according to some critics, the proponents of interpretive sociology at times take too much comfort in a sharp distinction between explanation and understanding, a distinction which doesn't seem helpful now that our conception of natural science has been revamped by the critics of empiricism. For material relevant to these points, see especially Richard Rorty, *Philosophy and the Mirror of Nature* (Princeton: Princeton University Press, 1979).

8. Stanley Hauerwas, who often follows MacIntyre rather closely in such matters, has given us a more generous account of medical care as a social practice in *Suffering Presence: Theological Reflections on Medicine, the Mentally Handicapped, and the Church* (Notre Dame, Ind.: University of Notre Dame Press, 1986), ch. 2. But his account also occasionally falls back into unhelpful hyperbole. It does this, for example, when Hauerwas says that "increasing technological power is an attempt to maintain the moral coherence of medicine in a morally incoherent society" and that "medicine gains its moral coherence by drawing on the fear of death, the one thing people still seem to have in common" (p. 51). It is hard to see, however, how medical care could be the social practice he describes elsewhere in the same chapter if our society really were "morally incoherent." And does Hauerwas really believe that fear of death is the only thing we still have in common? Do we not have in common the fear of prolonged and unbearable pain? Or the desire to maintain our autonomy in the face of the impassive medical bureaucracy? Or the hope for a meaningful and dignified dying?

9. Peter Dews, ed., *Habermas: Autonomy and Solidarity: Interviews* (London: Verso, 1986), p. 91. Richard Rorty, "Thugs and Theorists: A Reply to Bernstein," (forthcoming). Rorty's use of Habermas's definition comes as a surprise, given what he has said elsewhere in apparent praise of "instrumental reason"—for example, in "The Priority of Democracy to Philosophy."

10. Cornel West, "Neo-Aristotelianism, Liberalism and Socialism: A Christian Perspective," in *Christianity and Capitalism: Perspectives on Religion, Liberalism and the Economy*, ed. Bruce Grelle and David A. Krueger (Chicago: Center for the Scientific Study of Religion, 1986), p. 79.

11. John Dewey, *The Later Works 1925–1953*, Vol. 5, ed. Jo Ann Boydston (Carbondale: Southern Illinois University Press, 1984), pp. 106, 103.

12. Ibid., pp. 84–85. This theme from Dewey's writings is stressed by Richard J. Bernstein in "Dewey, Democracy: The Task Ahead," in *Post-Analytic Philosophy*, ed. John Rajchman and Cornel West (New York: Columbia University Press, 1985), pp. 48–58.

13. Quoted in Bernstein, "Dewey, Democracy," p. 56.

14. I have been influenced here by Steven Tipton's idea that a division of moral labor assigns separate tasks to different kinds of moral reasoning. Tipton developed this idea in a paper delivered at the American Academy of Religion in 1985.

15. This is the major theme of my first book, *The Flight from Authority* (Notre Dame, Ind.: University of Notre Dame Press, 1981).

16. "The Priority of Democracy to Philosophy," unpublished draft, p. 39. Exactly what Rorty means by "instrumental rationality" in this context I have not been able to determine. But recall his willingness, in "Thugs and Theorists," to accept socialism as Habermas defines it.

17. Christopher Lasch is right to point out that we are hardly bereft of interesting and useful sociological literature on practices. See his essay, "The Communitarian Critique of Liberalism," *Soundings* 69/1–2 (1986): 75.

18. Martha Nussbaum writes, "Virtually any woman or man who both works and raises children is bound to face many conflicts between work and family; many times this person will have no choice but to neglect something that he or she values doing, and would have done had the world arranged things differently. Many of these conflicts could indeed be removed by a juster and more rational public culture (by more equity in salaries, by better schemes of child care). But they will not all be removed this way. For the only way to guarantee that the demands of a child's love never encroach upon one's professional life is to deny the child's love—to arrange for it to be raised, and loved, by someone else. This is what many men have frequently done. And it seems important to stress that these conflicts are present as much for men as for women—though until now fewer men have acknowledged that (for example) in spending little time caring for their children they are missing something of intrinsic value. There is a cost in recognizing how many things are valuable: it is that one also sees how often the world makes it impossible to do everything that is good." "Women's Lot," *New York Review of Books* 33/1 (30 Jan. 1986): 11. This passage is quoted by William Werpehowski in his essay, "The Professions in Ethical Context: Vocations to Justice and Love," in *Proceedings of the Theology Institute of Villanova University*, ed. Francis A. Eigo, O.S.A. Werpehowski, in the course of a perceptive discussion of these issues, also quotes a powerful passage from Ellen Goodman about the tension between being a good doctor or lawyer and being a good spouse or even an admirable person. See Ellen Goodman, *Keeping in Touch* (New York: Summit Books, 1985), pp. 21, 46–47.

19. Lasch is therefore right to insist that we need "to make it possible for everyone to take part" in the political conversation and that we must do something about "the social and economic inequalities tolerated by liberalism," which deprive "large classes of people of an effective public voice." "The Communitarian Critique of Liberalism," p. 75. Why Lasch considers this an objection to my position I do not know.

20. It is largely because I am concerned about this sort of problem that I remain reluctant to jettison the language of rights, which has been especially useful in opposing unjust attempts to exclude people from social practices. Lasch, who shares my concern, believes "the vocabulary of right to be fundamentally incompatible with the vocabulary of virtue." ("The Communitarian Critique of Liberalism," p. 75.) He doesn't say why he believes this. I am hoping that my attempt to detach rights-talk from its usual philosophical set-

tings and to connect it instead with my notion of a provisional *telos* will persuade people like Lasch that they can have it both ways. It is very important to recall that rights-talk was not invented by philosophers and has in fact survived in remarkably varied intellectual contexts.

21. Jefferson and King play important roles in both *Habits of the Heart* and Rorty's essay, "The Priority of Democracy." Rorty in particular calls attention to the ease with which the Civil Rights Movement combined apparently disparate moral languages; see pp. 13–14. The example should make clear that the kind of eclecticism involved need have nothing to do with what some of Rorty's critics think of as decadent postmodernist *jouissance*. King was a master at combining modern notions of rights and dignity, civic republican notions of citizenship, and prophetic themes from the biblical tradition. But he was equally masterful in modulating his use of biblical categories when addressing audiences outside of the black church. And he knew how to invoke religious language, when appropriate, without *presupposing* a full-fledged system of religious belief. This is what people fail to take account of when making the now-familiar comparisons between King on the one hand and Jerry Falwell or Pat Robertson on the other—comparisons meant to lump together all clergymen who "mix religion with politics."

LEXICON

In referring to books already discussed above, I shall do without notes and give only abbreviated citations in parentheses. The full citations should be easy enough to find by consulting notes to previous chapters. Only books and articles not yet referred to will receive full citations here.

1. Richard Rorty, "Deconstruction and Circumvention," *Critical Inquiry* 11 (1984): 3.

2. Alasdair MacIntyre, "The Relationship of Philosophy to Its Past," in *Philosophy in History*, ed. Richard Rorty, J. B. Schneewind, and Quentin Skinner (Cambridge: Cambridge University Press, 1984), p. 45.

INDEX